Be a Person

Everything you need to build your enterprise social presence online — Fast!

The Social Operating Manual for Enterprises

Social Media Performance Group, Inc.

Mike Ellsworth
Ken Morris
Robbie Johnson

Buy this book online at: http://bit.ly/BeAPersonEFull

See other books in the Be A Person Series at: Order them all: http://bit.ly/OrderBeAPerson

ISBN-13: 978-1463729813

Table of Contents

Table of Figures

What is Social Media? Social Networking? Social Computing?

"Social media are online communications in which individuals shift fluidly and flexibly between the role of audience and author. To do this, they use social software that enables anyone without knowledge of coding, to post, comment on, share or mash up content and to form communities around shared interests."

Joseph Thornley, CEO of Thornley Fallis

First off, we're going to use these three terms interchangeably throughout this book — social media, social networking, and social computing — because they all really mean the same thing — online activities involving three major components:

- User Generated Content (UGC)
- Participating in online communities
- Sharing opinions and ratings with others

Most organizations are struggling with the effects, threats, and promise of social media these days. Many are reaping huge benefits from social media. Others are dipping a toe in the water. And perhaps the majority are wondering why they care what some Twitterer had for lunch. (We don't and frankly, nobody does.)

This book will straighten this all out for you. It not only gives you a solid foundation in the strategies and the "Whys" of social media, but also a firm grounding in the "Whats" of creating your organization's social media presence. You'll learn the rules of the social media road, how to create a social media strategy before you start using the tools — our **No Tools Before Rules**™ concept — and tips and techniques for maximizing the effectiveness of your social media use.

Social networks really aren't that new. Many recognize the Website SixDegrees.com, launched in late 1997, as the first social network site.[1] SixDegrees allowed users to create profiles, list their Friends and surf the Friends' lists.

Figure 1 — SixDegrees.com's First Main Page — First Social Network

Others point to the ancient discussion groups on USENET (begun in 1979), the pioneering online community the Well (AKA Whole Earth 'Lectronic Link — started in 1985), the communities on CompuServe (1979) and Prodigy (1988), and Internet Relay Chat (IRC — started in 1988) as early social networks.

While all these examples did indeed constitute online communities, they may not quite fit the modern definition of social networking for a variety of reasons, including the limited number of social features and their integration into the communities. However, they did fulfill our three requirements for a social network: They enabled, encouraged, and facilitated User Generated Content; they were online communities; and although sharing opinions and ratings with others was not usually formalized, commenting was generally fully supported.

So social networking has been around at least since 1979, when Duke University graduate students Tom Truscott and Jim Ellis, and Steve Bellovin, a graduate student at the University of North Carolina, created the USENET software and installed it on the first two sites: "duke" and "unc," which were connected by a relatively new network (created in 1969) called the Internet.

---

[1] See Boyd and Ellison's fascinating research paper on social networks at: **bit.ly/91Xxhn**

What's with the bit.ly stuff?

We've used a link shortener to make it easier for you to copy the links in this document by hand. Just copy bit.ly/ and then the nonsense letters and numbers into the address bar of your Web browser.

But in reality, you probably already belong to the oldest social network of them all: email. Electronic mail began in 1965 as a way to send messages on a mainframe computer. Modern email was invented by Ray Tomlinson, one of the forefathers of the Internet, in 1971.[2] The only one of our three social networking criteria that email doesn't obviously fulfill is: participating in online communities. If you've ever been part of an email group (AKA a listserv) or email newsletter, you know email can provide online community.

So **you** are a veteran user of social networking!

Social Sites Defined

Social networking sites will come and go, but the approaches to going social that we describe in this book can be adapted for any site. With that said, let's take a look at some of the most popular and useful social sites and concepts out there, and give some quick definitions.

Facebook

Facebook is the largest social networking site by far, with more than half a billion users. Many of its users use the site to keep up to date with friends and to "follow" celebrities, popular TV shows and movies, and causes. However, many use Facebook for serious purposes such as recruiting talent, selling products, and creating communities around brands or products.

The major features of Facebook include **friending** — connecting with other users so that you can see their activities; **posting statuses** — short blurbs about what you are doing or interested in; reading what others are posting in your **News Feed**, a constantly updating timeline of the comments and activities of your friends; and **playing online games** such as Mafia Wars and Farmville.

If you want to learn more about using Facebook, see the section *Setting Up Facebook* on page 313.

LinkedIn

LinkedIn is the most professional of the popular social networks. Users tend to be more affluent and influential, and more of their interactions involve some business purpose rather than being purely social. LinkedIn is a great place to prospect for talent, find partners and customers, and find volunteers and donors. LinkedIn is organized around your user profile, which is like a

---

[2] Read a conversation with Tomlinson: **bit.ly/d0tWEj**

resume on steroids. In addition, users' profile pages feature a News Feed similar to Facebook's as well as any number of plug-in applications such as Reading List by Amazon, SlideShare, blogs, and others.

LinkedIn has many features that enable you to find and connect with other users, but you are limited in the number of people you can contact directly and/or connect with. LinkedIn uses a principle of three degrees of separation: those you are connected to are your first degree network; those that your connections are connected to are your second degree network; those who are connected to your second degree network are your third degree network. You can only directly contact your first degree network, but can ask those contacts for help in connecting to people in your second or third degree network.

We explain this concept in more detail in the section *Setting Up LinkedIn* on page 243

One of the most useful aspects of LinkedIn is their **Groups** function. Anyone can create a group and invite like-minded people to join. It's a great way to meet others who share your interests. Another useful function is **LinkedIn Answers**, which enable users to ask and answer questions on any subject.

Twitter

Twitter is what is known as a microblogging social network. Members post messages of up to 140 characters (known as tweets) and those who follow them see the messages in their News Feeds. Often derided as shallow, trivial, and boring, Twitter is used for talent acquisition and all sorts of business and professional functions, including organizing online and offline events, and spreading the word about products and brands.

People who follow your tweets are called followers, and if they like a tweet they may retweet it — repeat it — to their followers. You can find people to follow by using the Twitter Website's search function to search for words or phrases, or for special keywords called hashtags. Hashtags are created by putting a pound sign (#) in front of a word, for example #nonprofit. People do this so their tweets can be associated with others on a similar topic. For example, many recruiters post their job openings on Twitter using the hashtag #job.

Twitter is often used to call attention to a Website or a blog or other online destination. With only 140 characters to play with, it's hard to say anything complicated, and thus Twitter often serves as an advertisement for lengthier treatments of a subject.

There's more about using Twitter in the section *Setting Up Twitter* on page 287.

Twitter Directories — WeFollow, Twellow, etc.

Twitter has spawned its own universe of related sites, including many different sites dedicated to helping users find tweets and tweeps (people on Twitter) of interest. Directories like WeFollow and Twellow enable users to list themselves, add tags describing their interests, and use tags to search for tweeps that share their interests.

Tweetups

A tweetup is not a site, but rather an offline gathering organized via Twitter. Organizations as diverse as NASCAR,[3] NASA,[4] and non-profits such as GiveMN[5] and Maui Food Bank[6] have used tweetups. Tweetups offer a chance for people who may only know one another virtually to meet in person. It's a great idea for enterprises because it can solidify interest and support for your cause.

YouTube

YouTube is a free service that lets people post short videos. Users can create a **channel** to house multiple videos, and other users can subscribe to the channel, **tag** videos within it, and **comment** on them in text or by posting a video reply. In most cases, users can **embed** (insert) videos on their Websites without the poster's permission, thus providing a free source of content for their own Websites.

YouTube is largest video service of its kind, but there are lots of others. YouTube tends to be in the forefront of the social networking aspect of video.

There's more about using YouTube in the section *Setting Up YouTube* on page 351.

StumbleUpon, Delicious, Digg, Flickr

These sites are known as social bookmarking sites. Each provides ways for people to discover Websites, videos, blogs and pictures of interest based on the efforts of other users, who tag sites of interest with keywords that others can find via searches. StumbleUpon will email you with suggested sites in categories that you select. Delicious and Digg enable you to search for keywords

---

[3] NASCAR Tweetups: **exm.nr/fH5zR4**

[4] NASA Tweetups: **bit.ly/hp0LXm**

[5] GiveMN Tweetup: **bit.ly/dLTwXt**

[6] Maui Food Bank Tweetup: **bit.ly/ggP0Tt**

and suggest general interest items. And Flickr specializes in photos, enabling you to post and tag photos and share them with friends.

Blogs

Short for Weblog, blogs are a way to post longer-form articles that may include pictures and videos. The average blog post is not terribly long — perhaps 400 to 700 words — that usually treats a single subject. Some blogs are user's everyday thoughts, like a diary, and others examine technical, philosophical, or religious topics. The most popular blog site is the Huffington Post (now part of AOL), which examines political topics, but there are also popular blogs that follow celebrities (TMZ, Perez Hilton), technical gadgets (engadget, Gizmodo, TechCrunch), or post satirical takes on current events (Gawker, The Onion).

Anyone can create a blog, and tens of millions have. A blog is a particularly good way for enterprises to engage with their communities.

There's more on blogging in the section *Setting Up Blogging* on page 375.

Google Alerts, Blog Search, Reader

Google has a wealth of tools to aid you in monitoring what people are saying about your organization on social media sites.

Google Alerts are automated searches you can set up that will search for keywords and email you the results regularly. At the very least, your organization should have some Google Alerts set up.

Google Blog Search does, guess what? Blog searches. It's another great way to keep tabs on the conversation.

Google Reader enables you to subscribe to RSS feeds (see below). Most blogs have feeds that Google Reader can consolidate into one place for you to read, sample, or skim.

Google+

At press time, Google+ was a young network with features similar to Facebook but with a more-effective way to organize your friends into "circles." The network exhibited phenomenal growth, attracting more than 10 million mostly male users in its first two weeks of operation. While many of its features are derivative, Google+'s Hangouts feature, which enables users to create ad hoc meeting spaces, may force other social networks to create their own equivalents. The site's Sparks instant messaging feature may even give Twitter a run for its money.

Google+ has a real potential to challenge Facebook for social networking dominance. A related effort, Google's 1+ equivalent to the Facebook Like button, released in March, 2011, achieved broad acceptance in a phenomenally short period of time, and has been especially spurred by the release of Google+. By the beginning of July, 2011, four percent of the top 10,000 sites had added a +1 button to their homepages, up 33% since the beginning of June.[7]

Google combination of a social network with its search engine dominance may help it eat into Facebook's impressive social media prominence.

RSS Feeds

Standing for Really Simple Syndication, RSS is a way for users to "subscribe" to the updates of a site or a blog. Subscribing means that whenever the content changes on the subscribed-to site, an update is made available. You can keep up with the update by subscribing to the RSS feed using an RSS feed reader, like the free Google Reader. That way you don't have to constantly revisit the site to see if anything has changed. You should consider implementing an RSS feed for your own site and social media properties.

Social Aggregators — Plaxo and FriendFeed

Started in 2002 as an address book synchronization service and purchased by Comcast in 2008 for $150 million, Plaxo added social aspects including the ability to follow multiple social media News Feeds from more than 30 sites (like Twitter, Yelp, Flickr, Facebook, and LinkedIn), a birthday reminder and e-card service, and user profiles. Plaxo's 20 million social members (and 50 million address book users) tend to be business-oriented. Although it's not often thought of for its social networking features, Plaxo is worth considering for use by enterprises.

FriendFeed enables social media friends to follow one another's' feeds from more than 50 social networks in one place. FriendFeed pulls friend activity from other sites and assembles it into a News Feed on its site. Users can thus just check the FriendFeed without having to visit several social sites to keep up with their friends.

---

[7] Adotas *Google's +1 Shows Impressive Pub-Adoption Rate*: **bit.ly/rsZdlZ**

Personal Curation

An emerging type of social media site allows users to create and curate their own publications based on their social media activity and feeds. The resulting magazine-like electronic publications feature articles harvested from, for example, the activity of a user's Twitter followers and Facebook friends. Paper.li, for example, daily assembles an electronic publication containing links to articles, blogs, pictures, and videos from your social media accounts. The publication has a front page and multiple "departments" containing material in categories such as technology, business, and politics. See an example at **bit.ly/MEDaily**.

Summify is much simpler, presenting your top five news stories from your social networks, and delivering it by email, web or iPhone. Storify is less-automated, and enables you to curate your own publication by selecting specific material from Twitter, Facebook, Delicious, YouTube, Google searches, RSS feeds, and other Storify publications via a simple drag-and-drop interface. PearlTrees takes a little different tack, installing a brower plug-in to enable you to publish "pearls" — little pointers to Webpages or other resources. PearlTrees users can navigate "pearltrees" — organized connections — link to them, or collaborate on creating them.

As the torrent of social information grows, more tools to enable users to filter and curate information will crop up.

Location-Based Sites – FourSquare and GoWalla

With the rise of the smart phone, location-based sites have gone wild. FourSquare allows users to "check in" either manually or automatically at real-world locations such as bars, restaurants, and other venues. The idea is to help provide a real-world connection for social-world friends. But detractors say the information these sites provide about where people are right this moment is an invitation to burglary or worse.

You'll want to consider whether to make location-based sites part of your social media strategy.

Expert Sites – Squidoo, About.com, eHow

There are lots of expert sites on the Web. Some are heavily curated (About.com has editors assigned to most of their expert areas); some are automated (Squidoo aggregates lots of content on a single topic); others are organized around how-to areas (eHow has articles and videos that show you how to do almost anything).

You should review these sites to see if they're talking about you and your cause, and to determine if they might include your organization in their materials.

White Label Sites – Ning

White label social media sites provide the tools for you to build a standalone social media site for your organization. One of the oldest and best is Ning ("peace" in Chinese), which hosts more than four million sites. Incidentally, cofounder and Ning chairman Marc Andreessen created the first insanely popular Web browser, Netscape, back in 1996 and sold it to AOL for $4.2 billion in 1999.

Your organization can get started on Ning for a few dollars a month. Of course, first you need to know whether your community needs (another) place to go, and whether you're ready to commit to the effort necessary to create and host a community.

Orkut and Bebo

Social media is a worldwide phenomenon, and while a large percentage of Facebook's membership lives outside the US, there are also social networks like Orkut and Bebo that focus on non-US members.

Orkut is owned by Google and has more than 100 million users. After starting as an invitation-only network in the US, its largest proportion of users now come from Brazil, where it is one of the most popular Websites, and from India.

Acquired by AOL in 2008 and then sold to hedge fund operators Criterion Capital Partners in mid-2010, Bebo was also started in the US and now has more than 40 million users, a quarter of which are from the UK.

If your organization wants to reach outside the borders of the US, consider using social networks such as these.

Knowem

Knowem is one of many sites that will allow you to reserve your organization's presence on hundreds or even thousands of social media sites. You can use the site to do this even if you have no plans to create a presence on hundreds of sites. It's a good idea because a) you may someday want to join one of the obscure sites and b) you may want to prevent others from usurping your identity on social sites.

Knowem is also a good way to research specialty social media sites where your community may have an active presence.

Social Media Badges

Many sites provide badges, little graphics that represent the site or some achievement, to supporters who then post them on their blogs or other sites. One example of this is on LinkedIn. When you join a LinkedIn group, you have the option to display the group's badge on your profile so others see you're a member.

Badges are also given by sites like FourSquare to signify some achievement or status. It's a good way to enable and encourage evangelists.

There are also other types of badges that recognize achievements of your supporters, such as "Top Blogger" or "Most Valuable Evangelist."

Why Social Media?

"One of the things our grandchildren will find quaintest about us is that we distinguish the digital from the real . . . In the future that will become literally impossible."

William Gibson, author

You're reading this book because you're at least curious about social media. You probably want to know why there's such a fuss about it, and you'd like to find out if it can help your enterprise. We'll get to all these topics, but first, why should you care at all about social media?

One reason is it is the fastest growing segment of the Internet, having overtaken online games and email as the most-used category of applications on the Internet.[8]

Think of how much you use email, and how much those around you use it. People are using social networking more often than they are using email.

In fact, here are some statistics on various social media properties:

YouTube is now 10 percent of all Internet traffic[9]	1.5 million blog posts per day (17 per second)[10]
YouTube & Wikipedia are among the top brands online[11]	Five of the top 10 Websites are social[12]
There are more than 152 million blogs[13]	More than 175,000 new blogs launch every day[14]

---

[8] Nielsen Online: **bit.ly/bkJZvx**

[9] Source: Ellacoya Networks — **bit.ly/8YKzTr**

[10] Source: Technorati — **bit.ly/9eXgAj**

[11] Source: brandchannel.com — **bit.ly/aMurzT**

[12] Source: Alexa — **bit.ly/dzCkL5**

[13] Source: Blogpulse via Royal Pingdom: *Internet 2010 in numbers*: **bit.ly/rk8vMB**

[14] Hmmm. Apparently Technorati said this as long ago as 2008, but this seems to be an accepted bit of Web lore at this point: a stat everybody quotes, but has no findable source.

Not convinced yet? How about some more statistics?

- One in four social network users knowingly follow brands, products or services on social networks. For those who use these sites and services several times per day, this figure increases to 43%.[15]
- Americans spent an average 5 hours 35 minutes a month on social networking sites in 2009
- If Facebook were a country, it would be the world's third largest,[16] with 750 million people, having overtaken the US, at 308 million[17]
- Facebook users shared 30 billion pieces of content (links, notes, photos, etc.) per month in 2010[18]
- Online communities are visited by 67 percent of the global online population, which numbered 1.8 billion at the end of 2009[19]
- Nearly two-thirds of US Internet users regularly use a social network (and almost two-thirds of all Americans are on the FTC's no-call list!)[20]
- Nielsen Netview found that in 2010 social media use by Americans dwarfed other online usage by more than two-to-one

---

[15] Edison Research and Arbitron *The Social Habit II: Internet and Multimedia Study 2011*: **slidesha.re/oZ9JJB**

[16] For a light-hearted take on what this means, see: **bit.ly/alnzw2**

[17] **bit.ly/biGYNr**

[18] Royal Pingdom: *Internet 2010 in numbers*: **bit.ly/rk8vMB**

[19] **bit.ly/AKbO5**

[20] Nielsen, Social *Networking's New Global Footprint*: **bit.ly/ILH53L** and Switched, *FTC's 'Do Not Call' List Hits 200-Million Mark, but Telemarketers Still Call*: **aol.it/lqY9Fh**

Figure 2 — Source: Nielsen Netview, June 2010[21]

Managed security company Network Box found in an April, 2010 survey[22] that social media sites dominate Internet usage by businesses. According to the company, employees watching YouTube videos accounted for 10 percent of all corporate bandwidth during Q1 2010 — up two percent over the previous quarter.

The top five bandwidth Websites, and the percentage of all bandwidth they used, were:

- YouTube — 10
- Facebook — 4.5
- Windows Update — 3.3
- Yimg (Yahoo Image Search) — 2.7
- Google — 2.5

Business usage of YouTube and Facebook sucks up almost 15 percent of the average organization's bandwidth! This brings us to another reason to be interested in social media: It's already here. Your enterprise is already dealing with its effects. You need to understand it, plan for it, and create a social media strategy for your business, if only in self-defense.

---

[21] Nielsen Netview: **bit.ly/bkJZvx**

[22] Network Box survey: **bit.ly/dBffUl**

And if that doesn't do it for you, consider the fact that Amazon recently was granted a patent[23] for "A networked computer system [that] provides various services for assisting users in locating, and establishing contact relationships with, other users," — in other words, social networking. When the big boys get this serious, you know something's going on.

We'll show you lots of other good reasons to be interested in social media throughout this book.

---

[23] Amazon granted a social networking patent: **bit.ly/cyB3p8**

How is Social Media Relevant to Business?

"We now have indisputable proof that online marketing,
YouTube and Twitter and all that it encompasses
is meaningful and has arrived.
We are seeing real consequences to a mistake.
If [social networks] didn't matter, you wouldn't
see this type of reaction from J&J or consumers
[over the Motrin Mom faux pas]."

**Gene Grabowski, chair
crisis and litigation practice,
Levick Strategic Communications**

Grabowski is referring to one of the entries in our Social Media Hall of Shame.[24] That entry reads as follows:

In fall of 2008, pain reliever brand Motrin posted a short video as part of an ad campaign aimed at young mothers. In an attempt to identify with its intended audience, the ad featured a young woman speaking in an irreverent tone about the "fashion" of wearing one's baby, and the back pain associated with the practice.

Some online moms found the tone patronizing and felt they were being mocked. The video went largely unnoticed for 45 days, but then on Saturday, November 15, one mother, Jessica Gottlieb, tweeted her disapproval using the Twitter hashtag[25] #motrinmoms.

---

[24] Social Media Performance Group's Social Media Hall of Shame: **bit.ly/HallOfShame**

[25] See the definition for hashtag on page 20.

By Sunday afternoon, #motrinmoms was one of the hottest hashtags on Twitter. Mommy Blogger Katja Presnal created a nine-minute YouTube video comprised of angry tweets from moms with baby carriers.[26] In all, however, fewer than 1,000 people posted using the hashtag. But this was a very vocal minority.

By social media standards, Motrin was slow to respond to the outcry. Yet by Sunday evening, they pulled the campaign, temporarily shuttered their Website, and apologized. Instead of engaging with the protestors on their own turf, however, Motrin reverted to an Old Media response: They tried to remove all traces of the video and ad campaign and offered a corporate apology in response: "We have taken immediate action to respond to these concerns and have removed the advertisement from our Web site."

By November 20th, they had pulled themselves together a bit more, and published a response with a much better tone. Kathy Widmer, Vice President of Marketing for McNeil Consumer Healthcare, offered a new apology that followed our mandate: **Be a Person**.

> So…it's been almost 4 days since I apologized here for our Motrin advertising. What an unbelievable 4 days it's been. Believe me when I say we've been taking our own headache medicine here lately! We are parents ourselves and we take feedback from moms very seriously.[27]

Much, much, **much** better!

Motrin's mistake was in not using the negative attention to engage in a dialog with the angered moms. By taking them seriously and listening to their concerns, Motrin could have probably defused the uproar and possibly turned the furor into an advantage. Engaging in a dialog would have enabled Motrin to explain that they were trying to be funny, and they were sorry that hadn't worked.

Ironically, Jessica Gottlieb, author of the original tweet, said that she felt the ad did not need to be pulled. What if Motrin had originally addressed her directly and enlisted her help?

We can learn two things from this object lesson:

- Social media can bring a powerful company to its knees in the space of less than a week
- With great power comes great responsibility[28]

---

[26] The video *Motrin Ad Makes Moms Mad*: **bit.ly/bZvjBR**

[27] Read more about the Motrin debacle at **bit.ly/awmztq**

[28] Spider-Man: **bit.ly/lnBePi**

We don't tell this tale to scare you, but rather to impress upon you the power and potential of this new communications medium. We also hope Motrin's story demonstrates that using social media without a strategy and a plan may seem easy to do, but like juggling chainsaws, the outcome is much better when you're trained and prepared.

Plenty of enterprises have produced great results through the use of social media. We've written this book to help you become one of them.

On the positive side of social media, take a look at the Blendtec YouTube videos,[29] one of the keystone case studies from our Enterprise Social Media Framework (ESMF).[30]

Blendtec makes powerful blenders, and so someone got the bright idea of doing a series of short videos called *Will it Blend?* Starting way back in 2006, and featuring Blendtec CEO Tom Dickson, each video — designated either "Try this at home" or "Don't try this at home" — blends a range of items from 50 marbles and a handful of golf balls to a new iPhone.

It was the iPhone blend video that went viral, racking up more than 9.8 million views, and counting. Combining the fetish power of the game-changing mobile phone with the eccentric idea of obliterating things with a blender equated to tremendous viralocity. Since the first iPhone bit it, the company has trashed a series of iconic electronic gadgets, including an Olympus digital camera, an iPad (11 million views), and an iPhone 4.

Was it planned this way? No. It was just a wacky — and cheap — bid for attention from a small company with a small marketing budget. It went viral because . . . well, just because it was bizarre, over the top, and cool, we guess. For almost no money, Blendtec has reaped more than 161 million YouTube views, 380,000 subscribers (making it #40 on YouTube's all-time list), and a 7X increase in sales.

So why do we mention this? Did you see the part about "almost no money?"

You could go viral as well. But to do so, you must be hooked into the zeitgeist[31] of your community, and the larger society. Offbeat, quirky ideas are what generally go viral. But if you try too hard (we're looking at you, LonelyGirl15[32]) you could do more damage than good.

Contrast BlendTec's success with the fact that the #3 result from a search on YouTube for Comcast is a video called *A Comcast Technician Sleeping on my Couch.*[33]

---

[29] Blendtec's YouTube channel: **bit.ly/9pHXlh**

[30] Enterprise Social Media Framework: **bit.ly/auxUYA**

[31] Google zeitgeist: **bit.ly/cy2fhg**

[32] LonelyGirl15's YouTube channel: **bit.ly/dBib9J**

(There's more about going viral in the section *Aim to Influence* on page 196.)

Talk about incredible results, both good and bad! Social media is here, it works for enterprises, and chances are good it is affecting your business today.

Social Media and Your Business

Now you may be thinking, "That's great and all, but my enterprise sells to businesses (or sells services, or is in a regulated industry, or . . .), and I can't see how funny YouTube videos will help me sell my product."

You're not alone in being skeptical about the potential effect of social media on your business. But more and more businesses of all sizes are starting to embrace it.

A 2011 Frost and Sullivan study[34] (see Figure 3) showed that of 200 C-level execs, 69 percent were closely tracking social media. That's amazing in and of itself, but executive interest in social media was greater than interest in other important technology trends, such as telepresence, VOIP, shared team spaces, soft phones, and even unified communications and unified messaging. Half of the respondents said social media is already used within their organization, and 41 percent

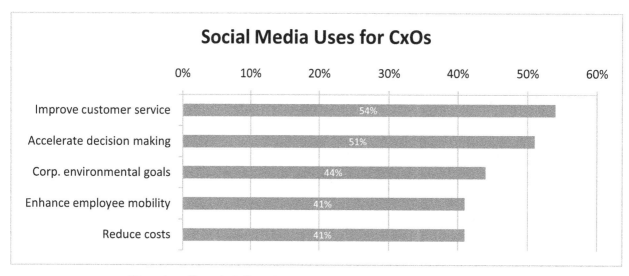

Figure 3 — Frost & Sullivan Survey - Goals for CxOs Who Plan to Increase Social Media Use

said they were using the technology personally.

---

[33] A Comcast Technician Sleeping on my Couch: **bit.ly/jPRrHZ**

[34] Frost & Sullivan report: **bit.ly/I7FMin**

How is Social Media Relevant to Business?

Social media expert Josh Bernoff of Forrester Research, writing for the Harvard Business Review,[35] divides large enterprises' use of social media into four groups:

- **Dormant** — Fewer than one in five large companies are in this group. They haven't really gotten started with social media.
- **Testing** — About one third of enterprises are just starting out. They usually begin with listening (monitoring social chatter) and talking on Twitter and Facebook.
- **Coordinating** — Another third of large companies have moved on to coordinating multiple social efforts around the company. Bernoff recommends, and we definitely agree, that the right strategy is not to put all the social efforts under one manager. He recommends appointing "shepherds" to help lead social media across teams in marketing, customer support, HR, and IT.
- **Mastering** — The remainder of companies, the smallest group, have mastered social media use. They face challenges in scaling and optimizing social efforts.

  Bernoff points to Dell as a leader. Manish Mehta is Dell's VP, Social Media & Community. Just having an executive position with a name like that indicates how seriously Dell takes social media.

  Bernoff says Mehta "has a weekly teleconference with managers throughout the organization who are responsible for the hundreds of social applications the company deploys, from the Twitter feed @DellOutlet that promotes overstock computers to IdeaStorm, the online community that solicits ideas for new Dell products. Coordinating measurement is also key: at financial services company USAA, for example, social media managers have proven that ratings and reviews generate a 17% increase in click-throughs to product purchase pages."

So it's early days, but despite that, many enterprises have seen real benefits from engaging with social media.

But it's not all about sales and marketing, as you can see from the preceding. In fact, we believe that sales and marketing are not even the most impressive things social media does. Savvy businesses use social media to:

- **Track what customers and prospects are saying**, what they're interested in, and how they buy
- **Create flash focus groups** online to get real-time, real-world feedback on customer likes and dislikes
- **Recruit new talent** — many companies are turning away from posting job requisitions to searching social networks like LinkedIn and inviting highly-qualified people to apply
- **Increase employee engagement**, satisfaction, and retention — McKinsey and MIT surveys found between 7 percent and 20 percent improvement in employee retention due to social networks[36]

If that's all social computing could do for your business, wouldn't that be enough?

[35] Harvard Business Review: **bit.ly/kCuVFK**

[36] Allyis blog: **bit.ly/k2TD3m** and McKinsey: **bit.ly/k8hl1q**

Our contention that most businesses miss the real point and much of the potential of social media is supported by a recent white paper published by the Harvard Business Review.[37] HBR did a survey of 2,100 companies, and these were some of their findings:

> Despite the vast potential social media brings, many companies seem focused on social media activity primarily as a one-way promotional channel, and have yet to capitalize on the ability to not only listen to, but analyze, consumer conversations and turn the information into insights that impact the bottom line.

> For instance:

> - Three-quarters (75%) of the companies in the survey said they did not know where their most valuable customers were talking about them
> - Nearly one-third (31%) do not measure effectiveness of social media
> - Less than one-quarter (23%) are using social media analytic tools
> - A fraction (7%) of participating companies are able to integrate social media into their marketing activities

> Only a small group — 12 percent — of the companies in the survey said they felt they were currently effective users of social media. These were the companies most likely to deploy multiple channels, use metrics, have a strategy for social media use, and integrate their social media into their overall marketing operations.

By using this book in your organization, you can learn how to become part of the successful 12 percent.

Let's Face It

They're talking about you online (if you're lucky).

That's right, there are probably people talking about your business online right now, via social media. What are they saying? Are they supporters or detractors? Shouldn't you listen to find out?

What are people who are interested in your business talking about online?

Of course, it varies depending on the business you're in, but you can count on the chatter being both positive and negative, just like offline conversations about you. The difference is, you can join in on these conversations and possibly influence them.

---

[37] Harvard Business Review, "The New Conversation: Taking Social Media from Talk to Action" **bit.ly/I9hNpQ**

How is Social Media Relevant to Business?

Regardless of what people are saying about you, shouldn't you be aware of the online conversations? What if Motrin had ignored what the Mommy Bloggers were saying? What if people are right now, this very minute, spreading misinformation or rumors about your company on Facebook?

Wouldn't you want to know?

Social media changes the way cheers and raspberries are distributed. Two of our favorite quotes about how much social media changes positive and negative conversations come from trailblazing broadcaster Edward R. Murrow and Paul Gillin, author of The New Influencers.

> The fact that your voice is amplified to the degree where it reaches from one end of the country to the other does not confer upon you greater wisdom or understanding than you possessed when your voice reached only from one end of the bar to the other.
> — Edward R. Murrow[38]

> Conventional marketing wisdom long held that a dissatisfied customer tells ten people. But…in the new age of social media, he or she has the tools to tell ten million.
> — Paul Gillin[39]

Social media hasn't changed people, just as Murrow says; it has amplified their voices far beyond what Murrow could have imagined in 1958, to the point that mass media is accessible to the average person, as Gillin's quote demonstrates.

OK, OK, social media is the next big thing. How can you start to take advantage of it?

Well, one thing you shouldn't do is go off into this new land of social media without a map. You need to channel social media's power to support your business's strategy. To harness the power of Social Media, you need a strategy, and a plan.

---

[38] Edward R. Murrow at the RTNDA Convention (Radio-Television News Directors Association and Foundation) in Chicago on October 15, 1958: **to.pbs.org/Id0Mvy**

[39] Harvard Business Review, "The New Conversation: Taking Social Media from Talk to Action" **bit.ly/I9hNpQ**

So What's Your Strategy?

Like anything that's worth doing well, it's best to have a strategy for using social media. You may be tempted to listen to those in your business who have a "Hey kids! Let's put on a show!" kind of mentality regarding social media. It's so easy to get started, you may decide to listen to these folks and start creating a Facebook page, a Twitter account, or a YouTube channel right away.

We hope you will resist the temptation to jump in with both feet until you have understood why you are using social media, and how it is going to support your overall strategy.

To maximize social media benefit, you need to align your business's strategy with both your external and internal social media strategy.

The difficulty in writing a book about social media and business is that there are so many kinds of enterprises, each with unique missions and goals. We could give advice for a medical device manufacturer, for example, which may not be appropriate for grocery distributor. On the other hand, most businesses face similar challenges such as selling, marketing, recruiting and retaining employees, gaining brand recognition, and so on.

Thus you will need to take the general principles in this book and apply them to your own enterprise. Without working closely with you, we can't identify for you the best social media goals, strategies, sites, and techniques for your business. Only you can do that, and you should use your overall mission, strategy, and goals to determine your social media strategy.

There's more detail later about creating strategies. First, we'd like to lay out the general concepts, and get more specific in the chapter *Create Social Computing Strategies* on page 65.

A good social media strategy:

- **Effectively communicates** goals and benefits of social media internally and externally

- **Guides selection** of the right tools to use

- **Ensures sustainability** of your social media endeavor

- **Involves regular reviews** of people, processes, and tools to ensure that your business stays relevant

The first step is to review your business's goals and strategy. Make whatever changes are necessary to your strategy to bring it up to date and ensure that all stakeholders support it before taking a look at social media. Identify the most important elements and start to think how social media can help, especially in ways other than sales and marketing.

Plan an Internal Social Media Strategy

It may be easier for you to start by focusing on creating an internal social media strategy. It's less scary, and you might have an easier time coming to agreement on the internal strategy. Some internal goals to think about include:

- **Empower employees** to advocate
- **Improve employee engagement** and retention
- **Encourage collaboration**, innovation, problem solving
- **Improve communications**
- **Manage risk** to your reputation
- **Improve your hiring process**
- **Improve your market research and competitive intelligence**

We elaborate more on this concept in the *Create an Internal Social Computing Strategy* section on page 67.

There's more information about engagement, advocacy, and evangelism in the sections *Engage Your Community*, *Find and Create Online Evangelists*, and *Create Buzz*.

Plan an External Social Media Strategy

Once you understand how social media can support your business's overall strategy, it's time to create your external social media strategy.

You need to go where your community is. Identify constituent groups to target — prospects, customers, influencers, evangelists, opinion leaders — and find out if they use social media. Delve into specifics. Are they reading any particular blogs? Are they on Twitter? Facebook? Find your community and study them to see what their concerns are. We examine this process in depth in the section *Find Your Community* on page 103.

Base your strategy on what you find through this research. If your target group is on Facebook, you may want to set up a business page. If your community tweets, you may want to set up a program of daily updates on Twitter.

If you haphazardly approach this task, you can spin your wheels without gain. No one will hear your message. Be sure to tie your implementation ideas directly to your external social media goals.

External goals to consider include:

- **Educate**
- **Inspire** to action
- **Create strong relationships**
- **Share internal culture** with external audience
- **Thought leadership**
- **Community involvement**
- **Sales**
- **Marketing**
- **Publicity**

We elaborate on this task in the section *Create an External Social Computing Strategy* on page 69.

Create a Social Media Mission Statement

After reviewing your goals and strategy and creating drafts of your internal and social media strategies, create a mission statement for your social media efforts. This needs to be one sentence that everyone in your business can recite from memory. Doing so will help sharpen your thinking about your strategies and guide the creation of plans to support your social media goals.

Here are some examples of social media mission statements you can learn from.

> "Our mission is to drive forward the adoption of social media across Europe in order to improve the quality, access, value and effectiveness of healthcare delivery to patients."

> — Health Care and Social Media in Europe

This is an easy one to get started with. This non-profit exists to spread usage of social media. But notice that they directly tie this social media goal to a specific non-social-media goal: "to improve the quality, access, value and effectiveness of healthcare delivery to patients." In other words, the organization doesn't just want to spread social media usage for its own sake; it wants to do so to achieve a real-world goal.

A great example of a very short and to-the-point mission statement is Ford's:

> "Humanize the Ford brand and put consumers in touch with Ford employees."

> — Scott Monty, Ford Motor Co.

You may have noticed that we don't even mention social media in the main title of our book, and this is intentional. The challenge for any business in the age of social media is to **Be a Person**, not a faceless entity. Scott Monty gets this. Ford wants to **Be a Person** — to humanize their brand, and connect with their community: their customers. So they put this in their social media mission statement. How can you get this concept into your statement?

Here's another statement that explicitly states what kind of person the business wants to be:

> "Instill trust in the brand, and highlight that the people behind the brand are parents too."
>
> — Lindsay Lebresco, Graco

Brilliant! Our employees are parents too; they can relate to you and your problems; they can create products that connect with your needs, because they share your needs. Wow.

Of course, delivering on your mission statement is the trick, isn't it?

Here's a general template to get you started on your social media mission statement:

> "The purpose of our social media efforts is to [*do something*] for [*someone*] while [*improving, furthering*] our [*business strategic objective*]."

Play with it until you think you've got it, and then get your staff involved in fine-tuning your statement.

Create Social Media Metrics

A strategy needs goals, and goals need measurement. Ensure that your social media goals can be measured. There's lots more about measurement in the section *Measure Results* on page 147, but for right now, you should think about real, concrete goals that are measurable.

We also talk much more about measuring the Return on Investment (ROI) of social media in the section *Measuring Social Media, Influence, Brand* on page 155, but here's a quick table of some of the things you can measure with social media:

Table 1 - Social Media Measurements

Blog posts	Google trends
Reader comments	Search results
Twitter mentions	Inbound traffic
Twitter followers	Video views
Facebook fans	SlideShare views
Links	Tags
RSS subscribers	Diggs

Don't worry too much if you don't understand what some of these elements are at this point. Most will become clear throughout the rest of the book.

Determine Who is Responsible

When creating your social media strategies, you should consider who in your business is going to be responsible for social media activities. We can't really do this for you, but here are some suggestions:

- Please don't just make it just marketing or public relations staff!

- Please don't make it just one person!

- How about anyone who touches clients?

- How about your leadership?

Determine How Your Clients Will Benefit

If you can't quantify this, you need to rethink your whole strategy. If the answer is truly that you see no benefit for external stakeholders, that's OK. Just be sure you understand that social media only provides internal benefits for your business. As we've discussed, those benefits can be enough.

Plan to Evolve Your Strategy

Accept that you're going to make mistakes. You're going to learn what works and what doesn't, and so you need to figure out how you are going to incorporate continuous improvement into your social media strategy and practice. One important element of improvement is to be open to innovation from your staff. Chances are good many have significant experience in social media and can help suggest improvements.

First Steps Toward a Social Media Strategy

"Social Media Performance Group's motto is: **No Tools Before Rules**. We believe that before you use any powerful tool, you should not only find out its capabilities and dangers, but also create a plan for its use. Beginning to use social media without a strategy would be like tossing the keys of your SUV to your 10-year-old."

Social Media Performance Group

The Social Media Performance Group strategy process begins with an enterprise social media readiness assessment. You need to understand how ready your staff, leadership, board, and other stakeholders are to make the changes that will be necessary to embrace social computing.

Although you may not realize it at the planning stage, successfully implementing social media to support your strategies will require organizational changes, some large, some small, and some that may be upsetting or controversial. For example, if you're a business that has a strict command and control hierarchy where every external communication is approved at a high level, you'll need to change to be able to fully leverage social media. The legal department of one enterprise we know recently approved 40 tweets. Yeah, that'll work.

If the idea **Be a Person** scares you, you'll need to do some organizational transformation before social media is right for you.

Of course, not all businesses are ready for social computing. In fact there are some who have ingrained styles and tendencies that will make adopting social media impossible, if not actually detrimental. How can you tell if your business is one of them?

Top Ten Signs You Should Avoid Social Media

Lisa Barone, Chief Branding Officer of Outspoken Media, put together a somewhat humorous collection[40] of indicators of organizational dysfunction that would make adopting social computing a risky business. We've adapted and expanded them in the following list.

You have no social skills (and don't want to fake them)

If your organization has problems relating with staff, customers, or other stakeholders, those problems are likely to be magnified by using social computing. Be honest with yourself when assessing your organization's readiness to openly relate with a large group of your stakeholders.

You have no sense of humor/can't handle criticism

A sense of humor often doesn't make it onto the list of things to consider about social computing, but it should. If your organization gets stirred up by the least little bit of criticism, or has a habit of misinterpreting humorous comments, think twice before adopting social media. Using social media means you are opening yourself up to unvarnished dialog with both your supporters and your detractors. If you don't think you can handle it, social computing is not for you.

You're going to forget about it in the morning

Social computing takes a commitment. It can't be a start and stop kind of thing. Once you engage with your community, you aren't going to be able to go back to ignoring them. So be sure you have a long-term, sustainable commitment to social computing before venturing forth.

Openness is a problem for you

This one is pretty much self-explanatory. If your organizational style emphasizes secrecy, security, and a lack of sharing, you're not going to succeed with social computing. Ask

---

[40] Outspoken Media provides online marketing services. Barone's list is at: **bit.ly/ctidjS**

First Steps Toward a Social Media Strategy

yourself what you're hiding, and why, and whether you can open up before getting involved with social media.

You're only there to sell

If you think social computing is just about selling, or marketing, or pushing messages into just another media channel, better to forget it. Remember that social media involves relationships and two-way conversation, and that you must respect your community's point of view to be successful. You should also be wary if your leadership plans on having others masquerade as them online. Social media is about transparency, not facades.

You view social media as a numbers game

This is a common attitude toward social media. You see it on LinkedIn among the LIONs (There's more on that in the *What is a LinkedIn LION™?* section on page 255.) The number of followers on social media is generally not what your business should concentrate on. The quality of your interactions with your community is vastly more important than the quantity.

You sometimes resort to name calling

We decided to edit this one. Barone**'s** original number 7 was: *You're inclined to call people's wives "douchettes."* Apparently, a CEO actually did call someone's wife a douchette,[41] although not online. Nevertheless, if your business has folks in it who might be inclined to disparage others, think twice about bringing this sort of thing to social computing.

You think Twitter is a social media strategy

We hope you know by now that we think you shouldn't get into social computing without first understanding how it can support your organization's strategy, and without creating a social media strategy to guide your usage. There are lots of consultants out there that

---

[41] Hear the audio at: **bit.ly/cymXi7**

think putting together a Twitter campaign, or a Facebook page, or a few YouTube videos is a great way to get started with social media. Tell that to Motrin.

You don't have a "social" culture

There are lots of signs of an anti-social-computing culture. The tendency to run everything by the lawyers. Endless rounds of revisions with final approval by top executives. A prohibition of social media site usage while at work. Blocking YouTube. Some of these tendencies can be overcome, and some might be enough to indicate problems with social computing acceptance. If your general organizational culture emphasizes tightly controlling the message, you're not likely to succeed with social media.

You don't have permission

In Barone's list, this item refers to staff who attempt to speak for the business without authorization, but we turn this around a little bit to mean, "Can you give your stakeholders permission to represent your business?" When you think about it, your staff, customers, and other stakeholders DO represent your business, every day, and can work on your behalf. But it's sometimes a hard step for an organization to let go enough to enable them to do the same on social media. Be sure you can let go before engaging with social media.

Do a Quick Survey of Your Stakeholders

To help determine if you're ready for social media, a social computing assessment can identify those who will embrace social computing, and who will resist. It also helps identify those who are willing but need training on how to use social computing.

The assessment can be done online using the Social Media Performance Group's free Social Media Readiness Survey™ [42] or via pen and paper using the version reproduced on page 51.

---

[42] SMPG's Social Media Readiness Survey: **bit.ly/smpgsurvey**

Do a Quick Survey of Your Customers

It is important to know what customers and prospects already know about social media so you can target your efforts to their ability to respond online. If your target audience is largely offline, you will want to use social media inside your company rather than externally.

It's important to realize that, due to socio-economic differences, many groups may not have regular access to social computing, which obviously can significantly alter your strategy in engaging them online. In your survey, you may want to segment prospects and customers by socio-economic status, which may affect how easily you can reach them via social media.

If your audience doesn't have computer-based online access, you may be able to reach them online via their mobile phones. In this case, you should consider using the Social Media Performance Group's free *Mobile Social Media Use Survey*.[43] The survey can also be found in the second part of the Social Media Performance Group Social Media Readiness Survey™, reproduced in the next section, and live at: **bit.ly/smpgsurvey**

After your survey is done, take a look at the results and divide the respondents into at least two groups: those who are likely to respond to social media, and those who probably won't. You'll need to base your social media plans on the composition of these groups. If, for example, the non-social-media group represents the majority of your stakeholders, you may want to consider educational approaches to help them learn about the benefits of social media. On the other hand, if the social-media-using group is large, you may want to consider more-sophisticated approaches to identify and enable your supporters via social media.

Assess Related Businesses

Identify closely-related businesses and partners you deal with on a regular basis, especially those with similar or complementary missions, particularly in your region. Find out what they are doing with social media. Not only might this give you ideas for your own approach, you may be able to team up with them to help further your social media reach.

---

[43] Social Media Performance Group's Mobile Social Media Use Survey: **bit.ly/c48q61**

SMPG Social Media Readiness Survey™

What is your comfort level with social networking/ media as of today?

___   I consider myself extremely proficient and knowledgeable in social networking/ media. I use it on a daily basis both professionally and personally.

___   I am comfortable with social networking/ media in a professional setting. I use social networking/ media frequently for business purposes.

___   I am comfortable with social networking/ media in a personally setting. I use social networking/ media frequently in my personal life.

___   I am familiar with social networking/ media but I am a casual user at best and I use it occasionally.

___   I know of social networking/ media but I don't use it at all.

___ I don't know anything about social networking/ media and as of right now, I am not comfortable with it and see no real value in it.

Please circle the appropriate answer as it applies to you.

I am very interested in learning more about social networking/ media, especially as it applies in a business setting.

Yes   No

I believe I would use social networking/ media more if I had a better understanding of it and how I could apply it in my professional life.

Yes   No

I believe that it is important to understand social networking/ media as it applies to business.

Yes   No

If I could see how other professionals are using social networking/ media in business I would be interested in learning more.

Yes   No

I believe social networking/ media is for personal use only and doesn't really apply to business.

Yes   No

I have no real interest in social networking/ media.

Yes   No

Social Networking/ Media Tools

How familiar are you with the following social media sites?

I'm a User	I Know of	None	Social Media Site
___	___	___	Linked In
___	___	___	Facebook
___	___	___	MySpace
___	___	___	You Tube (User: create content, Know Of: have used to watch videos)
___	___	___	Twitter
___	___	___	Blogging (I regularly read blogs or have my own blog)
___	___	___	Wikis (I regularly use wikis (such as Wikipedia) or have my own wiki)
___	___	___	Instant Messaging
___	___	___	Forums (I regularly participate in or have my own forum)
___	___	___	Ning
___	___	___	Business Social Networking Other (please list others) _____
___	___	___	Other personal social networking sites/ groups _____

Mobile Phones and Data Plans

Do you have a mobile phone?

Yes   No

Do you have a texting plan?

Yes   No

Do you have a smart phone with a data package?

Yes   No

How often do you do these activities on your mobile phone?

Daily	Weekly	Seldom	
___	___	___	Text
___	___	___	Email
___	___	___	Mobile Internet — Going to Websites
___	___	___	Using Social Media

I sign up to be on email lists from companies

Yes   No

I sign up to receive text messages from companies

Yes   No

What kind of information do you find valuable and would want to receive via text message from companies?

Coupons   Sales   Special Events

Company Updates   For Social Purposes

I believe that mobile phones are very personal and I use mine for business because I have to.

Yes   No

I believe that mobile phones are personal and I don't want to receive anything on them other than phone calls from people I know.

Yes   No

Take the survey online at **bit.ly/smpgsurvey**

Is Your Organization Ready for Social Media?

There is a wide variety of skill sets required to be successful at social media, whether your organization is just you and your computer or includes thousands of employees spread over several continents. Whether you're committing a couple hours a week, or you're hiring a social networking czar, your success will depend on the abilities of you and your team.

To find out if your organization has the right stuff, consider giving your leadership and key stakeholders the following test, adapted and expanded from Ron Shulkin's blog.[44] Score one point for each "Yes" answer. Answer "Yes" if you or your team currently has the relevant ability or skill set.

On Your Marks

1. Are you passionate about social media and able to inspire your team and your community?

2. Are you willing to commit a significant percentage of your time to the social networking effort?

3. Can you objectively evaluate the readiness of your internal culture to adopt social media?

4. Can you establish marketing plans and an organization social media strategy with clearly-identified, measurable goals?

5. Can you articulate and sell-in a comprehensive social media strategy? (Comprehensive doesn't mean, "Let's try this and try that" rather how you'll use social media throughout your organization.)

6. Can you take responsibility for the success of your organization's social media plan?

7. Can you marshal the organization's resources as required to execute the social media plan?

Get Set

8. Can you ensure daily updates to blogs and other social media that you are targeting by coordinating writing, publishing, promoting, and swift approvals?

9. Can you identify the software tools required to monitor your organization's social media activities and track progress toward measurable goals?

---

[44] Ron Shulkin is Vice President for North America at CogniStreamer: **bit.ly/dCfTWl**

10. Do you have a reliable resource on staff that has a public relations or marketing degree or equivalent experience?

11. Can you find an excellent verbal and written communicator to be the public face of your effort?

12. Do you have experience with other successful online community building?

13. Do you have experience building and running a Website?

14. Are you well-versed in search engine optimization?

15. Do you have leadership and project management skills?

16. Do you have the stamina and patience to shepherd your organization through the social media learning curve over a sustained period of time?

17. Do you have a strong familiarity with Facebook, LinkedIn, Twitter and YouTube?

18. Do you have in-depth knowledge of currently-available social media tools and the ability to use them to their best benefit?

19. Do you know what kinds of social media your target demographic uses most often?

Go

20. Do you stay current on the latest and best social media tools?

21. Can you provide guidance to your team members on social media best practices?

22. Can you define the rules of social media engagement for your organization?

23. Do you have a plan to provide consistent messaging and brand promotion to those on your team who are engaging with your community?

24. Do you have relationships with industry-expert bloggers?

25. Do you have a plan and the means to develop videos, photographs, graphics, applications, and other digital multimedia presentations?

26. Are you a creative thinker who can develop interactive, intriguing and interesting ideas that can go viral?

27. Can you productively engage with detractors online rather than taking offense or responding emotionally?

Test Scoring:

26–27 points	You're ready! Get cracking!
23-25 points	You can start your planning
18-22 points	You're almost there, but will need to recruit some expertise
14-18 points	Plan on taking a few months developing your team and preparing your internal culture
13 or fewer points	Read this book. Twice. Be certain to ensure stakeholder buy-in because it will be six months or more before you're ready.

Decide What Your Business Will Do About Social Computing

"Not to decide is to decide."

Harvey Cox, American theologian

There's a huge opportunity out there for your business. Based on your organizational intentions and the assessments we've encouraged you to do, you have three choices:

- **Ignore** social media

- **Monitor** social media

- **Engage** with social media

Let's examine each of these choices in turn.

Ignore Social Media

Obviously, we think you shouldn't ignore social media, and a quick review of some of the risks of non-engagement should be sufficient to convince you that you must at least start to monitor social media.

Regulatory Risk

If your business has anything to do with securities or other types of regulation, you can't afford to ignore social computing. If you have large securities holdings, you may face restrictions on certain types of disclosures. If you aren't monitoring social media, you may not be aware of disclosures that involve your organization's staff and which may run afoul of regulations.

Your business may cite regulatory constraints as a reason to avoid getting involved in, or even monitoring, social media activities. Be sure that the risks of this approach don't outweigh your responsibility to ensure disclosures are proper.

Reputation Management

A related issue is reputation management. Your business may not have a formal reputation management effort, but every organization needs to be concerned with the subject. If you've ever subscribed to an article clipping service, you've been engaged in reputation management.

Social media is one of the largest and the fastest growing forums for people's opinions. You can't afford to ignore what people are saying about you online.

Ask these famous brands if ignoring social media was a good idea:

- **Domino's disgusting video**[45] in which a couple of immature employees with a video camera caused a huge crisis

- **United breaks a guitar**[46] and the customer gets even with a YouTube video

- **Nestlé's Facebook Fan Page Heist**[47] where people reacted to Nestlé's heavy-handed attempt to get a critical video removed from YouTube by posting altered versions of the firm's logo, culminating in a boycott

- **KFC and Oprah's Free Chicken**[48] — Winfrey announced that her show's Website would let visitors download a printable coupon for free Kentucky Grilled Chicken. Web servers were overloaded, and supplies of free chicken were exhausted. Bloggers reported that store managers were turning away coupon-holders. KFC chairman Roger Eaton posted a video message explaining that KFC would not be able to redeem the coupons still at large

There are lots more examples of dumb social media moves in our Social Media Hall of Shame, online at: **bit.ly/HallOfShame**

---

[45] Domino's video: **rww.to/9LYuMs**

[46] United Breaks Guitars: **bit.ly/abJdu5**

[47] Nestlé Facebook Heist: **bit.ly/drkXqb**

[48] KFC free chicken: **bit.ly/dan6ol**

Legal Issues of Disclosure

Chances are your business has some confidential information, whether it is client records or minutes of sensitive meetings or the like. We're sure you have policies that instruct staff and others on how to keep this information secure.

At the very least you need to update your policies to cover social computing. But you'll also probably want to monitor social media to detect any disclosures that do happen. In fact, it's even possible that failure to do so may leave you open to charges of negligence. Consult a lawyer for information about your responsibilities regarding social media disclosure.

Other Legal Issues

While everything in the following list from New York Employment Law Letter via HRHero.com[49] may not pertain to your enterprise, many items affect all businesses, profit or non-profit, large or small.

You can face potential liability from employee use of social networking sites or blogging in a variety of ways:

- **Slander, defamation, and libel** — Your company could be held liable if an employee posts negative statements about another person or a competitor on a Website or blog.
- **Trade secrets and intellectual property infringement** — The disclosure of certain trade secrets can destroy the "confidential" status of the information, and the disclosure of a third party's confidential information could lead to an action for trade secret misappropriation or intellectual property infringement.
- **Trade libel** — Misstatements or misrepresentations about a competitor could lead to claims of trade libel.
- **Securities fraud and gun-jumping** — Publicly traded companies can face sanctions for securities fraud if material misrepresentations are posted. Any postings plugging the registered company could violate federal securities law.
- **Employment actions** — Employees may try to sue you for wrongful termination or discrimination if their employment is terminated because of postings that reference personal aspects of their life (*for example,* marital status or sexual orientation).
- **Harassment** — Language that is harassing, discriminatory, threatening, or derogatory could prompt a lawsuit.

As always, you should seek legal counsel only from a lawyer and not from a book such as this or the Web.

---

[49] HRHero.com: **bit.ly/9Xiop5**

Your Community Might Expect Social Media Responses

As the social computing movement gains momentum, it is becoming more and more common that stakeholders expect a response to complaints or other comments made online. Depending on your business, you may not be in this position today, but you will probably be in the near future.

This is especially true if you've dipped your social media toe in the water and have a Twitter or Facebook account that you don't monitor. Being on social media sets up an expectation that you will monitor and respond. As we've said before, don't get involved until you're ready to make a commitment for the long term.

Thinking Social Computing is Irrelevant

Despite our enthusiasm, and the probable enthusiasm of some of the people around you, you need to take all this social media stuff with a grain of salt.

At the present moment, it's very possible that what works online may work just fine offline as well. However, the two environments, while they do track closely on many fronts, are not identical.

The big brands have taken notice of this fact. In a 2009 article[50] in Advertising Age, Abbey Klaassen talks about the difference between what the general population is interested in versus what Twitter users are interested in:

> For example, in the past month [April, 2009], the Twitter community has been titillated by South by Southwest, AT&T, "Lost" and the redesign of Skittles.com. Missing from the list are things [that] the Communispace and Lightspeed surveys, both separately commissioned on Ad Age's behalf, found that the general population is fired up about, such as the AIG bonuses and the bank-bailout plans.

So offline does not equal online, yet.

Given the risks, however, social media shouldn't be ignored. But it also shouldn't be treated as the be-all and end-all for your organization. And as time goes on, the growth of social media will continue, and the two worlds will track much more closely. So if you do choose to ignore social media for now, don't do so for too long.

---

[50] Using Social Media to Listen to Consumers: **bit.ly/bGFtdl**

Monitor Social Media

If you decide that you aren't ready to engage with social computing but you can't afford to ignore it, a low-risk option is to merely monitor what is being said about your enterprise online.

There are lots of free and paid options for monitoring social media and some of them are quite complex, allowing for the semi-automated determination of a concept called sentiment.

Sentiment generally measures how people who are talking about you online feel about you. Social monitoring tools can recognize angry, sad, positive, happy, and a variety of other sentiments by extracting terms from online text.

Monitoring of message texts and sentiment is a key component to measuring the effect of your social media efforts, and it can also help you get acclimated to listening to your community. We talk about this in greater detail in the sections *Listen to Your Community* and *Measure Results*.

We recommend that you start monitoring social media well in advance of any initial attempts to use it. Once you start listening, you may be surprised at what people are saying, both negative and positive.

One of the great things about social computing is you can potentially see everything people are saying about you online. One of the sobering things is you might not like what you see.

If you're an organization of any size, you've had people bad-mouthing you for your entire existence. No business is perfect, and there are lots of people who do nothing but find fault. Before there was online, people were talking negatively about you, but you couldn't always hear.

With social media, not only you can hear the bad things people are saying, you can respond and engage with the speakers.

Isn't that great? We think that's fantastic! For the first time in history, you have the opportunity to engage with your detractors, and perhaps change their minds or mitigate their effect. See a good example of how doing so can turn a negative into a positive in the section *Engage and Clarify* on page 211. Being able to answer your critics is an unprecedented advantage for your enterprise, and how you deal with it will be important for your success with social media.

We strongly recommend that if you cannot productively engage with naysayers, you should ignore them. If you engage with them in a non-productive way (denying their validity, calling them names), you can do way more harm than good.

If you're just in monitoring mode, of course, you won't start engaging; you'll just be listening to what people say about you. You may be tempted to engage, but we recommend that you wait until you've listened for a while, and until you've got a plan for how to approach both the supporters and the detractors. Get your social computing strategy together first before engaging. It's too risky to do otherwise.

What if you are listening and no one is talking about your business? How do you get them to start talking? Well, first you start by engaging with social media.

Engage with Social Media

Obviously, we think you should engage with social media, but only if your organizational assessment determines that you can make it a positive experience both for the enterprise and your stakeholders.

Josh Mendelsohn, Vice President of Chadwick Martin Bailey, sums it up nicely:

> While social media is not the silver bullet that some pundits claim it to be, it is an extremely important and relatively low cost touch point that has a direct impact on sales and positive word of mouth.
>
> Companies not actively engaging are missing a huge opportunity and are saying something to consumers —intentionally or unintentionally — about how willing they are to engage on consumers' terms.[51]

Mendelsohn's company surveyed 1,500 consumers and found those who are Facebook fans and Twitter followers of a brand are more likely to not only recommend, but also more likely to buy from those brands than they were before becoming fans/ followers.

So there are some pretty compelling reasons to get engaged.

If you've been through the assessments and caveats we've presented above, and you think you're ready, then begin with an examination of your current organizational strategy, and fit your social computing strategy to it. The next section can help guide you in this process. After you have created your social computing strategies, see the section *How to Engage with Social Computing* on page 91.

---

[51] Chadwick Martin Bailey is custom market research and consulting firm: **bit.ly/izHMWz**

Create Social Computing Strategies

"Over and over again, connecting people with one another is what lasts online. Some folks thought it was about technology, but it's not. "

Seth Godin, interactive marketing expert

Let's say you want to remodel your kitchen. A contractor visits and begins to describe his approach: "I'm going to use a screwdriver and some screws; a hammer and some nails; a saw and some wood; a sledgehammer and a crowbar."

Another contractor visits and shows you the plans for the new kitchen, a list of materials you'll have to buy, and a project plan with a timeline and a cost.

Which contractor would you trust your kitchen project with?

It's the same with social media. You may encounter social media consultants who talk about LinkedIn, and Facebook, and Twitter, and YouTube, and Flickr, and Digg, and blogs and on and on. They may express great enthusiasm about the latest cool tools, and may encourage you to just try social media — do a quick project and just see what happens.

Hey, kids! Let's set up a Twitter account! Just as with the kitchen renovation, you're better off having a strategy, a plan, and a design before you consider the tools you'll use to engage your community via social media.

Social Media Performance Group's motto — **No Tools Before Rules**™ — means take the time to first determine what social media can do to support the strategy and goals of your enterprise. Then create a social media strategy, and map it to all the areas of your organization, inside and out. Only then should you begin to talk about tactics and tools. Your CEO's 20-year-old nephew might seem like a good option to help you get started, but he's not likely to have the depth of understanding of your strategy, and of social media strategy, to ensure that you won't just waste your time and money on an ineffective Facebook fan page, for example.

With social media, like a lot of things on the Web, you can't build it and expect them to come.

So how do you get started? First, think about the makeup of a good social computing strategy.

Elements of a Social Computing Strategy

As we've said, your social computing strategy should map social computing activities to your enterprise's overall goals and objectives. As we've stated previously in this book, a good social computing strategy:

- **Effectively communicates** goals and benefits of social media internally and externally
- **Guides selection** of the right tools to use
- **Ensures sustainability** of your social media endeavor
- **Involves regular reviews** of people, processes, and tools to ensure that your business stays relevant

Specifically, a social computing strategy addresses how your enterprise will:

- **Approach social media**
  - o Create the messaging
  - o Handle community responses, positive and negative
  - o Create and maintain social computing policy
  - o Maintain the connection between organizational strategy and social computing strategy
- **Join the conversation**
  - o Determine how to **Be a Person**, not an organization — who gets to speak online?
  - o Determine how to listen
  - o Find community members
  - o Engage your community
    - Ask for their help
    - Who manages your community?
  - o Measure your social computing success
- **Ensure safe social computing**
  - o Manage legal issues
  - o Manage your online reputation
- **Brand your business online**
  - o Determine how your main Website supports your social computing initiatives
  - o Determine kinds of online branding campaigns to focus on
  - o Manage the connection between online and offline branding
- **Find and create online evangelists**
  - o Determine the kinds of people to cultivate as evangelists

- o   Support evangelist development and sustain existing evangelists
- **Create buzz**
  - o   Examine types of online and offline promotions
  - o   Manage and sustain online buzz
- **Attract and convert new customers, staff, and evangelists**
  - o   Create online rules of engagement
  - o   Prioritize outreach techniques
- **Encourage and manage eCommerce**
  - o   Plan prospect conversion
  - o   Foster recommendations, ratings, and research
  - o   Coordinate with offline techniques

You can use this list as an outline as you create your organization's overall social computing strategy. We elaborate on many of these points in later sections of this book.

Create an Internal Social Computing Strategy

Many people think of social computing as an externally-oriented thing. The popularity of the various large social media sites — Facebook, LinkedIn, Twitter, YouTube — encourages enterprises to think social media is only about external relationships.

In reality, one of the more powerful ways to use social computing is inside your organization. In fact, as we've said, we believe that sales and marketing may be the least impressive things that social computing does. Social media can help build a sense of community among your employees, help improve internal communications, and greatly increase staff retention.

As we've mentioned, beginning by following an internal social computing strategy may be a lower-risk way to get started with social media. Whether this is your attitude or not, you should definitely create an internal social computing strategy. This strategy should support your enterprise's overall strategy and your external social computing strategy. And if the community you address has challenges in getting computer-based access to social media, you should also create a mobile social computing strategy.

Create your internal social computing strategy to help:

- Communicate with your base
- Energize your base
- Help your base communicate your enterprise's goals and objectives
- Create evangelists

Your internal social computing strategy should communicate to all stakeholders:

- What the business is
- How each stakeholder supports the mission — and each other
- How to use internal social media
- Policies
- How-to's
- Their responsibility in creating internal and external community

Your internal social computing strategy should:

- **Leverage your assessment** of staff's strengths and weaknesses so you can assign tasks accordingly
- **Create an internal communication system** to quickly and easily communicate social media strategy, tactics, and techniques
- **Ensure that employees create profiles** within chosen social media tools and actively use them
- **Identify one or two people** to be in charge of social media (both internal and external)
- **Ensure your enterprise** keeps a unified voice to the outside

Some of the organizational pain points you might want to address with your internal strategy include:

- **Inefficient Communications** — Communicating among staff or between staff and partners may rely entirely on email. This can often be inefficient as large files get emailed or recipients forget where or if they have them, resulting in redundancy and inefficiency. Consider how using social computing techniques such as internal blogs or wikis could help.

- **Ineffective Collaboration** — If your staff must collaborate on projects by, say, jointly revising a document, the back and forth of changes, and the difficulty in collecting and applying them can be challenging. In addition, reporting status via email may be prone to confusion if everyone doesn't follow the email thread. Using social computing features such as document repositories and project-based collaborative blogging may help.

- **Rampant Rumor Mongering** — One way to know if your organization seems disconnected from its leadership is the quantity of rumors that circulate within it. A leadership blog can help establish a connection between management and staff. Enabling comments on the blog can help leaders get a pulse on staff attitudes as well as foster innovation.

These are just a few ideas on ways social computing can help your enterprise. When crafting your internal strategy, look for these and other ways you can foster the social cohesion and communication of your company using social computing.

For example, as we've mentioned, using social media internally can greatly increase staff satisfaction at a relatively low cost.[52] Using forums and Twitter direct messaging can help your teams

---

[52] Just one example of the many articles and studies that support this: SocialTimes' *How to Connect With Your Employees Using Social Media, Email and Some Common Sense* **bit.ly/9o1vnP**

communicate better and in real-time. Using a wiki can help you capture the organizational knowledge that often walks out the door when an employee quits.

Create an External Social Computing Strategy

Create an external strategy to:

- **Communicate with prospects and customers**
- **Recruit new evangelists and influencers**
- **Create a network of partners** to multiply the effect of your own sales and marketing efforts

It is becoming well-accepted that today's social-media-savvy users do not respond as readily as they once did to pushed marketing messages (TV, radio, newspapers, magazine advertising).[53] Social media transforms an old sales platitude — "People do not like to be sold, but they love to buy" — into "People love buying from their friends. Make someone your friend and they will buy from you."

The advertising industry knows this, according to the Chief Creative Officer of the world's 4th largest ad agency, Craig Davis of J. Walter Thompson:

> Audiences everywhere are tough. They don't have time to be bored or brow-beaten by orthodox, old-fashioned advertising. We need to stop interrupting what people are interested in & **be** what people are interested in.[54]

So it's likely that your average prospect is barraged daily with appeals and pitches, which they can become quite adept at ignoring. Social media, on the other hand, creates value by fostering a relationship with an organization and a brand, rather than creating another loud member of a clamoring crowd.

A social computing strategy has become a must, particularly for large enterprises, and incorporating social media into an organization's overall strategy ensures that social media becomes an integrated driver of relationships, brand loyalty, and sales, rather than a less-effective afterthought.

---

[53] Fournaise Marketing Group, **bit.ly/bAkvPe bit.ly/dmwcg9**

[54] Exist.com: **bit.ly/kj6p4I**

Social Media Performance Group Approach

Our approach to creating a social computing strategic plan is designed to first and foremost integrate with your organization's strategic goals. We believe attacking a point opportunity ("Let's do some tweets about our new product") or a tactical implementation ("Let's drive traffic to our YouTube client testimonials") without alignment with your enterprise's strategy not only misses much of the value social media can bring to an organization, but also risks becoming counterproductive.

In addition, if all social media efforts are not coordinated with clear objectives and metrics, your organization runs the risk of wasting money and effort and losing effectiveness.

We lay out the elements of a successful approach to a social computing strategy in the sections that follow.

Review Business Strategy

As a first step, as we've indicated in previous sections, conduct a review of your enterprise's strategy, goals, and implementation plans to ensure alignment of the social media strategy. Next, work with your organization's senior leaders to create an enterprise-wide strategic blueprint. Determine how social media will support your operations, employees, sales, service delivery, and so on.

During this process, you should examine all the potential social media touch points for your enterprise, both internally and externally. We suggest you look beyond the usual suspects when thinking about how social media can help your company.

Who are the usual suspects? Typically, the leading purveyors of social media solutions in businesses of all sizes are public relations and marketing, and it's likely the same for your organization. The *2009 Digital Readiness Report*,[55] found that PR and Marketing lead the vast majority of social media engagements inside businesses of all types and sizes:

- In 51 percent of businesses, PR leads digital communications compared to 40.5 percent where marketing leads
- PR is responsible for blogging at 49 percent of all businesses vs. marketing's 22 percent
- PR is responsible for micro-blogging (think Twitter) at 52 percent of all businesses vs. 22 percent for marketing, for a combined 74 percent

---

[55] Produced by iPressroom, a hosted content management software platform, with support from the Public Relations Society of America: **bit.ly/djp0cw**

We think this state of affairs misses the point of social media, which, for us, is about relationships between people, not pushing PR and marketing messages.

Social media expert and author David Meerman Scott says:

> At every one of my speeches, I say PR people are spammers. That gets everyone's attention so I have an opportunity to explain what I mean … I get several hundred unsolicited press releases and PR pitches every week. Well over 99% of them are not targeted to me, instead they are sent to me because I am on various PR people's lists …

Scott is far from being alone in this situation. Way back in 2006,[56] writer Tom Foremski called for the death of the press release:

> Press releases are nearly useless. They typically start with a tremendous amount of top-spin, they contain pat-on-the-back phrases and meaningless quotes. Often they will contain quotes from C-level executives praising their customer focus. They often contain praise from analysts, (who are almost always paid or have a customer relationship.) And so on...

> Press releases are created by committees, edited by lawyers, and then sent out at great expense through Businesswire or PRnewswire to reach the digital and physical trash bins of tens of thousands of journalists.

> This madness has to end. It is wasted time and effort by hundreds of thousands of professionals.

With all due respect to PR professionals, the typical public relations approach is to scatter a million seeds, hoping some will find fertile ground. From their perspective, this makes sense. From a recipient's perspective, it doesn't. Those who groan under the load of all the messages wonder why you don't know them better. Why can't you establish at least a profile, and at best a relationship, so you understand what they want and are interested in?

The answer is because public relations has never had a tool that enables relationships. They've got a seed-scatterer.

The cool thing is social media provides a better way: relationships not messages. The further cool thing is you've got people all over your organization who can create relationships. PR professional Todd Defren responded to Foremski's cry to kill the PR by creating a template for a social me-

---

[56] Foremski's *Die! Press release! Die! Die! Die!* **bit.ly/nwPtwB**

dia press release.[57] That's a good start, but using this tool with a standard PR distribution system still misses the point.

Our point is that, no matter how enlightened they may be about social media, letting the PR and marketing folks in your enterprise dominate your social media use, might cause you to miss lots of places where social media can contribute to your organization, and as a result, you'll scatter a lot of seeds on fallow ground.

Enterprises that have understood the real potential use social media inside and outside their organizations successfully. When we help enterprises realize the value of social media, we do this based on our proprietary Enterprise Social Media Framework™ (ESMF). The ESMF maps your organization's structure to social media best practices and includes dozens of illustrative case studies pulled from the experiences of non-profit and for-profit organizations from all over the world. Insights derived from the ESMF help enterprises fully utilize the potential of social media.

---

[57] *MultiVu - SHIFT Communications Debuts First-Ever Template for "Social Media Press Release"*: **prn.to/pE7XNd**

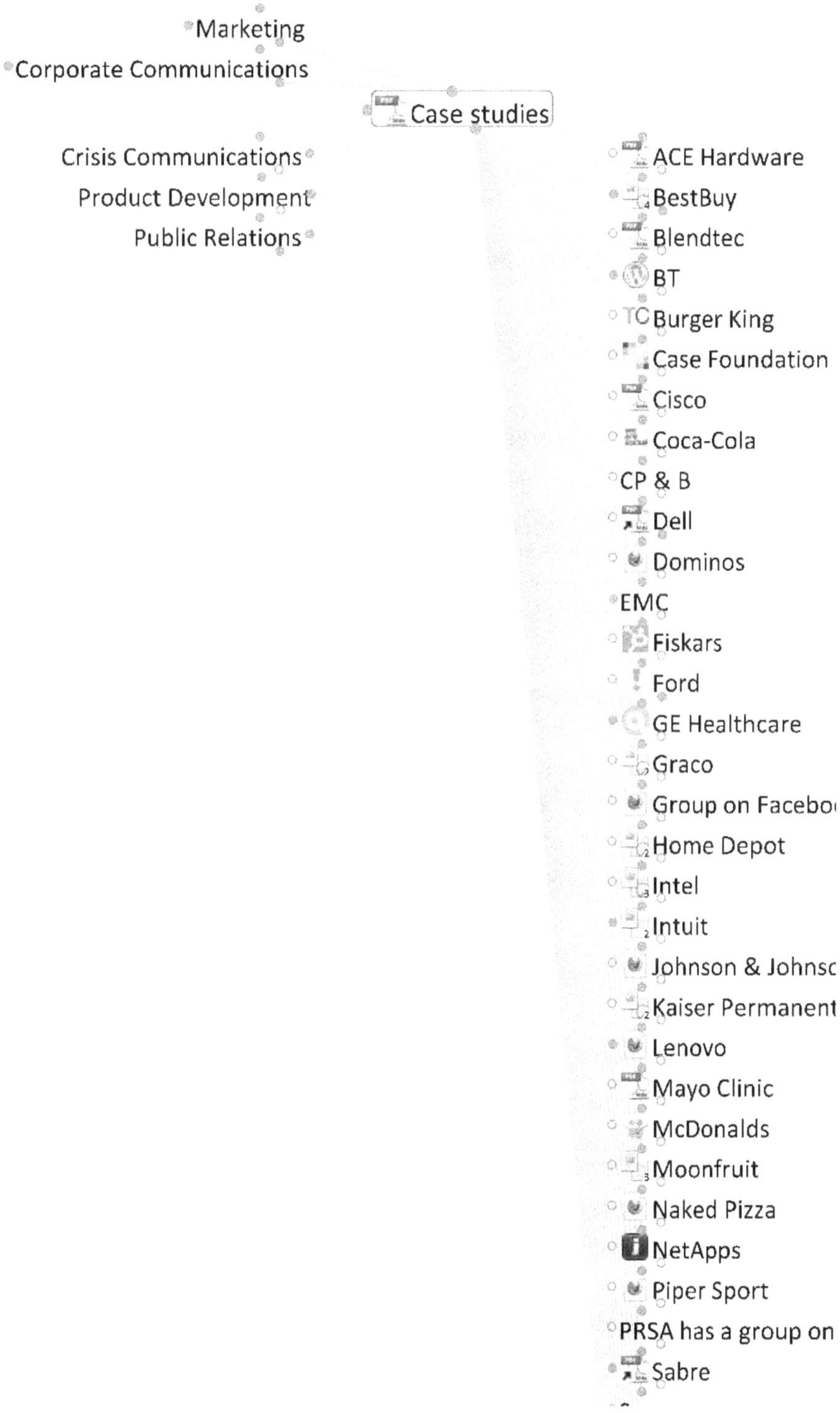

Marketing

Corporate Communications

Case studies

Crisis Communications

Product Development

Public Relations

ACE Hardware

BestBuy

Blendtec

BT

Burger King

Case Foundation

Cisco

Coca-Cola

CP & B

Dell

Dominos

EMC

Fiskars

Ford

GE Healthcare

Graco

Group on Facebo

Home Depot

Intel

Intuit

Johnson & Johnsc

Kaiser Permanent

Lenovo

Mayo Clinic

McDonalds

Moonfruit

Naked Pizza

NetApps

Piper Sport

PRSA has a group on

Sabre

Figure 4 — A small section of the Case Studies area of SMPG's ESMF

You can contact us if you're interested in learning more about ESMF. Otherwise, take a look at what has been successful for enterprises like yours and think about how the advantages of social media can help you beyond PR and marketing.

Finally, decide which opportunities to address first, and develop implementation plans.

Comprehensive Strategic Approach

We propose that you take a comprehensive approach in which you:

- **Analyze the competition** — Ensure that your enterprise is positioned to succeed against competitors' efforts

- **Create a comprehensive social media strategy** — Develop a social media strategy that is intimately bound to your objectives and current implementations

- **Create a social media tactical plan and structure** — Be sure to iterate out all implementation details to create a turnkey social media infrastructure including:

  - A community space on your organization's Website where users can comment
  - A facility to capture client reviews, suggestions, and testimonials
  - Presence on all relevant social media sites along with tactical plans for using them
  - A model for involving partners in coordinating social media campaigns
  - Social media monitoring services

- **Ensure social media training for your enterprise** — You'll need to assess and train your organization as well as designating community manager(s) and others who will implement your tactics. If you're interested, you can outsource ongoing community management and other social media execution to Social Media Performance Group, or we can train your staff to fulfill these functions.

Integrate Search with the Social Media Strategy

Social media must be integrated with Search Engine Marketing (SEM) and Search Engine Optimization (SEO) efforts. Your enterprise may not be involved with such efforts at this point. That may be a mistake. SEM and SEO are critical to the success of any Website these days.

With recent moves by Google to index Facebook and Twitter, social media's influence on online search is accelerating to the point that leading-edge firms are increasingly talking about a new term, Social Search Optimization (SSO). [58] We talk about social search in the section *Real-Time Social Search* on page 208.

All your Websites should follow good Search Engine Optimization processes, so you should review current practices and determine how social media interacts with SEO. (We cover this in the *Find Your Community* section on page 103.) Among the areas that you should address are page content, titles and metadata, content positioning, underlying codebase, site navigation, sitemap, and URL structure.

Create and implement a Social Search Optimization strategy, including identifying keywords and analyzing competitive sites. See the sections *Advanced Google Searching* and *Optimizing for Google* for more information on using Google and SEO.

Writing Your Social Media Strategy

Work with your organization to identify and implement your organization-wide social media strategy and associated implementation plans. The following are the main social media areas that will require development and implementation.

Determine Important Points

Develop a set of talking points that will be used to engage potential evangelists and supporters using social media. The points may change over time, as you learn more about your community.

The talking points should emphasize the special qualities of your business's services and foster a personal relationship with your brand. They should sound natural if delivered by an average person and should appeal to the emotional connection that your best customers feel with your enterprise's products or services. However, the message needs to be customized by audience as much as possible, so you may need to develop several groups of talking points.

Identify Influencers

All people using social media are not equal in their ability to influence others. Identify those who are already talking about and recommending your products or services, especially those with a significant online and social media presence. You may, for example, start with your organization's customer support people and concentrate on those who actively work with your clients.

---

[58] Some Social Search Optimization resources: **slidesha.re/dTdBDM slidesha.re/dQ68z3 slidesha.re/igunmG**

Create talking points for these influencers and think of other ways to enable them to help spread the word. The message will spread better if it is more easily found, and influencers can help your business's messages and products place higher in search engine results as well.

The goal is to quickly develop a number of evangelists, those who feel passionate about your products and your business and who will, with a little support, happily pass on information and help to convert others.

Create a Brand for the Social Media Effort

A good online movement needs a name. The name should be short, catchy, and communicate the goals of the effort. Building on the research efforts above, create the name and then use it to brand all campaign efforts. Your organization's site and partner Websites must help support the branding, and prominently feature selected user-generated content (UGC) in support of the campaign.

A great example of this was Yum! Brands' *Crash the Super Bowl* campaign[59] which encouraged people to submit ideas for Doritos commercials to run during Super Bowl XLV. Some of the user-generated ads were celebrated as the best presented during the entire broadcast.

Now this was a glitzy, highly costly campaign — especially considering the $1 million price tag for an advertising slot. But your enterprise might do a similar campaign, for far less money, to encourage your supporters to offer you ideas for your YouTube channel. This type of approach is called crowdsourcing, and we talk about it later in this book.

Establish a More-Effective and Coordinated Social Media Presence

The best way to get into social media is to start to participate (after creating a strategy and first listening for a while, of course!)

The best way to participate is to engage people one-on-one through active listening, rather than pushing advertising messages at them.

This strategy involves building on any existing enterprise social media assets such as customer stories and testimonials, YouTube videos, Twitter accounts and other sites. Create presences on popular social networking sites as well as engaging with those who are already using social media to discuss your products and your business.

All these efforts should be coordinated, and revolve around the talking points. Consider creating a branded social networking site that enables user-generated content, either standalone or as part

---

[59] Crash the Superbowl: **bit.ly/hAlYld**

of your organization's site. You should recognize, however, that this is a substantial undertaking. We talk about architecting your own community in the section *Building Your Community* on page 393.

Capitalize on Existing Relationships

Ensure that all stakeholders whom the enterprise touches regularly — your organization's sales and marketing folks as well as customer service and product management — are kept up-to-date via social media and other means.

This means leveraging any existing Internet assets such as email lists as well as other established marketing and public relations partners and also encouraging stakeholders to reach out to those they can influence.

Leverage Traditional Media Resources

Fold the social media campaign in with traditional marketing efforts such as press releases and other media contacts. Ensure that the campaign's brand is extended into traditional media. And remember: Don't stop doing anything you're already doing just because you're now doing social media. Ensure that all your efforts reinforce one another.

Enable Direct Supporter Actions

Provide media assets such as videos, screensavers, and special badges[60] to evangelists and other supporters. This concept extends to all forms of user-generated content, including blogs/posts, audio, and especially email.

Create a Mobile Social Computing Strategy

Many of your prospects may not have regular access to computers or the Internet, and others may prefer mobile devices for their daily social media use. You may want to create a non-Web-based social computing strategy to leverage:

- Smart mobile phones
- Tablets such as iPads and Android pads
- Texting

---

[60] See the definition of badges on page 26.

Mobile social computing is becoming a very important way users are interacting with social media. According to Facebook, in mid-2011 more than 250 million people were using Facebook from their mobile devices every month.[61] That represents a growth of 384 percent in less than two years, as there were just 65 million[62] users of using Facebook Mobile[63] in September 2009.

In fact, a recent study[64] by Ground Truth found that US mobile users spend almost 60 percent of their time on social networks.

Percent of Time Spent on Mobile Internet Usage by Category

Category	Percent
Social Networking	59.83%
Portals	13.65%
Operator	9.02%
Messaging	7.35%
Mobile Downloads	1.27%
All Other	8.88%

MySpace and Facebook were the top destinations cited in the study, which brings up an interesting point: Mobile users may not be the same demographic as computer-based social media users. Facebook has many times the number of members as the fading MySpace, yet MySpace was the most popular destination for mobile users, followed closely by Facebook. No other highly-popular social media sites were in the top 10 in the study.

MySpace's demographic skews young, with a generally higher proportion of high-school-age and younger users. However, with the sale of MySpace in mid-2011, you may want to watch carefully how the site evolves with new owners.

So if you want to reach mobile users, you'll need to adjust your approach and your messaging.

There is even research that indicates that mobile social media use is more popular than computer-based usage. A study by Ruder Finn in February, 2010[65] found:

- 91 percent of mobile phone users go online to socialize compared to only 79 percent of traditional desktop users

- Mobile phone users are 1.6 times more likely to bank online compared to traditional desktop users (62 percent versus 39 percent)

---

[61] Source: Facebook **on.fb.me/biGYNr**

[62] Source: Facebook **bit.ly/9fE4qn**

[63] Facebook Mobile: **on.fb.me/bpiCmQ**

[64] Ground Truth is a mobile computing research firm: **bit.ly/oaaE65**

[65] Ruder Finn is a public relations firm: **bit.ly/djlLb8**

Based on these statistics, you may find that you need to create a mobile social computing strategy that is slightly different from the rest of your external strategy. Since many social media sites are not optimized for the restricted bandwidth and small screen size of mobile phones, you may want to concentrate your efforts on sites that better-support these devices. Facebook has been a leader in this area.

Where to Go from Here

There's much more on these social computing strategy components in the latter part of the book, along with a lot of how-to advice.

But for now, let's take a look at some overall rules for using social computing, in the next section.

The 10 Commandments of Social Computing

"I think our nature is to be active and engaged.
I've never seen a 2-year-old or a 4-year-old
who's not active and engaged.
That's how we are out of the box.
And if you begin with this presumption,
you create much more open, flexible arrangements that
almost inevitably lead to greater satisfaction for individuals
and great innovation for organizations."

Daniel Pink, media theorist

Social Networking, Social Media, Social Computing — whatever you call it, it's big, it's new, and it's growing rapidly. We've collected several rules for using social media as the 10 Commandments of Social Computing.[66]

---

[66] For other folks' 10 commandments, see:
bit.ly/c2L97N
bit.ly/9NWATb
bit.ly/c5s1ZT
bit.ly/ceUjEs
bit.ly/8ZNxQG

Thou shall not social network for the sake of social networking

Social Media is Not:	Social Media is:
A Fad	Relevant to Enterprises
Just For Kids	For Everyone
About New Channels to Push Messages	About Creating Conversations
About the Tools	About Strategy
About the Techniques	About Planning and Execution
A Numbers Game	About Creating Relationships
A Replacement	A Supplement to Existing Techniques

Thou shall not abuse social networking

Quick Tips

- Don't push, push, push
- It's a conversation, not a soapbox! (we'll talk further about this)
- Avoid over-updating

    o Example: being 1 of 200 friends on Facebook, but making up 25 percent of updates — You're not that important!

- Constant nagging to join groups or causes
- Sending out multiple requests to join your cause — If they want to join, THEY WILL!
- Too many email blasts

Don't Push, Push, Push

People who do marketing are used to pushing their message out indiscriminately, hoping to somehow connect with those who will respond. In the traditional marketing environment, there is little way to identify ready recipients of the message, and marketers spend billions each year trying to segment the market and deliver the right message to the right person.

Social Media is different in three important ways:

- You can have conversations with prospects
- You can know more about your prospects and understand better how they will respond
- You can actually more-directly measure the effect of your efforts to attract and inform them

Because the medium offers these advantages, social computing users do not respond as well to the traditional push style of marketing. They may even be insulted if you blindly push your message at them.

Increasingly, online users respond better to relationship marketing. It's a conversation, not a soapbox!

Avoid Over-Updating

If you're constantly updating your status, posting to your blog or otherwise creating a high volume of messages in your social media venues, fellow users are likely to see you as annoying.

For example, if your Facebook activity comprises more than your fair share of the discussion, your friends may either tune you out or hide your updates.

It's not all about you. It's about the relationships and community that you build.

Similarly, if your messaging is one-note — join my cause, donate to my cause, write your congressperson about my cause — people will stop listening. You must balance your overt messaging with other messages of interest, either on or off topic. You'll need to discover the exact proportions that work for your community for yourself, but a good rule is to contribute four times for every time you ask for something.

Imagine you're at a cocktail party. You are making the rounds and you start to talk to someone who, although he's talking about a topic you're interested in, totally dominates the conversation and constantly asks you to come to his seminar and learn more.

Do you hang out with this person, or do you find an excuse to move on, and never re-engage with him?

Social media is like a big cocktail party. The boring monologists often end up speaking only to themselves.

How do you know if you're over-sharing? Ask. Often. But not too often!　【ツ】

Thou shall focus on connections and community

People join social networks to be a part of something bigger than themselves. So it follows that most of the time, that something bigger is not you (personally) or even your cause. Remember, no matter how successful your community or your Website is, people will spend 99 percent of their online time elsewhere. So be careful to give them what they expect, and what they want, while they're at your place.

One of the main things people want online is for their voices to be heard, especially by others who are passionate about a cause, issue, or topic. Enable that. Support their desire to be heard, to be valued, and to connect. What you say is important; what they say is essential.

Everyone is looking for a group that accepts them for who they are. Your job in creating a social media space is to foster that acceptance by giving them the tools, the space, and the permission to become a cohesive, self-sustaining group. That's the Holy Grail.

People want relationships that translate into the real world, not just online! Nobody spends all their time online (well, they've at least got to answer the door and pay the pizza guy). Many people look to make their online time and relationships meaningful in TRL (The Real World). There are many ways you can encourage these offline connections:

- Have real-world meetups[67] where virtual friends can press the flesh
- Show your followers evidence of how their commitment to your cause benefits others by providing testimonials — written and via video or audio — from people you have helped
- Encourage your followers to share details from their own lives, and the positive effect their commitment to your cause has on those they interact with offline

---

[67] Meetup.com allows people to organize real-world networking meetings online: **bit.ly/btNB8n**

Thou shall not commit social networking narcissism

Narcissus was so in love with his image that he gazed at it all day, to the exclusion of other activities. Sound like anyone you know online?

The Web is full of people who are full of themselves — the kind who might say, "Enough about me. What do you think about me?" Many organizations act the same way online, showing an alarming sense of self-absorption. They may be talking with you, but conversation is one way — all about them, their organization, their fund drive, their issues and obstacles, their successes.

One sign of social networking narcissism may be constantly updating your status on Facebook, Twitter, LinkedIn, or other social sites. This is like push advertising and your contacts will soon tire of hearing all about you, especially if your status is boring trivia such as, "The line at Starbucks is long" or "My cat just rolled over" or "Going up the stairs." Yes, these are all real tweets!

Of course, you may be over-sharing about your cause as well. Remember, it's not all about you, your group, your cause! People spend most of their time elsewhere. You need to be interesting first, and interested always. This means you comment on other people's posts; you send them messages asking how they're doing; you help develop and sustain a relationship with your contacts.

Narcissism, self-promotion, and boring/excessive status updates are often cited as the top reasons people "unfriend" or disconnect with others online.[68]

Finally, the form of your communication also counts. Don't just make statements; ask questions, and especially open-ended questions, even if they're off-topic: What's your favorite movie? What's your best idea for promoting our cause? What could we be doing better?

---

[68] Reasons to unfriend: **bit.ly/asCI5j**

Thou shall balance business and pleasure in social networking

Social networking is supposed to be fun; don't make it all business. Don't be ultra-serious all the time. Sure, your cause is serious, and important, but acknowledge that there are other sides to life, and don't be afraid to have fun. Make a stupid pun. Link to the latest stupid LOLCat picture (**bit.ly/dspJnq**) or dumb YouTube video (**bit.ly/9SQgex**). It's all about adding value, and sometimes that value is bringing a smile to your contacts' faces.

Remember, you are competing with all sorts of entertainment, online and offline. You may find that a light and humorous tone may attract more followers or deepen existing relationships.

Be a Person! Be personal. Share things about yourself. Ask others for their opinions.

The more real you are, the better the online and offline relationship!

Thou shall be relevant

It's not about your agenda — Talk about what's important to your audience.

Sure you want to make your points about your cause, but do so in relation to your audience's needs and interests.

One of the keys to social media success is providing what they want, not necessarily pushing what you want. Be relevant to their lives, even if it means straying off point. You want a relationship, a true, two-way understanding with your community. Think of the significant relationships in your life. How many of them are one-dimensional, built only upon a common interest in bowling, fishing, novels, disaster movies, or whatever?

Chances are in your best, most significant personal relationships, you connect on many levels. Ensure that you do that via social media as well.

Thou shall customize your strategy for your target groups

Before you even start using social media to improve your relationship to your followers, be sure you know who they are, how they differ, and how they want to be addressed.

How can you find these things out? Ask them.

Take the example of Fiskars, the Finnish manufacturer you probably know, if you know of them at all, as a maker of scissors. Scissors. A pretty boring category. Who cares what brand of scissors you buy? How utterly, utterly dull.

Well, if that's the way you feel, you couldn't be more wrong.

Think about Fiskars' audience. What are they doing with the scissors (and punches, shape cutters, stampers, craft trimmers, embossers, knives and multitools, edgers, and other craft tools)?

They're scrapbooking and doing other crafts.

If you know any scrapbookers, you know they can be very passionate, even fanatical. And they are inherently social. They like to get together IRL (In Real Life) and swap ideas, and work on their projects together.

So Fiskars did a very smart thing, way back in 2006: They created the Fiskateers social media site.[69]

How did they start their site? They found four women who were committed to scrapbooking and made them the heads of a nationwide campaign to create online and offline places (retail stores) for people bound by this common interest to gather and share ideas and community.

The site won awards. It generated results:

- 6,250 members in 50 states
- 1,000 certified volunteer demonstrators
- In craft stores where Fiskateers are involved Fiskars has three-times-higher sales growth than in non-member stores
- 13 new product ideas/month
- 85 percent of "Fiskateers" likely to recommend the product to a friend[70]

And, by the way, Fiskars spent less than $500,000 on this effort.

So you need to understand the segments of your target market. And you need a strategy for dealing with each. For sure there are some you will not be able to reach online. But a surprising number will not only respond to you online, they're already there and talking about you and your cause. Find their communities, listen, and tailor your approach to their needs.

---

[69] Fiskateers site: **bit.ly/9oBR3R**

[70] Adam Singer, blogging about Jackie Huba's (Church Of The Customer) Keynote at MIMA Summit Oct 5th, 2009: **bit.ly/cPol5P**

So your question is: Can you find four women?
(Or eight men. 【ツ】)

Thou shall balance online activities with real world activities

For best results, social networking relationships should translate into real world action of some kind. This action may be face-to-face (F2F) meetings, commitments to act on behalf of your cause, or some other action such as donation.

Social networking is a way to stay connected in between real world events. If your organization has periodic events, social networking can keep participants connected and top-of-mind in the intervals between real world community meetings.

Social networking is a dynamic way to quickly get the word out about real world events. Combine it with your normal online promotions, such as email lists, newsletters and online advertising.

If you put all your eggs in the social networking basket, you may one day realize that you've lost some of the real world connections you built up over the years.

Thou shall not try to control everything

As we've discussed, social media is about the community, not about you. And that implies that you have to give up some control in order to do social media. You may be used to thinking you're in control of your brand, your message. Well, you never really were. What people think about you has always been your brand. Leroy Stick, the anonymous person behind the satirical, faux BP Twitter account, @BPGlobalPR, perhaps said it best:

> So what is the point of all this? The point is, FORGET YOUR BRAND. You don't own it because it is literally nothing. You can spend all sorts of time and money trying to manufacture public opinion, but ultimately, that's up to the public, now isn't it?[71]

People have always talked about you (if you're lucky), and sometimes they say bad things about you. Now their talk is visible on the social Web, and you can see, perhaps too vividly, what your brand is, and what messages your community produces about — you!

To engage the community, you're going to need to give up control.

---

[71] Leroy Stick's blog post on StreetGiant: **bit.ly/btswHj**

You won't control the conversation. You won't control the venue (close your site and they'll go elsewhere and bad-mouth you). You won't control how people react to you.

Giving up control is the toughest thing for all organizations — You're not alone!

Social networking is dynamic; it belongs to the participants; it's not about control, it's about empowering people and energizing them to act on your behalf.

Social networking is about relationships, and relationships are based on a level of trust, not control.

But what if people are saying bad things about me, you ask?

Face it, if you act in the world, you'll always have detractors. The difference social media brings is that now, for the first time in history, you can not only see what people are saying about you, you can react, in real time, and, by engaging them, perhaps change their minds.

This capability alone is worth giving up some control, isn't it?

Thou shall enable people to become online evangelists

Not only can you find the naysayers online, you can also find your supporters.

Your goal should be to identify, cultivate, and empower these supporters to become your evangelists.

That requires training, teaching them how to use tools, and how to bring the message to others.

The goal of social networking is not to be a one-person show, but to create an army of people to take the message out.

According to Jeremiah Owyang, formerly of Forrester Research and now with Altimeter,[72] "An evangelist's role is to go beyond understanding and get others to believe in your product or service. This is beyond just communication and advertising and gets to the fundamental root of human communications, building trust."

People are many times more likely to take a friend's recommendation than a stranger's. Building an army of trusted friends will multiple your current efforts many fold.

---

[72] Quoted by Ashley Lomas: **bit.ly/8YRqmf**

How to Engage with Social Computing

"Audience Engagement is the proportion of visitors who participate in a specific marketing initiative by contributing comments, sharing or linking back"

Web Analytics DeMystified/Altimeter

The Holy Grail of social media is engagement. You'll see lots of blogs, comments, studies, and other discussion on the Internet about social media engagement. Everyone assumes this is the highest goal one can achieve using social media, because an engaged community is more likely to hear your message, do what you request them to do, and in general hang around and say nice things about you. But what actually is this elusive thing: engagement?

What is Engagement?

Oddly, for a medium that talks a lot about improving engagement, there's not a lot of consensus on exactly what the term means. We present one definition — by two analyst firms, Web Analytics DeMystified and Altimeter — in the quote that begins this chapter, but it, like many definitions out there, actually seems to be more about defining the ways you can measure engagement than engagement itself. In their excellent report, *"The world's most valuable brands. Who's most engaged?"*[73] Altimeter joins with fellow analyst firm Wetpaint to measure major brands' level of social media engagement. Not once is the concept explained or defined. They obviously expect their audience of brand marketers to implicitly understand the term.

---

[73] Altimeter / Wetpaint report: **bit.ly/csC04K**

They're not alone. Lots of other really smart social media folks also seem to think engagement is merely a way to measure success. Lee Odden, online marketing and search engine master at Top Rank Online Marketing, says:

> Linking, bookmarking, blogging, referring, clicking, friending, connecting, subscribing, submitting inquiry forms and buying are all engagement measures at various points in the customer relationship.[74]

With all due respect to Odden's enormous expertise, blogging is a measure? We think it's an activity. That engaged people do.

Others talk about the rewards enterprises can reap from the engaged. Social media guru Brian Solis points to statistics about engagement's effects on sales: "An impressive 51 percent of Facebook fans and 67 percent of Twitter followers indicated that they are more likely to buy since connecting online."[75]

Along these same lines, social media expert Jason Falls simplifies the definition, but perhaps a little too much: "Did you get something from your audience that can make your business better?"

Online community expert Amber Naslund gets a bit more specific, and a bit closer to an actual definition of engagement, saying[76] it involves one or all of the following:

- Interaction with unselfish intent
- Conversation
- Acknowledgement that we've been heard
- Responsiveness
- Unique contributions
- Personalized connection

The rest of the definitions we've seen run from the simplistic, and not all that helpful ("Conversing with others online in public and branded spaces" for example)[77] to lists of things to do to engage your community (provide high-quality content, answer questions, participate in conversations, provide great customer service to customers and potential customers, go off-line, meet in person).[78]

---

[74] Quoted by Jason Falls: **bit.ly/bhqZbg**

[75] Solis: **bit.ly/djsMvj**

[76] Amber Naslund runs social monitoring company Radian6's online communities: **bit.ly/9ax9pM**

[77] SayItSocial, who define themselves as Social Engagement Consultants. bit.ly/bD6b3J

[78] In a post entitled, ironically, "Six Ways to Define Social Media Engagement": **bit.ly/aReh54**

How to Engage with Social Computing

We don't really mean to tweak all these experts, but it is a sign of the new and maturing nature of social computing that so many talk about engagement, but so few attempt to define exactly what the term means. Apparently it's like art: We can't define it, but we know it when we see it.

We define social media engagement as interacting with a community that is:

- Listening
- Trusting
- Responding
- Communicating
- Acting

They are listening to you, maybe not all the time, but regularly or periodically. They trust what you say because you've built a rapport and a relationship with them. They respond to you, either by means of comments or other online participation, or by telling others about you. They are communicating their concerns, needs, passions, and interests to you; thus you can know them better. And, most importantly, they are acting. They may be buying your products, telling other abouts them, commenting, recommending, rating, or taking any of the myriad of actions you provide for them to get involved.

If your community is doing these things, they are engaged. And that's pretty much all you need to know about that.

Joining the Conversation

As we've seen in earlier chapters, if you're a company of any size with sufficient history, people are already talking about you.

Do you ignore the conversation?

Or join in?

Well, if you've read this far, we hope you've decided that ignoring is not smart, and joining in is a real possibility. Let's talk about how you engage those who are talking about you or your enterprise.

Social Media Performance Group Social Media Approach

You'll find lots of prescriptions for social media success out there on the social Web, and many of them are known by snappy acronyms: The Five A's, the Four C's, 5x6, and so on. We couldn't come up with a slick acronym; didn't really try. What we have are five action verbs for execution (FAVEs? Oops. That one just sort of happened!) that you should keep in mind as you begin to engage with your community.

Here are the FAVEs in short, and we detail each of these in subsequent sections.

Listen

This one's first for a reason. Many businesses forget that you must listen before you speak. You must offer before you take. You must engage before you ask for action. Spend the first month or more of your social computing engagement process just listening to what people are saying. Restrain yourself from responding, even (especially!) if you see things you don't like. Gauge the tenor of the conversation. What words do they use? How are they feeling? What gets them upset? What goads them to action?

During this phase, follow the old adage: It is better to be silent and thought a fool than to open your mouth and remove all doubt.

While you're listening, start sorting your community into segments. Who are the loudmouths? Who are respected? Who are emotional about your product? Who are skeptical?

You'll want to devise different approaches to the groups you find. The beauty of social computing is it enables you to address different groups differently. Start planning your engagement strategy while you listen. We talk more about listening in the chapter *Listen to Your Community* on page 99.

Find

OK this one logically comes first. How can you listen until you find who's speaking? But we think you see why Listen has to come first.

Mark Zuckerberg, the young creator of Facebook, famously said, "Communities already exist. Instead, think about how you can help that community do what it wants to do."

There's a community out there talking about you or your business. You need to find it and engage with it. Help it do what it wants to do. You probably won't have to look hard, but you

---

should realize the community may exist only online, only offline, or both. If it's only offline, you've got a bit of convincing to do to get them online.

To find your community, ask around. Ask others in your field. Google your business, products, product category. We've got more ideas in the *Find Your Community* section on page 103.

Engage

Engaging with your community means — at last! — joining the ongoing conversation. Don't think that you can land like a ton of bricks and start dominating. Follow the 4-to-1 rule: Comment on four posts for every post that you write. Give — invest — in the relationship before you ask for anything.

A great personal example of the need for giving before getting came after we did a seminar for a job seekers' group. After the presentation, an engineer came up to us and said, "LinkedIn doesn't work for job search." We asked why he thought this. "Well," he said, "I did what you said and joined the same LinkedIn group as someone who worked at my target company. I sent her a connection request, and she accepted. So I sent her a message asking her to introduce me to the hiring manager. And she refused! When I asked why, she said, 'I don't know you.' So LinkedIn doesn't work."

So what our engineer friend didn't realize, and what you need to always keep in mind, is that it's **social** networking. Approach it as you would approach building a relationship in real life. You may be able to meet more people online, but they're still people, and will develop a relationship with you over time, not immediately.

Once you have the hang of participating, you can begin to be more active — starting topics, offering more information about your business — but until your community is comfortable with you, don't get too heavy. Your early aim is to get people to check out your Website.

Which means you're probably going to need to renovate your Website. You need to make it social-media-aware and social-media-friendly. We talk about some ways to do that in the section *Engagement on Your Site* and we get more detailed about engaging in the section *Engage Your Community* on page 113.

Ask

After you've earned your stripes with your community, you can start asking for action. Your first Ask shouldn't be as bold as, "By our product," or "Give us your number and a sales person will call." You've just met these people! It would be like arriving at a party in a beautiful mansion and asking, "So how much did you pay for this dump, anyway?" You could say that to your best friend, but you aren't best friends with your community yet.

Make sure your Ask is appropriate to the reputation and amount of social capital you've amassed through your participation. By no means should you immediately set up your own community and ask everyone to join. That step comes later, much later, if ever, and you'll probably know when it's appropriate.

Nonetheless, there's no harm in having lots of Asks on your existing site, and inviting your community to come by for a look. If people want to take an action, you need to make it easy for them. We explore asking in the section *Ask for the Commitment* on page 141.

Measure

You'll read a lot about social computing measurement on the Web. It's an obsession among certain people, many of whom swear it's not possible to measure social media outcomes.

We think social media is the only medium where it is possible to measure outcomes exactly.

You'll hear people claim, "I know exactly how much money I'll raise if I do this direct mail campaign." And they may be right. Through trial and error, they've discovered an approach that works. But can they tell you which of their messages go immediately into recycling? No, because if they could, they wouldn't mail those pieces out in the first place.

It's the same with TV and radio advertising. It's an old saw in the advertising world: "I know half of what I spend on advertising is wasted. I just don't know which half." Heh. Not really that funny considering you're talking blithely about wasting more than $209 billion annually in the US alone.

Online you can connect your actions with the response. Don't let anyone tell you any differently. It may not be a snap to do, but it's possible. We discuss how in the *Measure Results* section on page 147.

Where to Go from Here

Each of these components of our social media approach is further explained in subsequent sections. Also later in the book is a wealth of how-to advice and tactics for creating your presence on popular social media sites, including the following chapters:

- Setting Up LinkedIn
- Setting Up Twitter
- Setting Up Facebook
- Setting Up YouTube
- Setting Up MySpace
- Setting Up Blogging
- Building Your Community
- Community Building Checklist

You can find information about other versions of **Be a Person**, including the enterprise executive version, on the Social Media Performance Group Website at: **bit.ly/OrderBeAPerson**

Listen to Your Community

"[Social media is] a shift in how people discover, read, and share news and information and content.
It's a fusion of sociology and technology, transforming monologue (one to many) into dialog (many to many)."

Brian Solis, FutureWorks

In preparing to engage your online community, you'll want to collect lots of information. Here are some tips on how to do that.

Study Your Offline Community

Listen to the conversations inside your organization and in your real-world community. What kinds of things are the people you engage with on a daily basis talking about? What concerns do they face? Chances are very good that your online community will mirror these topics, but you may find they place the emphasis differently.

Make lists of topics of interest to your real-world community discusses — the things you, your staff, your volunteers, and your clients talk about every day. We suggest keeping a log for at least a couple of weeks. Determine what kinds of information your community seeks from you and start thinking about how you will provide it online.

If appropriate, create an outline indicating subtopics and different points of view on common subjects. Organizing the topics in some sort of framework will help:

- Guide you in constructing your own community framework
- Enable you to construct positions and responses on the issues you'll face in building your community

Examine the framework you create and determine what your positions are on all the issues and questions, if you haven't already. Once you've done that, you're ready to create the talking points that will form the basis of your social computing strategy. At the same time, you'll want to extract the unwritten rules about how your community converses. Are there forbidden topics? Is there a preferred style of discourse? Do people avoid sensitive topics, or is there an accepted way to discuss them? Is there a line between too much info and just enough?

In essence, you're creating the first draft of the operating manual for your online community by understanding the communication styles, rules, and needs of your offline community.

Study Existing Online Communities

Find online communities discussing your product category and/or your organization. See the section *Find Your Community* on page 103 for ideas on this. But, in general, you'll probably find interesting blogs and forums of interest via a simple Google search for the name of your product category. Twitter and Facebook searches can provide additional information.

Lurk for a while. (Lurking means reading the material, but not responding or calling attention to yourself.) Be a wallflower, but take notes and update your community manual based on the new information you discover. Note any differences in the way people communicate online versus offline. Modify your framework as necessary.

After awhile, you might consider reaching out to influential bloggers[79] or other community leaders and influencers and asking their advice. Cultivate good relationships with these folks because you may want their help in launching your community later on. Be helpful, but be careful. If you approach them in the wrong way you could do more harm than good.

During this period, you should be thinking about how and where you're going to create your community. Are you going to create it (or find it) on an existing social media site such as Facebook or MySpace? Will you create a private space on your Website?

Or will you use sites like Ning,[80] Grou.ps,[81] or Qlubb[82] to create a branded community apart from your Website? Do you want an offline and online hybrid such as Meetup?[83] If you have lots of offline events, you'll want a way for people to discover, sign up, and help promote them.

---

[79] For an example of how to reach out to bloggers, read Chris Brogan's great analysis of the perfect social media press release: **bit.ly/cVBi8G**

[80] Ning: **bit.ly/dnx5Ck**

[81] Grou.ps: **bit.ly/ajDTN4**

[82] Qlubb: **bit.ly/9nqf04**

[83] Find out more at: **www.meetup.com**.

One thing you should definitely assess: Is your community so attached to their current online home that trying to entice them to yours will alienate or anger them? Do existing communities completely satisfy their needs, or is there an opening for you to fill? Can you achieve your social media goals by contributing on existing communities, or does your contribution require its own defined, sponsored space? If you created your own community, what would be unique about it? Can you identify and market this uniqueness to attract members?

This assessment is critical to your future community success. You can waste much time and money trying to muscle your way into a completely functioning and satisfying community. Many organizations fail to consider the possibility that everyone in their right mind may not naturally flock to their community offering.

Profile Your Community

By now, you know a lot about your community, offline and online. You may have, or can collect, other information on your community that can help you sharpen your approach, such as:

- **Demographics** — You may want to consider characteristics such as gender, age, race, income, marital status and so on and use them to design different approaches

- **Psychographics** — Data on values, attitudes and shared cultural experiences of the community can help you better understand your community's mindset and better address their everyday issues and concerns

- **Geographics** — Your approach to your community may need to take into account their geographic location and how it informs members' viewpoints

If you focus on this data, you'll want to research the social media literature to see if others have developed targeting and segmentation approaches you can adopt. There are great resources for finding out more about social media included in the *Resources* section starting on page 423.

Finally, you need to do an honest assessment of your organization and its commitment: Do you have the time, resources, and dedication to create or participate in a community? Can you be in it for the long run? Are you prepared to react if things get rocky?

If all is in order, you're ready to start to engage.

Find Your Community

"Social media is no more than an extension of what we do naturally."

**MC Hammer, formerly-famous rapper
and creator of DanceJam, a social network for music/dance
with more than 100,000 visitors**

Google is your friend. Using Google you can find your community, if you do a little thinking about the keywords that community members are likely to use.

For example, if your product category is small business accounting software, Google that term.[84] Currently, that search, without quotes, yields more than 12 million results. OK, that's a bit hard to put your arms around. If you try the term as a phrase, by surrounding it with quotes, you get under 800,000 results.[85] That may seem a bit more manageable, but it still may not give the results you can use to locate places where your community is talking.

Incidentally, you'll notice when you type a search string into Google, a little window drops down from the entry area with suggestions for similar searches and Google instantly shows you results based on what it thinks you're looking for. You also may notice that after you do a search, little ads — call AdWords — appear on the right side of the search results. Refer to the next figure to see what we mean.

---

[84] Google search for small business accounting software, with no quotes: **bit.ly/poUVZM**

[85] Google search for small business accounting software, with quotes: **bit.ly/ocs9Sf**

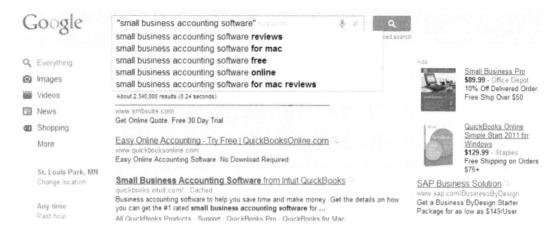

Figure 5 — Google Query with AdWords Sidebar — Example

You may find interesting search suggestions when Google offers them. If not, be sure to take a look at the AdWords on the right side. These organizations might be worth investigating, as could be potential partners, and visiting their sites may give you ideas for how to find your community online.

Be aware that each time you click on an AdWord, somebody pays Google some money, from cents to dozens of dollars. If that bothers you, you can copy the Web address from the AdWord into your browser's address bar and visit the site for free.

Back to our example. What you really want to do is to find people talking about small business accounting software on social media sites. So one thing you can do is to restrict your search to social media sites. This tip works with any type of site. Simply append a qualifier similar to the following to tell Google to only search a certain site:

site:facebook.com

Substitute any site after the colon and Google will only search the information it has indexed from that site.

Adding site:facebook.com to the Google query we're working on produces 3,800 results. OK, now we're getting somewhere. Here's what we got when we ran that search:

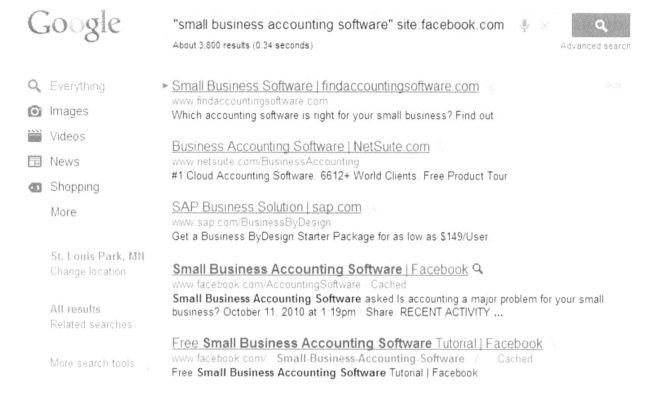

Figure 6 — Restricting a Google Search to Facebook Only

From these results we can see that people are indeed talking about small business accounting software on Facebook. Following the various links yields a group entitled "DIY Tax Accounting Software group," with more than a hundred members. If you make small business accounting software, you've just found a potential place to engage with your community.

You can repeat this exercise with other social media sites. Doing it with LinkedIn yields 206 people you'd probably like to know. Doing it with Twitter yields dozens of posts. Doing it with YouTube produces more than 575 links to videos.

You get the picture. Google is your friend, and using the site qualifier — and other advanced features available either by clicking Advanced Search up at the top of the page or clicking More on the left-hand column — you can tailor a search to find where your community is talking.

Advanced Google Searching

No matter what you're searching for, you should be sure to check out Google's More button. It offers a wealth of ways to specialize your search, including searching for:

- Maps
- News
- Shopping
- Books
- Blogs
- Updates
- Discussions

Clicking "Show search tools" offers you ways to restrict your search by time and type:

- **Any time**
- Latest
- Past 24 hours
- Past week
- Past month
- Past year
- Custom range...

- **All results**
- Social
- Nearby
- **Standard view**
- Related searches
- Wonder wheel
- Timeline

- **Standard results**
- Sites with images
- Fewer shopping sites
- More shopping sites
- Page previews
- Translated search

Wow! Be sure to check out the additional search types; they're pretty interesting. Here's a result for our "small business accounting software" search as a timeline. It would be great if you're doing a history of the subject.

Figure 7 — Google Timeline Search Example

As interesting as these options are, the one we really want to concentrate on is a relatively new one: Google's Social Search.

If you're active in social networking, you may have noticed that you often see little notices below the search results, like in the following figure. You can make this explicit by selecting "Social "by dropping down the "More" in the left column of Google search results. This causes Google to present results based on what those in your social network have tagged or otherwise recommended.

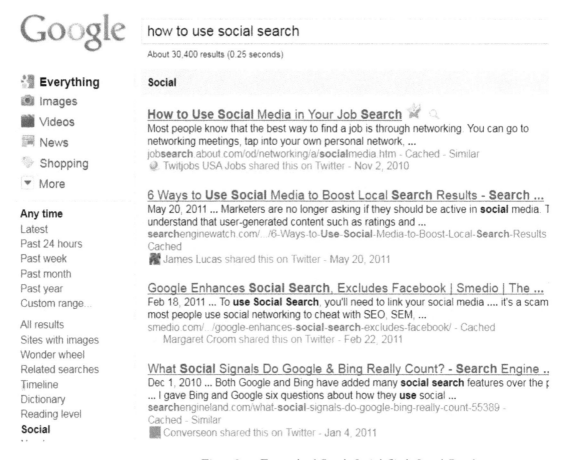

Figure 8 — Example of Google Social Circle Search Result

The concept that seeing results from people you know is going to be more interesting and relevant to you is called social search. (There's a bit more on social search in the *Real-Time Social Search* section on page 208.) Knowing that people in our social network have written or tagged related articles might make us more likely to click on these results. And any traffic generated to their sites was not so much due to any SEO techniques discussed in the previous section, but to their connection to us.

How Social Search Works

For social search to work, Google first has to know who you are. If you've logged in to any of Google's services — from Gmail to AdWords — or created a Google Profile,[86] Google knows who you are. Think about that for a moment.

OK, if it didn't creep you out, you're probably a GenY'er[87] <smile>.

So they know who you are. They can then connect up with all your Google accounts to find your friends. Of course, your Gmail address book is a primary source of information about who your friends are. Here are the areas from which Google says[88] it gathers information about your social circle:

- People in your Gmail (or Google Talk) chat list
- People in your Friends, Family, and Coworkers groups in your Google contacts
- People you're publicly connected to through social sites, such as Twitter and FriendFeed that appear on your Google profile or in your public Google Buzz stream.
- People you're following in Google Reader and Google Buzz
- People who are connections of those in your immediate, public social circle. This means that if you have a friend on Twitter, and he follows five people, those additional five people may also be included in your social circle.

Google uses your social circle to give you social search results from:

- Websites, blogs, public profiles, and other content linked from your friends' Google profiles
- Web content, such as status updates, tweets, and reviews, from links that appear in the Google profiles of your friends and contacts.
- Images posted publicly from members of your social circle on Picasa Web and from Websites that appear on their Google profiles
- Relevant articles from your Google Reader subscriptions

If you want to see more such results from people in your social circle, click More Search Tools on the left panel of the search results page and select Social to filter your results.

Here's what Google says about the privacy (!) of the information they use:

- **Public**: Public social connections that appear on your Google Profile are visible to your friends and the Internet at large. Because all of these connections are public on the web, your connection to some of these

---

[86] Create your Google Profile here: **bit.ly/bgn3s2**

[87] GenY defined: **bit.ly/bfh9bz**

[88] Google's social search page: **bit.ly/anrcsb**

people may be included in another person's social circle when appropriate. For example, if you follow Bob on Twitter, a friend of Bob's may see you in his social circle.

- **Private**: Private social connections like your Google chat list and Google contacts are not shared by Google. If you and Adam are chat buddies, we won't use that connection to expand anyone else's social circle. You cannot see Adam's other chat buddies or Google contacts, and he can't see yours. However, if you are connected to some of Adam's other chat buddies through other public networks, they may still appear in your social circle.

Google used to have a way to see your social circle in a beta test mode, but as of this writing they appeared to have pulled it, possibly in preparation for releasing Google+, their own social network.

Depending on whom your friends are, you might find the social search content interesting, inspiring, or insipid. Google has a nice introduction to social search on YouTube[89] that can help you better understand how it works, but the company is relatively mum about its further plans for the feature.

If you want to use Google social search to help market your organization, Debra Murphy[90] has a good blog post on the subject that we adapt below. It suggests you:

- Create a quality Google Profile and include all your important links
- Stop worrying about personal vs. professional connections being mixed together. Connecting with your customers and clients is critical.
- Don't fall for SEO companies claiming they will get you first page results — the game has changed and first page search results will be different based on **who you are, where you are and who you are connected with**

Take a look at Debra's last point above. Your best approach online, whether you believe all this social media stuff or not, is to ensure that who you are, where you are, and who you connect to reflect your online goals, because search is going social, whether you like it or not.

If you have a large online social circle and you post content relevant to your organization and cause, you are almost guaranteeing that anyone in your circle who searches for relevant terms will see your information on the first page of search results. Organizations pay hundreds to hundreds of thousands of dollars per month to get on the first page, so having a large, relevant social circle can create essentially free targeted advertising.

---

[89] Google's YouTube video about social search: **bit.ly/ael.BCI**

[90] Debra Murphy is a marketing coach: **bit.ly/catyrM**

If Google's hypothesis is correct — that people will trust content from people in their social circles more than they trust random search results — social search will be even more effective than traditional targeted ads or SEO techniques.

Think about that for a minute. At least in these early days, you can beat the large brands with huge marketing budgets just by tending to your community. The next section talks about reaching out and connecting with that community.

Reaching Out to Your Community

Once you find your constituency online you need to determine how to reach them. Your objectives in this phase are to determine:

- Networks your community is using
- How engaged your community is on these networks
- The conversations already happening about your organization or cause, and where they aren't happening
- Types of interactions your community is having within each network
- What others in your field are doing online

Based on the research results, you can:

- **Measure** the average frequency of relevant conversations
- **Identify** the more active hubs and communities
- **Recognize** the context of the conversations in order to determine time and variety of resources required

Once you've found where people are talking, you can determine the magnitude of the ongoing effort to monitor what they're saying. In his free e-book, *The Essential Guide to Social Media*,[91] Social Media expert Brian Solis lays out a formula calculating the effort necessary to stay current with what's going on the relevant communities and the pertinent conversations.

Now the following formula looks complex, but it's actually quite simple, so bear with us.

Solis' formula is:

$$\frac{Cn * Qc * 20}{60} = t$$

And it is calculated this way:

- The number of average relevant conversations per day per community — *Cn*

[91] Brian Solis' free e-book: **scr.bi/uzYfb**

- Multiplied by the quantity of relevant communities — Qc
- Multiplied by *20* (minutes required to research and respond and also monitor for additional responses. You may increase or decrease this based on your experience.)
- Divided by *60* (minutes)

The calculation results in *t*, the amount of time you'll need to spend monitoring social media.

For example, let's say your community produces 100 relevant conversations per day per community, and you need to track 10 communities. The formula is thus:

$$\frac{100 * 10 * 20}{60} = 333 \; minutes$$

That means, in this example, your organization must spend five and a half hours per day monitoring your community. Obviously, your mileage may vary, but this simple calculation indicates that to really get a pulse on your community requires a not-insignificant amount of time.

Applying Your Research

Throughout the research process, you'll undoubtedly see that relevant conversations occur across disparate networks that:

- Are representative of a sweeping variety of related topics
- Require varying responses
- Usually map to specific departments within your organization (those most qualified to respond)

    o Marketing and communications
    o Customer service
    o Executive management

Taking time for this research allows you to:

- Keep a pulse on relevant conversations
- Feed them, intelligently, to the right people internally
- Guide these people on the required response
- Follow-up to ensure that the interaction is more meaningful and helpful
- Distribute the responsibility across existing resources.

Once you've figured out what you'd like to say to your community, it's time to engage.

Engage Your Community

"There is no demand for messages."

Doc Searls, The Cluetrain Manifesto

Creating community is one of the hardest things to do, online or offline.

Yet online, communities can easily and spontaneously form, grow, age, and disappear in a matter of days. So forming communities is one of the easiest things to do online, right?

Confused as to what these opposing effects mean for your community? You're not alone.

Despite what you'll read online, and even in this book (see the section *Building Your Community* on page 393), there is no foolproof method for creating a community. There are some principles that seem to be tried and true, but the reality is the personalities who inhabit your community will have more effect on its viability and effectiveness than you will. Of course, you're one (or more) of those personalities, and controlling your actions and activities is extremely important if you are going to have a chance of being successful.

This means think before you post.

We suggest you create a poster of the slogan below and distribute it to everyone in your organization.

Think Before You Post

Many people have alienated others online through ill-considered statements and toxic encounters. To avoid making a mistake, never say anything online you wouldn't want

- Your own family to see
- To see on a billboard
- To be published on the front page of the Wall Street Journal

You also need to consider the heft your enterprise may have. What you say matters when you are a "someone." Your enterprise stands for something. Thus, people are likely to listen closely to what you say. Think before you Tweet/post — and think this: "If someone said this about me, would their organization or good name be harmed?"

Another thing to remember: Inauthenticity is the enemy of your social media effort. This means you need to truly understand the difference between using social media as just another one-way communication channel, and truly engaging your community.

One of the main techniques your community will hate is known as sock-puppetry: the disingenuous use of a real or fake user to parrot the enterprise's party line — just like sticking your hand in a sock puppet and expecting to be immune to criticism.

We collect a rogue's gallery of bad social media moves in our Social Media Hall of Shame at **bit.ly/HallOfShame**. It's a good primer on what not to do with social media. As far as what you should do, first you should create an engagement plan.

Elements of an Engagement Plan

Your engagement plan is the tactical realization of your social computing strategy. As such, each tactic should tie back to a strategic initiative — increasing sales, spreading the word, encouraging legislative action, increasing brand awareness, and the like.

You should consider including the following elements, as appropriate, in your engagement plan.

Goals for Engagement

You can expect various types of results from engaging with your community, and they can be categorized broadly into the following:

- **Listen and Identify** — Learning about your community via audience analysis that identifies what your community values and will respond to
- **Inform** — Increase the knowledge about your company within your community
- **Consult and Involve** — Band your community together to improve and amplify your enterprise's activities — a related concept is known as the wisdom of crowds:[92] the ability of masses of people to suggest accurate or innovative solutions to problems
- **Collaborate and Empower** — Encourage community participation and effectiveness by working together and providing empowering tools online and offline, for example, to brainstorm new ideas and approaches, collaborate on messages and themes, or to enable supporters to tell their stories and help recruit new evangelists

Chances are good your types of engagements will fall into the following categories:

- **Identification of problems, opportunities and issues** — Use community to keep a pulse on your market
- **Policy consultation** — Get your community's opinion on the direction of your organization, or about desired policy changes in government
- **Customer service and service delivery** — Find out what you're doing right, and wrong, and how you can improve your service to your clients
- **Marketing and communications** — Inform your community about significant activities of your enterprise or related entities in close to real-time (Twitter) or through regular updates (Facebook, blogging)

Ensure that your plan covers the following topics.

- **Guiding principles** — Lay out your target audiences, target outcomes, what you are offering, your key messages and success metrics. Example guiding principles:

    - Relationships sustain our community. Nurture them.
    - Action is more important than endless discussion
    - Our members are at the center of our community, and control its development

---

[92] The concept of the wisdom of crowds (defined: **bit.ly/a9cUC3**) was articulated by James Surowiecki in his 2005 book, *The Wisdom of Crowds* (**amzn.to/buJIFO**). Further discussion of this intriguing concept is beyond the scope of this book.

- **Channels** — Determine how you're going to use complementary on- and offline channels (print, TV, other social networks, ads, etc.) to let people know about and get them to contribute to your community. Examples of complementary channel use:

    - Include your social media presence in PSAs
    - Link your Facebook status to Twitter
    - Run a print promotion for a Facebook-based event

- **Activities** — What kinds of actions can your community members take on your site and elsewhere? You'll want to make these actions easy to find and easy to accomplish. Design your calls to action and the high-value interactions you are trying to encourage accordingly. Examples of activities:

    - Tell a friend
    - Like your Facebook page
    - Invite a friend to an event

- **Incentives** — Consider offering prizes, points, rebates and other benefits to community members who visit, contribute, or help other members use the site. Examples of incentives:

    - Special achievement badges members can display on their blogs
    - Two-for-one admission to your next event
    - Enter those who comment in a prize drawing

- **Roles and responsibilities** — Determine who is responsible for content creation, animation, promotion, outreach, tech support and other functions. Design the production and approval workflows. Ensure that all participants are well-informed about this process. Example roles and responsibilities:

    - Management funds the social media effort
    - The community manager manages social day-to-day activities
    - Outreach crafts the messages for distribution via social media

- **Messages** — Well in advance of launch of your social media effort, draft all the on-site and e-mail messages you're likely to need as you get started. Example messages:

    - Use AddThis[93] to add the ability for Website visitors to comment about you on social media
    - Embed YouTube videos on your Website and ask for comments
    - Include announcement of your social media effort in email newsletters

- **Timeline** — Any well-run project needs a plan that specifies what gets done when. Be sure to include all activities, including a periodic evaluation of success metrics (see the section *Create Social Media Metrics* on page 41 for ideas).

---

[93] AddThis: **bit.ly/d6oL2B**

- **Do's and don'ts** — Create a style guide for your staff to use in order to present a consistent voice. Be sure to address at least the following:

  - How often will the content be updated and posted to social media sites?
  - What type of content will be posted (topics, categories)?
  - How and who will approve content?
  - How will the site look? How is your logo to be displayed? What is the color palette?
  - How will you ensure the site is usable? Accessible (Section 508 compliant)?
  - How will you launch? We recommend a gradual, soft launch so you have time to work out the kinks.

  - How will you collect and safeguard Personally Identifiable Information (PII)?94

    - Does the site have privacy and legal disclaimers? What kinds of content need legal review? What legal jurisdictions do you need to take into account?
    - Ages of community members? Do they need to be 18 or over? How do you filter out the kids?

There's a lot more about pre-launch activities in the *Community Building Checklist* section on page 403.

Before you launch you should understand and plan:[95]

- **Goals** — What and why? Participation?
- **Outcomes** — How does this support your business?
- **Target Audience** — Who?
- **Research** — What is possible?
- **Pilot** — What small piece can you implement first as a pilot? What will you learn and apply to full plan?
- **Training** — Does anyone need to be trained in order to implement?
- **Capacity** — Who will implement? Outside expertise needed? Training?
- **Culture Change** — Once you have an initial plan, how do you get the enterprise to own it? How do you deal with resistance? How do you deal with legal department?
- **Implementation** — Who needs to know when problems arise? What about ongoing training and support?
- **Evaluation** — How will you know if you were successful? What did you learn?

After you've figured all this out, create an operating manual based on these policies and procedures and distribute it to all stakeholders. Take a look at Microsoft's Channel 9 Doctrine,[96] for a good example of how to organize this document.

---

94 Definition: **bit.ly/aX2Swd**

95 After Chris Brogan, as modified by We Are Media: **bit.ly/axqDVb**

96 **bit.ly/90OqYW**

Microsoft's Channel 9 Doctrine

Microsoft's Channel 9 Website hosts videos, podcasts,[97] and screencasts[98] about Microsoft products and initiatives. As you can see from their doctrine, the intent is to inform, not to sell. Note particularly the second and eighth bullet points.

- **Channel 9 is all about the conversation**. Channel 9 should inspire Microsoft and our customers to talk in an honest and human voice. Channel 9 is not a marketing tool, not a PR tool, not a lead generation tool.

- **Be a human being**. [We call this **Be a Person**.] Channel 9 is a place for us to be ourselves, to share who we are, and for us to learn who our customers are.

- **Learn by listening**. When our customers speak, learn from them. Don't get defensive; don't argue for the sake of argument. Listen and take what benefits you to heart.

- **Be smart**. Think before you speak, there are some conversations which have no benefit other than to reinforce stereotypes or create negative situations.

- **Marketing has no place** on Channel 9. When we spend money on Channel 9 the goal is to surprise and delight, not to promote or preach.

- **Don't shock the system.** Lasting change only happens in baby steps.

- **Know when to turn the mic off**. There are some topics which will only result in problems when you discuss them. This has nothing to do with censorship, but with working within the reality of the system that exists in our world today. You will not change anything by taking on legal or financial issues, you will only shock the system, spook the passengers, and create a negative situation.

- **Don't be a jerk**. Nobody likes mean people.

- **Commit to the conversation**. Don't stop listening just because you are busy. Don't stop participating because you don't agree with someone. Relationships are not built in a day, be in it for the long haul and we will all reap the benefits as an industry.

This doctrine is short and sweet, and this format is excellent for easily communicating your core online principles. It is not, however, a substitute for a detailed operating manual that people can refer to for answers for answers to technical, tone, and policy questions.

---

[97] Podcast definition: a series of digital media files (either audio or video) that are released episodically: **bit.ly/dx7K1U**

[98] Screencast definition: a digital recording of computer screen output often containing audio narration: **bit.ly/dxoWFE**

Create Your Internal Social Media Policy

Here are some suggested headings for your enterprise's social media policy. There's lots more advice on some of these topics in later chapters, especially in the *Community Building Checklist* section on page 403.

- **Company Philosophy** — Clearly define why your organization is using social media, what its goals are, and its general approach — formal, informal, collegial, peer-to-peer. Use this to ensure that all social media participants have a common understanding of the basics of your approach.

- **Definition of Social Networking** — It may not be immediately apparent what kinds of sites or activities your policy refers to. Is tagging photos on Flickr[99] included? How about helping create a wiki on someone else's site?[100] Be sure all involved understand the domain your policy covers. You may decide the policy covers all Internet activities, including email and instant messaging.

- **Identifying Oneself as an Employee of the Organization** — This could get tricky for some enterprises, especially if you are in a regulated industry. Should you require employees to identify themselves as part of your organization? When? Should all who speak in your name post disclaimers (comments do not reflect the opinions of [enterprise])? We recommend that you limit this type of requirement because we think the best way to use social media is to **Be a Person** (see the *Social Media Approach* section on page 177.)

- **Recommending Others** — You may want to have a policy about recommending others outside your enterprise. You may be concerned that the common social networking practice of recommending others may be construed not as a personal recommendation by a staffer, but as your organization recommending the person or group.

- **Referring to Clients or Partners** — Your enterprise may have guidelines about referencing clients, especially about revealing Personally Identifiable Information. Similarly, you may have a policy about revealing the identity of, or otherwise referring to, your partners. Make sure you cover these policies in your social media policy.

- **Proprietary or Confidential Information** — Your organization probably has a policy about revealing proprietary of confidential information. Incorporate this policy explicitly into your social media policy.

- **Terms of Service, Privacy, Copyright and other Legal Issues** — If you create social media areas of your enterprise's Website, or if you create your own online community, you'll want to spell out the terms under which you provide services. Google "terms of service" to see how other providers handle this matter. You'll also want to post a privacy policy and a notice of copyright if it is appropriate. Note that if you don't want to restrict all uses of the material in your social media site, you can use the Creative Commons

---

[99] Flickr is an image and video hosting website and online community: **bit.ly/9O2NeP**

[100] Wiki definition: a Website that allows the easy creation and editing of interlinked Web pages via a Web browser, generally around one or more common themes. The most famous wiki is Wikipedia: **bit.ly/b4hlR7**

Copyleft process, which allows you to reserve only some rights to your content, while encouraging others to otherwise use or modify it. Find out more at the Creative Commons Website.[101]

- **Productivity** — Pretty much every enterprise worries about the affect social media can have on the productivity of its workers. There are lots of studies that prove that generally the negative impact is non-existent or negligible.

  A July, 2009 study[102] by Nucleus Research found that companies who allowed employees to access their Facebook sites during work hours could expect to see total office productivity decline by an average of only 1.5 percent.

  On the other hand, an Australian study[103] showed an increase in productivity among social networking users. "People who do surf the Internet for fun at work — within a reasonable limit of less than 20 percent of their total time in the office — are more productive by about 9 percent than those who don't," said Dr Brent Coker, from the University of Melbourne's Department of Management and Marketing.

  Because of the potential benefits of staff use of social networking, we recommend a policy that stresses that social media use should not interfere with normal duties, and spells out how much use is acceptable.

- **Disciplinary Action** — Going hand in glove with the acceptable use policy should be a policy on discipline for staff whose productivity suffers due to excessive social networking use.

Your organization may develop other policies for social media use, but if you cover the points above, you should have a good basis for your initial social media policy. Like everything else regarding social computing, you'll probably revise your policies as you and your enterprise learn how best to use this technology.

---

[101] Creative Commons is an alternative to copyright: **bit.ly/dfZ5dM**

[102] Nucleus Research is global provider of research and advisory services: **bit.ly/clpklx**

[103] "Freedom to surf: workers more productive if allowed to use the internet for leisure," University of Melbourne: **bit.ly/aUCblU**

Here's an example of a short and sweet social media policy we wrote for one of our clients:

Discretion

Staff have discretion in responding to comments posted on our commenting system. However, where possible, post pre-approved responses to Frequently Asked Questions.

Tone

Be a Person. Respond in a friendly way. Do not use emotion.

Be Accurate

Make sure that you have all the facts before you post. It's better to verify information with a source first than to have to post a correction or retraction later. Cite and link to your sources whenever possible.

Think Before Posting

Don't be in a hurry to respond. Make sure you have the facts and you are not responding with emotion.

When in Doubt, Do Not Post

Associates are personally responsible for their words and actions, wherever they are. As online spokespeople, you must ensure that your posts are completely accurate and not misleading. Exercise sound judgment and common sense, and if there is any doubt, DO NOT POST IT.

Long, Repetitive Threads

If a comment thread gets too long and repetitive, ask the poster to take it offline by sending their contact info to our email address.

Commit to the Conversation

Don't stop listening just because you are busy. Don't stop participating because you don't agree with someone. Relationships are not built in a day. Be in it for the long haul and we will all reap the benefits.

Keep Records

It is critical that we keep records of our interactions with participants in our commenting system. The system keeps all posts, so this is usually only comes up when you must delete a post. Copy the offending post into a call record before deleting.

Negative Posts

When encountering a negative post (that does not violate the terms of service), encourage the poster to explain him or herself. Often they will reveal the source of their frustration. Use the Air Force blogging decision tree to guide your response. If a response to the negativity is not covered in the FAQ, let the subject matter experts respond.

Troll Policy
A troll is someone who repeatedly posts inflammatory, extraneous, or off-topic messages. Ignore trolls. Do not engage them. If they violate our terms of service, request management approval to delete them from the community.

We discuss creating policies, including the Air Force blogging decision tree, in a bit more detail in the section *Create Your Policies* on page 408.

Technical Support for Engagement

In addition to the general policy framework we've been describing, you'll need to think about the technical framework for your community. If you are using existing social media sites, be sure you understand all that the sites offer to support your goals. If you are creating your own community, either as part of your existing Website or as a standalone social media community, you'll need to decide which of the following technical functionality you require.

- **Rich media** — Rich media refers to a wide variety of technical capabilities such as the ability for members to control the format of their posts (bold, italic, add hyperlinks), add videos or podcasts, participate in games, and upload documents

- **Widgets** — Widgets are little pieces of functionality that allow you to embed features from other sites into your community site, such as LinkedIn polls, Facebook Ads, members' Twitter feeds, and so forth

- **Landing page calls to action** — Your main page may be the place most of your prospects land. You may also want to create special pages, called landing pages, for visitors who may come to your site via a Google search, from Facebook, or from a partner site. Consider crafting language and calls to action specific to these arriving visitors. You'll also want to offer opportunities for them to register for the site, and for your newsletter as well as:

    - Creating special videos
    - Offering coupons and special materials
    - Offering free trials or free demos
    - Enable "send to friend," call us, talk to an expert, and so on.

- **Thank you pages** — Whenever someone takes an action, send them to a thank you page. This is an opportunity to further engage with them and keep them on your site. Use the landing page techniques described above to offer them more value and entice them to stay

- **E-mail auto replies** — If visitors fill out a form to get something of value, offer secondary calls to action to continue the dialog by setting up an autoresponder. An autoresponder sends out an email automatically to the user when they submit a form. This email is another potential touch point that can help draw the visitor into a deeper relationship with you.

- **Viral/social/advocacy calls to action** — You may have seen little social media logos for Twitter or Facebook on other sites. These icons allow users to click and then comment about your site on the relevant social media site. Be sure to enable members and visitors to forward your site to a friend, post about you to their blog, tweet about you, post to Facebook, and thus spread the word. See the section *Add a Like Button to Your Website* on page 335 for more information.

- **Capturing leads** — Everyone who fills out a form or otherwise gives you contact information is a lead. Decide what you do with these leads. When do you follow up? How do you track them categorize them and escalate them? Consider obtaining a customer relationship management (CRM)[104] system to manage these leads.

Determine Engagement Readiness

OK. You think you're covered all the above bases, but are you ready to create your engagement plan? What else do you need to think about before you know you're ready to execute? Consider the following areas.

- **Budget for engagement** — Experts say you should expect to spend at least as much on your first two years of running a social media effort as you did on building it. Ensure that every stakeholder understands that the enterprise needs to be in it for the long haul, and that you're unlikely to be an overnight success. You'll need to plan to continue investing at a significant level for some period of time, and you should budget for this support.

- **Assess your resources** — Realistically assess your available resources. Determine the size of the team you're going to need to make your social efforts a success. Try to avoid minimizing the work that is required to be successful. Remember Solis' formula in the *Reaching Out to Your Community* section on page 111.

- **Plan your capacity** — Make sure you can accomplish the task of launching a successful social computing effort with paid staff and existing, proven evangelists. Don't count on new community members to do any essential tasks.

---

[104] CRM defined: **bit.ly/bwl0b7**

- **Encourage comment on your plan** — Put your draft plan on a private wiki[105] and ask for comments from your staff, managers, and board

- **Create some buzz** — See if you can include something that will make people say, "Wow!" to begin to create buzz. Promote this to engage visitors, bloggers, media, and potential contributors. There's more about buzz in the section *Create Buzz* on page 231.

- **Have some fun** — If your social media effort is dull drudgery you'll have fewer followers. Emphasize the fun of spreading the word about your business via social computing.

Create Your Engagement Plan

Based on your listening and the preliminary planning based on the foregoing, lay out how you're going to engage with the online community.

Your first step is a simple one: **Determine Who, What, and Where**.

You might try a format like the one on the next page.

---

[105] A *WIKI* is a Website that allows the easy creation and editing of Webpages, usually following a common theme, by a community of people. The most famous wiki is Wikipedia.

Social Media Community Targets

- **My communities are...**
  (Online and offline communities you want to reach and who will support you)

- **My audiences are...**

Internal   External

- **My opportunities are...**

- **I will know I'm successful when...**

Three new things that I can do with social media to create buzz about my enterprise in my communities...

Engage Your Community

Once you have defined your community, and the internal and external audiences you want to reach, think about:

- In what ways can we use social media to communicate with each of these audiences?
- When should we communicate (Year round? During other events or activities?)
- What are some opportunities we may be missing?
- What resources do we need?

Create a worksheet answering the first two questions for each of your audiences similar to the following.

Audience _____

Social Media Venues and Frequency

	Facebook	Twitter	LinkedIn	YouTube	flickr	Other _____
Daily	❏	❏	❏	❏	❏	❏
3x/week	❏	❏	❏	❏	❏	❏
Weekly	❏	❏	❏	❏	❏	❏
Monthly	❏	❏	❏	❏	❏	❏
Quarterly	❏	❏	❏	❏	❏	❏
Email only	❏	❏	❏	❏	❏	❏

Messaging

_____

_____

Call to Action

_____

_____

Objective: _____

Metrics
❏   Request coupon
❏   Like Facebook page
❏   Tell-A-Friend
❏   Make a purchase
❏   Sign up for Newsletter

Design Effective Community Processes

Think about how your community is going to interact with the social computing platform, whether it's a public platform like Facebook, a do-it-yourself platform like Ning, or your own customized platform. If the user experience is frustrating, people won't stay. It's worthwhile to hire professionals to help you design the look and feel of your site and to test its usability. And by the way, this advice goes for your main site as well.

Good examples of user experience principles you should consider are contained in the following table, abridged and adapted from the excellent Australian Government 2.0 Taskforce handbook, *Online Engagement Guidelines*.[106]

User Experience Principle	Description	Anti-Pattern Examples (What Not To Do)
Show me what's in it for me?	Reduce uncertainty about participation. Enable community members to understand the purpose of the online engagement, and to have visibility into the process itself. Members need certainty about the activities and engagement process before they commit to participation.	Forcing users to register before they can view activities. Hiding aspects of the engagement process because it is not time yet for that step. Deploying a particular technology used for on-line engagement in isolation.

---

[106] Available under a Creative Commons license: **bit.ly/9k3jim**

User Experience Principle	Description	Anti-Pattern Examples (What Not To Do)
Make it easy to contribute	People who want to contribute may be busy, may be inexperienced or cautious computer users, or they may simply be nervous about contributing. Help them participate by: • Streamlining the process for contribution by, for example, minimizing the number of steps for registration by allowing people to log in using their Facebook or other sites' credentials,[107] or eliminating it altogether. • Providing different methods for participation such as multimedia, video, active mechanisms (such voting against comments) or passive mechanisms (based on activity, such number of views). • Allowing collaborative methods of contribution, for example using a forum or a wiki. Moderation processes such as requiring approval for all posts may also make it harder to participate. See *Where are we up to?*	Forcing users to register separately before they can contribute. Not providing a rich text editor. Separating the submission of content step from the viewing of contributions. Not allowing participants to contribute directly.

---

[107] You can ask your techies about using Open Authentication or Facebook's Social Graph API, and also see the *Connection* section on page 187 for a practical use of this technology.

User Experience Principle	Description	Anti-Pattern Examples (What Not To Do)
Let me tell my friends	Allow users to share information and activity through their own social networks. Make it easy for participants to share content and their activities, for example, by adding a Facebook "Like" button or an AddThis button to your site.[108] For closed or offline engagement activities, it may still be beneficial to provide mechanisms to share information about the engagement process itself or participation in an activity. (Also see *Help me keep up with activities*)	Not providing functionality to share on social media or social networking sites. Not providing activity stream feeds. Not allowing the online engagement solution to be indexed by search engines. Not providing static URLs to pages and anchors to individual participant's contributions.
Where are we up to?	If the online engagement process involves any kind of asynchronous step — such as registration, submission of content (including comment moderation processes), tally of results, competition results, etc. Participants must be kept informed about progress. This will not only help to manage the expectations of participants about the particular step but will also encourage them to stay engaged with the process. Also see *Show me what happened?*	Moderating comments to a blog without providing any indication about how long it will take for comments to be approved. Asking people to sign up for an event with limited places, but not indicating how many places are left.

---

[108] Point your techies to: **bit.ly/bzw78P**

User Experience Principle	Description	Anti-Pattern Examples (What Not To Do)
Help me to keep up with activities	Keeping people up to date with activities is critical to ensuring ongoing participation throughout the engagement process. Multiple methods and channels should be supported, including, email, Real Simple Syndication (RSS),[109] mobile phone messaging (SMS),[110] microblogging[111] (Twitter and others), activity stream sharing[112] and instant messaging.[113] Mobile and other access channels should also be supported. Whenever possible (and appropriate) content and information should be delivered to participants, rather than forcing them to visit the site where it originated.	Only providing a single mechanism for receiving updates — for example, email only. Not providing participants with the option to select which activity, how much, how frequently or what information streams they want to follow — for example, all or nothing approach.

---

[109] RSS definition: a family of formats that provide a way to publish frequently-updated works—such as blog entries, news headlines, audio, and video—in a standardized format. Users can subscribe to RSS feeds and read them in an RSS feed reader, such as Google Reader, without having to check each site they subscribe to for updates: **bit.ly/cdx3Wx**

[110] SMS definition: The text communication service component of mobile phones. SMS text messaging is the most widely used data application in the world (**bit.ly/9ftmze**), with 2.4 billion active users, or 74 percent of all mobile phone subscribers. SMS text messages are generally limited to 160 characters: **bit.ly/cE356R**

[111] Microblogging definition: Generally, posting very short messages or comments as opposed to longer blog posts. Twitter is the most famous; others include Tumblr, Plurk, Emote.in, Beeing, Jaiku and identi.ca: **bit.ly/bJ9nPs**

[112] Techies should see: **bit.ly/ddnlJ1**

[113] Instant Messaging definition: Also known as online chat, IM is real-time text-based networked messaging, typically relying on computer-installed clients that facilitate connections between specified known users. Examples include AOL Instant Messenger (AIM), Windows Live Messenger, and Yahoo! Messenger. Some social networking sites, such as Facebook, have integrated their own instant messenging: **bit.ly/dx2iPW**

User Experience Principle	Description	Anti-Pattern Examples (What Not To Do)
Show me what happened?	Report and provide access to outcomes of all online and offline activities. Providing easy access to the outcomes or steps of an engagement process, regardless of whether it was ultimately completed on- or offline, will help to support both the legitimacy and value of that engagement. Doing so will also help to encourage participation in the future.	Archiving or restricting access to content and activities generated during the engagement process as soon as it has been completed. Waiting until long after the process has completed before sharing information with participants.

Engagement on Your Site

Embracing social media will almost inevitably require you to make changes to your enterprise's current Website. Thus it's a good time to think about how your current site is organized, how effective it is, and how your site's visitors are they going to find your social networking features.

Try to avoid the corporate underpants approach. The term, apparently coined by user experience consultant Tamara Adlin, refers to sites that are organized completely around the structure of the enterprise, rather than in a way that will satisfy the goals and interests of the site's visitors. You'll know you're showing your corporate underpants, Adlin says, "when your org chart shows up in the primary navigation of your Website."[114]

Do your site's visitors really want to know your enterprise is organized into departments, or regions, or brands and sub-brands? Why should they care?

Think about why a person would come to your social media site (OK, any of your sites).

Adlin gives an example of a travel site: "We knew we wanted to go on a 'trip' or 'travel somewhere' [. . .] but, when we arrived on the site, we just accepted that 'flights' and 'hotels' and 'cars' should be thought of, and booked, separately."[115]

What do your visitors want? Give it to them quickly and plainly. You only have 10 seconds.[116]

---

[114] Hide Your Corporate Underpants — Using Personas in UX Design: **blt.ly/drZ0fG**

[115] Process Pantylines: Why SEO and UX should share a cubicle: **bit.ly/d3sb6j**

How you do this depends on your business. A consumer packaged goods company is going to have a different approach than medical device business, or a bank. But let's say you have several marketing initiatives. You could organize your community site around these initiatives, with special areas for each. Always make sure you put somebody in charge of responding to questions or comments in each of the sections. People always feel better if they can get a real human to respond to them.

There's lots more to say about renovating your current site, but it's beyond the scope of this book Suffice it to say that if you think you can just graft a blog onto your existing site, you may find that nobody visits it, and conclude that social media doesn't work. It's better to integrate social media functions into the fabric of your site, and while you're at it, take the time to examine your assumptions about the effectiveness of your current site.

Engagement Plan Contents

After doing the thinking and your preliminary goal and audience identification, you're ready to create the engagement plan. The following are questions you should ask, as well as other recommended elements your engagement plan should include:

- **Reasons for Using Social Media**
    - What do you have to offer?
    - What problem are you trying to solve (reaching an audience, encouraging evangelism, improving sales)?
    - Why are you using social media to accomplish your goal?

- **Social Media Approach**
    - There are three basic approaches to using social media. Lay out how you'll use them, singly, in combination, or simultaneously:
    - Participate where conversations are already happening (for example on Facebook, Google+, YouTube, or Twitter)
    - Use, enhance, or create social media aspects of your existing Website
        - Create new a social network that stands alone — using, for example, Ning or other white-box social network software to create an online venue that you control

---

[116] You have only 10 seconds to make a good first impression: **bit.ly/cTz8sV**

- **Content Plan**
  - What kind of content will you publish?
  - What are the style guidelines for content creation?
  - What are the rules of engagement with community members?
  - Will you syndicate content from/to other sites? If so, where, how, and why?

- **Design Plan**
  - Determine your design parameters
  - How will the site look?
  - How will it work?
  - What features will it have?
  - Create a usability test plan

    - Recruit real users and have a professional do a test

- **Release Plan**
  - Avoid a single big-bang release; release incrementally
  - Start small

    - Start with low-risk contributions, for example, by posting to existing social net-working sites — see the section *Your First Contributions* on page 137 for more information

  - Coordinate final release with marketing efforts

- **Resource Plan**
  - Identify/assign resources, including writers and a community manager
  - Create the required internal processes for ensuring adequate staffing
  - Create a budget for start up and the first two years
  - Indicate supporters and what they will contribute

- **Training Plan**
  - Do a social media readiness assessment
  - Create a plan to fill the gaps
  - Ensure advanced social media training for staff assigned
  - Assess the amount of culture change involved in using social media and create change management plans to address

- **Metrics Plan**

    - What does success look like?
    - What measures will tell you your progress toward your goals?
    - What success factors are the most important?
    - What metrics assess those factors best?
    - How will you collect these metrics?
    - What metrics are related and should be analyzed together?
    - What kind of analyses are valid for the metrics?
    - How reliable are the metrics?
    - How reliable is the analysis? What specific tools will you use to measure activity and community engagement?
    - What corrective actions are triggered when metrics are bad?

- **Outreach/Promotion Plan**

    - How will you promote online?
    - What bloggers/online influentials will you target for cross promotion?
    - How will you fold the social media message into your traditional marketing efforts?

- **Listening Strategy**

    - How will you monitor what others are saying about you?
    - How will you engage them?
    - What will you do about negatives?

- **Community Management Plan**

    - Communities require care and feeding. Determine who is responsible, their duties, and the support they'll need.
    - Develop contingency plans for foreseeable problems such as dealing with trolls (excessively disruptive, negative, or argumentative community members) — there's lots more on trolls in the section *Dealing with Trolls* on page 213
    - See the *Community Building Checklist* on page 403 for much more on this subject

These sections should get you started on your plan. Throughout the rest of this book we'll give you tips and tactics to fold into your Engagement Plan.

Your First Contributions

Before considering a large undertaking such as modifying your site with social media features or creating a do-it-yourself standalone social media site, dip your toe in the water and gauge the tenor of your community. After you've listened for an extended period, you can start engaging by posting on existing communities. Here are a few suggestions for your first contributions:

- Be low-risk, for example, by posting interesting, non-controversial news, comments, or events
- Know who the champions are in your community and acknowledge them visibly, perhaps by commenting on their posts
- Share professional/personal information
- Share a professional problem and ask if somebody has the same problems/interests
- Highlight content from well-established community members more often than content you create. You'll build good will.
- Refresh your content often, but not TOO often: Performing A/B split content analysis using Google Analytics can help you figure out how often — see our discussion of this technique in the *Optimizing for Google* section on page 369

Once you're a familiar face, consider asking the community to help you design your enterprise's social media presence. If appropriate (and your legal counsel approves), you can conduct contests that invite ideas and let other members help judge them. This is a technique called crowdsourcing (see footnote 92 on page 116 about the wisdom of crowds, and also **bit.ly/cpyFhG** for more information), and it is an effective way to encourage people to not only contribute ideas, but to take a stake in them.

Keep It Fresh

Change the content on your social media sites regularly. How you define regularly depends on your community, but you should shoot for at least weekly updates. The surest way to ensure the death of a community site is to let it get stale. This goes for the content you generate, and the discussion and other material your members generate. Mix it up. Give people a reason to come back, or to follow your feed, or to seek you out wherever you are.

Promote the Community via Other Venues

Social media should not exist in a vacuum, or even only online. Feature your social media presence in your newsletter, in your advertising, at your events, anywhere you're doing public relations or marketing.

Even if you decide to focus on social features of your enterprise's Website, or on a standalone social networking site that you build, also engage members and donors where they are (Facebook, Twitter, LinkedIn, MySpace, and YouTube)

And of course, don't forget to promote your social media activities on traditional media.

Synergistic Promotion Activities

We've said previously that you shouldn't stop doing anything you're currently doing just because you've started to use social media. Even more important: Fold your social media efforts into your other efforts so they reinforce one another. Here are some ideas along those lines.

- **Social network outreach** — If you have your own community or are sponsoring online events, use social networks like Facebook, Twitter and MySpace to promote your activities and gather feedback

  - **Blog outreach** — Create a plan to involve influential bloggers and get them to write about your organization. Be sure to designate someone to follow and engage bloggers. Read Fanscape and the Word of Mouth Marketing Association's white paper, *Pitching to Bloggers*.[117]

  - **Email** — Identify e-mail lists you can encourage to pass your message on. Ask staff, managers, and board to consider informing their personal contacts about your social computing efforts.

  - **Personal networks** — Ask staff, managers, community members and supporters to tell their personal networks (online and offline) about your social media activities

- **Traditional media outreach** — Fold in links to your social media presence and promote your online events along with your offline events. Ensure that your current media personnel are well-versed in what you're doing online.

  - **Online ads** — Although online advertising is no longer as effective as it once was, you may still want to leverage it. Consider buying ads on search engines, such as Google AdWords, and ads on Facebook, LinkedIn and other social sites. Determine whether you will you hire professionals to produce the creative and manage the ad buy.

  - **Offline ads** — How will you promote via broadcast advertising? Will you do print ads -- even if it's just including your URL in another ad for your enterprise or brand?

---

[117] The Word of Mouth Marketing Association's white paper, *Pitching to Bloggers:* **bit.ly/bXLN7F**

- **Direct mail** — If you do regular mailings, integrate your online messaging and URLs

- **Collateral** — If you produce written materials or trinkets, be sure to promote your social media presence

- **Partnerships** — Ask partners to spread the word to their customers, members, or constituencies

- **Other established channels** — Consider telling your social media story wherever you communicate with people, for example, your telephone hold music

Ask for the Commitment

"Social Networking that matters is helping people achieve their goals.
Do it reliably and repeatedly – so that over time people
have an interest in helping you achieve your goals"

Seth Godin

You're using social media for a reason. You want something. It may be attention; it may be sales; it may be brand awareness. The best-designed social media sites feature calls to action — click to get our newsletter; click to find out more; click to buy.

Your site should ensure that your audience knows what it can do to help, and can take a positive action online. "Click to email a salesperson" isn't going to cut it. "Click to chat with a live person" is much better. "Click to buy" is even better. "Click to recommend this site to your friends," however, may be the best outcome.

Based on the goals you identified in your engagement plan, design interactions that explain the participation options, and entice people to get involved, right now.

The old saw that salespeople must practice ABC — Always Be Closing — is applicable to online as well. But what it means to close may be different. If you're that obnoxious sales guy always asking, "Are you ready to buy now? How about now? Now?" you're not going to be successful online.

While it doesn't pay to be obnoxious, you also don't want to be shy. It's best online to give before asking, and it's also best to gradually draw your audience in to a more intimate relationship.

Perhaps you start off by offering information on your business, and then ask for a small commitment, like entering an email address to receive a white paper, or a newsletter, or a bumper sticker. Then perhaps you ask them to email their friends about your social site. Later you may ask them to sign up for a newsletter, or come to an event, or take action in some other small way. It's a conversation. It's relationship building, and you don't want to go too fast, yet at the same time you want to enable those who are really excited to proceed at a faster pace.

How you ask and what you ask for at what time is more art than science. You can take your learning from offline efforts and try to apply it online. Just be sure you keep your ears open. Ask those you're involving how they'd like the relationship to progress, and don't fall into the offline ways of constantly pushing messages as a passive audience.

Regardless of your other online goals, most businesses share a common goal: Increase sales. Buying online now has a long history, and is rather sophisticated and well-developed. Social media definitely offers new ways to reach and inform prospective customers while drawing them into an ever-more-intimate relationship with your business. We take a look at this topic in the following section.

Social Media Relationship Stages

To encourage a relationship with your customers and prospects through social media, it will take more than placing a simple "Buy" or even a "Like" button on your home page or social media site. As we've discussed, one of your online goals should be to draw existing and potential customers into a relationship that will be productive for both parties. The basic steps, to paraphrase online marketer Seth Godin, are to:

- Turn strangers into friends
- Turn friends into customers
- And then... do the most important job: Turn your customers into evangelists

The trick is to do this without resorting to traditional marketing tactics that may turn off your online community.

Traditional marketers refer to the gradual process of enticing the public to become buyers as the marketing funnel. Lots of folks go in the top; only a few fall out the bottom as customers. Godin thinks this metaphor is all wrong for online marketing. In his free e-book targeted at non-profits *Flipping the Funnel — Give Your Fans the Power to Speak Up*,[118] Godin gives advice that enterprises can benefit from as well:

> The math is compelling. Most of the people in the world are not your donors [customers]. They haven't even heard of you, actually. And while many of these people are not qualified buyers or aren't interested in supporting your organization, many of them might—if

---

[118] *Flipping the Funnel — Give Your Fans the Power to Speak Up:* **bit.ly/9r3Psa**

　　　　　　　　　　　　　　　　　　　Ask for the Commitment

they only knew you existed, if they could only be persuaded that your offering is worth investing time and energy and passion and money into.

But how on earth are you going to get them to know about you?

We're living in the most cluttered marketplace in history. Whether you are curing cancer, encouraging faith or educating people in need, people are better at ignoring you than ever before. You don't have enough time to get your message out.

Godin goes on to say that most organizations have underused assets: your friends and your supporters.

Godin's idea is to flip the marketing funnel and turn it into a megaphone. You give the megaphone to your fan club: the people who like and respect you, and who have a vested interest in your success.

Social Media is the Megaphone

And your supporters are the speakers. Encourage them to:

- **Tag** you on delicious.com, digg.com
- **Upload** relevant photos to flickr.com
- **Blog** about you
- **Tweet** about you

Godin describes the power of the Internet, and of giving your supporters the megaphone:

The Internet changes everything. Now, one person armed with a keyboard can reach millions. One person with a video camera can tell a story that travels around the world. And one person with a blog can sell a lot of computers.

The trick is this: you need to give your fan club some leverage, an amplifier — a megaphone.

Your former patrons, the aggrieved ones, the critics — they've already found the web. They're the ones who have managed to post play-by-play accounts of your misdeeds and missteps. They're motivated and they're already embracing the medium.

A diligent marketer, however, can make it easy for your fan club to get the word out as well. And to do it in an authentic, uncontrolled, honesty way.

This is why you don't censor comments about you online: There are supporters as well as detractors out there. If you get all paranoid about nasty things the haters (or trolls) say, and feel tempted to remove them, it helps to remember that your supporters see these posts as well. And if you've enabled them — handed them the megaphone — you may find they'll rush to your defense.

This won't work, however, if you insist on approving all posts on sites you control.

Doing so stifles the ability for your supporters to quickly respond to negativity. It also breaches the trust you hope to establish with your community. If community members feel they must think twice before posting — taking into account whether Big Brother will approve their posts — you lose the ability to find out what they really think, and violate the implicit contract you established with your community when you decided to engage with them.

Enable Social Tagging

Another way to enable your community involves social tagging.

There are lots of social tagging sites, but two of the most popular are Digg[119] and del.icio.us.[120] Social taggers who find an interesting Webpage can easily tag it — mark it as interesting for other site members to see. Only a minority of people actually tag pages, while a much larger number cruise the tagging aggregator sites looking for interesting topics and pages. This gives the taggers an enormous influence for their size.

Encouraging your community to tag your information and media can dramatically improve your visibility, even if your site does not perform well in Google searches. Godin did a search on "diabetes" on Delicious. The search led him to a site filled with white papers on diabetes.

While this site would likely not show up on the first page of Google results, because eight people had tagged that page, Godin was able to easily find it through social bookmarking. Therefore, instead of spending vast amounts of time and resources on SEO techniques to influence Google search results, if an organization can manage to get even a handful of their advocates and supporters to tag their pages, their visibility on the net would increase dramatically.

Godin puts it like this:

> The Acumen Fund [a non-profit global venture fund working to solve the problems of global poverty] has hundreds of pages on its site — yet most of them are essentially invisible. If the organization made it easy for donors and supporters to start tagging pages, the most important messages would rise to the top. The same thing is true for art museums,

---

[119] Digg: **bit.ly/0T3tk4**

[120] Delicious: **bit.ly/ceCC9l**

religious groups and the ACLU. In every case, there are pages, buried and doomed to decay into obscurity. But if a few surfers tagged the pages appropriately, though, other surfers would find it. And the word would spread. The big secret of del.icio.us is that the percentage of users who do the tagging is tiny. Most of the traffic to the site is looking for the tagging done by a tiny minority. This is the essence of online leverage.

Think about how you can leverage your supporters by encouraging social tagging. It's a great way to drastically improve the impact of a small group of supporters.

Don't Sweat the Hierarchy

Godin also stresses that, since the nature of social media is distributed, non-hierarchal, and definitely not top-down, command-and-control, this have can implications for how your business is organized. He states that the huge non-profit United Way has underperformed in the last decade, and looks to the way they are organized as one of the keys.

> The United Way is a classic top-down approach. By creating arrangements with the Fortune 500, they were able to do payroll deduction on millions of paychecks. That, all by itself, was key to their scale. But what happens when those relationships aren't as important? Because people rarely talk about the United way and its work, the word of their great efforts doesn't spread as far and as fast as it might. As a result, it's hard for them to catch up when the payroll-deduction approach loses juice.

> Compare this to the brilliant peer-to-peer gimmick embraced by Nike and Lance Armstrong. [...] [T]he Armstrong LiveStrong idea spread so far, so fast precisely because of their side-to-side, not top down approach. In our ever faster, ever more selfish world, the chances of growing a non-profit with a top down approach are tiny. It's just too hard, we're to busy and you don't have enough time or money.

We discussed social media's effects on organization styles in the section *Understand the Social Media Maturity Stage of Your Organization* on page 169. Consider Godin's recommendations along with ours as you prepare to engage with your community.

Give the Megaphone

Ask your supporters to commit. This goes beyond the kind of commitment represented by merely buying your product. Make it easy for your supporters to pick up the megaphone and tag your site, blog about it, "Like It" on Facebook,[121] 1+ it via Google, tweet it on Twitter, and so on.

You'd be surprised how effective committed supporters can be:

- Dell estimates[122] that a Dell detractor costs the company $57, and a promoter generates $328
- A study across 20 brands by analyst firm Syncapse[123] found:

  o The average annualized value of an individual fan on Facebook is $136.38; the range is from $270.77 in the best case to $0 in the worst
  o On average, fans spend an extra $71.84 they would not otherwise spend on products they describe themselves as fans of, compared to those who are not fans.

    o McDonald's saw the largest variability, with Fans reporting spending $159.79 more per year than non-fans
    o Oreo saw the lowest value with a difference of $28.52

  o Fans are 28 percent more likely than non-fans to continue using a specific brand
  o Fans are 41 percent more likely than non-fans to recommend a product they are a fan of to their friends
  o An average fan may participate with a brand ten times a year and will make one recommendation. But, an active fan may participate thirty times and make ten recommendations.

- On the other hand, social media management firm Vitrue found that a Facebook Fan is worth $3.60 of media value

  o Vitrue determined[124] that on average, a fan base of 1 million translates into at least $3.6 million in equivalent media over a year at a $5 CPM (meaning, that a brand's 1 million fans generate about $300,000 in media value each month)

Of course, there are lots of ways to give your supporters the megaphone, and we cover many more techniques in the chapters that follow.

The key is to **give** the megaphone, not hog it.

---

[121] See the section Add a Like Button to Your Website on page 335 for more information.

[122] Dave Chaffey: **bit.ly/cA0uLs**

[123] Gigaom's *How Much Is a Facebook Fan Really Worth?* **bit.ly/pw924D** Link to the report PDF: **bit.ly/mV67os**

[124] Real Time Marketer's *A Facebook Fan is Worth $3.60. Really?* **bit.ly/pNPe9K** A dissenting view from The Future Buzz's *More Absurd Social Media Analysis - The Value Of A Fan* **bit.ly/oi6QD7**

Measure Results

"The social medium creates many artifacts, or digital breadcrumbs, that are directly measurable as people participate. It isn't just a medium with a message, but it is also a medium which contains and records actions."

Marcel LeBrun, CEO, Radian6

As part of your engagement plan, you determined what success looks like, and how to measure it. Without this key exercise, you can easily waste lots of time and money on ineffective use of social computing.

It's often said, if you can measure it you can manage it, and it's true. You'll meet many people who insist that you can't measure the value that social media brings. These people are only right in a sense — you can't use many of the old measurements designed for traditional media, and you may need to modify some (cost per thousand impressions or CPM, for example) to make them work with social media.

However, the idea that the online environment — the first man-made environment in history that can totally close the loop between causation and result — is somehow not measurable is dead wrong.

We discussed previously (see the Measure section on page 96) the idea that half of advertising is wasted. And it's a crying shame that a fraction of a percent of direct mail has the intended result. Why do others prefer these media? Because they've managed to achieve predictable results due to a mature measurement system. A marketer we know said, essentially, "I know if I drop $75,000 on a direct mail campaign I'll get a sales bump of X percent. I don't know what my investment in social media buys me."

It's true. The field of social media measurement is in its infancy compared to the giant, mature advertising industry. But there are still very good ways to measure your success.

Why Should You Track Social Mentions?

Tracking what people are saying about you online is the first step in creating Key Performance Indicators (KPI) that you will use to determine the success of your social media efforts. Setting KPI objectives help you realize when your approach needs modification, or merits increased effort and resources because of their success.

Marketing analyst firm Aberdeen Research[125] used the following four key performance criteria to distinguish the use of social media by what they term Best-in-Class companies:

- 93 percent improved ability to generate consumer insights
- 82 percent improved ability to identify and reduce risk
- 75 percent improved customer advocacy
- 63 percent decreased customer service costs

Aberdeen's survey found that those enjoying the best social media results had a variety of characteristics in common, including:

- 63 percent have dedicated resources devoted to social media monitoring
- 47 percent have a process in place for sharing customer insights gleaned from social media with key decision-makers

Aberdeen found that organizations received the following benefits from social media monitoring:

- **Risk reduction** — Social media monitoring helps identify and respond to external threats in a defensive (and even pre-emptive) manner, limiting the spread of negative opinion, including false rumors, information leaks, and even illegal online distribution of proprietary materials. This practice can help with reputation management as well.

- **Customer advocacy** — Using social media monitoring to identify and engage with top influencers can lead to increased positive word-of-mouth referrals. For most organizations, little is more efficient and effective than customer advocacy. There are a variety of metrics to track influence, including likelihood-to-recommend scores such as the Net Promoter Score® (NPS). There's more on NPS in the following section.

- **Community insights generation** — Organizations can get insights by observing as their communities discuss their experiences as well as their future wants and needs. The ongoing analysis of community--generated content can produce insights into what products and services you should develop, what your marketing messages should be, and what partners you should pursue.

---

[125] Aberdeen Research's *The ROI on Social Media Monitoring — Why it Pays to Listen to Online Conversation:* **bit.ly/dIPAJg**

- **Customer service cost reduction** — Online communities serve as public knowledge repositories comprised of thousands of question-and-answer pairs often monitored by very enthusiastic volunteers. This can lessen the burden on your staff to answer frequently asked questions about your business and your services. In fact, for many organizations, effective Return On Investment (ROI) for social media monitoring may lie not in marketing, but in customer support. To demonstrate ROI, measure your costs for content development for customer care without social media and determine the content savings for user-generated contributions. Other metrics involved determining what the online solve rate is, based on user-generated versus in-house-authored content.

As you can see, it is possible to measure success for social media.

Changing What We Measure

Here are a few real-life metrics from advertising legend Katie Delahaye Paine[126] that organizations have used to measure success:

- Best Buy measures 85 percent lower turnover as a result of its Blue Shirt community
- State Farm measures its internal blog by the improvement in morale
- Zero-budget YouTube videos about Barack Obama were seen by 120x the audience of Hilary Clinton's multi-million dollar "largest town hall meeting in US history"
- IBM receives more leads, sales and exposure from a $500 podcast than it does from a traditional ad
- ASPCA traces on-line donations and increased membership back to its social media efforts

Paine proposes measuring discussions in an objective way and proposes a classification of online discussions in the following table.

---

[126] Adapted from *Measurement & engagement: why engagement is really the only thing that matters*, Katie Delahaye Paine: **bit.ly/9R0Q3F**

Table 1 — Paine's Possible Classification of Discussions

Acknowledging receipt of information	Making a joke
Advertising something	Making a suggestion
Answering a question	Making an observation
Asking a question	Offering a greeting
Augmenting a previous post	Offering an opinion
Calling for action	Putting out a wanted ad
Disclosing personal information	Rallying support
Distributing media	Recruiting people
Expressing agreement	Responding to criticism
Expressing criticism	Showing dismay
Expressing support	Soliciting comments
Expressing surprise	Soliciting help
Giving a heads-up	Starting a poll
Giving a shout-out	

Start out by assigning values to each of these communication types and tracking them in your community. By assigning negative numbers to the apparently negative interactions and positive numbers to the desired interactions, you can create a score for your social media effort. Adjust your scoring and then begin to measure your social media campaigns by how they affect the measures. With some experience, you can tie the score with your goals.

Of course, doing all this by hand is quite a chore. Luckily, there are a variety of social media monitoring tools you can use to automate your metrics.

Use Social Media Monitoring Tools

You can use automated social media monitoring tools to find social media mentions on a variety of social media platforms and track them over time. Some tools are quite expensive, including IBM's SPSS-based tool[127] and other high-end tools such as Radian6.[128]

All social media monitoring tools have basically the same function: to find out what people are saying online. Some also help you categorize conversations and calculate various metrics.

---

[127] IBM SPSS Modeler Professional: **bit.ly/bWbTel**

[128] Radian6: **bit.ly/byCdlN**

You first steps should be:

- **Assign** someone to manage the tools and listen
- **Establish** goals and Key Performance Indicators (KPIs) to track them
- **Regularly measure** and communicate your progress

There are many good free tools, but the most powerful tools can be expensive.

Three free general monitoring services are worth checking out follow.

Social Mention[129]

- Set up a profile to get email summaries of social media posts based on keywords
- Daily digest option
- Install the buzz widget on your site or blog
- See an example at **bit.ly/smperformance**

BlogPulse[130]

- Run by Nielsen
- Search blogs on any topic
- Follow topic trends
- Find top bloggers
- Check top:

    - Videos
    - Posts
    - Blogs
    - Phrases
    - News Stories
    - News Sources

---

[129] Social Mention: **bit.ly/2QLVaT**

[130] BlogPulse: **bit.ly/ufS2g**

BlogLines[131]

- Check top:

    - Videos
    - Posts
    - Blogs
    - Phrases
    - News Stories
    - News Sources

Google Tools

Google provides a lot of free tools to track social mentions. They also have scads of services as part of their AdWords program that you can use if you create an AdWords[132] account. AdWords are those little text ads you see on the right of a Google results page. You can bid on terms to get your ad to show up in search results. However, you don't need to create an ad campaign to create an account and use Google's tools to see how popular various keywords are on Google.

Here are some other useful, free Google tools for tracking social mentions.

Google Alerts[133]

- Set up alerts for keywords
- Get emails sent once a day or once a week with search results for those keywords

Google Video Search[134]

- Follow popular trends in videos
- See who's posting videos

Google Trends[135]

- Analyze trends in conversations

---

[131] BlogLines: **bit.ly/3SyBH**

[132] AdWords: **bit.ly/92bBsj**

[133] Google Alerts: **bit.ly/3fbcHD**

[134] Google Video: **bit.ly/xZuX**

[135] Google Trends: **bit.ly/2BPQgl**

Google Webmaster Tools[136]

Google provides a wealth of interesting tools to find out about your Website, its performance, and who is visiting, including:

- Search queries
- Links to your site
- Keywords
- Internal links
- Subscriber stats

Backlink Checkers

A backlink is a link from another site to your site. Backlink checkers show you who's linking to you. An advanced Google search query[137] can also provide similar information. Simply place the keyword "link:" in front of any site or Webpage to see how many sites link to it.

Here are some free backlink tools:

- **iWebTool.com**[138]

    - Free for up to 5 requests per hour
    - Shows what sites are linking to your site
    - Often too busy to respond

- **SEOChat**[139]

    - Requires you to enter a CAPTCHA (**C**ompletely **A**utomated **P**ublic **T**uring test to tell **C**omputers and **H**umans **A**part — those squiggly words you often see on pages) to check a page

- **SEOLogs**[140]

    - Not only a backlink checker, but lots of other free tools for Search Engine Optimization

---

[136] Google Webmaster Tools: **bit.ly/2QzqN**

[137] Google Advanced Search: **bit.ly/ddOlHi**

[138] iWebTool: **bit.ly/aOVFdF**

[139] SEOChat: **bit.ly/aU4Bz0**

[140] SEOLogs: **bit.ly/9SNRC1**

- **BackLinkWatch**[141]

    - Did not find all links in a test we ran

- **Domain-Pop**[142]

    - Requires CAPTCHA for each check

Measuring Online Video

Social media expert Jeremiah Owyang has an excellent list[143] of video measurement and deployment tools that we adapt and excerpt below:

Tubemogul

- Free service that provides viewership-related analytics for those that publish and monitor online video
- Free account features:

    - Video Deployments 100/month
    - Unlimited Storage
    - Five Custom Video Groupings
    - Basic Cross-Site Analytics
    - Video Transcoding (transforming a video from one format to another)
    - Email & Embed Reports
    - Submit to Social Networking Sites
    - Link Intelligence
    - Update Social Networks

Visible Measures[144]

- Comprehensive video experience measurement solution

---

[141] BackLinkWatch: **bit.ly/b0MMfm**

[142] Domain-Pop: **bit.ly/bR1cCh**

[143] Companies that measure or compare Online Video: **bit.ly/cS6ixS**

[144] Visible Measures: **bit.ly/bieuFC**

Mochibot[145]

- Traffic monitoring tool for Flash content; Flash is an animation tool from Adobe — YouTube videos and lots of those moving or interactive elements on Webpages are done in Flash

VideoCounter[146]

- Upload and distribute your videos to multiple video sharing sites like YouTube, MetaCafé, Dailymotion or Facebook
- Counts the number of times your videos are watched on Dailymotion, Sevenload, iFilm & Co.

Measuring Social Media, Influence, Brand

Jeremiah Owyang also has a list of sites that measure social influence.[147] Once again, we extract, augment, and adapt the list.

Monitoring Service	Description
BoardTracker bit.ly/dw9sFu	A search engine dedicated to indexing forums and online message boards. Can set up alerts, or save favorite threads to view later. Both options require a free registration.
HowSociable? bit.ly/bePnFc	Measures social media visibility and enables users to track an overall visibility score and how visible your organization is within the sites they track. Free currently but will soon have a Pro version.
Icerocket bit.ly/cYQMlW	Real-time search engine that searches blogs, social networking sites, and news. Free.
Technorati bit.ly/9P2O14	A blog search engine indexing more than 126 million blogs and more than 250 million pieces of tagged social media. Free.

---

[145] Mochibot: **bit.ly/akMpMi**

[146] VideoCounter: **bit.ly/aPL1u8**

[147] Jeremiah Owyang's *Companies that Measure Social Media, Influence, and Brand*: **bit.ly/bBN1NS**

Monitoring Service	Description
Trendrr **bit.ly/bh939h**	Identifies volume, sentiment, location, demographics and influencers for product or brand. Offers a free version as well as a paid pro version.
Tweetscan **bit.ly/cR8euR**	A live search engine for Twitter postings. Free.
Twitter StreamGraphs **bit.ly/aVpnUc**	Creates graphs of a Twitter stream based on a keyword or a twitter ID. Free.

Find more ideas at the New PR Wiki[148] maintained by Constantin Basturea. Also check Ken Burbary's Social Media Monitoring Wiki.[149]

Replacing ROI

You'll see lots of discussion about Social Media ROI (Return On Investment). But as you know, there are lots of everyday activities that are essential to the success of your organization whose value may be hard to quantify. Online wags have asked sarcastically, "What is the ROI of putting on your pants?" Or "What is the ROI of your phone?" Or even more cheekily: "What's the ROI of your relationship with your mom?"

Sarcasm aside, there are a great many activities in the offline world that have a tenuous connection with ROI, including one of the mightiest and most-ingrained metrics in the offline advertising world: Cost Per Thousand Impressions (CPM).

In the classic print advertising model, deciding not to measure CPM would be career suicide. CPM is the mainstay of the advertising world despite the fact that it is actually a very gross measure.

For example, to calculate the CPM for a newspaper, take the cost of an ad divided by the newspaper's circulation in thousands. However, this assumes that everyone who gets the newspaper has seen the ad, which is preposterous.

---

[148] New PR Wiki: **bit.ly/cFVTPe**

[149] Social Media Monitoring Wiki: **bit.ly/co2NZX**

Measure Results

This offline measurement has been transferred to the Web, calculating the number of impressions (in thousands) of an ad being shown in a browser and dividing it by the cost of the ad.

The problem with CPM is it doesn't close the loop — directly linking the impression to the desired behavior (typically a purchase). Online and offline, organizations forge links between the number of impressions and purchasing behavior in a way that involves lots of assumptions (such as that an impression has one direct effect — purchase stimulation — rather than a variety of possible effects — tell a friend, improved opinion of the product, long-term attitude change, and so on).

Online, CPM doesn't actually make a lot of sense for another big reason: The thing that causes the impression — a blog post, a Facebook post, and to a lesser degree, a Tweet — persists. Forever. Or at least as long as there's a Google.

This means every action you take in social media has what is termed a long tail — a declining residual effect that may continue for years.

Here's an example: Janet Fouts, a social media coach and speaker,[150] wrote a post about Twitter manners on her blog that received 86 clicks when she tweeted about it. In her Twitter post, Fouts included a link to the blog post that was shortened using the Bit.ly service, which tracks the number of times people click on the shortened link. (You'll notice we use Bit.ly for the links in this book!)

Fouts says:

> Over the next three months, the shortened link [. . .] was clicked 10,383 times. That means that once the link went out, people shared it in some way. It could have appeared in an e-mail, been re-tweeted on Twitter or another microblog service, or mentioned in a blog post. Of course that 10,000 click rate doesn't begin to tell us what [the number of views] of the Twitter post was, but if we're guessing there was a 20 percent click-through rate, then it may have been viewed 51,915 times so far.

So instead of measuring the effectiveness of that blog post by counting the 86 initial clicks, you need to factor in the long tail of more than 50,000 viewers.

Because of the long-tail effect, one of the first things to understand about measuring social media is that it takes time to see results. Since the metrics involved with social media are in their early days, you'll want to experiment with various social media tactics, and their associated measure-

---

[150] *Measuring Social Media's Return on Engagement* by Janet Fouts: **bit.ly/aKuwu1**

ments. And you'll want to be patient, trying various measures to craft the proper KPIs for your organization.

Social media theorist Brian Solis lists[151] various attempts to replace ROI as the dominant social media metric, including:

- **Return on Engagement** — The duration of time spent either in conversation or interacting with social objects, and in turn, what transpired that's worthy of measurement

- **Return on Participation** — A metric tied to measuring and valuing the time spent participating in social media through conversations or the creation of social objects

- **Return on Involvement** — Similar to participation, marketers explored touchpoints for documenting states of interaction and tied metrics and potential return of each

- **Return on Attention** — In the attention economy, we assess the means to seize attention, hold it, and measure the response

- **Return on Trust** — A variant on measuring customer loyalty and the likelihood for referrals, a trust barometer establishes the state of trust earned in social media engagement and the prospect of generating advocacy and how it impacts future business

To Solis' list, we'd like to add Net Promoter Score® and Online Promoter™ Score, which we cover in the next sections.

Using Net Promoter Score®

According to **netpromoter.com**:

> Net Promoter® is both a loyalty metric and a discipline for using customer feedback to fuel profitable growth in your business. Developed by Satmetrix, Bain & Company, and Fred Reichheld, the concept was first popularized through Reichheld's book *The Ultimate Question*, and has since been embraced by leading companies worldwide as the standard for measuring and improving customer loyalty.

NPS is based on the value of a single customer to an organization. For example, Dell estimates[152] that their average consumer is worth $210 over five years. And as we mentioned in the last chapter, a Dell detractor costs the company $57, and a promoter generates $328.

---

[151] *The Maturation of Social Media ROI* by Brian Solis: **bit.ly/axgv4v**

[152] Dave Chaffey: **bit.ly/cA0uLs**

NPS divides online contributors into three categories by asking simply: How likely is it that you would recommend [organization] to a friend or colleague? Based on the answers on a 0-to-10 point rating scale, individuals are categorized as:

- **Promoters** — Score 9-10 — Loyal enthusiasts who will keep buying and refer others
- **Passives** — Score 7-8 — Satisfied but unenthusiastic people who are vulnerable to competitive offerings
- **Detractors** — Score 0-6 — Unhappy people who can damage your reputation and growth through negative word-of-mouth

Tracking these groups helps you get a picture of your organization's reputation and performance through your clients, prospects, and supporters' eyes.

To calculate your organization's Net Promoter Score, take the percentage of people who are Promoters and subtract the percentage who are Detractors.

You should know that, like many new social media metrics, Net Promoter remains somewhat controversial, with studies denying and confirming its effectiveness. Nonetheless, just by making the effort to measure promoter activity, you will know a lot more about your community, and thus the effort is likely to be worthwhile.

According to Wikipedia: [153]

- General Electric uses NPS to evaluate process excellence for its customers, and plans to use NPS as a metric to decide the compensation of its leaders
- Procter and Gamble uses NPS to measure consumer reactions to its brands
- Allianz uses NPS to maintain what it calls "customer-centricity"
- Verizon Wireless uses NPS in all business channels including their call centers and retail stores

---

[153] Wikipedia: **bit.ly/bGFS3R**

Using Online Promoter™ Score

One metric that has been shown to produce a positive correlation between online promoter measures and sales is **Online Promoter™ Score (OPS),** developed by Northwestern University and MotiveQuest.

According to MotiveQuest, OPS measures the number of people online who are recommending your brand to others combined with sentiment measures, which are a way to determine the attitude — sentiment — expressed in online postings. MotiveQuest says OPS differentiates persons who discuss more than one product and assigns a score to their most-favored brand.

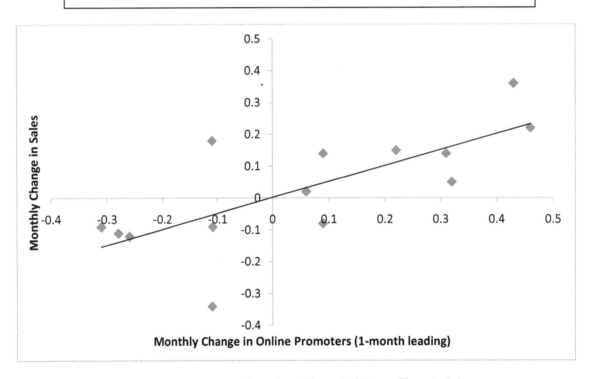

Figure 9 — Change in OPS vs. Change in Sales

MotiveQuest did an analysis[154] covering 16 months of data from January 2006 through April of 2007 for car company Mini USA. The graph above shows the correlation of the monthly change in online promoters for the previous month versus the change in sales. MotiveQuest claims that statistical analysis gives 99.8 percent confidence that the metrics are positively correlated.

---

[154] MotiveQuest analysis: **bit.ly/90gewK**

Other Metrics

In 2008, the Interactive Advertising Bureau, an advertising industry group, created its Social Media Ad Metrics Definitions.[155] The IAB breaks social media into three categories, and applies different measures for each:

- **Social Media Sites** — Defined by inherent functionality that facilitates the sharing of information between users within a defined network
- **Blogs** — Used by individuals, groups or business entities to publish opinions and commentary on various topics
- **Widgets & Social Media Applications** — Social media software programs designed to work on one or more platforms, for example, Facebook apps like Mafia Wars or Farmville

The social media metrics IAB defines comprise a whole long list that you can find online. We excerpt a few of the measures here to give you a flavor.

- **Unique Visitors**

  - A unique individual or browser which has accessed a site or application and has been served unique content and/or ads. Reported unique visitors should filter out bots.

- **Cost per unique visitor**

  - The total cost of the ad placement or application, divided by the number of unique visitors.

- **Return Visits**

  - The average number of times a user returns to a site or application over a specific time period

- **Interaction Rate**

  - The proportion of users who interact with an ad or application.

- **Time Spent** (section, microsite, community)

  - The amount of elapsed time from the initiation of a visit to the last user activity associated with that visit. Time spent should represent the activity of a single cookied browser or user for a single access session to the Website application or other property. Most publishers consider a session continuous if and only if not broken by more than 30 minutes of inactivity.

---

[155] Interactive Advertising Bureau Social Media Ad Metrics Definitions: **bit.ly/asRNe2**

- **Conversation Size**

    - Number of Conversation Relevant Sites
    - The count of sites in the conversation whose content contains tracked conversation phrases
    - Number of Conversation Relevant Links
    - The count of links to (in-links) and from (out-links) content that contains tracked conversation phrases across all sites identified for and/or supporting the campaign plan

- **Conversation Reach**

    - The number of unique visitors (monthly) across sites in the conversation

- **Author Credibility**

    - Number of Conversation Relevant Posts on the Site
    - The number of posts on the site with content containing tracked conversation phrases
    - Number of Links to Conversation Relevant Posts on the Site

As you can see, there's lots to measure, and lots of ways to tie metrics to your efforts. If you want to learn more about social media metrics, read Tia Fisher's excellent survey of measurements on the eModeration blog.[156]

But we'd like to talk about a couple of other measures that are getting some interest: Return on Engagement and Share of Conversation. That's what the next section is about.

Emphasize Return On Engagement

Metrics such as Net Promoter Score, Online Promoter Score, and Return On Engagement attempt to do a very difficult thing: measure the quality and effect of relationships.

Think about that. Could you put a monetary value on your relationship with your friends? How about with your coworkers? Just as it is hard to quantify the strength and positive effect of your personal relationships, so it is difficult to measure the value of online relationships.

Add to this the very different nature of social media, including the Long Tail effect and you can see why there is controversy about how to measure social computing's effects.

Return On Engagement is relevant not only for your external social media efforts, but also for your internal efforts. According to a 2008 study by Gallup, about 54 percent of employees in the

---

[156] eModeration blog: **bit.ly/9450vS**

United States are not fully engaged, and 17 percent are actively disengaged. Only 29 percent are engaged.[157] The Gallup organization says:

> Research has shown that engaged employees are more productive employees. The research also proves that engaged employees are more profitable, more customer-focused, safer and more likely to withstand temptations to leave. Many have long suspected the connection between an employee's level of engagement and the level and quality of his or her performance. Our research has laid the matter to rest.

Disengaged employees are more than inert drains on your resources. Employee disengagement is estimated to cost the U.S. economy as much as $350 billion per year in lost productivity, accidents, theft and turnover.

Positive management of internal ROE also will affect your success in your external endeavors, including social computing efforts. Gallup created the following graphic to show the effect of internal engagement on external engagement.

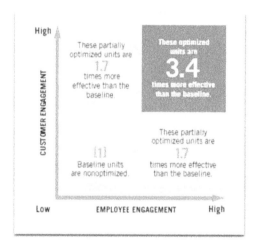

Figure 10 — The Interaction of Employee and Customer Engagement — Gallup

So the concept of ROE is useful outside and inside your organization, making it a doubly useful metric.

---

[157] Many of the stats in the section come from the excellent article by Enterprise Engagement Alliance called *ROE: Return on Engagement* **bit.ly/adtOW6**

One thing to remember is that Return On Engagement (ROE) is not a numbers game; it's a quality of interaction game. It's not how many followers or community members you have that counts. It's how well you do know one another? How likely are they to recommend you or to become evangelists for your organization? These are the returns you get from your engagement with your community. You'll notice they differ from the typical Return On Investment types of measures you may be familiar with.

ROE's differences from ROI are aptly summed up by Amy Sample Ward:[158]

Table 2 — ROI vs. ROE

ROI	ROE
Asks how many Facebook fans you have	Asks how many people are "liking," commenting and sharing your Facebook content
Asks how many staff and how many hours	Asks how many posts, updates, replies or individual responses
Asks how many email subscribers	Asks how many people send you emails
Asks how much money you raise	Asks how many people are campaigning on your behalf

Your organization may need to adopt a very important attitude shift in order to fully benefit from measuring ROE. It's one of the organizational transformations that effective use of social computing demands: the shift from pushing out messages to engaging in conversations. Put bluntly: You can't measure engagement if you aren't engaging your community.

This is a lesson that many organizations have to learn as they transition from offline marketing to leveraging social computing. The differences in measurement mirror the differences in attitude summed up by Mike Valentino,[159] CEO of media promotion company TMPG Inc.:

> Return On Engagement (ROE) is a concept that begs the question: Do you want your consumers to be active or passive. Put another way, do you want to pay X for a 30-second spot passively watched by 2 million prospects; or, for example, a special event, or a Web experience ignited by non-traditional radio techniques where 500,000 engage with the brand for seven minutes, then use Word of Mouth (WOM) to pass along their experience?

Valentino's rhetorical question begs us to answer, "The Web experience." Yet it may be hard for your organization to give that answer. Traditional push media — whether it be Public Service Announcements (PSAs) or push email campaigns — have worked for you before despite their

---

[158] Amy Sample Ward is a social media writer and consultant: **bit.ly/cBB6NK**

[159] Mike Valentino on ROE: **bit.ly/bZCJLo**

low engagement factor. You're comfortable with them, and changing modes to engage with your community, especially without the well-defined metrics you're used to, may be difficult.

Jeremiah Owyang provides a list[160] of somewhat informal ROE measures that demonstrates the powerful insights you can get when you start engaging with your community. We've edited the list slightly and adapted it:

- We learned something about our community we've never known before

- We learned something from our community that we didn't know before

- We connected with a handful of community members like never before as they talk back and we listen

- We were able to tell our story to community members and they shared it with others

- We have a blogging program where there are more community members talking back in comments than there are posts

- We have an online community where members are self-supporting each other and costs are reduced

- We learned a lot from this experimental program, and paved the way for future projects

- We gained experience with a new way of two-way communication

Ask yourself: If we were to receive these returns on our social media engagement, would that make our efforts worthwhile? The value of some of these insights is easily quantified in dollars (reduced support costs) others are hard to put a price on (learning something about your community you never knew — that could be priceless).

To derive benefit from using ROE, you need to decide what your goals are, and how to measure your performance against them.

Forrester Research's Brian Haven provides a list[161] of goals and metrics involved in achieving ROE in the following figure.

---

[160] *Why Your Social Media Plan should have Success Metrics*: **bit.ly/crzTy2**

[161] Forrester Research: **bit.ly/aybmAn**

INVOLVEMENT	INTERACTION	INTIMACY	INFLUENCE
What To Track			
• Site visits • Time spent • Pages viewed • Search keywords • Navigation paths • Site logins	• Contributed comments to blogs • Quantity/frequency of written reviews, blog comments, forum discussions, and UGC	• Sentiment tracking on third-party sites (blogs, reviews, forums, etc.) • Sentiment tracking of internal customer contributions • Opinions expressed in customer service calls	• Net Promoter (NP) score • Product/service satisfaction ratings • Brand affinity • Content forwarded to friends • Posts on high-profile blogs
How To Track			
• Web analytics	• eCommerce platforms • Social media platforms	• Brand monitoring • Customer service calls • Surveys	• Brand monitoring • Customer service calls • Surveys

42124   Source: Forrester Research, Inc.

- **Involvement:** How involved are your community members? How often does the average member visit? Are they subscribing to your blog? How many video views do you have? How often does the online community result in offline action, such as requesting information from a member of your team or attending an event?

- **Interactions:** How often are your community members posting, commenting? Are they contributing their own content (video, links to other sites, links to their own blogs)? Are visits to your fan page increasing?

- **Intimacy:** Intimacy involves measuring the sentiment of user interactions. Do your community members love you? Hate you? Feel comfortable with you? Are they talking about you on other community sites? What are they saying there? How many ratings are you receiving?

- **Influence:** Having identified the prominent influencers in your field, how many of them have you attracted to your community? How often are you getting retweeted by influencers? How often do they comment on your content? Perhaps most importantly, how much is your community influencing you — your policy, your strategy, your client support? How willing are people to recommend you?

We discussed one of the important measures of ROE — sentiment — in the *Monitor Social Media* section on page 63.

As Haven's list indicates, there are lots of ways you can measure ROE. One way is called Share of Conversation.

Emphasize Share of Conversation

We've seen that Return On Engagement is a social computing metric you can use to measure how you're doing with your own community. And that's great. But no matter how well you're doing, you must remember that your community members spend 99.99 percent of their time on other Websites.

Not only do they spend most of their time away from you, they may be talking about your business in other venues. Thus you may be able to learn a lot about how to improve your ROE by looking at how others are addressing the community.

Part of wanting to know about the competition is, frankly, driven by ego, and it's a story that started with a different type of measurement in the 1920s.

A young engineer named Art Nielsen was finding it hard to sell his concept of measuring sales by counting cans on drugstore shelves. (Yes, the term bean counter was coined to refer to Nielsen's auditors, who counted cans of Campbell's beans for Nielsen's first customer.) On a train ride on his way to make a sales pitch, Nielsen came up with a concept to overcome the objection he often heard from prospects: "We're doing just fine. Sales are good."

The concept Nielsen invented was market share, and it was a success because now the self-satisfied mogul could see that his competitor was selling more — had a bigger share — and his now-bruised ego caused him to sign the contract.

The market share concept has been expanded and adapted into the social media metric known as Share Of Voice (SOV), defined as the number of articles, posts, tweets, videos or images where a brand and its competitors are mentioned, can certainly be used to stoke the ego-driven competitive fires, and often is in the commercial online world.

For example, a seminal post[162] by Marcel LeBrun, CEO of social media measurement service Radian6, recounts a Share Of Voice study of social media discussions about painkillers that found the following shares:

- Tylenol 43.9 percent
- Aspirin 24.8 percent
- Advil 18.8 percent
- Motrin 12.5 percent

If you're Tylenol, you feel good; you've got a bigger share. You might think you dominate the online conversation.

---

[162] Share of Voice study: **bit.ly/2KI3qH**

If you're Motrin, you may set a target to improve your SOV from the paltry 12.5 percent measured.

But this is the same ego-driven thinking that gave birth to market share. Looked at from a social media perspective, however, we realize that it really isn't about the brands. It's about the people — the community — whose problems the brands exist to solve.

Looking solely at SOV limits the field of measurement to a handpicked set of competitors, and misses the larger context — and larger opportunity to use social media.

To understand this context, take a look at a slightly different metric — Share Of Conversation (SOC) — which may be a more honest assessment of social media influence.

SOC can be defined as the degree to which an organization is associated with the problem it seeks to solve. Put slightly differently, SOC is the percent of all people talking about a problem online that are talking about you.

Thus SOC has a broader scope than SOV. SOV focuses only on a brand and its competitors, rather than the whole range of discussions about the problem, making it of limited use in truly understanding the needs of your community.

In the Tylenol/Motrin example, you might broaden your social media listening to track all conversations, for example, about arthritis. When the SOV analysis is redone as an SOC analysis, you get very different results. Tylenol has a miniscule share — 1.7 percent — of the conversations about arthritis, versus aspirin's 98.3 share. The self-satisfied Tylenol brand manager who thought the brand dominated online conversations would be shocked to see Tylenol is barely in the game for arthritis.

The larger set of conversations is really where the opportunity is. Bob Pearson illustrates the difference between SOV and SOC in a great blog post:[163]

> I've measured hundreds of brands online and I can tell you that share of conversation is routinely 20-40x higher in volume than share of voice. Here's a few examples using Google search as a simple diagnostic tool, so you can do your own analysis after reading this post.
>
> If you search Orbitz,[164] you find 8.14MM results, but travel has 770MM. Salesforce.com has 3.03MM, but cloud computing has 31.3MM. I'm writing today on a Latitude E4200

---

[163] SOV and SOC: **bit.ly/sLC1v**

[164] Orbitz search: **bit.ly/d53RuB**

which has 3.14MM results, but laptops has 63.1MM. Even Google has 2.1 billion results, while search has 5.6 billion.

You can calculate Share Of Conversation for a given time period by counting the number of conversations about your business and the subset of these conversations which also mention you. Divide your total (or your competitors') by the overall total and express as a percentage.

But don't stop there. Aren't you curious about what people are saying in those conversations that aren't about you? You can learn a lot about your community by tuning in to those conversations, and that learning can help shape a more successful social media strategy.

Improved social media measurement necessarily leads to improved social media listening. The more you measure your effect on your community, the more you'll know your community, and the more you'll want to listen.

You may be convinced. You may be ready to get your organization on the Cluetrain,[165] and improve your social media use through listening and measuring. But is your organization ready for this? We consider this in the next section.

Understand the Social Media Maturity Stage of Your Organization

Social media expert Brian Solis (yes, he's one of our favorite pundits) argues that until an organization's social media practice has matured, discussions of the return social media delivers may be premature. Here are his ten stages of social media maturity,[166] as modified by us. Which stage are you at?

- **Stage 1: Observe and Report**
  We call this Social Media Listening — Your organization starts to track what is being said online and reports back to executives

- **Stage 2: Setting the Stage + Dress Rehearsal**
  You're beginning to develop your social media presence by creating accounts on the popular social sites. You may begin to track numbers of followers and set targets.

- **Stage 3: Socializing Media**
  We call this Joining the Conversation — You start to pay attention to how your community reacts to you and use this feedback to improve future engagement. You begin to converse with your community and identify supporters, and begin to track friends, fans, followers, conversations, sentiment, mentions, traf-

---

[165] *The Cluetrain Manifesto* is a must-read: **bit.ly/d3JKnQ**

[166] *The 10 Stages of Social Media Business Integration:***bit.ly/9fUxIG**

fic, and reach.

- **Stage 4: Finding a Voice and a Sense of Purpose**
  You begin to understand your community, their goals and interests, and start to integrate their ideas and energy into your efforts. You begin to track sentiment, including negative and neutral commentary, and monitor trends in responses and ultimately behavior. You begin to focus your efforts on particular social media areas that are most relevant and productive rather than trying to be everywhere.

- **Stage 5: Turning Words Into Actions**
  Characterized by empathy and sense of purpose, in this stage you begin to truly understand your community, their challenges, objectives, options, and experiences, and better connect with them. You start to communicate strategically as you better understand how the community reacts to you.

- **Stage 6: Humanizing the Organization and Defining the Experience**
  We call this Be a Person (Not an Organization) — You realize that your brand and your reputation is embodied in your people, and feel comfortable letting their voices be heard. Your story migrates from person to person, and evangelists are shaping it. In redefining the experience of new community members, prospects and influencers, you essentially make over aspects of your organization.

- **Stage 7: Community**
  Surprised that this stage is this far from the beginning? We've said earlier that community is one of the hardest, and most rewarding, things to create online. Solis defines community as an investment in the cultivation and fusion of affinity, interaction, advocacy and loyalty that is earned and fortified through shared experiences. You proactively reach out to ideal participants and potential ambassadors, becoming social architects, building the roads necessary to lead people to a rich and rewarding network, full of valuable information and connections.

- **Stage 8: Social Darwinism**
  Solis says that social media as practiced in the earlier stages is not scalable. To survive, the organization must integrate artful listening, community building, and advocacy that aligns with the organization's ability to adapt and improve its products, services, and policies. This means external collaboration cannot evolve unless internal collaboration with stakeholders inside and outside the organization keeps pace. Solis describes the transformation as an integrated and interconnected network of evangelists that must work internally to ensure that the organization is responding to its community.

- **Stage 9: The Socialization of Business Processes**
  Multiple disciplines and departments will socialize, and the assembly or adaptation of infrastructure is required to streamline and manage social workflow and develop a Social Customer Relationship Management (SCRM) system within the organization. The key concept is that all people in the community are equal, which is a concept far removed from the way most organizations operate today.

- **Stage 10: Business Performance Metrics**
  From the cry to find the ROI of social media, we've come to the realization that the metrics of the entire

organization must change to support the preceding transformations. Solis says, "make no mistake: Social is measurable, and the process of mining data tied to our activity is extremely empowering. Our ambition to excel should be driven through the inclusion of business performance metrics, with or without an executive asking us to do so. It's the difference between visibility and presence. And in the attention economy, presence is felt. [. . .] Stage 10 reveals the meaning and opportunity behind the numbers and allows us to identify opportunities for interaction, direction, and action."

You may be thinking this is more than you thought you signed up for when you decided to try to use social media in your organization!

It's very conceivable that Solis is mistaken in this vision of organizations transformed by going social. He could also be right. There are lots of social media thinkers who tend to agree that social media is, and will be, much more than just another communication channel for external relationships.

One thing is sure, however: You will find implementing social media for external relationships much easier and much more rewarding if you also adopt social media for internal relationships.

Just listen to Manish Mehta,[167] Dell's Vice President, Social Media and Community:

> Today's corporate leaders are struggling to figure out how to use social media to further their business strategy. At Dell, we believe this is backwards thinking. Social media isn't a means to further a corporation's strategy; it's a means to help determine it.
>
> So if you are wondering about how to leverage Twitter, Facebook, blogs, forums, and the company Website to achieve your organization's goals, perhaps you are starting from the wrong point. As with the corner store, if your business uses social media to engage in conversations on a human level, you strengthen your business and allow your strategy — both corporate and social media — to evolve based on customer feedback.
>
> "Mom and Pop" knew that their business was only as successful as their relationships with customers could make it. That's the value of the direct connection to your customer, and that's how every company can achieve success using social media -- by facilitating the conversation. No strategy necessary.

Make sure you thoroughly understand the commitment your organization must make to properly implement and benefit from social media. Half-measures taken by a less-than-committed organization could conceivably do more harm than good, as several examples we present in this book will show you (*Reputation Management* on page 60; *Social Media Approach* on page 177).

---

[167] *Isn't the Value of Social Media What Business Is All About?:* **huff.to/cUcQ7b**

Establish KPIs

Your Key Performance Indicators are not going to be the same as someone else's. You need to determine what your organization's goals are and how you are going to measure them. But to get you started, here's eConsultancy Editor in Chief Chris Lake's list[168] of 35 KPIs:

Table 3 — List of Key Performance Indicators

Key Performance Indicators	
Alerts (register and response rates / by channel / Click Through Ratio / post click activity)	Profile (for example, update avatar, bio, links, email, customization, and so on)
Bookmarks (onsite, offsite)	Print page
Comments	Ratings
Downloads	Registered users (new / total / active / dormant / churn)
Email subscriptions	Report spam / abuse
Fans (become a fan of something / someone)	Reviews
Favorites (add an item to favorites)	Settings
Feedback (via the site)	Social media sharing / participation (activity on key social media sites, for example, Facebook, Twitter, Digg, etc)
Followers (follow something / someone)	Tagging (user-generated metadata)
Forward to a friend	Testimonials
Groups (create / join / total number of groups / group activity)	Time spent on key pages
Install widget (on a blog page, Facebook, etc)	Time spent on site (by source / by entry page)
Invite / Refer (a friend)	Total contributors (and percent active contributors)
Key page activity (post-activity)	Uploads (add an item, for example, articles, links, images, videos)
Love / Like this (a simpler form of rating something)	Views (videos, ads, rich images)
Messaging (onsite)	Widgets (number of new widgets users / embedded widgets)
Personalization (pages, display, theme)	Wishlists (save an item to wishlist)
Posts	

---

[168] Chris Lake is Director of Innovation for eConsultancy: **bit.ly/cFjEe4**

Assign a Social Media Monitor

As you've probably gathered from the preceding, monitoring and measuring your social media effort can be a lot of work. You may be tempted to give these activities short shrift, and concentrate on getting your message out via social media.

Obviously we think that's a risky plan. Social computing can have a huge upside for your organization, if used correctly. If used incorrectly, it can have a huge downside. And if you plan on minimizing the effort you put into monitoring and measuring, you risk making it into our Social Media Hall of Shame.

The rogue's gallery of organizations in the Hall of Shame includes some of the most-savvy marketers in the world. Yet one of the things that all the members of the Hall have in common (in addition to not understanding the difference between push marketing and social media conversation building) is they didn't take monitoring and measuring social media seriously.

Using the various social media monitoring tools we've discussed you can automate much of the monitoring tasks. But you need someone to follow the conversations and report on significant ones. You also need someone to follow up with your community. They'll expect that, once you engage them.

We recommend that you:

- Assign a person or team to regularly review the monitoring services
- Assign staff to follow up:

    o Post comments on blogs, Facebook
    o Tweet
    o Follow groups on LinkedIn

The good news is that social media experts estimate that fewer than five percent of tweets and posts require a response. But you need to respond to those that need a response; that requires someone who is paying attention.

A good example of effective use of social media metrics in creating community is The Inner Circle customer community from tax preparation software company Intuit. Developed over a period of six years, The Inner Circle now boasts more than 25,000-members.[169]

After its first year, the Inner Circle community featured many social channels for customers to interact with, including a blog, user forums, an idea exchange center, and poll and survey ques-

---

[169] Intuit/Radian6 Social Media Case Study: **slidesha.re/oqVAnc**

tions scattered about the site. Like many enterprises, Intuit was a bit wary at first of having an unfettered conversation and kept a tight rein on community members and managers. Initially posts had to be approved by PR and a number of managers before going live. Once the Intuit team became more comfortable with the community, however, the approval process disappeared.

Intuit gave Inner Circle members special perks, including front-of-the-line support privileges through a special 1-800 number assigned just to them. The result of the developing relationship between Intuit and its community was a passionate group of evangelists who were willing to go above and beyond on behalf of TurboTax and Intuit.

Social media monitoring has played a large role in the growth and vitality of the community. The Inner Circle team created a series of alerts using social media monitoring software by vendor Radian6. The team tracks company mentions, comments, and customer passion, and regularly identifies and reaches out to non-members to invite them to the community. They also use Radian6 to keep tabs on regular commenters on Twitter.

Intuit's Ali McCourt says one of the key things she's learned is to strike a balance between serving the needs of your company and those of your community.

Based on input from the community, and the monitoring of social conversations within it and outside it, Intuit now performs annual product updates and regular improvements to its Turbo-Tax product based on comments and suggestions from its highly-engaged community members.

From this we can see that effective social media monitoring is a key to creating and maintaining your community, whether you create your own branded space, or create a presence on a public social networking site.

Executing Your Social Computing Strategy

"You've heard it said again and again, but I'll say it again.
Companies don't fail because their strategy is flawed.
They fail because their strategy EXECUTION is flawed."

Jennifer Johnston Canfield

"Your social media strategy execution should be in line with the company
innovation, future direction, reputation management, campaigns, customer
satisfaction improvements, and social CRM."

Debajyoti Banerjee

Yes, it's true. The best strategy in the world is only as good as its execution, and that's where many enterprises fall down. They may spend lots of resources creating a strategy only to have it sit in a binder, gathering dust on an executive's credenza.

If you've been following along in this book, by this time you've created your strategy or at least sketched it out. You may have begun listening, and perhaps measuring. Now it's time for the rubber to meet the road. You're ready to get started. But before you do, there's one more task you need to complete: integrating your social media strategy and tactics with your other marketing and public relations efforts.

Some organizations get the mistaken idea that using social media means they should stop doing what they're already doing. Far from it. You need to look at how your social computing efforts support your existing efforts.

Integrate Social Media

The following are some suggestions for how you can integrate your social media efforts with your existing offline marketing and promotion efforts.

- If you send out direct mail, continue, and:

    - Add social media URLs to your materials along with a call to action such as: Follow us on Facebook; Watch our videos on YouTube; Get the latest info on Twitter
    - Create events to entice recipients to join you online
    - Invite your offline followers to a Tweetup,[170] where online followers can meet one another in person

- If you send out newsletters, continue, and:

    - Add social media URLs and enticements
    - Enable immediate action by making URLs clickable

- If you do real-world events, continue, and:

    - Add a real-time social media component
    - Allow virtual attendance
    - Webcams
    - Live tweeting and blogging
    - Use TweetWally[171] to project on a wall a live Twitter feed based on a hashtag (more on hashtags in the section *Use Hashtags* on page 305)
    - Create an online giving meter[172] to get supporters involved
    - Research shows using social media components of live events boosts giving[173]

---

[170] HOW TO: Organize a Successful Tweetup: **bit.ly/dpWPpx**

[171] TweetWally: **bit.ly/cdS1oM**

[172] Fundraisingmom.com: **bit.ly/9MBEM7**

[173] Blackbaud white paper: *Making Event Participants More Successful with Social Media Tools*: **bit.ly/dk7f4G**

Social Media Approach

The first rule, the title of this book, and the most important tenet in your social media approach is simple to say, but hard for many enterprises to actually do:

Be a Person

This means many things, but in general, people prefer relationships with people, not organizations, not brands, and certainly not with marketers. And it is called *social* media, after all.

Let your people speak; speak as yourself, as a real person.

Not a fake person, as in the ill-fated Wal-Marting Across America campaign[174] way back in 2006.

Wal-Marting Across America purported to be a blog about a couple's journey across America in an RV, during which they encountered many Wal-Marts along the way. The blog was exposed as a Wal-Mart marketing gimmick, one that is called sock-puppetry (discussed in the section *Engage Your Community* on page 113).

Both Wal-Mart and famous marketing house Edelman took a hit due to the duplicity. They forgot the first rule: **Be a Person**, not a Brand.

---

[174] Wal-Marting Across America: **bit.ly/ciclJi** and **bit.ly/HwEDE**

Interestingly, the campaign was in direct violation of the Word of Mouth Marketing Association's Code of Ethics,[175] which Edelman helped create, and whose major tenets are:

Table 4 — Word of Mouth Marketing Association's Code of Ethics

TRUST	Promote an environment of trust between the consumer and marketer.
INTEGRITY	Comply with the requirements of applicable laws, regulations, and rules concerning the prevention of unfair, deceptive or misleading advertising and marketing practices.
	Promote honesty and transparency in practices and methods, such that all forms of consumer manipulation are rejected.
	Commit to avoid consumer deception purchasing decisions.
RESPECT	Promote and abide by practices that focus on consumer welfare
	The consumer, not the marketer, is fundamentally in charge and control, and the consumer defines the terms of the consumer-marketer relationship.
HONESTY	Do not support any efforts that tell others what to say or how to say it.
RESPONSIBILITY	Working with minors in marketing programs requires sensitivity and care, given their particular vulnerability to manipulation and deception.
PRIVACY	Respect the privacy of consumers, and use practices that promote privacy, such as opt-in and permission standards.

The lesson here is: Don't try to put one over on your community. You'll get found out, and it will hurt you. It's better to just be honest. And **Be a Person**.

Being a person also involves a few realizations about your community, such as how they really make decisions.

There's a great free e-book[176] from Network for Good and Sea Change Strategies called *Homer Simpson for Non-profits: The Truth About How People Really Think & What It Means for Promoting Your Cause* by Katya Andresen, Alia McKee, and Mark Rovner. In it, the authors assert a bit of common sense that many folks may not know they know:

Real people make decisions like Homer Simpson, not Spock.

Now although this book is geared toward non-profits, enterprises can learn a lot from the book and the Simpson/Spock dichotomy as well. Just as giving or supporting a cause is not influenced

---

[175] Word of Mouth Marketing Association's Code of Ethics: **bit.ly/MzH5T**

[176] Network for Good and Sea Change Strategies' free ebook — *Homer Simpson for Non-profits: The Truth About How People Really Think & What It Means for Promoting Your Cause:* **bit.ly/905R9y**

by cold rationality — the Spock side of us — neither are many purchasing decisions. For all kinds of decisions, we are more motivated by our gut, like Homer.

So to achieve your business's goals, do what people do when they're just sitting around: yack. Tell each other stories. Connect on a visceral level. And form relationships. That's what social media is all about.

Rather than present all the rational reasons why someone should take an action such as buying your product or telling their friends, engage with them on a personal level. Get people to care:

- About you
- Then about your business

Rather than pursuing supporters, in the traditional media way, online you need to attract supporters by offering Content, Context, Connection, and Community.

We talk a lot about these Four C's in just a bit, but before we do, we need to talk about who is going to do all this yacking.

Who's Going to Do It?

There's a social science theoretical concept called Dunbar's number[177] that posits a limit to the number of people with whom one can maintain stable social relationships. The generally accepted value for Dunbar's number is 150. This means the average human can maintain up to 150 stable social relationships.

But you want to have relationships online with many more. So how are you going to do that?

Well, if you accept the concept of Dunbar's number, and you want to maintain relationships with thousands of supporters, you're going to need lots of people, like:

- You
- Your staff, management, customers
- Your boosters and evangelists

Kind of scary, eh? Letting your staff represent your business without a filter or editor is an obstacle many organizations can never get over. Some enterprises worry about confidential material getting out via social media. Um, hello? Everyone in your enterprise has email, both business and personal, and probably several social media accounts. If they wanted to let cats out of the bag, they'd already be doing it.

---

[177] Dunbar's Number: **bit.ly/bgZ4jh**

The difference between what's happening now, and what we're encouraging you to let happen is you'll support your staff's online interactions, giving them policy guidelines, talking points and a schedule of initiatives. You get to plan it. Today you're not at all in control. You don't know what they're saying, and you have no real way of stopping them from saying it.

Don't believe us? Google your staff. Go ahead. We'll wait.

What did you find out? Hopefully nothing terrible . . .

We're betting you found that your staff is pretty engaged in social media. Great! You've got some expertise you can leverage. Now give them some action items, and guidelines, as they engage with your community. And begin leveraging the power of their commitment to your business.

How to Do It

To the First Rule, **Be a Person**, we add a few others, most of which are actually just variations of the First Rule:

- Be authentic
- Be transparent
- Be consistent
- Be patient
- Be careful

This last one requires a little explanation. The use of any powerful communication tool such as social computing carries with it certain risks. As Spider-Man says, "With great power comes great responsibility." When we say to get your staff involved, we don't mean encourage them to engage without rules of engagement. We talked about some of the legal ramifications of public speech on social networks in the section *Ignore Social Media* starting on page 59.

To this section, we add just two anecdotes:

- A judge was reprimanded after friending a lawyer in a case, and engaged in ex parte communications about the case
- A schoolteacher faced being fired after posting derogatory comments about her students on Facebook

If you deal in an area with regulations, ensure that all social media participants understand the limits on what they say and how.

You'll for sure want to craft an acceptable use policy governing your enterprise's use of social media. We talk more about this in the section *Create Your Policies* on page 408.

Online, Think Four C's

You'll find a lot of Four C's on the Web. Most have a few of the C's in common:

- Content
- Conversation
- Community
- Connection
- Collaboration
- Communication

But there are lots of other C's out there:

Conversion	Consistency	Character
Co-creation	Collective Intelligence	Commenting
Context	Creativity	Campaigning
Caring	Change	Collective Action
Collective Consciousness	Commerce	Commitment
Competitors	Complaints	Compliments
Constant Adaptation	Consultation	Consumers
Continuity	Contribution	Contributors
Cooperation	Count	Creators
Crowdsourcing	Cumulative Value	Curators
Customer support	Customers	

All of these C's are important to the use of social media. For some reason, social networking pundits are drawn to the letter. Some have proposed Five C's, and we even found one over-achiever promoting Seven C's![178] And the guy doesn't even appear to be a sailor. 【ツ】

But snarkiness aside, there's a long history of coming up with a set of alliterative words to describe marketing and media concepts. You may be familiar, for example, with the Four P's of

---

[178] 7 Cs of Social Media for Participation: **bit.ly/c3UQO1**

Marketing, introduced by Neil H. Borden in his seminal 1964 article, *Concept of the Marketing Mix:*[179]

- Product
- Price
- Placement
- Promotion

Internet marketing company Eyeflow came up with a way to add Five C's to these Four P's via a Fifth P in the diagram[180] on the next page.

Figure 11 — The 5 P's of Marketing, After Adding Participation

We'd put the participation between product and place, where a community may have more of an impact. It seems unlikely that a community could change price or promotion, although they could affect the product design and its distribution.

Despite the profusion of C's and P's out there, we kind of like the alliterative list approach, although our favorite Four C's are:

- **Content** — Yes, social media is all about content, and pretty much all of the Four C's include this one

---

[179] Borden's *Concept of the Marketing Mix:* **bit.ly/cmJD5D**

[180] Eyeflow's *The 5 C's and The Marketing Mix in the Social Media Era:* **bit.ly/aU6Hmk**

- **Context** — This is not one of the more popular C's in our survey, but we feel it is essential. The Web is awash in Content. Making sense of it requires Context, and we feel that's what social media does.

- **Connection** — This is one of the most powerful drivers of human civilization — the need to connect with others. We're all connected to something larger than ourselves, and social media is very good at fostering Connection, primarily through our final C, Community.

- **Community** — We stated earlier in the section *Engage Your Community* on page 113 that community is one of the hardest things to create online, yet, paradoxically, social media allows communities to spontaneously form in the blink of an eye

In the sections that follow, we examine each of our Four C's in turn.

Content

At the risk of you thinking we're getting too carried away with numbers of letters, we'd like to mention just one more set, concerning content: Paul Dunay's list of the Four S's of Social Media (oddly, in a post entitled *The 4 P's to Social Media Marketing*). It pulls ideas from four influential books on online marketing:[181]

- **Tell Good Stories** — think *Unleashing the Idea Virus*[182] by Seth Godin
- **Make them Sticky** — think *Made to Stick*[183] by Chip and Dan Heath
- **Package them to be Shareable** — think *World Wide Rave*[184] by David Meerman Scott
- **Launch them using all available Social Media** — think *Inbound Marketing*[185] by Brian Halligan, Dharmesh Shah and David Meerman Scott

Telling stories is what we do all the time, offline. This may take the form of gossipy tale-telling, "Can you believe what she said?" or "Did you hear about what happened to Jim?" or more well-developed yarns like "When we finally stopped the car we realized not only was the engine smoking, but we had two flat tires."

The best way to begin to engage with your community is to tell stories. Stories humanize us, and can set listeners at ease. But stories are just the beginning. You want to establish a dialog — to get your community involved.

---

[181] Dunay's *The 4 P's to Social Media Marketing:* **bit.ly/acF6Eu**

[182] Godin's Unleashing the Idea Virus: **amzn.to/bzLIYL**

[183] Heath's *Made to Stick:* **amzn.to/bWG5YB**

[184] Scott's *World Wide Rave:* **amzn.to/d9ptf9**

[185] Halligan, Shah, and Scott's *Inbound Marketing:* **amzn.to/9wuYxY**

Discussion vs. Dialog

Many people call what happens online a discussion. You'll see terms like "discussion group" used to describe places online where people congregate to talk. But discussion may not be the best term for the kind of interaction you want to foster. You may want something a big more intimate.

The physicist David Bohm developed an approach to conversation which he called dialogue. Bohm compared dialogue (derived from Greek words implying "a flow of meaning") with discussion (derived from Latin words implying, "a shaking apart").

The former is creative and collaborative, the latter analytical and often competitive. Bohm says:

> Dialogue is not discussion, a word that shares its root meaning with 'percussion' and 'concussion,' both of which involve breaking things up. Nor is it debate. These forms of conversation contain an implicit tendency to point toward a goal, to hammer out an agreement, to try to solve a problem or have one's opinion prevail.[186]

The following table, from a paper by Richard Seel[187] indicates some of the differences between the dialogue and discussion:

Dialogue	Discussion
Starts with listening	Starts with talking
Is about speaking with...	Is about talking to...
Focuses on insights	Focuses on differences
Is collaborative	Is adversarial
Generates ideas	Generates conflicts
Encourages reflection	Encourages quick thinking
Encourages emergence	Encourages lock in

Do you notice anything about the characteristics listed in the right column? They all have a lot in common with traditional push marketing — talking to, adversarial, encourages quick thinking, encourages lock in: This pretty aptly describes the modern television commercial.

In your content, and in your community spaces, you'll want to target the elements in the left column: listening, speaking with, collaborative, generates ideas.

To do so, make sure your content draws the reader in, rather than aims to make your points. Your content should encourage collaboration and idea generation, rather than focusing on differences

---

[186] Dialoque – a Proposal by David Bohm: **bit.ly/b1uCPT**

[187] Story & Conversation in Organisations: A Survey by Richard Seel: **bit.ly/dpnj4Z**

or being adversarial. Think of your community spaces as your living room, where, as Chris Brogan says, all the chairs face each other, not your lecture hall, where the chairs all face you.

In addition to these qualities, you'll want your content to be:

Type of Content	What?	Where?
Educational	Service features and benefits	Blogs, Website, Twitter, YouTube
Targeted	No spam (unlike broadcast media)	Facebook, LinkedIn, community ads, engage customers where they are online
Authentic	Client reviews and recommendations	Website, Blogs, YouTube, real success stories, your real staff!
Valuable	"How-To", Tips & Tricks	YouTube, Website, Blogs, Wikis, Communities — don't be afraid to entertain

Context

In that big list of C words we started this section with you may have noticed that context wasn't exactly way up there in the standings. It's puzzling how many social media list-makers leave out context. We think it's very important, perhaps even paramount, and certainly one of the things that makes social networking a unique medium.

In fact, in contrast to the old saw that content is king, we think context is actually king, or at least a duke.

Context is when you check out user reviews before buying something. Context is when you Google a current event and pass up CNN or the New York Times to get a blogger's perspective. And context is something you can't reliably count on getting from traditional media, hooked as it is on the 24-hour news cycle and reality shows.

So what is context? Context is when you surround and connect the unfamiliar with familiar touch points, thus enabling the user to better understand. It's providing a frame of reference, like the frame of a picture that adds to the enjoyment and understanding of the painting. It's the difference between seeing Jeff Smith's LinkedIn professional headline and seeing in his profile that he went to the same high school you went to and graduated when you did — chances are he's your old buddy!

More and more applications are adding social media context to their bag of tricks. For example, if you have a Gmail account, you can get a free Firefox or Chrome plug-in from Rapportive[188] that will show you the social media activity of the people you correspond with. Here's an example of what viewing an email in Gmail with the Rapportive plug-in providing social media context.

---

[188] Rapportive social plug-in: **bit.ly/b7GGE6**

Figure 12 — Rapportive Social Plug-in Example

The sidebar material in includes information from Mike's LinkedIn account as well as links to his tweets, Facebook, LinkedIn and Flickr accounts. To check up on what he's doing, we just need to click on one of the links.

Large online software vendors such as Salesforce.com are rapidly adding this type of context to their applications.

But context is definitely not only about apps. The human element online provides context for your community. LinkedIn provides a good example. Which of these connection offers would you be more likely to accept: one that uses the defaults "I'd like to add you to my LinkedIn network" or one that says, "I ran into a friend of yours recently and he said we both share an interest in racquetball. I see you also used to work at XYZ Corp. I'd like to connect and talk about old times at XYZ"?

The choice is pretty simple, isn't it?

Context is becoming so important on the Web that many thinkers are claiming sites will deemphasize Search Engine Optimization (SEO — a way to get your site highly placed on Google) and pay more attention to Social Graph Optimization (SGO — optimizing the people and their content that will refer traffic to your site).

According to Ryan Spoon[189] of Polaris Venture Partners, "The consensus was that context drives relevancy... and thus virality... and thus efficacy." To decode this, Ryan is saying that giving con-

---

[189] Ryan Spoon is a principal at Polaris Venture Partners: **bit.ly/aNA2vc**

text for a referral to a Website is more relevant to the user, and thus makes the user more likely to tell his or her friends, thus improving the ability of people to find your site.

Content that is more relevant (more contextual) is more likely to be forwarded on, tweeted about, and otherwise more likely to go viral (passed from person to person just like a cold).

So when you are dialoging with your community, be sure you understand their context and provide your content based on what they want.

Here are some tips to improve the context of your content:

Type of Context	What?	Where?
Help	Filter, aggregate, interpret, help your audience understand	All social media, Blogs, Website, Twitter, YouTube
Simplify	Your messages — don't overwhelm	Email, Blogs, LinkedIn Groups
Narrow	Your focus — but focus on behavior, not demographics	Appropriate messaging depending on site
Create	Targeted services — social media helps you identify niches	Audience research on all social media
Communicate	Frequently in short bursts — the average YouTube video is 2.7 minutes; average blog post under 500 words	Everywhere — Twitter, Facebook, YouTube, Website, Blogs, email

Connection

Of course connection has to be one of the Cs — it's really what social computing is all about: connecting with other people online. The key in this phrase is "people." People connect with people, not with corporations, or products, or even with causes. To create connection that is real, strong, and sustainable, you need to **Be a Person**, and that means getting your people involved.

People involved in social media people are looking online for opportunities to connect and exchange information with people who share their interests, not with brands or organizations or products.

It's not about me, me, me, the business with something to sell. It's about us, the folks who are connected because we like the product or service, or care about the problem you're solving. The community. Which probably already exists, so you need to connect to it first, before you can create relationships with its members.

Of course, a big thing to figure out is what will you do with the connections you foster? We've talked a lot about that so far in this book, and there's more later.

You do need to think beyond the one-to-one connections we've been talking about. Look at it from the community member's perspective. They go from site to site, and may have various relationships on various social media islands in the stream of the Web. But many of these connections are discrete — limited to the venue, such as Facebook, or Twitter, and not portable across all the places they roam.

There's a recent movement to offer context across these isolated connections. Facebook recently changed the way members can share the experiences they have on other sites. It used to be a site could offer a Share on Facebook button that would allow a Facebook member to click and comment on the site. It was generally a one-time thing. You see a site you like; you comment on it; it shows up in your timeline, and that was the end of it.

Facebook has changed this to a Like button[190] that does a lot more, and introduced the Open Graph[191] protocol, which is a fancy way of saying a standardized method for members of one site can share their experiences, enthusiasms and recommendations on another site. The site that offers the button can set up a lasting connection between the member's experience on the site and their Facebook experience.

Facebook explains it[192] this way:

> You can publish content from your site into the social graph to reach your users' friends. The Like button enables users to share your site's content back to their Facebook stream with one click. In addition, you can integrate pages deeply into the social graph via the Open Graph protocol.

So if content changes on Site A, it is pushed out to all Facebook members who have connected their Site A experience to their Facebook experience, and will show up in their Facebook timeline, and in their friends' timelines.

This is a very powerful way to connect the wide-ranging social media experiences of Facebook members, and serves to make Facebook the center of members' worlds, which is obviously great for Facebook.

But think of the implications for your enterprise. We talk about creating evangelists in the *Find and Create Online Evangelists* section on page 225. The new Open Graph process makes every user a potential evangelist, as their friends can discover information about their interests, leading to an interest in your site.

---

[190] Facebook Like button: **bit.ly/bQMlff**

[191] Facebook Open Graph: **bit.ly/aMUWV8**

[192] Facebook on the Open Graph: **bit.ly/b2uYU3**

Executing Your Social Computing Strategy

Several large social media sites have signed on to the idea, including the Web radio station Pandora, and as a result, Pandora users can:

- See all friends who use Pandora
- See the artists and songs that are liked by friends
- Import their Facebook pictures into their Pandora profiles, a key way to promote personal brand
- Listen to friends' stations (thanks, Andrew Eklund, for the great Medeski, Martin & Wood station!)

Pandora makes it easy to make the connection, as you can see in the next two figures. Simply click a button, answer some questions, and it's done.

Figure 13 — Pandora Connects to Facebook Using Open Graph

Figure 14 — Viewing Facebook Friends' Channels on Pandora

The Open Graph initiative represents a very strong way to connect the social media experiences of your community, creating a vast interconnected web (really) of information, recommendations, and discovery that you can use to communicate with potential new community members. Try putting the Facebook Like button on your site and see what happens. We tell you how in the section *Add a Like Button to Your Website* on page 335.

Here are some tips about making connections.

Table 5 — Connection What and Where

Type of Connection	What?	Where?
High Tech, High Touch	Keep human	Twitter, IM, YouTube, Communities
Two-Way	Conversation leads to conversion	Twitter, Email, Online Chat
Person-to-Person	Reveal yourself	Workers by name — see @cnnbrk, @comcastcares
Authentic	Don't spin	Everywhere

Community

Community is one of those things that everybody knows in their bones, but which defies being tied to specifics. You know what community means in your offline life — neighbors, town or city, worship partners, your golf league, your book club. It's easy to call them communities.

But when we talk about the insubstantialities of community online, even — or especially — the pundits can't agree. They use too many or too few words to describe the phenomenon, and spend more time ruling examples in and out based on their definitions than actually creating a useful definition. Notice how the following list from well-respected social media gurus range from definitions that emphasize the tools the community uses to broad descriptions that encompass online and offline communities:

- **Jeremiah Owyang**: "Where a group of people with similar goals or interests connect and exchange information using web tools."

- **Shel Israel**: "Communities are bodies of people loosely joined together by a common interest."

- **Howard Rheingold**: "[Virtual communities are] social aggregations that emerge from the Net when enough people carry on those public discussions long enough, with sufficient human feeling, to form webs of personal relationships in cyberspace."

- **Jake McKee** (the Community Guy): "A community is a group of people who form relationships over time by interacting regularly around shared experiences, which are of interest to all of them for varying individual reasons."

- **Tim Jackson**: "A strong community will be built around that shared experience or interest and passion will be at the heart of it — for a healthy community to survive anyway."

- **Ann Michael**: "Communities are groups of people that actively support each other."

- **Deb Schultz**: "Don't forget TRUST and a sense of commitment. To me it is not a community without the feeling (perceived? real) that other members have my back."

We like parts of all of these definitions. In particular, we like a key concept in Rheingold's quote: "sufficient human feeling." That's what makes the connection, the gut, not the brain, the Homer, not the Spock.

To create a community, you must foster the human feeling. This means in your messaging about your business, statistics may inform, but human stories will engage, and create the connection between your organization (**Be a Person**) and your community members. Make sure your staff and your supporters or evangelists tell their stories using social media. There's more on this approach in *The Importance of Stories* section on page 229.

We definitely need to add Ann Michael's and Deb Shultz's ideas about support and having each other's backs.

We also think there are important concepts in the dictionary definition of community: "A social, religious, occupational, or other group sharing common characteristics or interests and perceived or perceiving itself as distinct in some respect from the larger society within which it exists (e.g. 'The Business Community')."[193] Common characteristics — having cancer, for example — and common interests — wanting to save the world, for example — are what attracts people to form a group and helps define them as distinct from other individuals or groups.

Also important are the following basic community characteristics.

- **Organized Around a Shared Purpose**
  Communities need a reason for existing, and that typically is a shared interest or purpose. Community members generally have a common reason for joining.

  While some communities may be more general — YouTube, for example, or Facebook — these broader communities generally are hosts for sub-communities comprised, for example, by you and your friends on Facebook, people who like stupid human tricks videos on YouTube,[194] fans of a band on MySpace,[195] or members of your family tree on Ancient Faces.[196] Within these larger communities made up of members with weak attractions for one another (like viewing funny videos online, or having a lot of followers on Twitter), your community will be organized around your business or perhaps the problem it solves, and will include people who are interested — hopefully passionate — about it.

  Your community won't necessarily, or optimally, be organized around your business. It generally is not the content (videos, tweets, blogs) or the tools (blogs, messaging, friending) that create the bonds that tie the community together. It's the people, and their relationships.

- **Interactive**
  Interactivity is the whole point of community online: the ability to easily find kindred souls and interact with them. The job of the community organizer is to remove as much friction as possible to allow people to interact, while maintaining agreed-upon levels of privacy and confidentiality. The conversation is many to many, not top down to the crowd — two-way not one-way. Members support one another and defend each other if necessary.

  The basic interactive tool of a social media community is the contact, or friending, capability. By friending, people identify each other as connected in some way. Friending can be weak, as in Twitter followers, or strong, as in Facebook friends, who are allowed to see each other's more-personal information. Another basic community tool is commenting, which allows community members to react and respond to

[193] Dictionary.com: **bit.ly/aaqRyf**

[194] YouTube search: **bit.ly/9gK0zH**

[195] For example: **mysp.ac/blxYxr**

[196] Ancient Faces: **bit.ly/dxXclW**

each others' posts.

- **Everyone Can Contribute**
  Contribution is fundamental to a successful community: the creation of a system that supports and encourages all members to contribute, not just the organizers. Although lurkers may comprise the majority, all have permission to contribute.

  In your community, you should seek a balance between helping enable the dialog, and guiding it. Too much in one direction and the community degenerates into lawlessness. Too much in the other, and the community becomes just another place for you to push your messages. Remember that you don't need to be involved in every conversation, and you don't need to correct every misconception or misinterpretation yourself. Your community will often take care of that.

  On the other hand, your community will likely expect you to be present, and involved. You may be expected to respond to direct requests for answers or information within a particular timeframe. Make sure your community understands the service level they can expect in this regard. And be sure you have the resources to consistently deliver that level of service.

- **Evolving and Growing**
  You may start out with a goal and a plan for your community. Things may change as your community members evolve their relationships. However, members determine how the conversation and the community develop and grow, or die. Since one of the main principles of community is that the community is in charge, you may need to hold the reins very loosely. Remember, a mob is also a type of community. Online, passions can spike instantly, and people have the tools to express themselves immediately. See a good example of what can happen on the influential Techcrunch blog.[197] Co-Founder Michael Arrington provoked an angry response when he questioned a journalist on a video blog, resulting in a mob of angry people wishing him ill on the social site FriendFeed.

  Depending on your community, and how it evolves, you may need to worry about mob rule. Anonymous blog commenting is one of the ways social media can get out of control. We classify the people who comment on a blog post as a form of community, although others disagree. The posters often comment on each others' posts, and things can get out of hand and way off topic. What is your responsibility in this case? If you are too heavy-handed in ensuring posts are on-topic and polite, users can revolt, or simply leave.

  Another problem with blog commenting is the automated bots (short for robots) that look for blogs that don't require registration in order to post. The bots can slam one or a hundred spam posts into the comments, polluting the commentary, and turning off the community. You need to think about how you will implement specific features like this, and how you will react as your community evolves.

  In fact, the various bits of functionality your community offers, from commenting to friending to blogging

---

[197] Techcrunch mob: **tcrn.ch/cgKxr0**

or video uploading, the tech can have an effect on the direction and vitality of your community. Media theorist Marshall McLuhan said, "We shape our tools and thereafter our tools shape us." We definitely see this concept at work in online communities where the technology — be it YouTube's video or Foursquare's GPS tech — shapes the interactions and the arc of the community.

- **Multi-Threaded**
  Community is not a monologue. There are multiple speakers, multiple topics, and multiple ways community members can interact. One aspect of community management is to set policy for concerns off-topic posting. Some community managers delete off-topic threads, move them out of the main flow, or otherwise discourage them. We feel that a good amount of the attraction f a good community is the ability for its members to express themselves as they see fit. We recommend that you ask your community how they want to police off-topic posting, and enable them to solve such problems themselves.

  But there are other types of undesirable activity you'll need to deal with: trolls. The term troll refers to someone who posts inflammatory, extraneous, or off-topic messages in an online community.[198] Trolls deliberately create messages to foster responses of outrage or indignation. These are the people with an axe to grind, or who just enjoy stirring the pot. They may hijack threads and bend them to their agenda. We talk more about trolls in the section *Dealing with Trolls* on page 213.

- **Leaderless/Many Leaders**
  By this we mean there is usually no single leader in a community. You may think you'd like to be the leader, but what you'll find is that many leaders will emerge. And they may fight for dominance. To use your community properly, learn how to nurture these leaders and turn them into evangelists so they can spread their influence — and your messages — beyond your community. You may find, however, that some of the leaders are leading dissent. We talk more about handling negatives in the section *Dealing with Negatives* on page 209.

  In general, however, you need to govern your community with a light hand. Community members will expect to be involved in major decisions about your community, so you should clearly lay out your policies regarding the actions you can take unilaterally, and respond to community comments about them. You'll find that most community members will expect you to exert a certain amount of control, but be very careful about actions that could be construed as censorship.

- **Continuity**
  Generally, a community is a longer-term entity. However, some communities are quite ephemeral, coalescing around events or short-lived causes (for example, disasters like the Haiti earthquake in early 2010) or fads. To benefit, members may require a sense of continuity — the feeling that by investing in the community it will be there when they need it.

  Most communities generally have a core membership that interacts over a long period of time, and it's often the quality of their interaction that attracts and holds the rest of the membership together. A good

---

[198] Wikipedia definition of a troll: **bit.ly/bhHq1m**

example of this is the long-running Whole Earth 'Lectronic Link (the Well) that started in the San Francisco Bay area in the mid-80s (as a bulletin board for Grateful Dead fans) and is still running strong today. When I first joined the Well in 1993, all the leading lights of the Internet movement made their home there, including Howard Rheingold (previously mentioned in this section), Whole Earth Catalog creator (and Well cofounder) Stewart Brand, writer Bruce Sterling, usability pioneer Brenda Laurel, Lawrence Lessig, one of the founders of the Creative Commons Copyleft movement, and Caterina Fake, creator of Flickr and Hunch.

This is not to imply you need stars to keep your community going, but it doesn't hurt. Surely there are stars in your field. See if you can get them to participate.

Why are we going on and on about the definition of community? Well, to state the obvious, if you're going to build a community, it would certainly be helpful to know when you've achieved one. But also we feel a definition of community that states the characteristics of good, sustainable efforts will be the most useful in guiding your efforts to architect your community.

So to put all this into one definition, we'd say an online community is:

A group of people with a shared purpose in a longer-term relationship in which all voices can be heard, members support one another, and which evolves over time based on where its members want it to go.

Does that sound good to you? OK, we've defined what community is. Let's take a quick look at what it isn't.

What isn't Community?

- **An audience**

    - Chris Brogan says, "The difference between an audience and a community is which direction the chairs are pointing."
    - Do you want an audience to speak at, or a community to support and converse with you?
    - The community is not there to consume your messages

- **Leaderless**

    - You as a sponsor can lead, but in the best communities, leaders emerge
    - Those leaders can be your evangelists, but even if they aren't, they are critical to the community's success

- **A Place Requiring Equal Participation**
    - Many more will lurk than contribute, and that's OK
    - A small percentage will contribute the majority of content and interaction — cultivate them!
    - It's just important that everyone have the same opportunity to contribute even if they don't take advantage of it

Here are some quick tips about community:

Attribute of Community	What?	Where?
Not Just Geography	Affinity for your business	Ning, Plaxo, LinkedIn
Self-Forming	Already out there	Find existing communities, enable new ones
Enable Commenting	And don't censor!	Blog, Contact Us, Wikis, YouTube, Polls, Surveys
Invite Everyone, Even Detractors	Especially detractors, be proactive, answer all negative comments, actually fix problems	Blog, Website, Wikis

Aim to Influence

One of your goals for your online community — whether you create your own or use an existing social media site — is to influence people. We've talked about having goals for your social networking efforts, which involves figuring out what activities you want people to take. So how do you influence your community and spark them to action?

The first step is to be sure you invest before you make a withdrawal. By this we mean, don't just jump in with both feet and start asking for commitments. Remember, the point of social media is relationships, so a far better tactic is to start getting involved by establishing yourself as a resource.

Don't just post, engage with the community. Get to know various influential members, and offer advice, information and other value. You might, for example, give away something for free, perhaps a white paper, or maybe just a blog post that addresses common community concerns. Other ideas for contributing include:

- **Break news** — Draw people's attention to significant news about your product or service category or just in general can help establish your value to the community
- **Offer trial versions** — Depending on your community, and your business, you can add value for offering trial access to content, discounted access to events, or other freebies
- **Create How-To's** — Produce a series of how-to blog posts that are relevant to your community and that they will find valuable

It's a good idea when engaging in this way to enable community members to take action just as long as this is not seen as the primary reason for your interaction with them. When enabling action online, be sure to give details up front and ensure that the action is specific, and able to be completed online right away. For example, you can include a link to the eCommerce section of your Website in your signature for posts.

On the other hand, avoid pitching offline actions that take a bit more effort to complete. For example, if you want people to buy, include a Buy button rather than a message such as, "click here to email someone to find out how to buy" since this requires a more lengthy, or offline, follow up.

The bottom line is that you need to be a part of the community, and accepted by the community, before you start asking for commitment. Imagine two door-to-door donation solicitation scenarios. In one, a stranger appears at your door selling magazine subscriptions; in the other, your neighbor (or neighbor's kid) appears. Which would be more likely to get you to buy? It's the same online. Become a neighbor first before asking.

Partner and Cross-Promote

Partnering is even more important and effective online than it is offline. By choosing the right strategic partners, you can leverage others' traffic and followers and attract them to your community. You can also increase your prestige by associating with the right online leaders, creating a halo effect by borrowing their influence.

Social media is a good way to find new partners and create partnerships. In his *2010 Social Media Marketing Industry Report*,[199] Michael A. Stelzner reported that 53.1 percent of those who invested 6 to 10 hours per week over a few months with social media marketing found new partnerships.

The benefits of having online partners can be great. You can multiply your efforts and mutually enhance each other's success. You can offer a more compelling value to your community. You can benefit by associating with a partner, sharing in each other's prestige and reputation. Perhaps more importantly, by partnering with a larger or more established online business, you can reinforce your own legitimacy and community standing.

---

[199] Stelzner's *2010 Social Media Marketing Industry Report:* **bit.ly/abFxFX**

Prospect for Partners

There are many ways to find potential partners using online media. We recommend that, after you've established some goals for having a partner, you use the following procedure:

- **Determine the important keywords for your business**
  What are the first words that come to mind when you think about your business and your products? Write them down. Now put yourself in your community's shoes. What words would they use to find you? Add them to the list. Organize the list into primary keywords — those that you think most people would associate with your product category — and long tail keywords — those that may have meaning, but are more peripheral. (Incidentally, you'll probably want to use this list in your Search Engine Marketing (SEM) efforts.)

- **Search and see who controls the keywords**
  Plug your primary keywords into Google. Who comes up on the first page? Assuming it's not you, note the organizations and make a list of their names. Explore their Websites to determine how they might fit as a partner. Assign a 1 to 100 score based on their likelihood and desirability. Do the same for your long tail keywords. Then prioritize your list and use the top works in your content and to search for partners. Prioritize the resulting partner list and use it to make contacts.

- **Check sponsored results**
  While doing your Google research, also take note of any AdWords ads you see. AdWords are those text ads that appear to the right of search results on Google. There may also be some sponsored results at the top. Evaluate the organizations behind these ads and adjust their scores.

- **Create a list of the influential blogs/forums**
  Using your lists, search for blogs and forums that deal with your product category. You can use Google Blog Search[200] or the various tools we've previously discussed. From the number of comments, tweets, or other measures of influence, create a list of influential bloggers and forums.

- **Listen to the blogs/forums**
  Find out what people are saying about the organizations on your partner prospect list. If your prospects are participating, even better. You can start to engage with them on these sites. Research your prospects by finding out what social media sites they frequent.

Using this process, you've created a partner prospect list and been able to prioritize it. Now you can start to engage with these partners online, and draw them into a relationship. Start by commenting on their blogs or other posts and gradually introduce yourself that way.

In the *Finding Partners* section on page 249, we offer tips on using LinkedIn to prospect for partners.

---

[200] Google Blog Search: **bit.ly/dy7s5O**

Executing Your Social Computing Strategy

Facilitate Viralocity

You've probably heard a lot of talk about being viral online. It's not about infection, at least not bodily infection, but about getting people excited enough about you that they pass your messages on to others.

One of the earliest and most impressive successes in building a business using viral techniques is Hotmail. Now known as Windows Live Hotmail, Hotmail was started by Sabeer Bhatia and Jack Smith in mid-1995. By the end of 1997, when Microsoft bought Hotmail for $400 million, it had 8.5 million subscribers. How did two Silicon Valley wage slaves start the free email movement and make millions? At the bottom of every Hotmail email message, the service tacked on the following text: "Get your private, free email at http://www.hotmail.com." So every message their 8.5 million subscribers sent could go viral. The best thing about this technique is it didn't require any change in behavior by Hotmail users. They just went about their business, emailing people and spreading the word about Hotmail.

Many online marketers are absolutely obsessed with the concept of going viral, and many will profess to know how to be able to take your messages and make them viral.

But one thing to understand about viralness, virality, viralocity, or whatever you call it: It is not a technique. It's a destination. There are no tried and true techniques for creating viralocity. Most often, viral phenomena seem accidental.

Take the Blendtec YouTube videos[201] that we talked about back in the second chapter.

For almost no money, Blendtec has reaped more than 115 million YouTube views, 300,000 subscribers, and a 7X increase in sales.

You could go viral as well. But to do so, you must be hooked into the zeitgeist[202] of your community, and the larger society. Offbeat, quirky ideas are what generally go viral. But if you try too hard (we're looking at you, LonelyGirl15[203]) you could do more damage than good.

What you can do is enable your supporters to take viral actions, like embedding a link to your Website, Buy button, Facebook page, or other social networking site as signatures in their emails. Or enabling a Tell A Friend feature on your site, or add a social media sharing service such as

---

[201] Blendtec's YouTube channel: **bit.ly/9pHXlh**

[202] Google zeitgeist: **bit.ly/cy2fhg**

[203] LonelyGirl15's YouTube channel: **bit.ly/dBib9J**

AddThis[204] to your site so fans can bookmark you on Delicious or "Like" you on Facebook. You can offer your users branded badges they can add to their blogs or Websites

The first step to viralocity is to ask users to pass it on. We talk more about these techniques in the *Find and Create Online Evangelists* section on page 225. Other ideas include the following list, created by Dr. Ralph F. Wilson[205] way back in 2000 but still very relevant a decade later:

An effective viral marketing strategy:

1. Gives away products or services

2. Provides for effortless transfer to others

3. Scales easily from small to very large

4. Exploits common motivations and behaviors

5. Utilizes existing communication networks

6. Takes advantage of others' resources

These attributes of viralocity may be simple, but, as we've indicated, going viral is more art — and luck — than science.

Use YouTube

As we've discussed, YouTube can be a powerful way to influence your community, even if you don't think blending or blowing something up is your cup of tea.

YouTube is great for drawing attention, but it's also great for teaching. You can create short mini-documentaries about your business, products, or product category; you can create how-to videos about your products.

One of the great things about YouTube is that it's OK to be crude (in both senses). In a perverse way, a less-than-slick video is often seen as more real, more authoritative than polished efforts with Hollywood production values.

And one of the major feeders to YouTube turns out to be Facebook. Recently the site became the second-most-popular source of video referrals to YouTube, accounting for more than 16 percent

---

[204] AddThis: **bit.lv/d6oL2B**

[205] Wilson's *The Six Simple Principles of Viral Marketing*: **bit.ly/9be3Fg**

of YouTube's views.[206] In fact, Facebook itself is another good target for your videos, since it is the fifth-largest video provider.[207]

If you want to attract attention on YouTube — and have a chance at going viral — try being controversial or off the wall. Of course, this may not fit your enterprise's image, but that very fact may make an offbeat video that much more attractive to your community.

The most popular topics on YouTube tend to be:

- Cute — babies, dogs, animals of all kinds, smurfs and trolls
- Painful — think Funniest Home Videos and people getting hit in the groin
- Explosive — blowing stuff up is a perennial favorite

However, you may be surprised at how many educational or product-oriented videos are on YouTube. We talk more about the business uses of YouTube in the *Set Up YouTube* section on page 351.

Blog

A major way you can influence your community is by blogging. Don't let the sobering fact that tens of thousands of blogs are created each day stop you from starting your own. Make sure you know what you want to say, and what your point of view and style will be before getting started. You'll need to do more than just start a blog and hope they will come; you'll need to promote it. And once you get people to your blog, you must be sure you're giving them something of value, not necessarily just your opinion.

You should include a blog on your Website for sure, and also on as many blog sites as you can. It's OK to cross-post (not all agree with this), using a site such as Ping.fm[208] to put the same material on each site, but it's best if you modify it for the intended audiences on the other sites. There's a great free guide to cross-posting *How To Cross-Post Content To Other Sites and Social Media Platforms* by Movements.org: **http://bit.ly/oy40dU**

If you do blog to multiple sites, link them together by adding links between posts to introduce your audience to the other places your voice can be heard.

If possible, get yourself invited to be a guest blogger by a more-influential site. It's a great way for both sites to benefit, and for you to find an audience.

---

[206] RealSEO's *Facebook Is The 2nd Largest Referral Source for Online Video:* **bit.ly/c5qzMO**

[207] ClickZ's *Facebook Grows Video Presence:* **bit.ly/b4SXMf**

[208] Ping.fm: **bit.ly/dwbqG3**

You can even ask other bloggers to blog about you, but you should have a good reason why they'd want to.

When blogging, always remember, like all social media, blogging is not a one-way channel. It's not just a way for you to present your agenda and point of view. It's a way for your community to respond to you. So you should definitely enable comments. Doing this may cause you a little extra work — monitoring and responding, and even removing offensive posts — but you'll find the interaction not only stimulating, but traffic-building.

Everywhere you are on social media, think about making an offer of some kind, generally of help of more information if a reader takes some action. A good place to do this is as a standing part of your blog's author bio. It can be as simple as, "Email me for more info on _____" or as a link to your site for more information. You can also take a page from Hotmail's viral success and incorporate your offer into your email signature.[209]

Get Found

Yes, you'll need to do some work to get found on social media. There is no build it and they will come. The best way to get found is to provide something your community finds valuable. But that alone will most often not be enough. You'll need to use a variety of online and offline techniques to build awareness in your community.

We take a look at a variety of ideas for getting found in the following sections.

Run Contests

The most sure-fire way to attract users on the Internet has long been to give something away for free. Years ago, this caused us to create the aphorism: "On the Internet, everything devolves to free."[210] Well, what if you start out with free? Free is a crowd pleaser.

Years ago, Internet marketing guru Seth Godin promoted his book, *Permission Marketing*,[211] by offering the first four chapters to anyone who would email him at **free@permission.com**. He gave away 150,000 free copies. Was that stupid, or did it contribute to the book's success? Godin went even further with *Unleashing the Virus*:[212] He gave the book away for free — two million copies

---

[209] Advice on email sigs: **bit.ly/9eCOfM**

[210] Are we devo? **bit.ly/an3gnK**

[211] Godin's *Permission Marketing*: **amzn.to/bvbWjn**

[212] Godin's *Unleashing the Virus*: **amzn.to/dsGGpw**

worldwide. Sheer folly, right? Wrong. According to Godin, the hardcover edition went to number 5 on Amazon in the US, and reached number 4 in Japan.

So don't be afraid to give away valuable stuff for free.

One way to give stuff away, attract attention, and create a little buzz is to run a contest. We can't pretend to know what kind of contest you should run, but it should be fun, have a significant prize, and generate enough excitement that your followers tell their friends. In fact, make a secondary prize for the person who refers the most entrants.

Most of the time you'll be giving away prizes that cost you something. But you can also give away something that costs you nothing: prestige. The prize could be nothing more than bragging rights, and be represented by something as simple as the ability to display a badge or other notice of the honor as part of the winner's profile, or on their blog.

Microsoft figured this out more than a decade ago with their Most Valuable Professional (MVP) program.[213] MVP is an award presented by Microsoft for exceptional technical community leaders who voluntarily provide technical expertise within Microsoft support communities. This award has value to the awardees — helping convince potential clients that they know their stuff — and the winners invariably have given hundreds of hours a year in service to Microsoft by helping people solve their technical problems with the firm's software.

So your contest could not only be cost-free for you, but it actually could benefit your business.

Create Anticipation

If you're having an event or some other significant future initiative, one good way to attract followers is to create anticipation via a series of teasers. The masters of this technique are Steve Jobs and the marketing folks at Apple. Each year at their annual event Apple announces some great new device or service. However, rather than overtly tease, they make a big show of secrecy, yet somehow unconfirmed details leak out, causing lots of buzz, rampant speculation, and lots of traffic to sites devoted to technical gizmos.

You may not be as sexy as Apple, but these techniques can work for you as well. Just think of the blogosphere as a potentially huge echo chamber for your message and see if you can create anticipation and mystique around the things your organization does.

---

[213] Microsoft's MVP program: **bit.ly/drOKhY**

Establish an Inner Circle

Groucho Marx famously said, "I don't want to belong to any club that will accept me as a member." Most people don't feel that way, thankfully. Consider creating an exclusive club and offering some kind of benefit — perhaps only prestige — to its members. It might be as simple as first dibs on tickets to one of your events, or attendance at special briefings, or other exclusive access.

You might have various circles within the club, with the highest circle reserved for those who are your true evangelists, and who do the most to help build your community.

If you offer things for sale, consider creating a coupon club that lets participants get discounts.

Triangulate Your Social Media Presence

At the most basic level, what we mean by triangulation involves linking your social media properties together. So you should:

- Tweet about your blog
- Blog about your Facebook page
- Link your blog to your Website
- Link your Website to your YouTube channel
- Link your Twitter feed to your LinkedIn and Facebook statuses
- Put all your images on Flickr and link to them when you need images on your site or your blog

You get the idea: Send people who find you on one social site to your offerings on all your other sites. We mentioned the concept of social media as an echo chamber in a previous section. You're trying to set up your own echo chamber to reinforce your presence. Of course none of this will work if you're boring and don't add any value on all your sites.

Beyond this rather mechanical view of triangulation, though, are other considerations such as your online brand. On all your sites you should use consistent graphics. Have your graphic backgrounds and logos professionally created, and use the same graphics everywhere. Include photos of you and your staff to personalize your brand.

Include links to your social media presence everywhere:

- Email signature
- Company letterhead
- Traditional advertising

The idea is to maximize the ability of your community to find out all you're doing online even if they just happen to glimpse a single tweet and check out your profile. Not only will your Twitter profile point them to your other sites, but when they arrive, they'll see a consistent graphic and branding treatment. If they later run into another of your sites, this consistency reminds them of their previous experience and builds your brand.

Search Engine Optimization

It shouldn't be news to you that Google is most often the top way users find Websites. Your site will probably be no different. So you need to make sure that Google can find you and that when they do, they categorize you properly, and rank you highly.

The art and science of ensuring high placement on Google and other search engines is known as Search Engine Optimization (SEO). A related technique known as Search Engine Marketing (SEM) encompasses SEO and also adds online advertising on Google and other search engines. We talked about advanced Google usage to find your community in the section *Advanced Google Searching* on page 106. Now let's turn that idea — finding interesting people using keyword searches — around: How can you be found via keyword searches? That's what SEO is all about.

The basic goal of SEO is to ensure that when people use search words that are relevant to what you do they find you on the first page of search results. This is generally done, at least in part, by selecting a set of keywords that are highly relevant to your site, and then optimize your site to feature these keywords. We led you through this exercise in the *Prospect for Partners* section on page 198.

There are lots of SEO consultants out there that will guarantee first page placement, and some are quite good, while others haven't a clue, so it's best to have a basic understanding of SEO before you consider using one.

All of them do some combination of the following SEO techniques. We only scratch the surface of a very deep subject here, but many of these techniques you can do yourself without high-priced consultants.

We're indebted to a very fine post on ClickZ by P.J. Fusco[214] for much of the structure and material in this list. It's one of the most concise and comprehensive lists of SEO techniques we've read.

- **Optimize Title Tags**
  The title of a page is the part that shows at the very top of your browser window. It's the part that is above the toolbar. It must describe the purpose of the page and it should also identify your site.

---

[214] Fusco's *Site Redesign SEO Considerations for 2010*: **bit.ly/d5VTjh**

The title tag of every page should begin with a uniquely optimal keyword phrase and end with consistent branding, such as the name of your business, or the name of the site.

The words at the beginning of the title tag have more prominence and weight than the words at the end. The target length for title tags should be 65 characters (with spaces). The major engines recognize and index title tags beyond 120 characters, but only 65 characters are visible in the search results.

- **Ensure Each Page Has a Theme**
  Just as you were taught in school that every paragraph needs a topic sentence, so each Webpage needs a topic, or a theme. This helps the search engine categorize your page correctly. If you're tempted to dump all sorts of marginally-related information onto your yard-long pages, the search engines aren't going to like you.

- **Optimize Heading Tags**
  Second to the title tag, the <h1> is the most prominent location to accentuate your keywords. If you're not familiar with the HTML <h1>, or heading, tag, it's generally the first and largest heading on the page. It often is the title of a post or a section of a Website.

  There should be only one <h1> heading tag on a page, and like the title tag, it should begin with the optimal keyword phrase. Additional <h2> and <h3> tags, which denote secondary and tertiary heading tags, should help complement the targeted theme of each page. Unlike <h1> tags, there can be more than one <h2> or <h3> tags per page.

- **Optimize Body Copy**
  The text of each page should contain introductory copy or a summary of the page text. Body copy should consist of at least three sentences with a minimum of 150 words. You should try to mention your target keywords as many times as you can in your body copy, without becoming annoying or unreadable. The general rule is to try for four mentions of a keyword per page. Of course if you have a set of 10 keywords, the result could be gibberish, so here's where the art comes in.

- **Create a Meta Description**
  A meta description is an invisible page component that is part of the HTML page header. You see it only when your page shows up in search results. Each page should have a meta description even though having one won't improve rankings in the search engines. The major search engines ignore the meta description for the purposes of indexing your page. Having a good meta description can, however, increase the likelihood of users clicking on search results.

  Meta descriptions should be unique to each page and should contain no more than 265 characters. Typically, however, only the first 150 characters (including spaces) are displayed in the search engine results pages, so the meta description should include the relevant keyword phrases and end with a call to action.

- **Create Meta Keywords**
  Meta keywords, like the meta description, are invisible parts of the HTML page header. They are lists of

Executing Your Social Computing Strategy

words that the page author think are important to describe the content of the page.

Google and Bing pay no attention to meta keywords. Yahoo only reviews meta keywords for misspellings that might affect their indexing of the page. You should insert three or four keywords per page, ensuring that the words are pulled from the page. If they're not, don't bother producing keywords at all. Nonetheless, don't make meta keywords a critical part of your keyword strategy.

- **Optimize Alternative Attributes**
  You may have seen descriptions pop up when you run your mouse over a graphic or a link on a Webpage. These are known as alternative attributes, or alt tags for short. Create keyword-rich alt tags for all graphics and images. Also create mouse-over text[215] for any links on the page.

- **Optimize Videos**
  If you are embedding videos on your Webpage, follow conventional title tag and meta data standards as already outlined. Embed one video per page and organize video content around the structures of your pages, sections, and the site.

  If you are using a YouTube channel for hosting videos, ensure that you optimize the following YouTube fields using your keywords:

  - Title
  - Description
  - Tags

There are plenty of other aspects of SEO beyond optimizing your site and its content. One very popular and effective technique is to increase the number and quality of the inbound links to your site.

An inbound link is when another site links to you. Google assigns a rank to all sites, and if a more-highly-ranked site links to your site, it confers some of its rank — its prestige — to your site. Plus, the more inbound links you have, in general, the more highly you will rank. And the more highly your site ranks, the more highly placed it will be on Google search results. Google takes a dim view of such site and may penalize you for linking to them.

A common way to increase a site's rank is to run an inbound link campaign. This involves contacting other, highly-ranked sites, and asking them if they'll link to you. It can be tedious, but it can also be quite rewarding. Beware of those who want to link to you in return for a reciprocal link. Be sure the requesting site is reputable and not what is known as a link farm — a site that exists to try to game the Google system so that they'll get increased ad revenue.

---

[215] You've seen mouseover text when you've moved the cursor over a link on a page, and popped up a little description.

As we've said, SEO and SEM are very deep and complex topics and you really may need a consultant to move much beyond the advice we've given here. Just be careful of too-good-to-be-true claims. It generally costs hundreds or thousands of dollars per month to stay on top of search engine results. Those who claim to be able to do this for you for less may not be able to deliver.

There are few absolutes in the world of SEO, but one of them is that as soon as someone figures out how to game the search engines, they'll change their ranking techniques, and perhaps penalize previously-effective SEO techniques.

Real-Time Social Search

As the social computing phenomenon gains momentum, search engine experts are increasingly talking about the growing importance of real-time search, or social search, by which they mean search that can tell you what's happening on social media sites. Google recently revamped their search to add a real-time component, and reached agreements to index Twitter[216] and Facebook[217] content.

Some pundits worry that the primacy of traditional search engines like Google, and the cottage SEO industry they support, may be threatened by the rise of social search, wherein recommendations and referrals from within social networking communities outpaces the referrals from Google, et al.

For example, after the 2009 Oscars, celebrity gossip blogger Perez Hilton recorded a single-day high of 13.9 million page views, and the site's top traffic source was Facebook.[218] So what, you say? Well, Google is generally the top referrer for pretty much any site — the undisputed king. That Facebook dethroned King Google as the top referrer for a popular site was big news, and demonstrates the changing nature of search.

Google itself recognizes this trend, and has introduced social search features to its traditional search listings, as we discussed in the section *Advanced Google Searching* on page 106. To summarize from that section, if you belong to the popular social media sites, and if Google can identify you (by you logging in to one of their services, like Google Docs, for example), you may be presented with search results ranked based on information from your social network.

---

[216] ReadWriteWeb's article on indexing Twitter: **bit.ly/c1Rtd1**

[217] SocialBeat's article on indexing Facebook: **bit.ly/cnsF2p**

[218] GigaOm's article about Hilton's traffic: **bit.ly/9zUexn**

Dealing with Negatives

One big question that comes up almost immediately when enterprises start to use social computing is: What do you do about negative comments?

When dealing with this question, it's helpful to recognize that if you act in the world, you probably have detractors. People have more than likely been talking negatively about you offline for some time. You've never been privy to their conversations, and you've had limited or no ability to address them directly or to know their concerns. Now that social media has brought these negative conversations out in the open, not only are they spread more widely, but you get the chance to do something about the root causes. That's fantastic! You can find and address negativity, in real-time, for the first time in history.

The natural inclination of most enterprises is to try to suppress, delete, or otherwise eliminate dissent. In a world where access to broadcast media was expensive, restricted, and guarded by gatekeepers, this type of approach was effective. Enterprises could use libel laws or lawsuits, could pressure media outlets, and could use the media to confront and refute naysayers. Many enterprises employ these techniques in social media as well.

Often, however, the old tools for dealing with negatives not only don't work online, but can result in generating even more negativity.

A recent example of the traditional approach, and one that has made it into our Social Media Hall of Shame, involved international food giant Nestlé. Like a lot of large food companies, Nestlé is the target for various groups who disagree with their business and agricultural methods. Some of these groups had taken to posting defaced versions of the Nestlé logo on Nestlé's Facebook fan page as a critique and protest of the company's policies.

In series of posts widely seen as an attempt to silence or intimidate these critics, Nestlé posted, "We welcome your comments, but please don't post using an altered version of any of our logos as your profile pic — they will be deleted."[219]

This post breaks a cardinal rule about running online communities that we discussed in our *Community* section on page 190: Govern your community with a light hand. Your community members expect to be involved in major community decisions, and they certainly do not expect to be arbitrarily censored. We further discuss community governance policies in the *Define Your Goals* section of our *Community Building Checklist* on page 403.

---

[219] Bnet's *Nestle's Facebook Page: How a Company Can Really Screw Up Social Media*: **bit.ly/asqGGB**

The company also threatened action for trademark infringement if critics didn't comply. Incredibly, Nestlé also posted sarcastic replies to negative posts.

Nestlé's old-media attempt to stem negativity was, unfortunately, all too predictable, as was the result. Rather than doing anything to respond to, placate, dissuade, or even just acknowledge the dissenters, Nestlé whipped up a storm of protest that eventually made the mainstream media news — blowing up a relatively unpublicized group of protesters into media darlings.

Here's a typical post following Nestlé's blunder:

> [W]ould like to personally thank Nestlé for providing a place for all the people who see their unethical, disgusting and lethal practices for what they are to share their opinions. Finally we have a way to share how much we hate their practices. If you don't boycott Nestlé already, start now, please.

One poster stated she's not a fan — the posts were on Nestlé's Facebook fan page — and wanted to have a "Register My Disgust" button on the page. Another was a bit more reasonable:

> I like some Nestle products so I qualify as a 'fan.' I would like Nestle to make them even better by removing palm oil. I would like to enjoy my Kit-Kats without feeling responsible for rainforest destruction and orangutan deaths.

And this wasn't Nestlé's only social media blunder. When Greenpeace posted a critical video on YouTube, the company lobbied to have it removed based on use of its logo, generating lots of free publicity for Greenpeace.

The poor besieged person in charge of the Nestlé Facebook page did try to do some damage control, posting:

> This [deleting logos] was one in a series of mistakes for which I would like to apologize. And for being rude. We've stopped deleting posts, and I have stopped being rude.

This was a good move. It does three things: It acknowledges the mistakes; it pledges to stop deleting the logos; and it humanizes the company by taking personal responsibility for the action. Remember, our first rule for using social media is to **Be a Person**, not an organization.

So what went wrong here? Well, obviously, Nestlé has the right to protect its logos and trademarks. But was it really the best approach to sarcastically criticize and threaten the dissenters? What the company failed to realize is that social computing gives the same power to individuals as it gives to big enterprises. You need to keep that in mind whenever you make a decision to deal with negativity about your business.

By the way, you may be interested in the end of the story. After a two-month campaign led by Greenpeace against Nestle for its use of palm oil, the company gave in and announced in May 2010 that it will rid its supply chain of any sources involved in the destruction of rainforests.[220] There's no telling what role the bungled responses on YouTube and Facebook had in this resolution, but they sure didn't help.

Techniques for Handling Negatives

If Nestlé had truly understood social media, the outcome might have been different. We recommend a few techniques for dealing with negatives below. However, we have different advice for dealing with the chronic negative poster, called a troll. We cover this subject in the section called *Dealing with Trolls* on page 213.

Monitor for Negatives

If your enterprise does nothing else with social media, you need to start monitoring for negatives. People are talking about you. You'll never know what they're saying unless you listen. We've got a whole section on monitoring starting on page 150.

Forgive Negative Behavior

People are more likely to post when angry, and often a negative post is out of character for a community member. Consider ignoring the random negative post completely. In fact, our advice is, when in doubt, do nothing. An ill-considered response can set off an echo chamber of negative responses. If the negative behavior is persistent, but doesn't rise to the level of troll behavior — a repetitive, mindless, attention-getting pattern — you may want to address it. But in general, the best course of action is often to ignore the behavior.

Engage and Clarify

People can seem more negative online due to the lack of visual cues. If you feel you must respond to a post, try starting out with a clarifying question. This not only ensures you understand the intent of the poster, engaging with them may get them to moderate their negativity.

Here's a personal example. I responded to a tweet about a software package called Ektron:

---

[220] Mongabay: **bit.ly/aZLjio**

> @PROsocialmedia re Ektron > Joomla — IMHO Ektron's a toy and severely limited. We use Tridion and couldn't be happ[ier]. And I like Joomla 2

Relatively soon after, within less than two hours, a guy from Ektron responded. He didn't say, "You're a jerk; we're great." He said, "I'd like to know more about your experience with our product."

Now I was stuck. I hadn't actually used the product, although I had evaluated it as part of a purchasing decision my organization was making. My brother had, however, sold and implemented the product, and that's where I got the "toy" part of my post from. So, @ektronmatt had nicely called me out, and was interested in hearing what I had to say.

Great move. I felt I had to explain:

> @ektronmatt Most of my info is from my brother's experience as a VAR. You guys had a serious MS-related bug that went unfixed for some time.

By engaging me, ektronmatt got me to be more specific about my post. In the meantime, a typo in my first post — "couldn't be happy" instead of "couldn't be happier" — attracted the attention of supporters of a competitive product, Tridion, the one we had actually selected. They retweeted — repeated to their followers — my post and said they assumed I meant "happier."

Now I felt I needed to clarify that matter as well:

> @puf Heh! You're right — happier, not happy. Praise, not a dig. In defense of Ektron, I have no direct experience. My brother was a VAR.

But I was still bugged about passing on a secondhand opinion — something that I probably wouldn't have thought twice about if @ektronmatt had not engaged me. So I emailed my brother and asked him what he thought of Ektron's latest release. He said it was very much better. Now I felt really bad at having made a snarky comment with old, secondhand information. Once again, this is all due to a single question @ektronmatt asked me, which took him all of 30 seconds to post.

> @ektronmatt re Ektron opinion — I asked my brother and he actually likes your new release; said the improvements look good. So, good on ya.

And that's one way you can turn around negatives. Don't attack. Clarify and probe. It won't always turn out as positively as this incident did, but if you try to censor, quash, or attack negative posts, you'll never have this kind of outcome.

Delete/Ban Only as a Last Resort

It's hard to give you any hard and fast rules about when it's OK to delete an offending post, or, for that matter, kick a member out of your community. All we can say is, this is really the last resort.

If you must take this type of action, we suggest you discuss the matter with your community. Try to enlist support for the action — and be sure your community governance rules have spelled out your ability to take the action beforehand.

We suggest starting by merely deleting an offending post. Document your action to the community. If a pattern of behavior requires another deletion, do that in the open, too. Show a pattern of behavior that supports the ultimate step: banning the individual from posting, or removing them from the community. This last step is best reserved only for trolls, which we discuss in the next section.

When managing a community, always remember what founding father Benjamin Franklin said, "It takes many good deeds to build a good reputation, and only one bad one to lose it."

Dealing with Trolls

Trolls can wreck your community. And pretty much every community eventually has its trolls. Trolls exhibit negative, hostile, antisocial, and deliberately provocative behavior. They may have an axe to grind, or they may just be people who thrive on discord, on getting a rise out of people, and who may not really value the community. We say may not because there are some trolls who just can't help themselves. They may actually be the most committed members of your community. They just have the type of personality that produces antisocial behavior.

Offline, the troll might be the person in your book club who never shuts up. Or the busybody that, while often productive, needs to poke her nose into everything. Or the guy who always offers off-the-wall solutions during meetings and insists on bringing them up repeatedly, long after the decision has been made.

Online, trolls are empowered. If there are no policies and procedures in place to check them, they can dominate every conversation and sidetrack every productive dialog.

Types of Trolls

The Communities Online site[221] categorizes trolls into four types, which we adapt below, adding our own fifth category:

- **Mischievous**

  Mischievous trolls have a humorous intent. Often, they might be a regular community member playing a good-natured prank. They are not abusive and rarely create trouble. Generally there is no harm in responding to them. Some members may find mischievous trolls annoying, particularly if their presence leads to lengthy threads that distract the community from its true intent. Other members find that the troll's humor and light-hearted antics provide the community with an opportunity to laugh together.

- **Mindless/Attention Seeking**

  Mindless trolls have a tendency to post lengthy stories of questionable veracity, or commenting on every post with off-topic or provocative statements. Mindless trolls are generally harmless, although their activities can rise to the level of extreme annoyance. On rare occasion, the fictitious posts of a mindless troll may lead to insightful debate and discussion. There is generally no harm in you responding, but it is often best to simply ignore them. If response is necessary, let the community respond.

- **Malicious**

  A malicious troll is blatantly abusive to the group and/or specific individuals within the group. One of their characteristics is that within a very short time of gaining access they begin targeting and harassing members. In some cases, the troll has a prior history with the group or someone within the group. In other scenarios, the troll is simply looking for a fresh meat market. As a community manager, respond to such trolls carefully. Generally, community members will step up and enforce community norms themselves.

- **Destructive**

  Around 1999, destructive trolls began to appear in mail groups and online communities. The primary purpose of this type of troll is to completely destroy the group it has infiltrated. Destructive trolls may work on their own, or possibly in teams or gangs. As a community manager, you may need to directly confront this type of troll, and eventually may need to ban them. Be sure to enlist the support of the community to take any enforcement action. If the troll does actual damage to the community forums or software, feel free to immediately ban them, assuming you are supported in doing so by your published community policies.

- **Trollbots**

  Sometimes a troll is not actually a person, but an automated program called a trollbot. Generally, these bots are not interactive, and usually just post canned text as comments to other posts. An example of a recent trollbot was the Ron Paul trollbot from the 2008 presidential campaign. Such bots are an an-

---

[221] Community Online's *Communities Online: Trolling and Harassment*: **bit.ly/cuCoEG**

noyance, but if you run an open community — one that doesn't require registration and approval — you will get visited by trollbots. Enlist the community in identifying their posts and feel free to delete them.

General Approaches to Trolls

So how do you deal with trolls? Well, first you need to determine that the person is really a troll, not just a clueless newbie uninitiated in the norms of your community. This can be a difficult process, and so you should refrain from taking any action until the troll has established a body of work that has annoyed your community. Of course, that means letting a potential troll stir things up a bit first.

In the following we consider various strategies for dealing with trolls.

Ignore Trolls

Many online pundits recommend ignoring trolls. This, however, is easier said than done, although it can be a very effective approach. The problem is, everyone has to ignore the troll. If even one community member engages the troll, the chase is on. However, the community manager should respond to trollish posts with a gentle reminder of the community guidelines for behavior. You may want to repeat this a few times, after which you should counsel the community to ignore the troll.

Ignoring trolls works because the main need a troll has is to be recognized, and responded to. If the troll's posts are ignored, their behavior is not reinforced, and they may go elsewhere or fall silent.

But universally ignoring a troll is very hard to do. While long-time community members may recognize the troll's posts for what they are — cries for attention — new members may respond to the outrageous or off-topic troll posts and give the troll the recognition they crave.

Others recommend responding to troll posts with love and understanding. We think that any response is likely to reinforce the behavior. While it may be effective to take the discussion offline, where possible, and try to convince the troll that their behavior is self-defeating, this is an approach with a low likelihood of success. Remember, the troll is probably a troll in real life as well. You're not likely to be able to change a troll's personality (at least, without years of psychotherapy).

Do Not Confront and Out Trolls

There's a school of thought that confronting and shaming trolls will be effective in discouraging them. For example, blogger Kirsten Stanford recounted[222] how she dealt with a troll who personally insulted her: She exposed his email address and his network address:

> Everyone, say hi to Paul! [email address and IP address redacted] Paul left this wonderful comment for me recently. It left me feeling confused as to why someone / anyone would take the time to spew so much vitriol. It really makes no sense.

We do not recommend this approach. Stanford is not likely to change Paul's mind, and also not likely to convince him to stop harassing her. What is more likely is that Paul will change identities and network addresses, and step up his harassment.

But even more important, confronting Paul as Kirsten did runs the risk of making her look petty and vindictive. As Abraham Lincoln said, it's better to say nothing and be thought a fool, than to open your mouth and remove all doubt.

Ban Trolls and Troll Posts

If you're in charge of your community, you may have the power to delete troll posts and to ban members who are trolls. In fact, there are probably lots of things you can do about trolls:

- **Delete the post** — This can be a controversial move, and could harm the trust you have build with your community members. We recommend that before you delete troll posts, you ask your community to weigh in on the move. Of course, you should only take this step after ignoring the troll has not worked, or if you're unwilling to try that approach.

- **Ban the troll** — This can also be controversial. If you have control over the membership of your community, you may have the ability to ban a troll for a period of time, or to remove them from the community altogether. If your community requires new registrations to be approved, you may even be able to prevent the troll from coming back. Be sure you have community support before taking this action.

- **Moderate all posts** — Once again, if you have control, you may be able to require that all posts and comments in the community be approved before being published. This affects your entire community, and puts a big burden on your community manager. We recommend that this be a temporary solution at most. Requiring moderation for all posts will definitely affect community trust, and may cause defections.

- **First post moderation** — Moderate every member's first post. Once approved, the member is free to post anywhere. Depending on the level of control you have on your community software, you may be

---

[222] Sanford's *Dealing with Trolls*: **bit.ly/aOgy9L**

Executing Your Social Computing Strategy

able to require moderation for the first post in each forum the user posts in. This technique can help blunt the effect of trollbots, and it probably won't bother your community members as long as they understand its intent. But it will do nothing to prevent the chronic troll.

- **Let trolls become part of the conversation** — If your community can handle it, then let them handle it. It's probably the next best solution if ignoring doesn't work.

No matter how you want to deal with trolls, you need to create a troll policy as part of your community guidelines and make sure all community members understand it.

OK, here's a bit of troll humor:

- **How many trolls does it take to change a light bulb?**
  Three. One to change the bulb; one to severely criticize the bulb for going out; and one to insult your parentage for complaining about the dark.

Social Media Optimization

The term Social Media Optimization refers to techniques you can use to get the most out of your social media efforts. Rohit Bhargava of Ogilvy Public Relations coined the term, and explained it like this:

> The concept behind SMO is simple: implement changes to optimize a site so that it is more easily linked to, more highly visible in social media searches on custom search engines (such as Technorati), and more frequently included in relevant posts on blogs, podcasts and vlogs [video blogs].

Bhargava proposed *5 Rules of Social Media Optimization (SMO)*[223] which were later expanded to 16, and which we've adapted below:

- **Increase your linkability**
  Enable and encourage others to link to you, and you should aggregate and link to your other content as well
- **Make tagging and bookmarking easy**
  Enable others to tell a friend; list relevant tags on your pages
- **Reward inbound links**
  Enable permalinks (links to, say, a blog that will never change) and feature bloggers who link to you
- **Help your content travel**
  Submit PDFs or videos, and the like, to other sites to increase their reach

---

[223] Bhargava's *5 Rules of Social Media Optimization (SMO)*: **bit.ly/cbHXMh**

- **Encourage the mashup**

  A mashup is when someone else does something with your content; the classic case is the Google Maps Mashup[224]

- **Be a User Resource, even if it doesn't help you**

  The classic give to get; contribute to the community and it will come back to you; link users off your site if it will help them

- **Reward helpful and valuable users**

  Reward influencers and champions by promoting their works on the homepage, develop a rating system, or just drop them a quick note in private telling them you appreciate them

- **Participate**

  If you've read this far, you know why

- **Know how to target your audience**

  If you've read this far, you know why

- **Create content**

  While this seems like a duh moment, think about the content you create in terms of how it can be spread by your community

- **Be real**

  If you've read this far, you know why

- **Don't forget your roots, be humble**

  Just a good rule to live by, overall

- **Don't be afraid to try new things, stay fresh**

  Pundits from Jean-Baptiste Alphonse Karr (plus ça change, plus c'est la même chose) to Woody Allen (A relationship, I think, is like a shark, you know? It has to constantly move forward or it dies) have advised this

- **Develop a Social Media Optimization strategy**

  A Social Media Optimization strategy, like all strategies, involves defining objectives, setting goals, and tracking progress

- **Choose your Social Media Optimization tactics wisely**

  Don't do social media to keep up with the Joneses — the Joneses may have a different audience, different objectives, and different resources

- **Make Social Media Optimization part of your process and best practices**

  As we've stressed, don't graft social media onto your organization; assimilate it and make it part of your way of doing business

---

[224] Google Maps Mania: **bit.ly/an0Hly**

Brand Your Enterprise Online

You may employ branding tactics in your offline marketing, or you may feel that you either don't need to, or don't have the money to.

Online, you must pay at least some attention to branding efforts. A brand is a promise, and it's also a handle by which people can find you, refer to you, and talk about you online. We've said before that online, if you build it, they won't necessarily come. And if you have a haphazard, disorganized, or confused brand online, they may not come because they don't associate what you do with your online presence.

All your online marketing efforts should reinforce your brand, and aim to drive traffic to your Website, the center of your brand presence. It's great to get people to read your blog. It's great to have thousands of followers on Facebook or Twitter. The goal, however, should be to make your Website the hub of all your social media activities.

The first step is to ensure your domain name (the part after the www) is easy-to-remember, easy-to-spell, and content-appropriate. Make it simple, direct, and if possible, the first thing that comes into people's minds when they think about the problem your business solves. Don't be too clever.

For example, if your products deal with drinking water filters, ensure that the word "water" is part of your domain name.

If it's going to serve the purpose of being a hub of social networking activity, your Website needs to be optimized. At a minimum, your site must:

- Have a call to action
- Clearly describe your business, purpose, and products
- Enable users to bookmark, tag, or email your URL to a friend

Have a Call to Action

Of the Must Have Three, the call to action is the most important. If your site merely explains what you do and, somewhere buried on an interior page, allows your visitors to take an action to support you, it fails. Period.

Design your site to clearly communicate what visitors can do to help you, and give them a positive action they can take, whether it be a buy button, a "Like Us on Facebook" button, or at the very least, a newsletter signup button.

If you're not doing these things, don't begin using social media.

The reason is simple. Much of your activity on social networking sites can't actually enable a direct action. For example, the best action that can happen upon reading one of your tweets is for the reader to click on an URL to go somewhere else. That somewhere else is your Website. Other social media sites are similar: Blogs, tagging sites, photo sharing sites, and so on, all lack features to complete a significant action. They'll all lead people to your site, where you must make it easy for them to act.

We discuss the importance of a consistent social media branding and graphic presence in the *Triangulate Your Social Media Presence* section on page 204, and we talk a bit about site organization in the *Engagement on Your Site* section on page 133. These activities will help reinforce your online brand.

Here are a few other specific recommendations for "socializing" your Website:

- **Ensure that your About page clearly describes your business** in a way people will respond to. Yes, your board and your corporate structure is important, but is that the main thing you want people to know about your enterprise? Link to all your social media sites in this section.

- **Organize your site** from your users' perspective — If your site is organized based on your organizational structure it likely is not optimized for your users. This penchant for site structure mimicking organizational structure is called showing your corporate underpants, which we described in the *Engagement on Your Site* section on page 133.

- **Add commenting** to your site — You'll come to love it. And don't require approval before comments are posted. See the previous section, *Dealing with Negatives* on page 209 for reasons why. A nice, free option for adding comments is DISQUS,[225] but be careful of privacy concerns when users use Facebook or Twitter to log in to post comments. We use DISQUS on our site.

- **Add an RSS feed** to your site — RSS is short for Really Simple Syndication and is a way for people to subscribe to a page or a site and receive updates using an RSS reader such as Google Reader or others. It's what's behind those little orange icons ( ) you may have noticed on Websites. If your hosting software doesn't already provide the ability to add RSS feeds to your pages, you may need to get a techie involved. You can also use third party software such as FeedYes[226] and others.

- **Ensure your site is usable** — Usability is a deep and broad subject and beyond the scope of this book. But in general, use text and background colors that provide a lot of contrast; don't make text too small (especially if you want older folks to read your site); and avoid garish or distracting graphics. Also you need to think about your major navigation and whether it is logical to the typical user. And beware of putting important material in the upper right of pages. Users often ignore that area since it very often contains ad-

---

225 DISQUS: **bit.ly/cbLzqB**

226 FeedYes: **bit.ly/b7etvb**

vertisements.

- **Ensure your site loads quickly** — Sure, everybody in your organization might love the Flash movie that loads every time a user goes to your main page, but is it really worth a 30-second load time? And will it just annoy frequent visitors? Aren't the frequent visitors you want to optimize your site for?

- **Register your site** with all the top search engines — You need to be found.

- **Claim your blog on Technorati.com** — Technorati indexes tens of millions of blog, but to be sure you get into their directory, you need to claim your blog.[227] This allows you to specify categories your blog will appear in, and specify tags for the blog, enabling others to find it. In addition, Technorati will track the effectiveness of links you embed in your blog, calculating your Technorati Authority. If you don't have a blog yet or aren't really sure yet what one is, see the section *Setting Up Blogging* on page 375.

- **Search Engine Optimize your Website** — Use WebsiteGrader.com[228] to make sure your site is attractive to Google.

Once your main site is optimized, you're ready to start to build or improve your online brand.

Online Branding Campaigns

Let's consider: What is branding? There are lots of definitions, but one that we like was formulated by Chris Levkulich on the BrandingBrand blog:[229]

> Branding, in essence, is developing a plan of action that will make your product or company the ONLY solution to its targeted problems. Instead of making you stand out among the crowd of other products and having your product being chosen over the competitors as the best product, branding wants to promote the product as the only product. Like Kleenex.

This cheeky definition goes further than many others, but we like that it defines the ultimate goal of branding: To become inextricably identified with the problem you are solving as its only solution. Marvelous!

Then Levkulich goes on to declare that social media is the future of branding. While we won't go quite that far, certainly the ability for the real owners of the brand — the people — to affect the perception and the definition of the brand changes the game completely. No longer is the Coke or

---

[227] Find out more about claiming your blog at: **bit.ly/97muSS**

[228] WebsiteGrader: **bit.ly/bgrfgC**

[229] BrandingBrand blog: **bit.ly/c5o7K0**

Wal-Mart or IBM brand strictly what their branding experts say it is through their brand-building, traditional media tactics. Many aspects of a brand are now entirely in the hands of the people who use it, and who discuss it on social media.

When talking about brand, however, often people really are talking about brand recognition — how many people have heard of you? Obviously, social media has a strong role to play in brand recognition.

Every organization with any kind of presence in the larger world has a brand. It's more than just your name or reputation, it's what you're known for, and it's your promise — to solve a customer problem, to meet a customer need. If you're not already thinking about what your brand means to your community, it's time to start, because online, the opportunity for your brand to be known far and wide is great. And you don't want to fumble this opportunity.

Here are some characteristics you should take into account to build your brand online:

- **Inspire Trust**
  One of the best assets of a brand is trust. Let's face it. If your community doesn't trust your brand, you're out of luck. Everything you do online should build trust. This means doing what you promise to do, and refrain from negative activities, such as criticizing competitive brands or individuals.

- **Maintain Integrity**
  Integrity goes hand-in-hand with trust. Wal-Mart compromised its brand integrity with its fake-blogger campaigns (discussed in the *Social Media Approach* section on page 177).

- **Build Brand Confidence**
  Brand confidence is the result of positive brand trust and integrity. Your community is confident that you will deliver what you say you will. You become the go-to brand for your solution.

- **Deliver on the Promise of Your Brand**
  When you look at how brands originally came to be and how they evolved, you can see that the modern brand is a promise. Derived from the Old Norse *brandr*, meaning "to burn," branding began with livestock as a way to declare ownership. The first consumer brand was registered by Pears soap in the 19th century, but attempts to use branding to distinguish the quality of the product from others were common by the last days of Pompeii. It was the industrial revolution, and the extension of a maker's potential market beyond the local community that produced many of the modern components of brand — the promise of integrity and the beginnings of consumers' relationships to brand. More recently, a brand became a proxy for the unique selling proposition — the superior qualities of the product — and that aspect of brand is very important in social media today.

  So what is your promise? Can everyone associated with your organization put this promise into words? Understand your promise, deliver on the promise online, and ensure that your online efforts never betray it.

- **Personality/Personalness**

  In social media, we obviously think it is important to **Be a Person**. Thus your online brand should have a personality, embodied in the people who engage your community. There are, of course, risks in involving your staff in your branding efforts, but there's really no other choice. It can blow up as in our Nestlé example — a community manager who was insufficiently trained causing a ruckus — but it can just as easily have extremely positive effects, as in our Ektron example — a community manager who engaged with a negative poster and produced, in the end, an endorsement. No matter what you think about employee engagement online, your brand must represent your people, and not a faceless, monolithic enterprise.

Based on these qualities of the modern brand, your online branding campaigns should exhibit high integrity and emphasize the people involved in your business.

The ASUS entry in our Social Media Hall of Shame is an example of a brand campaign that failed due to integrity problems.

Computer-maker ASUS created a blogging competition at electricpig.com by picking six people and asking them to blog about products they'd been given for review. Readers were then to rate the blogs and the winner would be able to keep the reviewed products.

Things did not go the way ASUS managers hoped, however, since the readers picked an honest, but not perfectly positive, review by Gavyn Britton. Faced with endorsing and publicizing a review that revealed some faults in their product, ASUS changed the rules of the competition — several times. Instead of the ASUS community voting on the winners, the six bloggers themselves voted to decide the prize, resulting in Emma Hill winning.

It's incredible to think that an online community would be hoodwinked by this duplicity. When challenged by its community, ASUS said they had upgraded the prizes the bloggers got, but did not apologize for fixing the race.

ASUS is a little known brand in the US that doesn't spend as much as its big PC-maker competitors on building its brand. Chances are good they chose an online brand-building event due to its relatively low cost. Instead of positively building their brand, however, it can be argued they did damage.

What could ASUS have done differently?

- Acknowledge that their product is not perfect, perhaps while pointing out its advantages over their competition
- Commit to take the feedback from the winning blogger and make the product better
- Promise to update the community on how they fix product deficiencies
- Make a big splash when announcing an improved product, emphasizing the community's contributions

On the positive brand-building side, here's a case study from our Enterprise Social Media Framework[230] about a company that appears to get online brand building, and who took a big risk in a branding campaign: Burger King.

In this case BK leveraged a social media phenomenon — Facebook — to connect with its customers online in an offbeat and inside-baseball way. The company created a Facebook app called Whopper Sacrifice.[231] To participate in the campaign, community members agreed to unfriend (break contact with) 10 friends in order to get a free Whopper. Ordinarily, people aren't notified when someone unfriends them. But in the Burger King campaign, the removed friends got a notification that they had been sacrificed so one of their friends could get a free Whopper. This made the unfriended curious about the campaign, and this helped spread the BK Facebook app, and, Burger King hopes, builds loyalty to their sandwich.

This campaign is extremely sophisticated. It addresses the downside of a positive social media phenomenon: the fact that you may have, somewhere along the way, friended someone you wish you hadn't or that you may feel overwhelmed by the number of friends you have.

This is a pretty subtle perception on the part of Burger King. It shows a deep understanding of the social media space. And it struck a nerve. Before Facebook took down the BK app for privacy concerns, Burger King spent an estimated $50,000 on the campaign, received an estimated $400,000 in press/media value, and got 32 million impressions for its brand. Incidentally, it's likely Facebook pulled the app because it doesn't believe friends should be notified when they are unfriended.

The major difference between these two branding campaigns has to do with respect for, and understanding of, the community. ASUS thought they were in control, but when they exerted that control, they found out that, as is almost always the case, the community was in control. Burger King took the time to understand their online community and to design an edgy — and potentially dangerous if not handled well — campaign that appealed to community sensibilities.

ASUS forgot to act with integrity. Facebook forgot to let their users be in control. Burger King pulled off a risky approach and reaped the benefits.

Keep these lessons in mind as you create your own online branding campaigns.

---

[230] Social Media Performance Group's Enterprise Social Media Framework info: **bit ly/auxUYA**

[231] Whopper Sacrifice: **tcrn.ch/bW1aDS**

Find and Create Online Evangelists

As John Stuart Mill said, "One person with a belief is equal to a force of ninety-nine who only have interest." While all members of your social media community are important, the most important are those who passionately promote your business and its products. We call these people evangelists for a reason: These true believers often exhibit an almost religious fervor in backing you and your products (think Apple customers). The best online evangelists have a rich assortment of social media connections to enable their advocacy to reach far and wide.

You probably already have evangelists. They're your enthusiastic customers who recommend your products or serviceds, and who tell their friends about you. One of the most valuable things your organization can do online is to identify, cultivate, and enable online evangelists. Doing so multiplies your online efforts many fold.

In this section we consider ways to find and develop evangelists.

Creating Online Evangelists

One great source of potential evangelists are your best customers. They're generally easy to find, and they are likely to be motivated to help you spread the word and serve others. Use the following steps to harvest potential evangelists, and evangelistic messages, from customer groups.

- **Interview Satisfied Participants**
  Talk to those who use your products and get them to agree to participate in interviews.

- **Ask What Caused Them to Buy**
  What was it about your organization, products, or employees that made them buy? Try to distinguish between a commitment to your product and a commitment to your organization — the resulting messages you create may be different.

- **Ask What They See as the Value of Your Services**
  Get customers to put into words your value proposition. What makes your business or its products worthwhile? What distinguishes your enterprise from similar organizations? What is most important about the way you address the need you fill?

- **Ask How They Describe Your Products to Others**
  Ask them for the elevator speech — how they would describe your products to a stranger during an average elevator ride. You're looking for a statement that takes 30-60 seconds to deliver. You should already have written your version of your elevator speech. But you may be surprised what others come up with.

- **Write Down Their Answers Word for Word**

  Resist the temptation to edit what they tell you during these discussions. Aim to exactly record what they have said. If you pre-edit their contributions, you may miss a chance to learn an important nuance you might not have caught.

- **Use Their Material in Your Recruitment and Branding Messages**

  During your interviews, you have discovered how your community looks at you and speaks about you. Just as it is important to capture this material verbatim, it's also important to use it to fashion or modify your messaging. Ideally, the messaging you use for evangelist recruiting will be very similar to the rest of your messaging. Remember, using the voice of the customer will help you create the relationship and conversations with your community.

- **Test and Refine Your Messaging at Offline Events**

  Before designing online campaigns, test out your messaging offline. Be sure to gather reactions from a wide variety of stakeholders.

- **Use Your Refined Messaging in Your Marketing Materials**

  If it works online, it's likely to work through conventional marketing as well. Consider using your new approach in all your marketing materials, but not before you've proved it online.

Once you have an approach mapped out, you're ready to find evangelists.

Finding Evangelists

Chances are you already have some evangelists, or can readily identify candidates based on your offline community. There are probably lots of other active evangelists already online, and many of them are already using social media to proselytize for you.

As a first step in finding current and potential evangelists, you need to identify related blogs, Twitterers, LinkedIn connections, and Facebook people who have significant influence, followers and traffic. Here are some ideas about how to do this.

- **Google "I love [your product, organization]"** — If you've got the nerve, and want to know your enemy, also Google "I hate [your product, organization]"

- **Google Blog Search your product, organization** — You can use Google Blog Search[232] or any of the other blog monitoring tools we've mentioned

---

[232] Google Blog Search: **bit.ly/dy7s5O**

- **Search Twitter and Facebook** — Twitter's search has gotten a lot better. You can also now search tweets on Google as well. Facebook search is OK, and Google indexes it as well.

- **Set up Google Alerts and Twitter Alerts** — Google Alerts[233] can send you daily updates based on your keywords. You can set up and save a keyword search on Twitter but you'll need to manually run it. You can set up automated alerts using TweetBeep.[234]

Don't forget your staff! Reach out to them for ideas on finding evangelists.

Evangelistic Styles

Once you've found evangelist candidates, you'll want to begin to establish relationships with them. Before doing so, it's helpful to realize that there are various styles of evangelists.

- **Intellectual**
  Intellectual evangelists enjoy using rationality, ideas and evidence to persuade. They are typically analytical, logical, and inquisitive. They will most likely engage with your community by debating ideas and presenting rational evidence. They typically are more concerned with what people think than with what they feel.

  An intellectual evangelist is a good fit for communities or community members who like to engage on a rational level. If your organization's appeal is primarily visceral, this type of evangelist may not be a good fit.

  Support the intellectual evangelist with lots of facts, figures, and other empirical evidence. They are likely to respond well to objective manifestations of their success, such as awards, badges, and admission to special clubs and hierarchies.

- **Testimonial**
  This type of evangelist has been there and done that and is best used as a representative for products and services that change lives. They've used your products or services to solve a problem or improve their lives in some way. They have the war stories to establish credibility. But their experience doesn't have to be dramatic, based in life-changing events and conflicts. In fact, ordinary stories may connect with a larger range of people. Testimonial evangelists are generally good communicators as well as good listeners. They have a talent for connecting their experiences with your community's.

  A testimonial evangelist can be an asset to almost any organization, but particularly one whose business purpose is emotionally affecting.

  Support the testimonial evangelist with lots of case studies and personal stories from those you serve.

---

[233] Google Alerts: **bit.ly/3fbcHD**

[234] TweetBeep: **bit.ly/dduOQK**

They may respond well to objective manifestations of their success, but are likely to be more driven by the number and quality of their relationships.

- **Interpersonal**

  The interpersonal evangelist thrives on creating relationships with community members and influencing them via these relationships. They generally have a very conversational online style and are compassionate and sensitive. They are obviously friendship-oriented and have an ability to focus on individuals in the community and their needs.

  An interpersonal evangelist, like the testimonial evangelist, can be an asset to almost any organization. Organizations where interpersonal bonds in the community are especially strong can best leverage this type of evangelist.

  Support the testimonial evangelist with online tools that enable them to easily create and maintain personal relationships. They may respond well to objective manifestations of their success, but, like the testimonial evangelist, are likely to be more driven by the number and quality of their relationships and a personal relationship with your organization's staff and leadership.

- **Invitational**

  Invitational evangelists specialize in attracting new members to the community. This type of evangelist is a gatherer, identifying potential community members and bringing them into the fold. They are also extremely open, hospitable, and persuasive, and live for meeting new people. They are extremely committed and welcome opportunities to invite prospects to experience the community.

  The invitational evangelist fits best in an organization that has lots of online and offline events or other gatherings that the evangelist can help attract prospects to.

  Support the inherently social invitational evangelist by providing opportunities for them to work their magic. They are likely to respond to some objective measurements, such as number of prospects converted, but mostly to a sense of belonging to your organization and making a difference.

No matter the evangelism style your organization prefers, it's important to distinguish between an evangelist and a fanatic.

Famous online personality and former Apple evangelist Guy Kawasaki said, "Fanatics forcefully push their agenda whereas an Evangelist always puts the customer first." For customer in this quote we would substitute community. You don't really want fanatics. While their energy and devotion are not in question, they may lack a variety of other characteristics that would make them a good evangelist, notably subtlety. And their passion may actually get in the way of their effectiveness: think the overly-zealous salesperson who won't take no for an answer.

Supporting Online Evangelists

We've talked about the specific ways to support the different evangelism styles. Here are some general ideas for supporting your evangelists. Remember, not all will work with each type of evangelist.

- Give your online supporters tools to identify themselves

    o Avatars for Twitter
    o Badges for Websites and social network profiles

- Create specialized mailing lists for them to join
- Create a special online forum exclusively for evangelists
- Create fan pages and groups on Facebook and other social networks for them to join
- Enable evangelists to invite others to join
- Offer stickers, T-shirts, fabric badges, other trinkets
- Create contests with prizes

In the end, you'll need to ask your evangelists how you can best support them. Be sure to devote enough time to their care and feeding. They may be the most important people in your organization.

The Importance of Stories

Here's a good example of online evangelism and it comes from a non-profit.

I've known my friend Les LaMotte for a decade, but we hadn't talked in about three years. One night, Les opened a chat with me on Facebook and told me his story. I knew that he had been working with a non-profit he founded called Sudan Hope.[235] He told me the story of how, together with the Sudanese people, they had built a paved road and a boat, and brought wireless Internet to remote villages. He talked about his struggles and successes and told me he was seeking support for a movie on the plight of the Sudanese.

Over the next month or so, I must have told and emailed 15 of my friends about what Les was doing, and included a link to his donations page.

What's that worth? It took less than half an hour out of Les' day to multiply his reach 15-fold.

---

[235] LaMotte's Sudan Hope: **bit.ly/93wKuC**

What if your entire organization, and your entire community, was engaged in this type of evangelism, if even for half an hour a week? Think of how you would multiply your marketing and brand development efforts.

Characteristics of a Good Evangelist

No matter the style of the evangelist, you will probably value the following characteristics of a good one.

• Energy	• Good Leadership
• Community-Oriented	• Good Storyteller
• Empathy	• Confidence
• Inspires Trust	• Credible
• Loyal	• Open
• Accessible	• Warm

In his groundbreaking technology evangelism book, Selling the Dream,[236] Kawasaki created the following checklist to determine if you are an evangelist:

- Do you have a desire to make a difference?
- Do you fearlessly believe in a cause?
- Do you work for a cause for the intrinsic satisfaction that it brings?
- Do you give up other things to make a commitment?
- Do you enjoy fighting the mediocre, the mundane and the status quo?
- Do you get accused of being driven, showing chutzpah,[237] or having more guts than brains?
- Does your spouse threaten to leave you?

While we're not sure items 5-7 will be appropriate for all organizations, the first four certainly are.

For a good overview of online evangelism, read the three-part blog posts entitled, *Evangelism beyond boundaries*[238] by Tata Communications International's president, Vinod Kumar.

---

[236] Kawasaki's *Selling the Dream*: **amzn.to/98Tjsg**

[237] Chutzpah, or audacity: **bit.ly/cJGlEg**

[238] Kumar's *Evangelism beyond boundaries*: **bit.ly/c6vkCG**

Create Buzz

Buzz can help attract evangelists and other community members. Buzz is excitement; it's a feeling that people want to share. Buzz is required to make anything online go viral. Buzz is spread by word of mouth (WOM), and word of mouth is a phenomenon as old as communities. Social media removes the friction from buzz/word of mouth and, like a lot of other kinds of communications, greatly accelerates it.

Although we prefer the term buzz, much of the social media industry uses the term word of mouth as if word of mouth was always positive. Many things can be spread rapidly by word of mouth online, including misinformation and negative information. Buzz, on the other hand, is almost always positive.

Professors Del Hawkins of the University of Oregon and David Mothersbaugh from the University of Alabama define buzz as "the exponential expansion of word-of-mouth" communication.[239] You need more than a cute idea to create exponential expansion. You need to connect with the current zeitgeist[240] or with a common need. And you have to make it easy for people to tell one another about you.

What Creates Buzz?

The combined tactical approach Old Spice used effectively created buzz, but doesn't really answer the question "What creates buzz." Here are three answers to this question from respected sources:

- **A good experience, says Forrester Research**[241]
  According to a survey of 4,500 consumers, when asked about companies in 12 industries, more respondents reported talking about good experiences than bad experiences in eight of the industries. Forrester found that consumers reported positive word of mouth about retailers and banks while TV service providers have the most consumers saying bad things. Although there is a trend toward sharing positive feelings, consumers tell more people about a bad experience. GenX'ers and Older Boomers most frequently shared news about a negative experience. Word of mouth cuts both ways.

- **An offline relationship with peers, says BIGResearch**[242]
  According to a survey done for the Retail Advertising and Marketing Association, 20.6 percent of social

---

[239] From JPL Creative's blog: **bit.ly/ahXmEB**

[240] Zeitgeist is the spirit of the times or the spirit of the age. It's what people are talking about now.

[241] Forrester's *How Customer Experience Drives Word Of Mouth*: **bit.ly/a4yMkH**

[242] RAMA's *Social Media: An Inside Look at the People Who Use It*: **bit.ly/d0jGuq**

media users say they regularly seek advice from others when purchasing products or services. More than one-third (34.7 percent) give advice about purchases, compared to 28.4 percent of all adults. Offline relationships remain more important, however, with 71.8 percent of social media users spreading the word about a product or service in face-to-face conversations, while more than one-third (34.7 percent) do so over a mobile phone conversation.

- **A purple cow, says Seth Godin**

  In his book, *Purple Cow*,[243] Godin defines the remarkable bovine as, "Products, services and techniques so useful, interesting, outrageous, and note-worthy that the market will want to listen to what you have to say. No, in fact, you must develop products, services, and techniques that the market will actually seek out." The idea is to stand out from the other, boring cows. But to do so you need more than a regulation cow and some purple paint, or even a brilliant idea. You need to execute. In a Fast Company magazine article,[244] Godin flips an old superlative — the greatest thing since sliced bread — on its head:

  > Otto Rohwedder thought he had invented the greatest thing because he invented sliced bread. He thought that if he got a patent on sliced bread, he'd be rich. What Otto forgot was to ask a very important two-word question: Who cares? No one knew about sliced bread. No one cared. It wasn't until Wonder Bread came around and marketed it that sliced bread took off. It wasn't the bread that won, it was the packaging and distribution.

  > Ideas that spread, win. What we've been living through is the greatest culture of spreading ideas that there's ever been. At one level, that's great because it's easier to spread your ideas than ever before. At another, it's harder because we keep raising the bar.

Listen First

Like lots of things related to social media, the creation of buzz begins by listening. Proper listening can help you get in on emerging trends at the beginning, allowing you to be on the wave, not under it. Listening for buzz is different from running surveys, a technique you may be familiar with.

When you run a survey, you adopt various rigid methodologies about samples, and questions, and statistical analysis. For decades, traditional marketing has depending heavily on asking people what they think via surveys.

There's one big problem with surveys, however: People lie on them. And not only just on sensitive topics such as religion, politics, or sex. Survey experts are very familiar with how people's

---

[243] Godin's *Purple Cow*: **amzn.to/cmUk2q**

[244] Godin's *Purple Cow* article in FastCompany: **bit.ly/dbv15X**

need to please the survey taker or to appear to be part of the norm causes bias in traditional surveys.

So don't think you're going to track buzz by putting a survey on your site.

It's best to listen to people when they're just talking, as among friends on Facebook or via comments on blog posts. These conversations are more likely to represent the unvarnished thoughts of those involved than a stuffy, artificial survey. Of course, this is not to say there aren't plenty of surveys flying around on Facebook and elsewhere. And who knows if people are really being more honest on a social media survey, when their guard is down?

Regardless, part of your social media listening program should be to track hot topics, and try to identify new trends and buzz.

One of the reasons that the traditional marketing and advertising community isn't sold on online listening, according to Ed Keller,[245] author of the book *The Influentials*[246] and principal of the research firm Keller Fay Group, is that the offline and online worlds do not yet track exactly. In fact, according to Keller, offline discussion makes up around 90 percent of word-of-mouth for brands. In a recent study of the 100 brands most talked about online, only two of the top 10 and half of the top 50 most-talked-about online were also most-talked-about offline.

In about a third of cases, offline- and online-buzz volume correlates strongly for a brand, he said. In another third, online and offline buzz have a negative correlation. In another third, there's no clear relationship. In other words, on average, there's little correlation between online and offline buzz.

This lack of correlation is, we believe, primarily due to the relative youth of social computing, and the fact that those online are not perfectly demographically identical to those offline.

However, there is evidence that some groups actually trust online buzz more than they do advertising.

An April 2010 Sophia Mind[247] study of Latin woman in the US, Mexico, Argentina and Brazil summarized by eMarketer[248] showed that Hispanic female social network users rely on social sites for purchase decision-making. In the US, about 20 percent of Hispanic women said they made social network comments about purchase experiences all the time, and, 24 percent of US

---

[245] AdAge's article *ARF: Consumer Opinions Online Still Seen as Curse, Not Gift*: **bit.ly/bU8amo**

[246] Keller's book *The Influentials*: **amzn.to/bPEFNc**

[247] Sophia Mind: **bit.ly/cEjGT8**

[248] eMarketer's *Most Hispanic Women Trust Online Buzz More than Ads*: **bit.ly/cSzIpu**

respondents let their friends and connections know when an experience was positive, compared with just 11 percent who only complained.

Most importantly, bad comments were more likely to negatively influence purchases than brand messages or advertising were to help them. A fifth of Facebook users gave up on a purchase after seeing a negative remark on a social site. Compare this negative effect with the positive effect of promotional messages: According to the study, just 18 percent chose to make a purchase based on company messages on the same site.

Buzz is powerful, and for some groups it has a significant effect on online behavior. The effect of buzz on commercial behavior may indicate similar effects on behaviors your organization may be trying to encourage. No matter what the positive effect may be, you certainly want to avoid negative buzz.

Important Aspects of Buzz

While we can't pretend that we have a foolproof way to create online buzz (if we did, we'd be lounging on our own tropical island drinking umbrella drinks right now), there are a few very important aspects of buzz you should pay attention to.

Like most things social, creating buzz has to be genuine. Social media users can smell a fake a mile away.

Your campaign to create buzz must have the following qualities:

- **Trust** — As soon as your community feels you're trying to sell them something using old-style push marketing or that you're not treating them as individuals, you're sunk.

- **Accountability** — You must deliver on all promises, with no exceptions. All your activities must be aboveboard and visible. See Trust.

- **Credibility** — For effective buzz creation, you must first be seen as credible. Don't do anything to compromise that credibility during your campaign.

- **Transparency** — Let people know what's going on. If you need to change any of your promises or any of the rules, be forthright about it. See the ASUS entry in our Social Media Hall of Shame and previously in the section *Online Branding Campaigns* on page 221

Buzz Killers

While it's hard to say exactly what creates buzz, it's pretty easy to list what can kill it.

- **Banality** — The concept has to be interesting, not mundane

- **Self-promotion** — Don't make it about yourself or your products or organization

- **Old, hard-to-use, non-Social-Media-aware Website** — If you're successful, lots of new people will be coming to your site. Make sure it's ready to receive them.

- **No call to action** — Sure you've got a cool/funny/weird/attention-getting YouTube video, but what do you want us to do?

- **Controversial Topics** — This can cut both ways. You can create buzz by being controversial, but not too controversial. And some topics — and treatments of topics — should be off-limits.

- **Overload** — Don't overdo. If people get sick of seeing your campaign, the buzz is gone.

Buzz Creation Techniques

Since we're not writing this from our aforementioned island, you may take this section with a grain of salt. Buzz is like art: We know it when we see it, and most of us can't create it. But here are some things to try.

The first thing you must do to create buzz is to find a promotional hook, something that grabs your community's attention, like Godin's purple cow. If you're short on ideas, track the hottest conversations about your product category; ask opinion leaders in your community.

Once you have the hook, you need the story. Consider involving those you serve and get them to tell their stories. A kind of silly story, and some innovatived combining of old and new media, drove one of the most buzz-worthy ad campaigns in recent memory: the Old Spice body wash "The Man Your Man Could Smell Like" campaign. It combined quirky, high-tech television commercials[249] featuring an attractive and cheeky former NFL wide receiver with deft use of social media to enhance the buzz.

In addition to heavy rotation of the ad on TV, Old Spice posted 186 highly-publicized personalized response videos[250] on YouTube, and they amassed an incredible 34 million views and a bil-

---

[249] A sample Old Spice commercial: **bit.ly/a24H7d**

[250] A sample Old Spice response video: **bit.ly/bCQd0Q**

lion PR impressions in a single week. These videos responded directly to tweets about the product, including a hilarious "this has in no way been a cross-promotion for an affiliated Old Spice sister company" response to @Gillette.[251]

These videos helped make Old Spice, with 94 million views, the number 1 all-time most-viewed sponsored channel on YouTube.[252] In addition, Old Spice's Twitter followers went up 3200 percent; Google searches rocketed up 2200 percent; Facebook interactions climbed by 800-1000 percent; and traffic to the Old Spice Website increased 350-500 percent. Old Spice became the number 1 branded body wash, and sales increased 55 percent, with some product variations as much as 1900 percent.[253]

This brilliant campaign shows how to synergistically combine old and new media to achieve dramatic results. Old Spice combined a well-done TV ad campaign with use of Twitter and YouTube to increase buzz.

To create buzz, you first have to grab your target audience, either by entertaining them, as Old Spice did, or appealing to their guts. That's obviously easier said than done, and we can't possibly give you the specific advice you need about how to do it without knowing your situation and your goals.

So in lieu of that, here are three buzz-creation techniques you can use to create your own buzz:

- **Create a microsite** — a small Website, either part of your current site, or as a standalone — for the buzz campaign, and link to it from your home page. On the microsite, create a call to action that gets those attracted by the buzz to interact. Create reasons for them to give you their email addresses, blog addresses, Twitter handles, and other information.
- **Be sure to integrate the online promotion** — posting on YouTube, Twitter, blogging, and so on — with rest of your marketing plan.
- **Appear and be spontaneous** — Old Spice's idea to respond directly to comments on Twitter was inspired. Notice they responded with the persona of the guy in the commercial rather than as a corporation. Here's how their creative team accomplished this.

> We had two full days of real-time—creatives, digital strategists, community managers, developers and editors all sitting in the same area at the same time....

> We built a platform [that] allowed us to pull in comments from all over the Web. [. . .] These were prioritized by existing narrative, by some form of clout, and their creative potential—as they came in, the writers said, "I want to write to that."

---

[251] The non-cross-promotion: **bit.ly/aygCa3**

[252] AdAge's *How Much Old Spice Body Wash Has the Old Spice Guy Sold?* **bit.ly/abPJ5Z**

[253] MediaBistro's article *The Old Spice Campaign, By the Numbers*: **bit.ly/ck8SCQ**

> The creatives wrote the scripts. We sent those scripts to the teleprompter. Isaiah [The Man Your Man Could Smell Like] did shots, sometimes in a single take. Those were exported to editors, uploaded to YouTube, and then posted in Twitter…. All in under 15 minutes per spot.

Notice the emphasis on responsiveness, speed, and spontaneity.

Of course your budget may not permit the level of polish of the Old Spice campaign, but you certainly could use these tactics with dramatically fewer resources than Old Spice had at its disposal.

The Ante

If you're going to create buzz, or if you're just going to start to use social media effectively, there are certain things you should do first, some of which we've already mentioned. The ante includes:

- Create or update your Website
- Create microsites for significant specific events
- Create landing pages for YouTube videos or people responding to your various social media promotions
- Create a Google Profile
- Create a LinkedIn company page
- Create a Facebook page
- Create a Twitter account
- Create a YouTube channel
- Create a blog
- Join Plaxo
- Invest in SEO

That's quite a list, but you're in luck. The next several chapters give you tips on how to set up your social media presence on LinkedIn, Twitter, Facebook, YouTube, and blogging.

Set Yourself Up on Social Media Sites

"You will make mistakes.
If you are sincere about helping the community,
the authenticity will show and your mistakes will be forgiven."

**Zia Yusuf, executive vice president
SAP global ecosystem and partner group**

OK. You've decided to take the plunge. You've done your prep work as we've suggested in the sections *First Steps Toward a Social Media Strategy* on page 45, *Create Social Computing Strategies* on page 65, *How to Engage with Social Computing* on page 91, and *Engage Your Community* on page 113.

So now it's finally time to set your organization up on social computing sites. In the sections that follow we walk you through tips, tricks, and techniques for setting yourself up on:

- LinkedIn
- Twitter
- Facebook
- YouTube
- Blogging

Even if you decide not to use one of these sites right away, we strongly recommend you reserve it just in case. At the very least it will prevent others from camping on it, causing brand confusion and other problems.

In fact, as a defensive move you should even reserve your name on sites you not only have no plans to use, you've never even heard of.

Power Tool: Setting Up Sites

To check the availability of your preferred name or identity on lots of social computing sites quickly, you can use KnowEm[254] or other sites that search for availability of user IDs on multiple social computing sites.

KnowEm allows you to search for availability on more than 400 social sites with various levels of service from $99 to $599. It's a cheap form of insurance in case the next Facebook is already out there, ready to pop.

Find Where Others Are

Chances are communities organized around your cause already exist. Before you consider creating your own community, or investing a lot of effort on your own fan page for Facebook, for example, be sure you see where else people are talking about you and your cause. If you find existing groups, consider joining the conversation as a good way to get started with social media. We talk about that in the section *Find Your Community* on page 103.

Be Consistent

We discussed online branding and consistent graphics in the *Triangulate Your Social Media Presence* section on page 204. Other kinds of consistency are key to your social media presence. Here's a quick checklist to review as you prepare to start creating your sites.

All your sites should:

- Have a call to action
- Enable people to join your cause immediately
- Provide information on organization activities and plans
- Provide opportunities for people to get involved
- Get employees involved

    o Establish guidelines for engaging
    o Suggest topics for blogging

---

[254] KnowEm: **bit.ly/cfSBQL**

- Use consistent keywords — use the keyword lists you created in the section *Search Engine Optimization* on page 205 throughout all your sites

    - SEO
    - Blog
    - Twitter
    - LinkedIn
    - Facebook
    - YouTube

- Mimic the best techniques of your competition
- Be everywhere they are

With all this in mind, you're ready to start with your first site. Regardless of your other inclinations, we suggest you set up LinkedIn first. It's a great way to gain access to lots of people who can help you and your organization in many ways, as you'll see in the next section. Even if you don't want to set up LinkedIn, at least read the LinkedIn chapter first since it covers lots of basics that we refer to in the other setup chapters.

Setting Up LinkedIn

"Networking is not about hunting. It is about farming.
It's about cultivating relationships.
Don't engage in 'premature solicitation'.
You'll be a better networker if you remember that."

**Dr. Ivan Misner, bestselling author & founder of
Business Network International**

LinkedIn is a great place to market your business and to find evangelists. It's the most business-oriented social media site of the Big Three (Facebook, LinkedIn, Twitter) since it's designed specifically for business professionals, more than 100 million of them.[255]

LinkedIn Overview

While there are many possible business uses for LinkedIn, perhaps the most popular marketing-related uses are:

- Prospecting for customers
- Finding partners
- Searching for talent
- Brand building
- Using targeted LinkedIn ads

---

[255] While this book was being written, LinkedIn was adding about 5 million members a quarter, so the total is likely to be greater by the time you read this.

We'll talk about prospecting first, but before you attempt to do any social media marketing on LinkedIn, you need to do two things:

- **Ensure your personal profile is complete**
  LinkedIn says that users with complete profiles are 40 times more likely to receive opportunities through LinkedIn.[256] You can check to see if your profile is complete by editing it. There's a bar in the right column towards the top that indicates completeness. The top two reasons why your profile is not complete are:

  - **No picture** — Always have a picture, of you only, professionally done. If you're sensitive about your appearance, substitute a company logo, a high school yearbook portrait, or a caricature or avatar. (There are plenty of free sites to create one.) Note: LinkedIn's terms of service do specify that only a head shot of you can be used. This rule is widely ignored, but you could get in trouble for it, so, word to the wise.

  - **No recommendations** — Ask your past and current colleagues, customers, or vendors to recommend you. You'd be surprised at the importance a short recommendation can hold. Potential partners or prospects are likely to check out your profile when considering doing business with you. A buddy of mine recently sealed the deal on a job offer when the employer checked out his recommendations.

- **Create a company profile**
  Just like having a business card, a professional email account or a sign over a storefront, having a business profile on LinkedIn lends legitimacy (despite the fact that anyone can create one)

We'll show you how to create your profile in the section *Create Your LinkedIn Profile* on page 258.

Prospecting for Customers

Since LinkedIn is all about connections, before you can prospect, you'll need connections. You can upload your address book from the major services and send out invites, but resist the temptation to spam everyone you've ever met. That happened to me when I first joined LinkedIn, six weeks after it was founded in 2003. I checked the wrong box, and sent LinkedIn invites to my 3,000 contacts. It actually turned out OK, because I heard back from a lot of people, but I sure apologized a lot.

These days, you need to be careful whom you invite. Historically, LinkedIn would suspend you if you got too many IDKs (I Don't Know). However, with the mid-2010 and 2011 revisions to how connection invitations are handled, it's unclear if this is still so, or even if these actions should still be called IDKs, since the label has changed. There's more on IDKs in the section *What is an IDK?* on page 255.

---

[256] LinkedIn on complete profiles: **bit.ly/dtH4TT**

You'll also want to customize your invites, adding a personal note to the canned one LinkedIn provides. You are limited to 3,000 invites, lifetime.

Follow Your Connections

Once you have connections, their activities will show up in your timeline. Follow that daily. Use a contact's update as an excuse to reach out to them and comment. Remember, social media is about creating relationships, not bombarding people with commercial messages. Never spam your contacts with a sales pitch. Instead, update your status on a regular basis with information about what you're working on. This causes you to appear in your connections' timelines, keeping them informed of what you're doing in a subtle way.

Offer Value via Status Updates

Every time you change your LinkedIn status, that status appears in the timelines of your connections. Make sure you regularly update your status, and offer value in the form of links to interesting or timely information.

Ask Your Connections to Introduce You

To reach beyond your immediate network, you can ask your contacts to introduce you to people in their networks you'd like to know. Use this sparingly, and be sure you communicate a very good reason to want to connect with the contact's contact. We discuss introductions and other connection requests in the section *Types of Direct Connection Requests* on page 263 and *Finding People to Invite* on page 266.

Send a Connection Invitation after Meetings

If you have a meeting with a customer or a prospect and you're not already connected to them on LinkedIn, send them a connection request as soon as possible after the meeting. You will be fresh in their minds, and they will be more likely to connect with you right away.

It's also a good idea to look your prospects up on LinkedIn before the meeting, to learn more about them.

If you can't find them on LinkedIn, this is a good excuse to either bring up LinkedIn in the meeting or email them afterward and ask, "I wanted to connect with you but couldn't find you on LinkedIn. If you don't belong, I'd be happy to discuss the benefits of joining and help you get started." If they take you up on the offer, you've already expanded your relationship with them.

Even if they engage you to tell you why they think LinkedIn is a waste of time and energy, you've connected with them on a new level.

If your customer or prospect does connect with you, now you will (usually) be able to see their first order network. In that network there may be connections you have in common, and you can appeal to them for ideas on how to close your prospect or delight your customer.

Also in their network you may find people who have hundreds of connections whom you might benefit from connecting to.

Join LinkedIn Groups

A better way to get to know those you don't is to join LinkedIn Groups. There is a group for every conceivable interest under the sun. You can join 50 at a time, so be wise about those you choose. The cool thing about groups is that you can message fellow group members, either publicly by commenting on their posts, or privately. We discuss LinkedIn Groups in the section *Create a LinkedIn Group* on page 280.

Prospecting Example

To pull this all together, here's a great example of how to use LinkedIn for prospecting.

One of the Social Media Performance Group partners used to work for a $4M IT consulting company. He called a major multibillion dollar international company and inquired about getting on their vendor list. The purchasing guy actually laughed at the request. "We just sliced our vendor list in half to get rid of little companies like yours. You have no chance," the guy said.

Robbie was not to be dissuaded. He searched on LinkedIn (using the advanced search) and found several company employees to target. Since group memberships are often listed on people's profiles, he found and joined the groups they belonged to. If they contributed something to the group, he messaged them to ask a question about it, and otherwise found excuses to engage with them. He did no selling; he asked them about their challenges, offered interesting information, advice, and links, and eventually it was time to ask them to connect, and later, to have coffee.

After nine months of cultivating these relationships, one of his contacts said, "Hey, we've got a new project starting that you guys would be perfect for. I'll have the purchasing guy give you a call." And who eventually called him? You got it: the laugher. Robbie's company got the bid, and got on the vendor list of this huge company. He never once pitched any of his LinkedIn contacts.

Building Relationships on LinkedIn

Here are some steps you can take to build a relationship with an individual or an organization via LinkedIn.

- **Find people in the organization** — Obviously, your first step is to inspect the organization's Website to find relevant people to try to contact on LinkedIn. If this doesn't work, you can use Google to look for staff email addresses, and from that figure out people's names.

  Use a query of the following form: "*@nameoforg.org". Substitute the domain name (the part after the www in the organization's Website URL) for "nameoforg.org." This query will find email addresses that have appeared on the organization's Webpages or elsewhere on the Web, and from the email addresses, you can probably figure out their names. It's good to have the person's email address because one of the ways you can connect with people on LinkedIn is to use their email address.

  If you know the person's name, but don't have their email address, there are a variety of services, such as Email Dossier,[257] that let you input an email address and find if it is currently valid. The Google search previously mentioned should give you an idea of the format the organization uses for its email addresses, so even if the search doesn't turn up the target person's email address, you can guess at the format and use Email Dossier to see if it's valid. If your search didn't turn up the general format of the organization's email addresses, try using the following formats in Email Dossier:

  - firstname.lastname@domainname
  - firstname_lastname@domainname
  - lastname@domainname
  - firstname plus last initial @domainname
  - first initial plus last name @domainname
  - last name plus first initial @domainname

- **Look them up on LinkedIn** — Once you've identified the prospective contact, do a People Search on LinkedIn by simply typing their name in the search box at the top of any LinkedIn page. If you find them, go to their profile page. See what groups they belong to, or if anyone you know can introduce you. There's more on getting introduced in the section *Three Degrees of LinkedIn* on page 265.

- **Join the groups they are in** — LinkedIn Groups are a great way to get to know people. There are thousands of groups, and most are open for anyone to join. By joining a group you can find out more about your target person, and even directly contact them via LinkedIn.

---

[257] Email Dossier: **bit.ly/cg5ld6**

- **See if they've posted in the group discussions** — If so, start by commenting on the post item. If they've posted a lot, keep commenting on what they say for a few posts, then send them a private message (using the Reply Privately link shown at the end of the post) asking them a question about what they said.

- **Try to engage them in a conversation** — Once you've established a bit of a relationship, send your target a connection request, mentioning your common group membership and any discussions you've had. Do not just send the default invite; personalize it and give them a good reason to accept. There's lots more about connection requests in the section *Finding People to Invite* on page 266.

- **Once you are connected** — Download their vCard. A vCard is a contact information file in a standard format that most email programs can import. The vCard icon on LinkedIn is easy to miss. It's located at the bottom of the first main box on a connection's profile and it looks like the following figure. The vCard is likely to include their email address and not much else.

Figure 15 — LinkedIn vCard Icon

- **Email them** — Periodically (don't spam) email your contact with a bit of news or other information that they will be interested in, and ask for their comments.

- **Watch their activity** — The various activities that your connections take on LinkedIn show up on your LinkedIn main page in a timeline. If a connection changes their profile, changes their status, or joins a group, a notice appears on your LinkedIn home page. You can comment on these events and activities as appropriate and build your relationship with them.

- **Ask when the time is right** — Only after you've established a deep-enough relationship with your new connection should you start discussing the reason you wanted to know them. Exactly when and how to do this is something you'll have to figure out for yourself. Put yourself in their position: If they asked you to take an action, would you?

Finding Partners

If you're ready to find a partner — for a joint venture, for creating an event, or to form a new venture — you may find the experience is a lot like dating: Kiss a lot of frogs, and hope to get lucky. That's partly because meeting with a new potential partner is like a blind date. You know a little about each other, and may have some friends in common, but you don't have a relationship yet.

Well, there are more than more than 100 million frogs to kiss on LinkedIn, but one advantage of using the site is that you can get to know a lot more about your blind date before committing to dance with them.

You can start your search for a partner by using LinkedIn's advanced search feature. Along with normal things like location and company, you can search by all kinds of other relevant attributes such as:

- Function
- Seniority Level
- Company Size
- Interested In

This last attribute is very useful in finding members who are interested in making deals, and the seniority level attribute lets you search for decision makers.

Unfortunately, to use this and the other search attributes in the above list, you must upgrade from the free membership to at least the $24.95 a month Business level. But if you're serious about making a deal with a partner, it's not much money, and you can cancel at any time. Plus you get more InMails (ability to message random people to whom you are not connected) and search results limited to 300 instead of 100 items.

Even if you don't upgrade, you can use the advanced search to zero in on potential partners, or better still, use Google to search LinkedIn.

Power Tool: Google

An alternative to paying for better LinkedIn search is to use Google, which places no limits on the number of search results. Simply format your Google query like either of the following:

> site:linkedin.com +<name of your industry> +CEO +<your location>

> site:linkedin.com +<name of your industry > +"business deals" +<your location>

For example, the following query recently turned up 23,700 results — 23X the number you could get with the free LinkedIn account:

site:linkedin.com +CEO +"medical device" +Minneapolis

The "site:" modifier restricts the Google search to pages on the target site, in this case, LinkedIn. The plus sign means the keyword is required. In this case, both "CEO" and the phrase "medical device" are required. There are lots of other modifiers you can use with advanced Google searching as well. Remember, however, Google search is limited to LinkedIn members' public profiles, while the internal search looks at all member information.

Researching Potential Partners

Now that you have your candidate list, prioritize it based on the Google results and start visiting their profiles. Be sure to note the LinkedIn Groups the candidates belong to; you may want to join those groups so you can contact them. Also note whether you have second- or third-level connections who may be able to introduce you.

Once you've got a short list, be sure to Google each candidate and visit any relevant Websites you discover.

Making the Connection

There are many advantages to joining LinkedIn Groups. The most relevant one here is that you can privately or publicly message other group members. You can also use your group membership as a reason to send a connection request. So join the groups your short-listed candidates belong to, and start forging a relationship with them.

You also may want your current connections to connect you. We talk more about this manner of getting connected in the *Three Degrees of LinkedIn* section on page 265.

We recommend only trying to connect to second level contacts this way (friends of your friends). The positive effect of an introduction can be lessened with third level contacts (friends of your friends' friends).

Once you're connected, let the relationship begin! Here's hoping you get lucky!

Using LinkedIn to Search for Talent

If you're recruiting in the current economic downturn, you're well aware of the perils of posting a job requisition on even a single online job board. The result is likely to be dozens or hundreds of resumes, many of which not only not in the ballpark, but not even the same solar system as your requirements.

This growing deluge of eager jobseekers has accelerated an already growing trend in talent acquisition (AKA finding people to hire). More and more enterprises are de-emphasizing offline and online job posting and turning to social media sourcing, using social media sites such as LinkedIn to locate top candidates and invite them to apply, for free.

This new emphasis is akin to a fisherman changing from casting a wide net in hopes of catching a single prize fish to using sophisticated mapping and sonar to fish where the fish are.

LinkedIn is an ideal environment for finding those trophy fish.

If you're an enterprise of some size and you're serious about recruiting on LinkedIn, you can sign up for a LinkedIn Recruiter[258] account. This type of account drastically improves your ability to search on LinkedIn, adds the ability to create alerts, gives you 50 InMails (ability to email anyone on LinkedIn) per month, and allows you to check references instantly. As part of their Talent Advantage program, LinkedIn also offers features such as employment ads, annual subscriptions for job listings, and customizable company profiles you can use to display different job information to LinkedIn members based on their profiles.

Be prepared to shell out some money for these features, however. Although details on cost are sketchy, it's been reported that $29,800 is the minimum investment for the LinkedIn Talent Advantage Starter Package. You can go a bit cheaper by upgrading to one of LinkedIn's regular paid accounts, which range from $24.95/month to $499.95/month, with discounts for buying a full year.

If you'd rather not commit that much money before getting results, here are some less-expensive ideas for finding that perfect hire:

- **Advertise in Your Profile**
  If you're looking for talent, say so in your LinkedIn profile. Adding a simple line such as, "Looking for an outreach manager" or "Need a policy researcher," or even adding, "hiring" to your professional headline can attract interest. Of course, we assume you've already described your business in other sections of your profile, so prospective applicants can learn more. This is often more effective than blind job post-

---

[258] LinkedIn Recruiter page: **bit.ly/cjZwqU**

ings, and is more likely to attract passive candidates — those who are not actively looking for a job.

- **Ask Your Network for Help**

  If you're trying to fill a position, let your connections know. One good way is to change your LinkedIn status, indicating what kind of candidate you're looking for. Another good technique is to contact your connections, either through LinkedIn or via email, let them know about your talent search, and ask them to recommend people in their networks.

- **List Your Job in a LinkedIn Group**

  Most groups have an active Jobs section, where members post jobs and find jobs. It's free for group members to list a job in these sections.

Sort by: Relevance ▾   15 jobs

Assistant Brand Manager
National Importers - Vancouver, Canada Area - May 18, 2011
▸ 2 members shared this job
Save job · Share

TURNER PR   ### Sr.Agency Director
Turner Public Relations - Midtown Manhattan - May 11, 2011
▸ 1 person in your network at Turner Public Relations   ▸ 2 members shared this job
Save job · Share

 ### Sr Project Manager
Liberty Personnel - Freehold, NJ - Jun 4, 2011
▸ 2 people in your network at Liberty Personnel   ▸ 1 member shared this job
Save job · Share

Figure 16 — Example LinkedIn Group Job Listings

- **Post Your Job on LinkedIn**

  You may have noticed there's a Jobs link on the LinkedIn toolbar. You can post jobs on LinkedIn, but it will cost you $195 for a 30-day posting, or you can save up to 40 percent with a multi-job pack.

- **Use LinkedIn Answers**

  The LinkedIn Answers feature lets you ask a public question. Any LinkedIn member can answer the question, plus, you can directly message those who answer. So your question could be, "Who'd like to be my next Project Manager?"

- **Use LinkedIn's Email Signature Tool**

  LinkedIn has a free tool that helps you create an email signature — that bit of contact information you see at the bottom of people's emails. One useful function is the ability to include a **"We're hiring" link**. When an email recipient clicks on the link, it opens and searches LinkedIn Jobs for open positions at your company. Two other interesting links you can add are:

- "Professional Profile" link which displays your profile
- "See who we know in common" link which displays your profile, and focuses on common connections

All of these ideas, however, share one thing in common: They're very similar to the post-your-job-and-hope model of talent acquisition by casting a wide net.

One of the advantages of LinkedIn is that you can find out lots about other members from their public profiles. So to find those passive candidates, or to avoid getting inundated with resumes due to public job posts, use the techniques discussed in the previous section to find candidates to invite to apply for your openings.

In fact, you may find a passive candidate may be a better choice than one who is actively looking. A LinkedIn poll found that 60 percent of employers said that passive candidates made better employees. If you believe, as unfortunately many do, that the best talent is always employed, then you can understand these poll results.

One final tip: use Google to search for people with a particular number of LinkedIn recommendations. The following search produces a list of 24 highly-recommended candidates:

site:linkedin.com +"7 Recommendations " +"project manager" +minnesota

These 24 folks are likely to be not only highly experienced but, ahem, come highly recommended.

Power Tool: Mozenda

One technique you might use with LinkedIn involves scraping the results of searches right into Microsoft Excel. Using Mozenda,[259] a versatile screen scraper that starts at $99/month, you can run the LinkedIn people search and have results exported as a CSV or Excel file. Of course, since free LinkedIn accounts only return 100 name results per search, this is another incentive to upgrade to one of the premium accounts and get 300, 500, or 700 results per search.

---

[259] Mozenda: **bit.ly/nUCISj**

Who is On LinkedIn?

According to a study done in 2008,[260] the people on LinkedIn tend to be middle-aged (42), highly compensated ($100K+), and describe themselves as decision-makers. Now you must remember that these stats are all self-reported, so take them with a grain of salt.

Internet traffic measurement company Quantcast reported the US demographics[261] shown in the following figure in September, 2010.

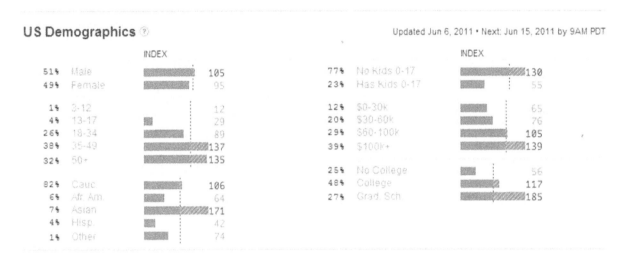

Figure 17 — LinkedIn US Demographics

Income represents total household income
An index of 100 represents the average across all Internet users

The average LinkedIn member has a pitiful 34-38 connections. Really, now, we'll bet you could sit down for five minutes with a pad and pen and come up with more than 40 current and former associates, classmates, and other connections you might know well enough to invite to connect on LinkedIn.

There are some people on LinkedIn who think it's all about the numbers, and they keep score by amassing hundreds of connections. Those who will indiscriminately connect with anyone are called LIONs.

---

[260] Summarized by TechCrunch: **tcrn.ch/dsZ1R4**; Anderson Analytics' report: **bit.ly/be9i11**

[261] For up-to-date demographics from Quantcast: **bit.ly/cAj0Z9**

What is a LinkedIn LION™?

LION™ stands for LinkedIn Open Networker. LIONs are not endorsed or supported by LinkedIn. In fact, the LION concept — connect indiscriminately — runs counter to LinkedIn's slogan: Relationships Matter. Nobody knows for sure, but there are probably well in excess of 16,000 LION members on the site.

LIONs connect with anyone. They don't care who you are, what you do, what they can do for you, or what you can do for them. They tend to crow that their networks are huge. But what does a huge network of people you don't know do for you?

You know what? We belong to a network that will allow us to ask anyone in the developed world a question.

It's called the telephone network.

We're about as likely to get help with a problem, or get referred to a valuable contact, by randomly dialing the phone as we would by using a LION's network.

There is an upper limit to LIONs' — and any member's — number of connections: 30,000. And you only are permitted 3,000 connection invitations, lifetime. That's why you'll see so many LIONs requesting that you send them an invite, rather than them inviting you.

One of the LIONs' codes is that a LION will never IDK you.

What is an IDK?

If you try to connect with a LinkedIn member and they don't remember you, they can IDK — I Don't Know — your attempt. It used to be quite obvious how to do this — I Don't Know was a button shown below the invitation. Since LinkedIn did a redesign in mid-2010, there's now an Ignore button, which removes the request from your queue, and a Report Spam button. If you can choose to Report Spam, that's the same as IDKing them. You should only do this if the person persistently bothers you to connect or is otherwise misusing LinkedIn.

Figure 18 — Example of Ignoring a Connection Request on LinkedIn

If you get a lot of IDKs — as few as five — LinkedIn black-lists you and can terminate your usage or suspend your account for up to 90 days. So it's a very good idea to not extend LinkedIn invitations to folks you barely know.

If a LION IDKs you, you are not penalized, supposedly, but this is hard to rely on, since LinkedIn doesn't condone LIONs.

Help! I've Been IDKed!

If you get even one IDK, immediately contact LinkedIn Customer Service and explain the circumstances. Conversely, limit your own use of the IDK to truly obnoxious people. If you don't want to accept a connection request, simply archive or ignore it.

Alternative to Being a LION

Being a LION can be exhausting work. Since you agree to connect with anyone, and advertise this fact in your professional headline, you generally get lots of connection requests, which you have to honor, one at a time. This can add up to quite a daily chore.

We recommend that, as an alternative, you find at least five LIONs in your industry, locality, or occupation and connect with them. This simple technique will grow your network exponentially, and it takes very little effort vs. being a LION.

We asked a certain LinkedIn Rock Star LION how many connection requests he had to deal with every day. He said generally dozens, with 120 pending at any one time. It took him more than half an hour each day to deal with them. We asked him how big his LinkedIn network was and he said, boastfully, 6 million.

Imagine his surprise when we told him that, using our strategy we had maybe one or two connection requests a day maximum, and a network size of 12 million (up from 8.3 million in less than nine months).

Be Careful Out There

Before we get into the nitty-gritty of setting up your profile and using LinkedIn, a quick consideration of other ways you can get in trouble on LinkedIn:

- **Name Field** — If it contains anything but your name, you can get your account restricted or even have it deleted

- **Spam or Abuse** — If you are accused of spamming or abuse, LinkedIn may restrict your account. Always remember that spam is in the eye of the beholder. If you think someone might misinterpret something you say — anywhere online — don't say it.

- **Page Views** — This is a weird one. If you view "too many" profiles, LinkedIn may suspend you for suspicion of intent to commit identity fraud. By the same token, be sure the information you share online doesn't reveal too much about you.

- **Non-Professional Profile Picture** — Don't show too much skin or wear something inappropriate. Even though in practice, you can use a logo or an avatar instead of a picture of you, LinkedIn policy says you can't. We're not too sure how tightly this is enforced, since we have several connections who use logos and many who use avatars. This policy is most likely used as just one more reason to ding someone who's being obnoxious in other ways.

Now that that bit of unpleasantness is over, let's get into creating your profile, your complete profile.

Create Your LinkedIn Profile

Completeness is the name of the game for your profile. It's not your resume. It's more properly considered as search bait. Think about it. How are people going to find you on LinkedIn? By searching, of course. So the more you have in your profile, and the more keywords you have in your profile, the more you're going to get found.

Here are some tips on creating your profile:

- **Current and Past Positions** — Put in all your jobs unless you're ashamed of any of them. It's better to be complete in case old colleagues suddenly want to look you up.

- **Education** — Include all the places you went to school, even if just for a few seminars or quarters. Again, for findability.

- **Photo** — As we said in the introduction to this chapter, include a photo of just you, taken by a pro. If you're sensitive about your appearance for any reason, consider substituting a high school yearbook photo, or a caricature or avatar.

- **Nickname or Maiden Name** — Include all the names people have known you by (OK, if one of them was Stinky, leave that out). This is so people can find you.

- **Summary** — Your summary is one of the most important portions of your profile. It's often thought of as your elevator pitch — the pitch you'd give if on an elevator ride with a prospective customer. However, you can feel free to make it a bit longer than that, since you also have to appeal to search engines.

  You should write, rewrite, and polish your summary. It should convey who you are, what you've accomplished, and what you're looking for on LinkedIn.

  There are two parts to the summary. Generally people concentrate the first part on a brief statement of experience, accomplishments and goals. While you don't want to write a novel, length is not as important as it may be on, say, a resume. Make sure you have a catchy opening, but don't feel bad if you can't distill yourself down into a single paragraph.

  The second part is called Specialties, and it's a great place to put a lot of keywords that will help attract other people to look at your profile. It's not really intended for humans to read, but rather search engines. Don't skimp on the keywords here.

- **Websites** — Include all of the Websites you may have been associated with.

- **Interests** — Be careful when adding interests. While it helps to show a rounded picture of who you are, be sensitive to including anything that might cause someone to have a bad reaction. Remember, this is first impression material. If you're into something off-the-wall — not that there's anything wrong with that — wait to discuss until you know your audience better.

- **Email addresses** — Including email addresses is controversial because if you do this, you're likely to get spam. If you want to include an email address — anywhere online — use the following format: you at wherever.com. By breaking up the address, it makes it harder for spambots to come along and harvest your email address to slap onto lists that are then sold and resold.

- **NO TYPOS!** — Nothing kills a buzz like a typo, especially if you're a professional. Have somebody else proofread your profile.

- **Use Industry-Specific Keywords** — Since it's all about search, make sure you use the buzzwords from your product category or industry.

- **Use Acronyms and Spell Them Out** — Use any relevant acronyms; spell them out so outsiders can understand what you're talking about.

Keywords, keywords, keywords! It's all about the keywords. Jam pack your profile with high-value words that people you want to attract will likely be using to find you. If you're stumped as to what to use for keywords, Google your product category to find good ones. You can also search for your industry on LinkedIn for ideas.

When you're done with your profile, there's one last, very important, step: Make your profile public.

From time to time we come upon people who have private profiles and we ask ourselves: Why are you here in the first place if you don't want to meet anyone? However, leaving that existential question aside for a moment, there is one supreme reason why you make your profile public:

It can be found on Google!

In fact, it's likely to be ranked highly on Google, because LinkedIn is a very popular site. Try Googling your name or the name of your enterprise before creating your profile and then again about a week later. We guarantee you'll see an improvement in your ranking.

Make and Get Recommendations

As we mentioned in the opening of this chapter, lack of recommendations is one of the main reasons why your profile is not complete. Perhaps the best way to get started with recommendations is to make a few first. Often those you recommend will return the favor, but be careful that all your recommendations aren't mutual, since that could look like mutual backslapping.

"Mike is a user-friendly IT consultant who designed our company website. He made it highly functional, easy to use and attractive even though our company was in the development stage and did not have a great deal of information to share with website visitors. He was responsive to our requests and issues in a timely manner. Mike provided training to me as web administrator (and to others) that allowed me to make necessary updates and changes and did so using non-technical terms wherever possible. Mike was very understanding of company finances and allowed our company very generous payment terms until we were able to get current with our payments. I am very pleased with the outcome and would recommend Mike to other potential users." May 29, 2009

Top qualities: Great Results, Expert, Good Value

(1st) Jerry Rice CPA(inactive),
hired Mike as a IT Consultant in 2004

"I've known Mike for three years, during which time I've known him to be an avid supporter of entrepreneurship in Minnesota (we serve on the board of directors of the Minnesota Entrepreneurs, Inc. together) and a whiz at installing wireless networks (he installed a network for me at my home office)." March 7, 2004

(1st) Eric Strauss,
worked directly with Mike at StratVantage Consulting, LLC

"Mike came to our firm and solved a networking problem that was three years old. In so doing he was efficient, polite, and cost-effective. He is now our "go-to guy" for any IT questions and/or problems." February 16, 2004

(1st) William Lehnertz
was Mike's client

"Exceptional knowlege of emerging technology. It's almost like he has a crystal ball." January 8, 2004

(1st) Dave Harkins
was Mike's client

Figure 19 — Sample Recommendations on LinkedIn

Recommendations are generally quite important for recruiters. In fact, we have a friend whose LinkedIn recommendations were reviewed by the CEO of a company in advance of a phone interview, during which he got the job.

Create a Company Profile

Once you've gotten your personal profile squared away, it's time to create your enterprise's profile.

Anyone can create a company profile, but it's important that the first person to do so for your enterprise has registered using the organization's email address. LinkedIn will search for other LinkedIn members that have similar email addresses (the part after the @ sign), so if you've registered with LinkedIn using a Gmail or other non-organizational email, get somebody else to create your enterprise's profile.

Figure 20 — Sample Company Profile on LinkedIn

After you put in a description of your enterprise, LinkedIn does a lot of work for you. They list:

All current and former staff members on LinkedIn

Employee career paths

New hires

Recent Activity

Headquarters

Type

Size

Website

Median Age

Gender Breakdown

Related companies

Common job titles — derived from staffers on LinkedIn

Recent Promotions and Changes

Key statistics, including:

Industry

Status

Founded

Top Schools (of LinkedIn members)

Median Tenure

Having all this information available on LinkedIn can be a big help in recruiting staffers and finding partners and prospects. And it's free.

Adding Connections

After you've created your profiles, the next thing you'll want to do is to make connections. As we mentioned, you start with 3,000 available invitations, lifetime, so, while that's a lot, you don't want to be frivolous with them, either.

Before you go sending out invitations, a word of caution. We mentioned the danger of getting an IDK in a previous section. When you first join LinkedIn, you may be tempted to enthusiastically invite all kinds of people whom you don't really know all that well. It's not a good idea, not just because they could IDK you, but because it's a bit rude.

Think about it. If someone you don't recognize invites you to connect, what is your reaction? Chances are you'll scratch your head, visit that person's profile and try to figure out where you may have run into them before. That person just took a few seconds or minutes out of your day, because they didn't give you the context for the invitation.

When you invite a contact while viewing their profile, LinkedIn suggests the text for the invitation, similar to the following figure.

Figure 21 — LinkedIn Default Invitation Text

Pretty minimal, huh? It gives the recipient absolutely no context.

Never use the default text unless you know the person really well, and they're expecting your connection request

---

Always include an explanation for why you want to connect, and a little bit about how you know the person. Not only do you avoid being rude this way, you'll also be much less likely to get an IDK. If you think the person might reject your request, some people append something like, "If you decide not to accept my invitation, I would appreciate it if you would archive the request rather than clicking I Don't Know."

We feel that if you really need to add a disclaimer, you should think twice about directly contacting the person, and opt for getting recommended by someone in their network, which we cover in the section *Three Degrees of LinkedIn* on page 265.

Types of Direct Connection Requests

When you first signed up with LinkedIn, it asked you if you wanted to upload your contacts from your email. This is a good idea to do, even if you don't immediately want to send invites out to the list. LinkedIn uses the list to remind you from time to time to think about connecting with folks you know.

Other than using a list, the best way to directly add connections is to click the friendly green Add Connections link at the top right of most LinkedIn pages:

Figure 22 — LinkedIn's Add Connections Link

When you do this, you'll see a form with a tab that allows you to search for connections on popular email services like Hotmail, Gmail, and Yahoo, import your contacts from Outlook or other email clients, or send invitations to people whose email addresses you know.

This is just one of the options you have for making connections, and one you should use judiciously.

Select the Colleagues tab to invite people who have worked at the same organizations as you have.

Remember when you were filling out your profile, and we told you to include all your previous jobs? Here's one place where this pays off. LinkedIn shows you LinkedIn members who also work or worked at the places you did. You can easily take a look at the lists and invite former colleagues to connect.

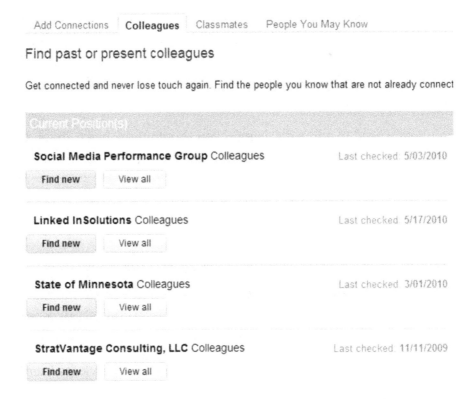

Figure 23 — Add Colleagues on LinkedIn

A third way to directly invite connections is to use the Classmates tab. LinkedIn finds members who attended the same schools as you did.

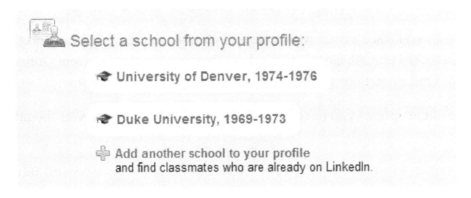

Figure 24 — Invite Classmates to Connect on LinkedIn

The final tab allows you to filter lists of people LinkedIn thinks you might know, based on connections of your connections, places they worked, and schools they attended.

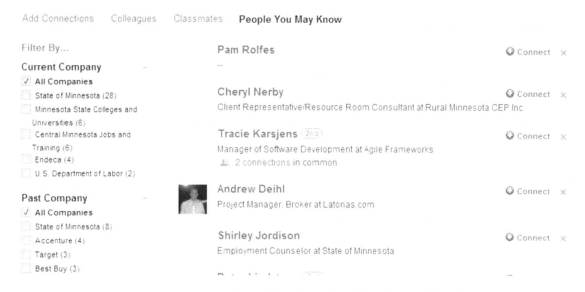

Figure 25 — Invite People You Know on LinkedIn

As you can see from the screenshot, you can filter the list by current and past company as well as schools. But what do those little numbers after the potential contacts' names mean? They indicate the degree of separation away from you, part of the three degrees of LinkedIn.

Three Degrees of LinkedIn

You've probably heard of the trivia game, *Six Degrees of Kevin Bacon*. The game is based on a concept that originated in scholarly analyses of offline social networks called six degrees of separation. The hypothesis behind the concept and the game is that everyone in the world is no more than six friend-of-a-friend jumps away from any other. A landmark study by famed psychologist Stanley Milgram actually determined that people in the United States were no more than three degrees of separation away from one another.[262]

There's no telling if Milgram's theories gave birth to LinkedIn's three-tiered networking policy, but regardless, that's how the site defines the size of your network.

People you are directly connected to are your First Degree network. When you visit their profiles or see them listed in a search, their names are followed by a 1st icon.

Your First Degree contacts obviously also have connections. These secondary connections are your Second Degree network, denoted by a 2nd icon. You can connect to these Second Degree folks by passing a connection request through one of your First Degree connections. That First

---

[262] Milgram's Small World experiment: **bit.ly/crdJBb**

Degree connection can decide whether or not to pass on the request, and you'll be none the wiser. If the request is passed on, the Second Degree contact is free to accept or reject the request just as if it had come from any other source. Obviously the number of people in your Second Degree network is larger than your First Degree population.

The Second Degree connections have connections themselves, and this is the limit of your addressable network: your Third Degree network. Just as with the Second Degree connections, you can pass a connection request along to a Third Degree by first passing it to a First Degree contact, who must decide to pass it to the Second Degree connection, who similarly must decide to pass it to the Third Degree connection. Confused yet?

When you add up all the people in your First, Second, and Third Degree networks, you have your total addressable network. Depending on the number of contacts each member in your addressable network has, you might be surprised at how many people you can be potentially connected to. (See our rock star encounter earlier in this chapter in the *Alternative to Being a LION* section on page 256.)

We recommend that when you want to contact someone you don't know at all that you use the method of passing your request through your network described here. It's like the difference between cold calling someone and getting introduced — being passed through a presumably trusted member of the target person's network implies a similar endorsement, and will be more likely to help you avoid getting IDKed. However, be aware that some have put the likelihood of getting introduced by a Second Degree contact at lower than 80 percent, and the likelihood for Third Degree contacts is vanishingly small.

Finding People to Invite

There are probably lots of interesting people beyond your LinkedIn network that might want to consider linking to — friends you haven't met yet. You can use various features and techniques to find those kindred souls.

One effective technique is to check out the Just Joined LinkedIn section of your Home page. It's down towards the bottom as in the next figure.

Just joined LinkedIn

COLLEAGUES
Evalubase Research
A. C. Nielsen
VirtualFund.com, Inc.
Linked InSolutions
Geneer
State of Minnesota
ACNielsen Company
StratVantage Consulting, LLC
Social Media Performance Group

CLASSMATES
Duke University
University of Denver

Figure 26 — Follow the Just Joined Section on LinkedIn

This section is updated daily and lists new LinkedIn users that worked or attended the companies and schools listed on your profile. Now what's the first thing a new LinkedIn user is going to want to do? That's right: Connect with other members. So even if you don't know or remember the folks in these lists, you might consider sending them a connection request, saying something like, "We both worked at XYZ Company, but I don't think we were there at the same time. I thought maybe you'd like to connect and talk about old times."

As a newbie, your potential contact is likely to welcome a friendly invitation. It's even better if you visit their profile first and mention some other common interests in your note. Also, since the member is new, they are less likely to IDK you.

In the following sections we discuss other ways to find people to connect with, and techniques for inviting them.

Search Titles

Using LinkedIn's advanced search, you can zero in on relevant members you might want to connect with. As we discussed previously, some of the most interesting and powerful search fields are reserved for use by premium members — those who pay money to belong to LinkedIn.

But take a look at the search form and we think you'll agree; it's still pretty powerful.

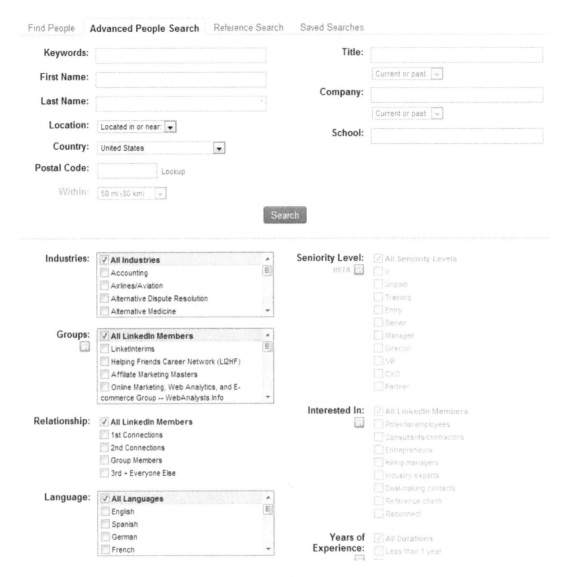

Figure 27 — LinkedIn Advanced Search Page

The various grayed-out areas are only available to premium accounts. You can still search by industry, language, location, title, company, and school. Of course, if you want to use Google as your search engine, as we demonstrated in the opening section of this chapter, you may be able to get at some of the premium attributes.

Here's a more-advanced example of a Google search of LinkedIn:

site:www.linkedin.com -inurl:answers -inurl:jobs -inurl:companies -inurl:directory YOUR KEYWORDS HERE

Let's take a look at this example bit by bit:

- **Site**: — Use this keyword to restrict Google's search to a particular site, in this case, LinkedIn

- **-inurl**: — This keyword, combined with the minus sign, excludes pages with certain keywords in the URL. In this case, we don't want to see results from the LinkedIn Answers section, the Jobs section, the company pages or company directory. If you do want to see answers in a specific section, change the minus sign to a plus sign.

- **Keywords** — put your keywords, using plus, minus, quotes, or AND or OR to further qualify the search

For example, this search:

> **site:www.linkedin.com -inurl:answers -inurl:jobs -inurl:companies -inurl:directory "project manager"**

finds 17 million project managers on LinkedIn. That's far better than the 100 search results the free LinkedIn account limits you to.

Once you find these folks, check out their profiles, and either use the connection request techniques we've already discussed, or use the two additional ones below.

Inviting People: Send InMail

InMail is a way to send a message internal to LinkedIn. You can message anyone on LinkedIn, not just those in your network. Sending InMail generally means upgrading your account. You can buy InMails for $10 apiece, or get three InMails a month with the Business premium account, 10 with the Business Plus account, and 25 with the Executive account. The various LinkedIn recruiting accounts offer more InMails.

Inviting People: Fellow Group Members

A far easier way to contact random people on LinkedIn is to join LinkedIn Groups. As we discussed earlier in this chapter, there are all sorts of groups on LinkedIn — hundreds of thousands of them. You can join 50 at a time, and you can message group members publicly by replying to their posts in the group discussions, or privately. The hitch here is that the group member must first post a discussion topic or comment on one.

If your target person is shy and doesn't post, go to the Members tab for the group, which enables you to invite any group member to connect or even send them a private message.

Search Companies

If you're more interested in finding companies, LinkedIn has a comprehensive company search.

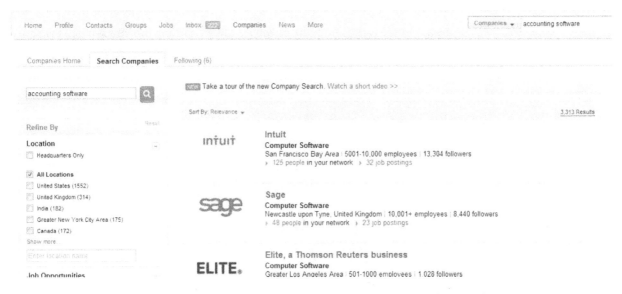

Figure 28 — LinkedIn Company Search Example

A simple search for the keyword "accounting software" finds more than 3,300 organizations. You can filter the results by industry, location, country, postal code, degree of connectedness to you, company size, and whether they're hiring.

Power Tool: LinkedIn Toolbars

Chances are you're not always going to have LinkedIn open in a browser on your computer. But if you use Microsoft Outlook for email, or either Microsoft Internet Explorer or Firefox as your Web browser, you can install LinkedIn toolbars[263] that give you instant access to LinkedIn features. LinkedIn also offers:

- **Email Signature tool** — Enables you to customize the emails you send in Outlook, Outlook Express, and Thunderbird

- **Mac Search Widget** — Enables you to search LinkedIn from your Mac Dashboard

- **LinkedIn Button for Google Toolbar** — Adds LinkedIn search to your Google Toolbar

The Outlook toolbar is worth it just for a single feature: the Grab button. This button allows you to highlight a signature block on an incoming email and instantly convert the information into an Outlook contact. No more laboriously cutting and pasting a new email correspondent's information into contact fields.

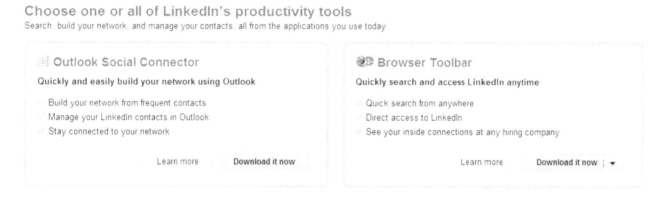

Figure 29 — LinkedIn Toolbars

The browser toolbar installs the JobsInsider function which pulls up a side panel when you view a job listing on many company and third party job sites. JobsInsider analyzes the contents of the job listing to find the employer's name and then determines how many inside connections you have to the job. The side panel lists people in your network who work at the company and enables you to view their profiles.

---

[263] LinkedIn Toolbars: **bit.ly/cllp0G**

Figure 30 — LinkedIn JobsInsider Shows People in Your Network

Developing Relationships

OK, you know how to find people and invite them to connect. Obviously that's a big first step, but unfortunately, many people stop there (especially LIONs). You need to do more than collect connections like charms on a bracelet of lives in a video game.

The real key to using any social network is building and nurturing relationships. In order to do this, you need to stay involved with your network. A good way to do this is to watch your contacts' status.

Your homepage features a timeline that shows you the various updates and activities your LinkedIn connections are engaging in. You should visit your page every day to keep tabs on what your connections are doing. It needn't take long to do so. Just bring up LinkedIn, scan your timeline for interesting activity, and decide if any of it is worthy of a quick comment.

The timeline shows activities in several categories:

- **Updates** — When a connection changes his or her status, the new status will appear here. Select More Updates to see the entire list of changes. Watch for these changes and note what your contacts are working on. If it's interesting or relevant you can either "Like" it, comment on it, or reply privately. This is a great way to quickly touch the people you know and build and maintain your relationship.

- **Company Updates** — When a connection starts following a company, this fact is noted in this section. You can click to see the company's profile, and then follow them yourself. You can also see who else is following the organization. You may be interested in connecting with them as well.

- **Profile Updates** — When a connection updates their profile, that activity shows up here. You can Like or comment on this activity. It's a good idea to view the profile to stay in touch.

- **Application Updates** — LinkedIn has several applications that you can add to your home page, including the following:

LinkedIn App	Description
Blog Link	by SixApart — With **Blog Link**, you can get the most of your LinkedIn relationships by connecting your blog to your LinkedIn profile. Blog Link helps you, and your professional network, stay connected.
Box.net Files	by Box.net — Add the Box.net Files application to manage all your important files online. Box.net lets you share content on your profile, and collaborate with friends and colleagues.
Company Buzz	by LinkedIn — Ever wonder what people are saying about your company? **Company Buzz** shows you the twitter activity associated with your company. View tweets, trends and top key words. Customize your topics and share with your coworkers.
E-Bookshelf	by FT Press — Tap into the insights of the leading minds in business, E-Bookshelf by FT Press-essential reading for success. Read quick, concise business and career lessons from the top experts. Read the content you want, when you want and at a great value.
Events	by LinkedIn — Find professional events, from conferences to local meet-ups, and discover what events your connections are attending.
Google Presentation	by Google — Present yourself and your work. Upload a .PPT or use Google's online application to embed a presentation on your profile.
Huddle Workspaces	by Huddle.net — **Huddle** gives you private, secure online workspaces packed with simple yet powerful project, collaboration and sharing tools for working with your connections.
Legal Updates	by JD Supra — Get legal news that matters to you and your business. (Lawyers, upload your articles and other content. Be found for your expertise on LinkedIn.)
My Travel	by TripIt, Inc. — See where your LinkedIn network is traveling and when you will be in the same city as your colleagues. Share your upcoming trips, current location, and travel stats with your network.
Polls	by LinkedIn — The Polls application allows you to collect actionable data from your connections and the professional audience on LinkedIn.
Portfolio Display	by Behance — Showcase your creative work in your LinkedIn Profile with the **Creative Portfolio Display** application. Free, easy to manage, and supports unlimited multimedia content.
Projects and Teamspaces	by Manymoon — Manymoon makes it simple to Get Work Done with your LinkedIn connections. Share and track unlimited tasks, projects, documents and Google Apps — for free!
Reading List by Amazon	by Amazon — Extend your professional profile by sharing the books you're

LinkedIn App	Description
	reading with other LinkedIn members. Find out what you should be reading by following updates from your connections, people in your field, or other LinkedIn members of professional interest to you.
Real Estate Pro	by Rofo — Access your local real estate and office space market. Follow active brokers, agents and professionals. Track new property listings and available spaces and stay informed of completed deals in your area.
SAP Community Bio	by LinkedIn — Display your certified SAP expertise on LinkedIn. The **SAP Community Bio** application allows you to add your SAP contributions and credentials to your professional profile.
SlideShare Presentations	by SlideShare Inc — **SlideShare** is the best way to share presentations on LinkedIn! You can upload & display your own presentations, check out presentations from your colleagues, and find experts within your network.
Tweets	by LinkedIn — Access the most important parts of the professional conversation with Tweets, a Twitter client you can use right on LinkedIn.
WordPress	by WordPress — Connect your virtual lives with the WordPress LinkedIn Application. With the WordPress App, you can sync your WordPress blog posts with your LinkedIn profile, keeping everyone you know in the know.

We recommend at a minimum adding Blog Link or WordPress so you can link your blog to LinkedIn; Reading List by Amazon to show what you're reading, which could spark connection requests and discussions; SlideShare Presentations, to feature uploaded presentations on your profile; and Tweets, to link your Twitter account to LinkedIn.

When your connections post something using an application, that fact is noted and you can Like or Comment on it.

- **Recently Connected** — Follow the connection activity of your contacts. You may find a contact in common that you may want to connect to also.

- **Group Updates** — You can easily follow recent activity in your groups from your home page.

One of your goals on LinkedIn is to show up in your connections' timelines on a regular basis. You can do this by changing your status by typing in the "Share an Update" box:

Figure 31 — Change Your LinkedIn Status Regularly

You can also trigger timeline updates by changing your professional headline or your experience. You don't need to make visible changes. Just adding a space or deleting and re-adding a word will do.

The last section of this chapter has another tip for changing your status. No fair peeking.

Never Can Say Goodbye

When we train on LinkedIn, one of the most common questions we get is "How do you drop a contact?"

It's pretty easy. Click Connections; select the connection; then select Remove. The connection is not notified that you have dropped them, but, of course, they may notice you're no longer in their list of connections.

Ask and Answer Questions

LinkedIn offers lots of ways to build your online brand (see the section *Brand Your Enterprise Online* on page 219 for more information on brand building). One very effective way is to ask questions and provide answers on LinkedIn.

LinkedIn provides an open forum for any member to ask or answer a question. You access it by clicking More on the top bar:

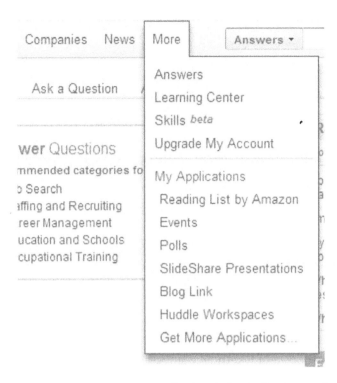

Figure 32 — Finding the LinkedIn Answers Section

You can ask a question, which is displayed for all to see, or answer questions. Once you have a question answered, you can rate the answers, selecting a best answer. Answerers accumulate points by the number of best answers they get. They then are listed on the This Week's Top Experts section. You'd be surprised how many answers it takes to get to the top of this list — often more than 500 answers a week! An added bonus is that every time you answer a question, you show up in your Connections' timelines.

Obviously, one way to build your brand is to get on the Top Experts list. But even if you don't want to spend the effort to do that, you can become known as an expert by answering lots of questions in your field. However, even asking questions can have very positive results, as we discuss in the next section.

Ask Questions

Asking questions on LinkedIn is very easy. Start by simply filling in the Ask a Question box:

Figure 33 — Asking a Question on LinkedIn

When you select Next, you'll see a menu asking for more information:

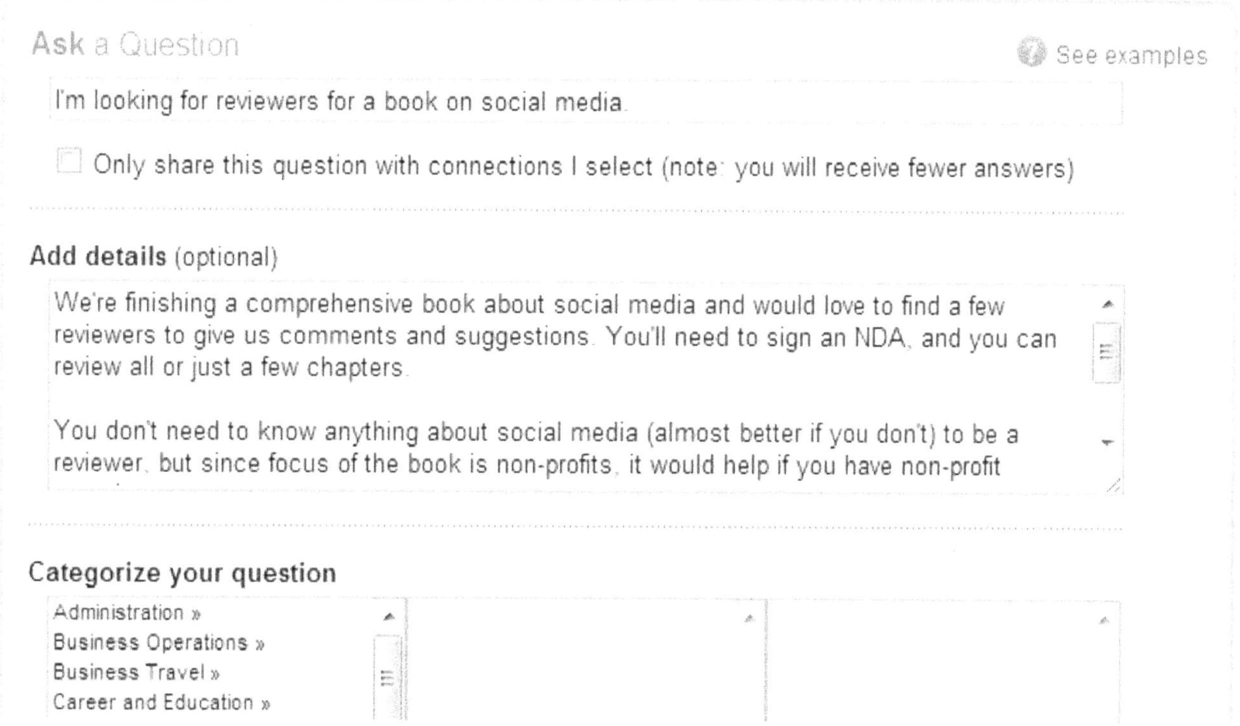

Ask a Question   See examples

I'm looking for reviewers for a book on social media.

☐ Only share this question with connections I select (note: you will receive fewer answers)

Add details (optional)

We're finishing a comprehensive book about social media and would love to find a few reviewers to give us comments and suggestions. You'll need to sign an NDA, and you can review all or just a few chapters.

You don't need to know anything about social media (almost better if you don't) to be a reviewer, but since focus of the book is non-profits, it would help if you have non-profit

Categorize your question

Administration »
Business Operations »
Business Travel »
Career and Education »

Figure 34 — Ask a Question on LinkedIn Detail Page

You provide more details and you can elect to make the question public or just send it to a select group of connections. When you process this page, you'll be given an opportunity to email the question to up to 200 of your connections.

So, when we train, at this point we ask our students, "What is the minimum number of connections you should have on LinkedIn?"

Can you guess the answer?

That's right, 200. There are various places in LinkedIn where you can include up to 200 connections in an activity, so you should aim for at least that many to maximize the impact of your LinkedIn brand.

Your question will remain open for seven days.

When framing your question, it's not necessarily a great thing to be too upfront: "Q: Will you buy our product?" Rather, think of questions you can ask that will provoke interesting or thoughtful responses. You can demonstrate your expertise in the description of the question, and in the on-going dialog that will happen as multiple people answer the question.

To demonstrate, we'd like to mention two questions we asked, and the results.

I asked a technical question about using Microsoft's ancient ASP Web technology: "What are the risks of continuing to use Microsoft Active Server Pages (ASP)?" Not only did I get a lot of free advice, within two hours, the link to the question was in the top 10 results on Google for a related query!

Figure 35 — Great Google Placement for a LinkedIn Question

Now that may not sound that fantastic to you if you're not familiar with how difficult it is to get into the top 10. Let's just say many companies spend thousands of dollars a month to accomplish this feat. Granted, it was a rather narrow subject, but it's still an impressive demonstration of the power of LinkedIn to build your online brand.

I asked another question that demonstrated how far LinkedIn members will go to give you a good answer. My buddy Don was having a problem with his Website. He'd done an update, and noticed that when he tried to print his Webpages, Microsoft Internet Explorer went into an infinite loop. He called me up and said he'd pay me to fix the problem. I took a quick look and determined the problem involved the style sheets that controlled the look of the page. Not being a style sheet guru, and not wanting to charge my friend a ton of money, I asked a question on LinkedIn.

Within a couple of hours, to figure out the answer, one respondent downloaded Don's site to his computer and analyzed the style sheet problem. He determined that there were two settings that were conflicting, and recommended the solution. I tried it, and it worked.

So my hat's off to Keith Tyler! He did this for no other reason that the intellectual challenge, and to be helpful. And I didn't charge Don a penny for the solution. There are hundreds of folks like Keith on LinkedIn, and all it takes to harness their brilliance is asking a question.

Answer Questions

Asking questions is one way to not only benefit from the expertise of LinkedIn members, but to build your brand. Obviously, a more direct way is to answer questions.

To get started, search for unanswered questions. You can search in various categories, and chances are very good you'll find questions you can answer. You can also subscribe to question categories using an RSS feed. (See the section *Have a Call to Action* on page 219 for more information on RSS.)

Use the advanced search to zero in on specific types of questions using keywords as in the following figure.

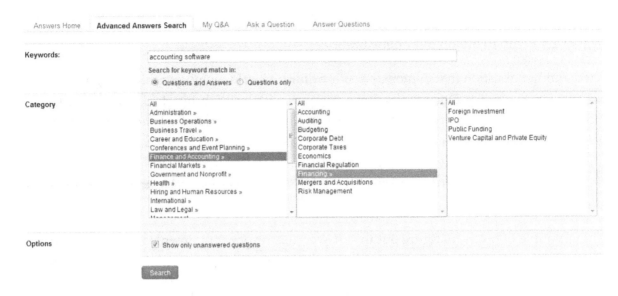

Figure 36 — LinkedIn Advanced Answers Search

Click the option to show only unanswered questions.

When creating an answer, avoid obvious self-promotion. The point of this service is for members to help members. If you're seen as being interested only in promoting yourself or your business, you're likely to provoke a negative response.

Create a LinkedIn Group

One great way to build your brand on LinkedIn is to create your own group. We don't recommend naming the group after your company unless you want to have a group for current or former staff. Rather, determine a concept or problem of concern to your target audience and create a group around that.

You should name the group using keywords, because it's all about search, especially since, according to a mid-2010 article on TechCrunch,[264] there are more 650,000 groups on LinkedIn, with the largest representing 200,000 members.

But don't create a group without a plan. By creating a group, you are making a commitment to your community, and you had better figure out what you're going to do before you take the plunge.[265]

---

[264] **tcrn.ch/9tebzu**

[265] LinkedIn guide on creating a group: bit.ly/mmQtVz

LinkedIn Group Strategy

There are two general types of groups on LinkedIn: open groups and closed groups. The choices are known as "Open Access" and "Request to Join" on the group creation form. More specifically, you can designate your group as:

- Alumni
- Corporate
- Conference
- Networking
- Non-Profit
- Professional
- Other

You'll be able to upload a logo for the group, so you should think about whether you need a new logo or if you'll use your enterprise's logo.

Group search is only done on the 300 word summary so make sure that summary contains key-words potential members are likely to use to find the group. Other important settings are:

- Display this group in the Group directory — If you want to be found, be sure to check this

- Allow group members to display the logo on their profiles — This is another great way to get found; often members will check out the groups their connections belong to; checking this also will send notifications to your connections about the group creation

- Pre-approve members with the following email domain(s) — This is especially useful if for alumni and corporate groups

Once you've created the group, you can explicitly invite 200 of your contacts to join. Be sure to do that.

Next, you'll need a plan to recruit members. Decide what kinds of people you'd like to join, and target them on LinkedIn using the techniques described in the earlier sections. It's a good idea to post a message on the group's discussion forum encouraging members to display the group logo on their profiles.

You also need to establish a policy on the types of posts that will be permitted on the group. As group manager, you have plenty of power to police the group, but you need to be sure group members understand your policies. See the section *Dealing with Negatives* on page 209 for more information on establishing community policies.

Among the policies you'll need to consider:

- **Preventing LION Invites** — LIONs love groups and often repeatedly cross-post invitations for members to connect with them on groups. You need to decide whether to prohibit this type of posting, and how you'll deal with LIONs in general.

- **Prevent Members from Repeatedly Posting the Same Post** — You'll find that some of your members will view the group solely as a way to promote themselves or their event. Establish a policy regarding this and other repetitive posts.

Finally, even if you're not too interested in creating a group, depending on your situation you may want to do so anyway, just to preempt someone else from doing it. For example, the ex-Microsoft employee group is run by an Apple recruiter. Think seriously about this if your business has a vocal opposition that might want to create a group under your name just to trash you.

Create a LinkedIn Ad

Our final LinkedIn tip for building your brand is to create a LinkedIn Ad.

LinkedIn ads are surprisingly affordable, and very targetable. Get started by clicking on Advertising on the footer of any page. There are choices for large and small budgets. It's probably wise to get started with LinkedIn DirectAds to learn how well LinkedIn can address your target audience.

Figure 37 — Example — Creating a LinkedIn Direct Ad

You can target the ad by company size, industry, seniority, gender, age, and geography:

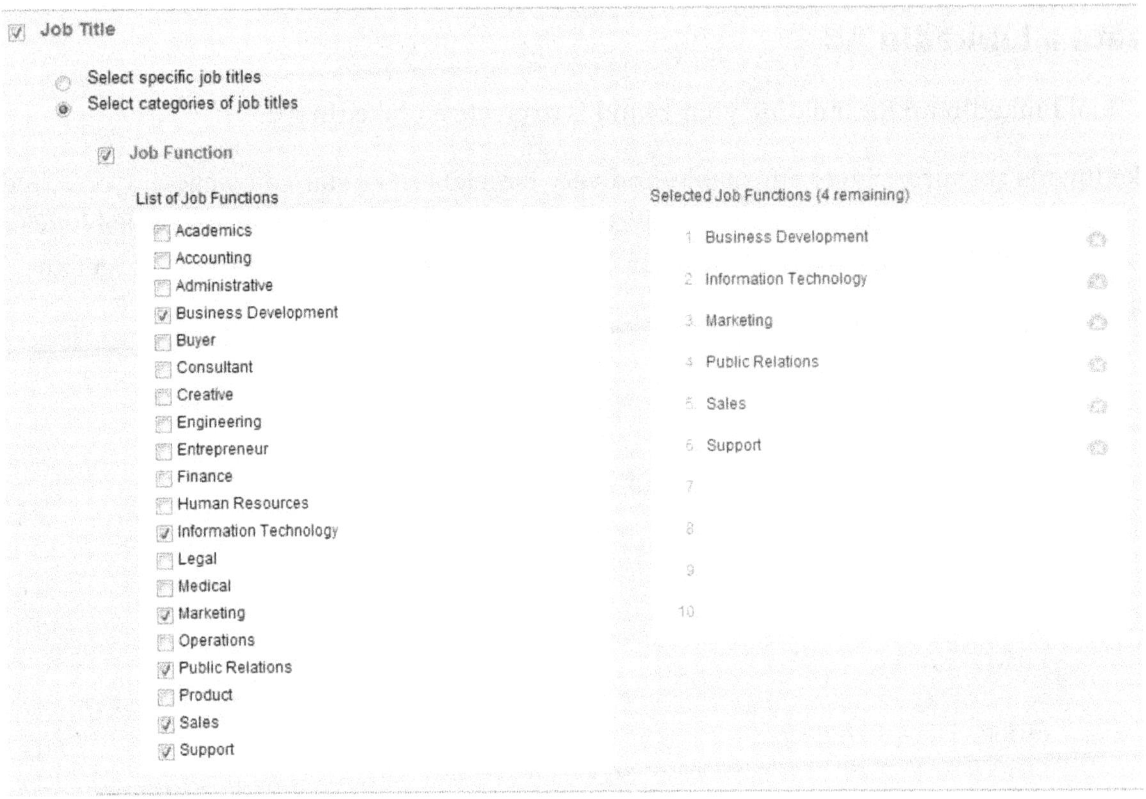

☑ Job Title

○ Select specific job titles
◉ Select categories of job titles

☑ Job Function

List of Job Functions	Selected Job Functions (4 remaining)

List of Job Functions:
- ☐ Academics
- ☐ Accounting
- ☐ Administrative
- ☑ Business Development
- ☐ Buyer
- ☐ Consultant
- ☐ Creative
- ☐ Engineering
- ☐ Entrepreneur
- ☐ Finance
- ☐ Human Resources
- ☑ Information Technology
- ☐ Legal
- ☐ Medical
- ☑ Marketing
- ☐ Operations
- ☑ Public Relations
- ☐ Product
- ☑ Sales
- ☑ Support

Selected Job Functions (4 remaining):
1. Business Development
2. Information Technology
3. Marketing
4. Public Relations
5. Sales
6. Support
7.
8.
9.
10.

Figure 38 — Targeting Linked In Direct Ads

You always want to select Pay-per-click, unless you really know what you're doing. This means you are only charged when a member actually clicks on the ad, rather than when they just see it displayed. You can also set your budget per click and per day, as well as scheduling your campaign period.

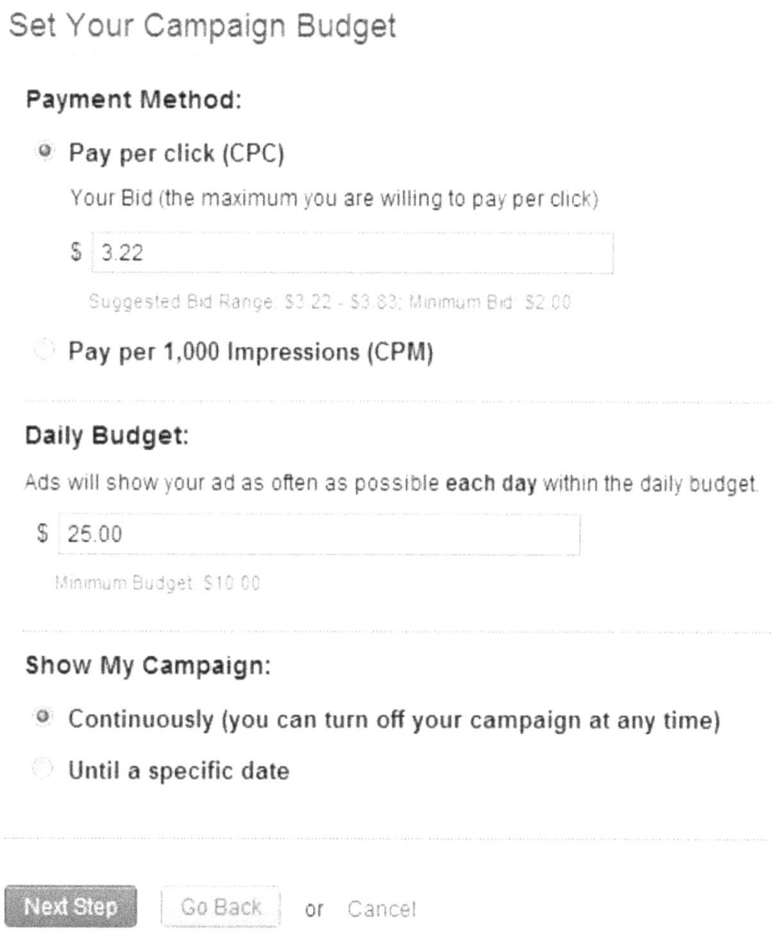

Set Your Campaign Budget

Payment Method:

○ **Pay per click (CPC)**

Your Bid (the maximum you are willing to pay per click)

$ 3.22

Suggested Bid Range: $3.22 - $3.83; Minimum Bid: $2.00

○ Pay per 1,000 Impressions (CPM)

Daily Budget:

Ads will show your ad as often as possible **each day** within the daily budget.

$ 25.00

Minimum Budget: $10.00

Show My Campaign:

○ Continuously (you can turn off your campaign at any time)

○ Until a specific date

[Next Step] [Go Back] or Cancel

Figure 39 — Always Pick Pay-per-click for LinkedIn Ads

Once you've selected all the parameters, your ad goes live immediately. You'll need to turn it off using the management menu if you don't want it to run yet:

Campaign	Status	Budget	Clicks	Impressions	Click Through Rate	Avg. Cost Per Click	Total Spent ↑
Total for All Campaigns			0	0	0%	--	**$0.00**
Linked In or Left Out	Off Turn On Hide	$25.00	0	0	0%	$0.00	$0.00
Linked In or Left Out	Off Turn On Hide	$25.00	0	0	0%	$0.00	$0.00
Social Media for...	On Turn Off Hide	$25.00	0	0	0%	$0.00	$0.00
Social Media for...	Off Turn On Hide	$10.00	0	0	0%	$0.00	$0.00
Social Media for Your Biz	Off Turn On Hide	$20.00	0	0	0%	$0.00	$0.00
Total for All Campaigns			0	0	0%	--	**$0.00**

Figure 40 — Managing your LinkedIn Ad Campaigns

Beyond LinkedIn Basics

There is a lot more to do on LinkedIn. We've given you the basics and some guiding principles to use on the site. Once you have gained some experience don't be afraid to try different approaches and features as they come on board.

One last tip: You can link your Twitter feed to your LinkedIn status so that everything you tweet shows up in your connections timeline. Don't have a Twitter account? Check out the next section.

Setting Up Twitter

"Twitter is a community of friends and strangers
from around the world sending updates about moments in their lives.
Friends near or far can use Twitter to remain somewhat close while far away.
Curious people can make friends.
Bloggers can use it as a mini-blogging tool.
Developers can use the API to make Twitter tools of their own.
Possibilities are endless!"

Twitter, 2007

That's the way Twitter described itself in 2007. Here's how Twitter described their service in 2009: "Twitter is a service for friends, family, and co-workers to communicate and stay connected through the exchange of quick, frequent answers to one simple question: What are you doing?"

Here's how Twitter described itself in 2010: "Discover what's happening right now, anywhere in the world. Twitter is a rich source of instant information. Stay updated. Keep others updated. It's a whole thing." And here's how it describes itself in mid-2011: "Follow your interests. Instant updates from your friends, industry experts, favorite celebrities, and what's happening around the world."

Four fairly different descriptions, but the Twitter service really hasn't basically changed in the last several years. Sure they've added features, and tweaked various aspects — most notably privacy settings — since the service debuted in 2006, but Twitter is still a way for you to send out messages of no more than 140 characters to people — called followers — who sign up to read what you write.

If you want to get up to speed quickly on Twitter, Commoncraft has a funny but very effective YouTube video called *Twitter in Plain English*[266] that explains the service in less than two-and-a-

---

[266] Commoncraft's *Twitter in Plain English*: **bit.ly/degile**

half minutes. In fact, the whole Commoncraft series of "plain English" videos is well worth your time.

You may be among those who are skeptical about using Twitter for anything useful. In fact, the most common comment we get from non-Twitter users when discussing the service is, "Why should I care what you had for lunch?"

It's true. Much of what is said on Twitter is trivial. There are lots of people tweeting about meaningless things. Our top worst Twitter tweets ever:

- "I'm going up the stairs now" — tied with "OMG, just saw something black going up the stairs behind me, please tell me its my cat! I'm gonna be looking behind me every 10 seconds now!"
- "My cat just rolled over" — tied with "*MY CAT JUST ROLLED OVER* onto me...cuddle time?:3"
- "Gee, the line at Starbucks is long" — tied with "What is the deal with the long drive thru line at Starbucks? My gas light is coming on people!"

So these scoffers have a bit of a point. There are plenty of self-involved people using Twitter to spout trivial inanities or unwanted details about their lives.

However, to condemn Twitter because some people say stupid things on it is like condemning the telephone network because people say stupid things on it. Both are ways for people to communicate. And both host a wide variety of conversations, some vapid and some deadly serious.

Examples of the deadly serious side of Twitter are quite compelling:

First Pictures of Flight 1549 Landing in the Hudson

 - There's a plane in the Hudson. I'm on the ferry going to pick up the people. Crazy.

2:36 PM Jan 15th, 2009 via TwitPic
Retweeted by 7 people   Reply   Retweet

jkrums
Janis Krums

Twitter Outage Delayed Due to US National Interest

During the Iran election protests of summer 2009, the US State Department asked Twitter to delay planned maintenance work to allow Iranians to communicate with each other. "We highlighted to them that this was an important form of communication," said a State Department official.[267] Twitter and Facebook were used to coordinate protests over the Iranian election's outcome. Worldwide supporters helped keep Iranians' access to Twitter running in the face of government censorship. English comedian Stephen Fry posted: "Our Iranian friends can access Twitter from 148.233.239.24 Port:80 in Tehran. Can avoid govt filters from here. #iranelection."[268] For Iranian protesters, access to Twitter might have been a matter of life or death.

Twitter Adds Twitter Business Center

At the end of 2010, Twitter released a Business Center that offers the ability to advertise and promote tweets and trends. Twitter also has a promoted account feature that helps automate finding followers. The site also offers advanced analytics which helps businesses track their promotions.

These features improve Twitter's use for business and will be welcomed by the millions of businesses that regularly use the service — from HealthPartners and their Petey PeeCup[269] kids' health outreach program to Comcast's Comcast Cares[270] customer service effort.

Twitter Activism is Growing

Environmentalists used the #coalash hashtag to discuss a Tennessee Valley Authority spill in 2008. (A hashtag is a way to tag tweets so people can easily find them.)

Activist Twitter accounts such as **@socialawareness**, **@ ClimateActivism** and sites such as **TwitterActivism** demonstrate the powerful organizing capabilities of the service.

If you still think Twitter is a toy for self-absorbed narcissists, perhaps we can convince you otherwise in the rest of this chapter.

---

[267] Reuters: U.S. State Department speaks to Twitter over Iran: **bit.ly/aFJcd6**

[268] Telegraph: Iran protest news travels fast and far on Twitter: **bit.ly/cYSNrW**

[269] HealthPartners' @Petey_P_Cup Twitter account: **bit.ly/ahlM0k**

[270] @ComcastCares Twitter account: **bit.ly/crtIQV**

Why Use Twitter?

Why should an enterprise use Twitter? For one thing, it's a very direct and immediate way to stay connected with stakeholders. Here are some other ideas:

- Establish connections with clients and donors
- Establish your brand online
- Establish your credibility and expertise

Take a poll of your stakeholders — perhaps through your regular newsletter — and ask how many of them use Twitter. You may be surprised at the response. Twitter is used all over the world as an organizing tool for social movements. Its use by the Obama campaign in the 2008 presidential election is a great example of Twitter's ability to mobilize, energize, and spur people to action.

You can use Twitter to help establish your online brand by making it a reliable source of the latest news pertaining to your products and your business. You may have other methods of keeping your community informed, but nothing beats the timeliness and immediacy of Twitter.

By becoming a trusted voice on Twitter, you can build your credibility and demonstrate your expertise to a larger audience than you are currently reaching. We discuss the demographics of Twitter in more depth in the next section, but there are more than 200 million Twitter accounts,[271] growing at a little less than 10 percent a month. Active Twitters who tweet at least once a month comprise 17 percent of the total, encompassing 10 million to 15 million active tweeters.[272] That represents a large potential audience to which you can spread your message.

Many enterprises have successfully used Twitter to advance their business. But few have realized the extraordinary ROI that Cisco did with its Aggregated Services Router (ASR) product launch.[273] The company went entirely virtual for the launch, shaving six figures off launch expenses delivering the following results:

- 9,000 people attended the social media product launch event – 90 *times* more attendees than in the past
- Saved 42,000 gallons of gas
- Nearly three times as many press articles as with traditional outreach methods
- More than 1,000 blog posts and 40 million online impressions

Twitter was a key piece of the launch, featuring 108 Cisco feeds with 2 million total followers.

---

[271] Just like with our numbers for LinkedIn, this number will likely have changed by the time you read this. Here's where we got the numbers: bit.ly/hqStPu

[272] Computerworld: **bit.ly/alcJMR**

[273] Social Media Examiner's *Social Media Launch Saves Cisco $100,000+:* **bit.ly/pRRv6F**

"It was classified as one of the top five launches in company history," said LaSandra Brill, senior manager, global social media. "It was the crossing the chasm point for us in the adoption phase of social media and helped us get over the hump of internal acceptance."

These few ideas should get you thinking, throughout the rest of this chapter, about other ways to use this real-time, urgent messaging system.

Who's Using Twitter?

Far from being a tool for teenagers, Twitter is widely used across all age demographics. Yes, the median age of a twitter user is 31, but take a look at some relevant findings from a recent Pew Internet & American Life Project[274] study that measured the percentage of online adults who have used Twitter or other status updating service:[275]

- 19 percent of American Internet users
- Male — 17 percent; Female — 21 percent
- Just 8 percent of online teens say they ever use Twitter[276]
- 9 percent of Whites, 15 percent of African-Americans, 16 percent Hispanics (English)

---

[274] Pew Internet: Portrait of a Twitter user: Status update demographics: **bit.ly/do6g9K**

[275] Pew Internet: The Twitter Question: **bit.ly/9y4821**

[276] Pew Research Center's Internet & American Life Project Report List and Summaries of Research on Teens and Technology Use (2007-2010): **bit.ly/ckiYK0**

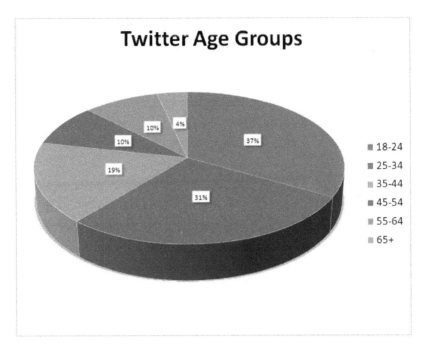

Figure 41 — Twitter Age Demographics

Not convinced it's for you? Take a look at a partial list of the Twitter handles of enterprises, large and small:

Table 6 — Enterprises Using Twitter

@ATT	@ATTCustomerCare	@ATTDeals
@BestBuy	@BlackBerry	@CiscoSystems)
@CMEGroup)	@Comcastcares	@DellCares
@DellEnterprise	@DellOutletUK	@Direct2Dell
@Ernst_and_Young	@FordCustService	@FordDriveGreen
@FordMustang	@FordRacing	@HRBlock
@Intel	@JetBlue	@KPMG
@Kraft_Cadbury	@Mayoclinic	@McDonaldsCorp
@MyStarbucksIdea	@Nikebaseball	@Nikegolf
@Nikestore	@Oracle	@PopeyesChicken
@SamsungMobileUS	@SonyPictures	@SouthwestAir
@Thehomedepot	@WholeFoods	

OK, assuming you no longer believe Twitter is trivial, let's see how to go about using it.

How to Use Twitter

First, you need to sign up for an account; it's free.[277] Use your real name for your Twitter name (also called a handle, a remnant from the "10-4 good buddy" CB craze of the late '70s and early '80s[278]) or possibly the name of your enterprise, although Twitter officially frowns on this. If you don't use either, select a good username using keywords or a brandable phrase (15 character limit). Pick something related to your cause to better brand yourself as an expert.

For example, let's say your enterprise is called XYZ Corp. If you're relatively well-known, you'll want to tweet as @XYZCorp. While using your enterprise's name can be a good idea so that your stakeholders can find you, you may want to broaden your effort to reach people who haven't heard of you, but might search for your product category on Twitter. Thus you might consider creating a Twitter account for your product category. Let's say that XYZ Corp. makes water filters. You could create an additional Twitter account for @WaterFilters, for example.

Be sure to create your profile, which is limited to 160 characters (20 characters more than a tweet). Include information about yourself or your business, and add a picture of yourself or your logo. All this information will be publicly viewable.

Make sure you have a secure password. There have been numerous examples of bad guys taking over people's Twitter accounts due to weak passwords. A strong password is at least eight characters long; uses upper- and lowercase letters, numbers, and punctuation; and is not a single English word.

---

[277] Sign up for Twitter: **bit.ly/aRhcIP**

[278] See a definition for handle at: **bit.ly/bOduGd**

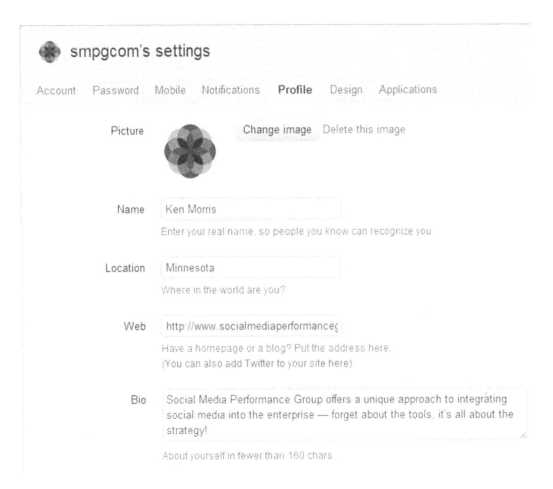

Figure 42 — Example Twitter Settings

You'll also want to create a background for your page. This background sits as wallpaper behind your Twitter account when others view it on the Web.

Here's what ours looks like:

Figure 43 — Example Twitter Background Graphic

Notice that we incorporate our logo graphic both as our Twitter picture and background. We discuss the importance of consistent branding in the *Triangulate Your Social Media Presence* section on page 204. You should consider having a professional designer create your graphics for your various social media sites.

Managing Your Accounts

Once you have an account, you can use it directly from the Website or via a variety of desktop tools, including:

- Tweetdeck[279]
- Seesmic[280]
- HootSuite[281]
- Clove[282]

---

[279] Tweetdeck: **bit.ly/de0lqe**

[280] Seesmic: **bit.ly/bVEyHc**

[281] HootSuite: **bit.ly/cHVqoL**

These applications allow you to more easily filter and sort your Twitter stream. And after you've started following more than a dozen tweeps, you're going to need one of these apps to keep things straight. You can create sections in each of these tools that enable you to follow one or more people specifically, monitor a recurring Twitter search, and they also enable you to post, reply, and retweet using your own Twitter account.

Bought for $40 million in mid-2011 by Twitter itself, Tweetdeck dominates the desktop Twitter/social networking market with Seesmic and Hootsuite close behind. All three are fighting for visibility on iPhone and Android phones.

Seesmic, Tweetdeck, and Clove are quite similar in look and feature set. Each allows you to set up columns representing a particular social media feed — your Twitter stream, Facebook stream, and perhaps a Twitter list as well as monitoring a particular keyword search. HootSuite's approach is a bit different, running in a Web browser, or integrating into the Firefox browser as a clickable widget, enabling you to monitor your Twitter feed wherever you are. Currently, HootSuite is winning the arms race, supporting the largest number of social networks.

Clove, a small startup out of Minneapolis, has a little different approach than either Seesmic or Tweetdeck. In addition to being able to track specific searches as the other platforms do, Clove lets you filter the results and combine columns into folders, called "scenes."

Clove offers sophisticated publishing controls that allow a central publisher to push scenes out to followers.

In addition to features Clove shares with other platforms such as the ability to manage multiple accounts and to auto-post to social networks, the application offers unique features such as the ability to:

- Combine feeds from different social networks
- Auto-expand short-URLs (like the URLs in the footnotes to this book) so you can check out where you're going before clicking
- Create an address book of contacts
- Synchronize your settings among multiple computers
- Displaying feeds as threaded discussions (showing posts along with replies and answers)
- Offline access (ability to store recent feeds on your computer so you can review them when you don't have Internet connectivity)

We prefer Clove for its flexibility and extensibility. TweetDeck is nice, but its little chirp sound effect when a new post comes in drives us crazy. Both Seesmic and HootSuite have their good points, and we use all four of these platforms at different times for different reasons.

---

[282] Clove: **bit.ly/d7eJgB**

How to Get Followers

Whether you use the much-improved Twitter Webpage or one of these applications, you'll want to start out by following interesting people. Following means you will see their tweets in your timeline, similar to the following figure:

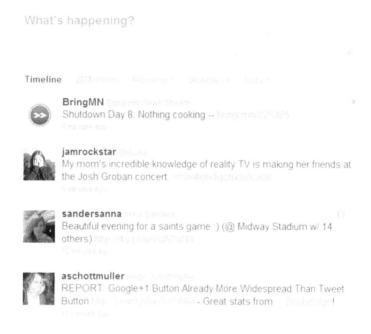

Figure 44 — Example Twitter Timeline

You can start by following us: @smpgcom. If you know a person's Twitter handle, you can go to their page on the Web by typing twitter.com followed by a slash and their handle, without the @ sign. For example, here we are: **twitter.com/smpgcom**.

One thing you'll find out once you start following people is that you'll magically get some followers of your own. That's because not only are your tweets now showing up on your followers' sites, but many people track new followers of people they follow, and decide to also follow. In general, the more people you follow, the more will follow you back. You can find likely people to follow by searching for keywords that interest you. We discuss Twitter search in more detail in the section *Searching on Twitter* on page 304.

When you're ready to send out your first tweet, start by saying something about what you're interested in. Just try not to make it about your cat, going up stairs, or how long the line at Starbucks is.

Incidentally, your followers are called tweeps, not twits.

Follow to Get Followed

As we said above, the best way to get followers is to follow others. Then watch their Twitter stream and you're likely to find other interesting people to follow, who might also follow you back. Of course, you should include your Twitter handle in your email signature and in other promotional materials.

Another handy way to find people to follow and encourage people to follow you is to use Follow Friday. This is a tradition on Twitter. Every Friday people recommend other tweeps as good people to follow by posting recommendations and including a hashtag, which is a quick way to create a keyword by putting a hash, or pound, sign at the beginning of a word or phrase (no spaces). In this case, people use the hashtags #ff, #followfriday, and a few others to mark their posts recommending cool people to follow. (There's more on hashtags in the *Use Hashtags* section on page 305.) Other people search for these tags and often check out the people recommended. Here's a recent sample of Follow Friday activity:

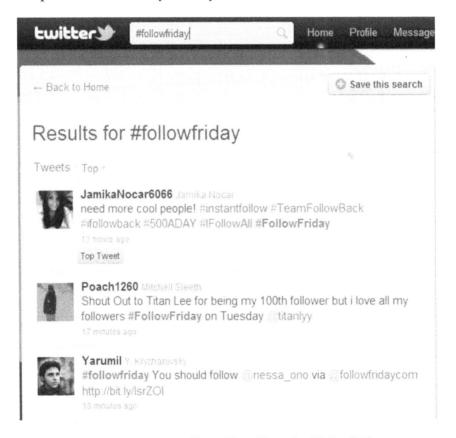

Figure 45 — Example of Follow Friday

Since you're new at Twitter, it's not likely anyone is going to recommend you via Follow Friday just yet. So start off by recommending others. People will be curious about you, and if you've created a good profile, they may decide to start following you. Of course it helps if you have a few interesting, pithy posts under your belt before you try this.

Create Twitter Lists

A great way to get people to follow you is to create a Twitter list in your account. A list is nothing more than a group of people you follow that you give a name. So for example, if you like the tweets of @abc and @mno because they are talking about water filters, create a list called Water_Filters and add these accounts to it.

It's easy to do. Go to your account on the Twitter Website, and select the Profile button. At the top of the page you'll see a button called Lists.

Figure 46 — Creating a Twitter List — List Button

Click New list. You'll see a box to fill in a name and description for the list, and to determine if it's a public or a private (only you can see) list.

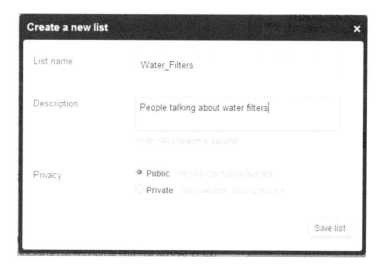

Figure 47 — Naming a Twitter List

Click Create list, and Twitter creates the list. Now you can to add followers (your tweeps) or others to the list on the next menu similar to the next figure.

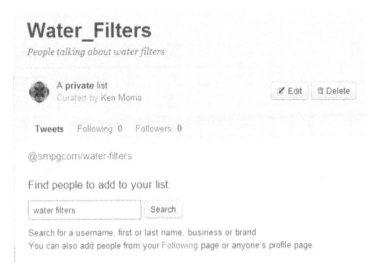

Figure 48 — Adding People to a Twitter List

After you do a search, you can easily add people to your list.

Each list is currently limited to **500 people**, and you can create a maximum of **20 lists**. When you view your list, you see the tweets from the people who are members of the list rather than a list of members. Those who you add to your list are passively notified that they are on a list, if it's public. They may notice at the top of their Twitter profile page, next to the lists indicating the number of tweet, number of followers and number they are following, that the number of lists they are on has increased.

If you've created a public list, and if your followers find it interesting, they may follow your list as well. Similarly, if someone just happens to be browsing your Twitter profile, and they see a list they like, they may follow you and the list. Your list also can be found on some Twitter Directories, like Listorious (see the section *Power Tool: WeFollow and Other Twitter Directories* on page 307 for more information about Twitter directories.

Setting Up Twitter

Unfollowing, Blocking, and Reporting for Spam

If you don't want a particular person to follow you — perhaps because you don't want to be associated with them, or they're a little creepy — you can block them. Blocking's a bit drastic. Perhaps you just don't want to see their tweets anymore. You may just want to unfollow them. To unfollow a user, go to your main Twitter page and click the "Following" link and select "View as a List of People." This brings you to a list of the people you are following.

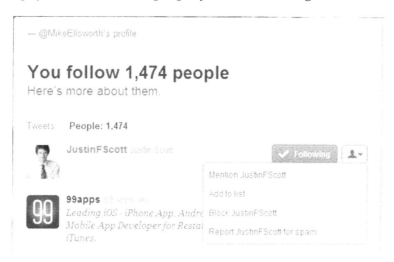

Figure 49 — Unfollowing People on Twitter

Find the person you want to unfollow, and click the Follow button to unfollow them. You can also use the dropdown to see various actions you can take, including mentioning, adding to a list, blocking, and reporting them.

If you really want to block the person from following you, you can select "Block." The block takes immediate effect, although you'll see an Undo link in the listing if you change your mind. You can also block a user by visiting their Twitter page and clicking "Block."

Twitter doesn't notify the blocked user, although they may notice they no longer can view your tweets in their timeline, but they will be able to view them on your public profile page. The main benefit is that they can no longer direct message you (we discuss direct messaging in the next section.) If the blocked user tries to follow your tweets again, Twitter displays a message similar to the following figure.

This user has blocked you from following them.

Figure 50 — Twitter Blocked User Message

You may also want to report users for spamming. This is a good idea if, for example, you and another user are mutually following each other, and they start direct messaging spam to your account.

Here's what Twitter considers to be spamming behavior:

- Posting harmful links (including links to phishing or malware sites)
- Abusing the @reply function to post unwanted messages to users
- Creating lots of accounts or using automated tools to create multiple accounts
- Spamming trending topics to try to grab attention
- Repeatedly posting duplicate updates
- Posting links with unrelated tweets
- Aggressive following behavior (for instance, mass following and un-following in order to gain attention)

To report this type of abuse, select Report for Spam on either in your list of followers or on the user's Twitter page. Reporting a user blocks them from following you and flags them for Twitter to review. A single report is not likely to cause Twitter to take action against the accused spammer. Here's Twitter's current statement about reporting spammers:

> Twitter's Trust and Safety Team looks at user reports of spam in combination with other signals for spam investigation. You may not immediately or definitely see this account suspended. Once you've reported an account as spam, it is no longer able to follow you or reply to you.

Twitter Commands

Anyone can find your messages by searching for keywords, so don't tweet anything private. Anyone can also see any replies you make to others' tweets — these replies begin with @theirhandle. Doing this saves the message in the recipient's Replies tab for later reference by the recipient.

If you want to send private messages, known as Direct Messages, or DMs, begin your post with D followed by a space and handle of the person you want to send to (with or without the @ sign.) For example, this sends a direct message to us "D @smpgcom Love the book." Don't make the rookie mistake of using DM at the beginning of a direct message (we've all been there). Everyone can see that message.

As a privacy measure, and to ensure that random people can't DM you with spam, you can only DM someone when you are mutually following one other.

One thing to especially remember about using Twitter: You don't have to read all the tweets.

Once you follow more than a dozen people it's hard to have a life and follow that many tweets, especially if those you follow love to yack. You may want to consider getting a Twitter app for your mobile phone if you want to keep close tabs on your Twitter feed. There are several, especially for iPhones.

Twitter Glossary

Like all social media, Twitter has its own specialized vocabulary. Here's a list of some of the more familiar terms you're likely to run into.

- **At Reply or @reply** — a reply to another user
- **DM** — stands for direct message, but use **D** to start a direct message, **not** DM
- **Failwhale** — graphic that appears when Twitter is over capacity
- **Hashtags** or # — marking a word as a keyword
- **Retweet** (or RT) — repeating another's tweet
- **Tweeps** — people who follow you on Twitter
- **Tweet** — sending a Twitter message
- **Tweetbacks** — the background for your Twitter Webpage
- **Twitterati** — A-list twitterers everyone follows
- **Twitterverse** — the Twitter community
- **Via** — instead of using retweet, use "via @username" when you paraphrase another's tweet

There are also a lot of cute or funny twitter terms such as Twapplications, Twaiting, Twalking, Twead, Twebay, Tweetheart, Twerminology, Twittectomy, Twittastic, Twittercal mass, Twitterfly, Twitterish, Twitterject, Twitterloop, Twitterphobe, Twitterphoria, Twitterstream, Twittertude, Twitticisms, but we won't bother to define them here, as they're generally not in wide use and most are, quite frankly, more than a bit silly, or SillyTwit, if you like.

Searching on Twitter

After having no real way to search for years, Twitter not that long ago added a decent search on Twitter Webpages, and at search.twitter.com or at **https://twitter.com/#!/search-advanced**. You can search for keywords or phrases and hashtags, and can also save searches so you can repeat them later. The advanced search is actually quite powerful. See the following figure.

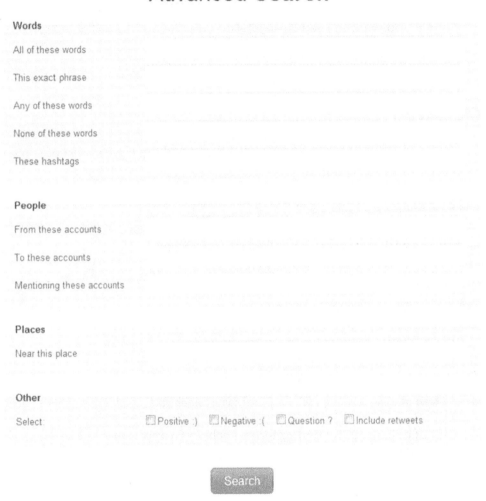

Figure 51 — Twitter Advanced Search

Twitter also has added a Trending Topics feature, which displays popular topics on Twitter, with links to searches that help you find the relevant tweets.

Use Hashtags

A hashtag is simply a way to tag a word as a keyword by preceding the word with a # sign (called a hash sign). Using a hashtag is a bit more specific that using a regular keyword and makes tagged tweets a little easier to find. Note that you cannot include any spaces in a hashtag.

Anyone can create a hashtag at any time. Whether anyone else uses it depends on how well-named it is, and how much you popularize it.

You may want to create or find a hashtag for your products or your enterprise. You can also "register" the hashtag at Twubs[283] or Tagdef[284] to make it easier to find. Doing so, however, does not mean you have exclusive use — or any rights — to use the tag. Anybody can use any tag for whatever use they like at any time.

Here's a recent search for the hashtag #enterprise as an example:

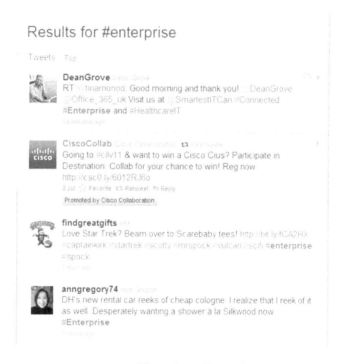

Figure 52 — Example Hashtag Search

---

[283] Twubs: **bit.ly/9YyzkU**

[284] Tagdef: **bit.ly/bBWELg**

Shrinking Long URLs

You may have noticed the odd URLs in the footnotes of this book. We are using an URL shortener called Bit.ly. Although URL shorteners have been around at least since the first popular one, TinyURL, launched in 2002, the length limitations of Twitter and other social media statuses have caused their use to explode. These free services take a long URL, such as, for example, the URL to one of our blogs — **http://www.socialmediaperformancegroup.com/index.php/blog/94-branding-in-the-social-computing-age** — and turn it into an URL that is much shorter, and easier to remember or type — **http://bit.ly/aaOk1J**.

When someone clicks on the shortened URL, their browser is directed to the shortener's site, in this case Bit.ly, which looks up the original long URL, and redirects the browser there.

With the dramatic growth of demand, shorteners like Bit.ly now provide other services, such as vanity short URLs — like **http://bit.ly/smperformance** — and usage tracking, allowing the creator of the URL to see how many people have clicked on it.

Since you need to include the lengthy http:// portion of the URL when you tweet, the shorter the name of the shortener site, and the fewer characters it needs to do the job, the better.

As an example, here are three ways **www.careeronestop.org** is shortened using different URL shorteners:

- **http://tinyurl.com/d6m6hu** — 25 chars
- **http://bit.ly/2lJGiH** — 20 characters
- **http://is.gd/pGDa** — 17 characters

Power Tool: WeFollow and Other Twitter Directories

On WeFollow,[285] you can register yourself and assign three keywords to your Twitter account. People who search on WeFollow can then see you in their search results based on the keywords. WeFollow also ranks registrants by influence. Here's a recent example:

Entrepreneur

Most influential

#1		aplusk	6,636,323 followers
		i make stuff, actually i make up stuff, stories mostly. collaborations o...	
#2	TC	TechCrunch	1,662,787 followers
		Breaking Technology News And Opinions From TechCrunch	
#3		tonyrobbins	1,948,033 followers
		The Official Tony Robbins Account	
#4		iamdiddy	3,640,867 followers
		KING COMBS	
#5		GuyKawasaki	345,931 followers
		Firehose that answers the question: What's interesting? Co-founder of Al...	
#6	Zappos	zappos	1,813,647 followers
		deliveringhappinessbook.com www.zappos.com blogs.zappos.com twitter.zap...	
#7		Jason	111,184 followers
		Yeah	
#8		UncleRUSH	755,524 followers
		@sasha1176 Happiness is a direct result of making others Happy. U ju...	
#9		jasonfried	60,963 followers
		Founder of 37signals. Co-author of REWORK. Credo: It's simple until you...	

Figure 53 — Example from WeFollow

The top person in this list, aplusk, is celebrity Ashton Kutcher, famous for challenging CNN to a race to 1 million followers. If you go to his profile, you'll see a new addition to Twitter's features: the Verified Account.

Here's what Twitter says about this new feature, which is very handy for celebrities, and others who might get impersonated on Twitter:

---

[285] WeFollow: **bit.ly/9Pj888**

Any account with a Verified Badge is a Verified Account. Twitter uses this to establish authenticity of well known accounts so users can trust that a legitimate source is authoring their Tweets.

Twitter now only verifies accounts of celebrities, their advertisers, and other prominent people. At one time they did allow the rest of us to request verification but no longer.

The following table lists some of the more popular niche and general Twitter directories that you might want to consider adding your account to. These directories can be a powerful way to attract new followers.[286]

Table 7 — Twitter Directories

Directory	Description	URL
GovTwit	Specialized government directory listing state and local, federal, contractors, media, academics, non-profits and government outside of the U.S.	bit.ly/9CXJsJ
Listorious	Lists "Experts" on Twitter. Also lets you search for Twitter Lists.	bit.ly/9QLVoT
My Twitter Directory	Claims 9,582,621+ Twitter profiles and 1.2 billion+ followers. Create extended profile, list yourself in multiple categories. Requires you to allow it to connect to your Twitter account	bit.ly/cMLtOa
Tweet Social	Directory of Twitter applications, tools, mashups and resources.	bit.ly/9fapTO
TweetFind	Has a nice "Around Me" feature that lets you find tweeps in your geographic vicinity. Requires you to allow it to connect to your Twitter account.	bit.ly/bDYCu4
Twellow	Twitter "yellow pages." Add links to your other social media profiles, create an extended profile, and easily follow other Twitter users from Twellow. Requires you to allow it to connect to your Twitter account.	bit.ly/aC0Ca2

---

[286] Check out this great list of Twitter applications by Social Media Today: **bit.ly/rbbi5G**

Promote Yourself: Get Retweeted

We've mentioned retweeting before — it's a great way to increase your audience when other people send your tweet out to their followers. It's the best possible outcome of a tweet. It's a way to cast your net wider and gather in supporters, and it should be your goal on Twitter. As Web celeb Guy Kawasaki once put it, "You don't know who the best evangelist will be for your product or service." So you need to figure out how to get retweeted.

Twitter recently made it much easier for users to retweet. As we discussed earlier, to manually retweet, copy the message and insert RT and the sender's Twitter handle at the beginning. Due to a new Twitter feature, you now can retweet any post from the Twitter Website by mousing over it. When you mouse over a post, Twitter provides several possibilities below the message:

Figure 54 — How to Retweet Example

If you select Retweet, you see a message pop up (in what is known as a light box) similar to the following:

Figure 55 — Retweeting Example

If you select Retweet, Twitter will send the message, verbatim, without any commentary from you, to your followers. If you want to edit the message or add your own thoughts, stick to manually copying it to your status window and adding at the beginning the RT and user handle, or using the "via @whoever" convention to indicate you've edited or commented on the original tweet.

To get others to retweet you, start off by answering the right question — not the original Twitter question: "What are you doing?" or its current incarnation, "What's happening?" Instead, answer "What's interesting?"

Guy Kawasaki is the master of finding interesting things to tweet about (with the help of his staff). My favorite — one that I retweeted almost immediately for no other reason than that it was really interesting — was "Taiwanese scientists bred glow-in-the-dark pigs."[287] How can you resist?

So what interesting things should you tweet about? Try tweeting about Twitter. Twitter users love to read about:

- What some analyst thinks of Twitter
- How to use it better
- Lists of companies on Twitter
- Lists of CEOs on Twitter
- What's wrong with Twitter?

You can also break news:

- Follow the Twitter newsbot of CNN (@cnnbrk), retweet its tweets, and get retweeted
- Find news from niche topics related to your product category
- If in doubt, tweet it. Most tweets are noise, so yours has as good a chance as any of standing out

Personal branding guru Dan Schwabel produced this list[288] of the most retweetable words and phrases:

1.) You	8.) Free	15.) Follow
2.) Twitter	9.) Media	16.) How to
3.) Please	10.) Help	17.) Top
4.) Retweet	11.) Please Retweet	18.) Blog Post
5.) Post	12.) Great	19.) Check Out
6.) Blog	13.) Social Media	20.) New Blog Post
7.) Social	14.) 10	

While this list is probably accurate, we're not sure how it actually helps! According to Dan's list, the ultimate retweetable tweet could say "Would you please help retweet my great free new blog post about Top 10 Social Media People to Follow and Check Out?" Perhaps you should write that blog post, and include a link to it at the end of this sure-to-be-retweeted tweet?

---

[287] Glow-in-the-dark pigs! **bit.ly/d1anvL**

[288] Dan Schwabel's list: **bit.ly/aJ1dOO**

How to Reply

We briefly touched on replying via Twitter — start your tweet with @ and the user's handle. Twitter automatically fills this in for you if you use the Website.

We'd like you to think before you reply, because by default, Twitter doesn't include the content of the message you're replying to. You should always remember when replying that your reply will be a public tweet, but without any context, nobody else will have any idea what you're talking about, like this actual tweet: "@puppydog: Maybe in Montana!!! LOL." That may be OK with you, but if your entire twitter stream is comprised of incomprehensible non sequitur replies to your tweeps, who's going to want to follow you?

Be sensitive to others who may be reading your stream when replying, and if it really is nobody's business what you're saying, make the tweet a direct message (known as a DM) by placing a D as the first character. Be sure to use a D and not a DM. If DM is the first characters of a message, the message is a normal, public tweet.

Be Careful of Direct Messages

You are not likely to have a personal relationship with all of your followers. You may follow them back because they seem interesting, or because you'd like to get more followers. Thus you need to be careful about clicking on links from DMs. There have been many spam and phishing attempts via DM, so be aware that the URL in the tweet — especially a shortened URL — could go to a malware site.

If you're not quite sure what we were saying in the last paragraph, here are some definitions:

- **Spam** — delicious pork product
- **Phishing** — messages pretending to be from a trusted source that try to get your account info
- **Malware** — viruses, spyware, keystroke loggers — any type of program with a bad intent

Twitter will help you see where you'll be taken if you click on a shortened link. Simply mouse over the link and up will pop a little balloon with the full URL.

Twitter Do's

- **Go for the Numbers** — Unlike some other social media sites, Twitter really is all about the number of followers you have. Go for numbers. You need to have lots of followers. You never know who will find you that customer or partner.

- **Follow Your Followers** — Twitter etiquette is that you automatically follow everyone who follows you. Not all agree with this, and we're among them. We were once followed by some randy girls from Australia who wanted us to view their Webcam feed. Didn't follow back.

- **Follow Your Followers' Followers** — If you want to build your numbers, consider following people your followers follow.

- **Create a Follow Policy** — Do you follow everyone back, or only those who meet your criteria? Do you use the number of followers the person has as a determinant? Most importantly, would following this person reflect badly on you, due to the types of people they follow and the messages they tweet? Many people, for example, don't follow tweeps who follow more people than they are followed by.

- **Create Goals and Metrics** — Like all social media, you should have a goal for using Twitter, and a way to measure how you're doing against that goal. The goal could be number of followers, status of your followers, or the number of retweets you get. You can determine this latter by using services — such as Retweerank[289] — that show how many times you've been retweeted.

- **Be Interesting** — The most important Twitter Do is, of course, to make interesting tweets. We think perhaps we've stressed this enough.

- **Share the Love** — Promote other people many times for each tweet promoting you or your enterprise. As on other platforms, your Twitter followers will tune you out if all you talk about is yourself. Also, reply directly, and publicly, to other people (tweet begins with the user's handle — @somebody). It shows you're engaged in the community.

- **Create Lists** — Twitter allows you to create lists to which you can add your followers. It's easier for you to catch up with those in the list, plus, users are notified that they are part of your list, and are more likely to check you out because of this.

- **Keep it Shorter** — Limit your tweets to 120 characters to leave space for others to retweet you and add their comments.

---

[289] Retweetrank: **bit.ly/9A5l4k**

- **Monitor Twitter** — You should monitor what people are saying about you by searching periodically for your Twitter handle and organization name, by watching @ replies, and by setting up automated alerts.

- **Tweet at the Right Time** — It's not enough just to create fascinating tweets. You need to pick the right time to tweet. In general, the best time to tweet to reach the largest North American audience is between 1 and 2 pm Pacific time. That's when the most people are active on Twitter. If you want to reach an international audience, 9 am Pacific time hits several major break times in people's days: arriving at work on the West Coast, lunchtime on the East Coast, and the end of the business day in London. If these aren't convenient times for you, consider using a tweet scheduler like SocialOomph[290] or others.

- **Put a Share Button on Your Website** — Make it easy to for your site visitors to share what they find on your Website by adding a Share on Twitter button. There are a number of free services that you can easily add to your site to accomplish this. One we like is called AddThis.[291] If you are permitted to use persistent cookies (ask your Webmaster), AddThis can also give you sophisticated tracking metrics about your visitors.

Twitter Don'ts

- **Don't be Boring and Don't be Obnoxious** – 'Nuff said. However, what other people find to be boring and obnoxious will vary. Widely.

- **Don't be a Showoff** – See previous. Always posting about how great you or your organization is can turn people off.

- **Don't use Poor Grammar or Spelling** – Seems pretty obvious.

- **Don't Get too Personal** – There's a fine line here. Of course, we encourage you to Be a Person, but the minutia of your life is likely not that interesting to the majority of your followers. Be careful what you share.

- **Don't Forget that a Tweet is Forever** – and Google is your permanent record. Watch what you say.

- **Don't Monopolize a Conversation** – Just like IRL (In Real Life) those who talk all the time are tiresome and boring.

- **Don't Reply to Every Single Tweet You Receive** – This point is similar to the preceding. Over-replying will make you look needy, over-anxious, and as if you are a tweetbot.

---

[290] SocialOomph: **bit.ly/cnbUCz**

[291] AddThis: **bit.ly/9K30P4**

- **Don't Over-Tweet** – Don't tweet more than, say, ten times a day, or more than five times an hour. Try to find a balance between staying engaged and being obnoxious and spammy.

- **Don't Brag** – about how many people follow you; about your Twitter rankings; about your Twitter milestones (This is my 1,000[th] tweet!).

- **Don't Retweet without Giving Credit to the original Tweep** – that makes you a tweetcreep.

- **Don't ask "Please Retweet" on All or Even a Majority of your Posts** – Save this type of request only for important posts. It gets annoying otherwise.

- **Don't Ignore a Genuine Direct Message** – Many people have automated replies to those who follow them or for other purposes. It's OK to ignore or respond to these as you wish. But if someone sends you a pertinent DM, failing to acknowledge it can harm a budding relationship.

- **Don't Include Hashtags in Every Post** – This can be seen as a pathetic bid for attention. However, including hashtags can expand your followers, so be judicious.

- **Don't be a Twitter-Stalker** – While it can be perfectly appropriate to jump into the middle of a public conversation between two or more people on Twitter, jumping into the same person's conversation constantly can get more than a little creepy.

- **Don't Take an Unfollow Personally** – and don't report on your Unfollows; Don't announce who you're Unfollowing; Don't tweet your rules for following and Unfollowing; Don't threaten to Unfollow your followers. Nobody cares.

Twitter – There's an App for That

There are lots and lots of free sites that provide tools for using Twitter. Here's a very short list of useful Twitter applications that may interest you. There are many, many more out there. Just Google what you want to do with Twitter, and you'll find some.

- **Twitalyzer** — analysis of your Twitter habits
- **Future Tweets** — schedule your Twitter posts
- **Monitter** — Twitter filtering, live streaming
- **Tweetgrid** — Like Monitter
- **TweetBeep** — free Twitter alerts by email
- **Tweetizen** — filter the daily influx of tweets

Setting Up Facebook

> "Communities already exist.
> Instead, think about how you can help
> that community do what it wants to do."

Mark Zuckerberg, founder of Facebook

Talk to the average adult about Facebook and you're likely to hear it dismissed as a place for the kids. Yes, that was its beginning — as a way for college students to find out who was that cute guy or gal on the quad. But today the site is much, much more.

You may know the lore: In early 2004, Harvard sophomore Mark Zuckerberg started — or stole the idea for, as subsequent lawsuits by the Winklevii have alleged — Facebook in his dorm room. Like a lot of origin stories this one's not 100 percent true. And neither is the movie, *The Social Network*,[292] by the way.

In fact, what Zuckerberg originally created was called Facemash, and, rather than mimicking a traditional face book — a printed pamphlet with pictures and names of students — the site was basically a knockoff of the then-popular picture-rating site, Hot or Not.[293] Instead of asking visitors to rate the hotness of a single portrait, Facemash's innovation was displaying two pictures side by side, and asking users to rate the hotter person.

Actually, there was one more innovation: Zuckerberg got the pictures by hacking into Harvard's dorm ID photo database. Harvard shut down the wildly popular site within days, and, in a harbinger of things to come, charged Zuckerberg with violating students' privacy. The college threatened to expel Zuckerberg, but eventually dropped charges.

---

[292] The Social Network movie: **bit.ly/9fCwlA**

[293] Hot or Not: **bit.ly/bbLRH7**

After putting up another unrelated site later that semester,[294] Zuckerberg released thefacebook.com in February, 2004 as an online face book. The domain name used today — facebook.com — was not used until it was purchased for $200,000 from the Aboutface Corporation in May 2005.

Figure 56 — Thefacebook.com's 2004 Main Page[295]

Originally encompassing only Harvard, within three months, thefacebook's membership expanded to other colleges in the Boston area, the Ivy League, and, in 2005, to other colleges and universities and even high schools. During the early years, a potential member had to have an educational email address (one ending in .edu) to join the site, effectively keeping the old folks out. But many (like your humble correspondent) found a loophole — using an alumni email address — and it became popular for parents to log into the community to see what their kids were up to.

---

[294] This is a great story in its own right. Zuckerberg was behind in his studies due to his work on the Web. He needed to be able to discuss 500 images from the Augustan period for his art history final. Up against the deadline, Zuckerberg built a Website featuring the images and a place for comments. Then he invited his fellow class members to share their notes on the images, like a digital study group. Not only did he do well, Zuckerberg claims so did the rest of his classmates. This is not only a slick Tom Sawyer move, but a great example of the power of social media. This story and other great info about the start of Facebook can be found in a 2007 Fast Company article. **bit.ly/bEkRUn**

[295] See Facebook pages through the ages: **bit.ly/a3bd60**

So what's the real story here? That a smart college sophomore first rips off a popular photo site, then takes a standard college staple — the face book — digital, quits school, moves to Silicon Valley in mid-2005 with no car, no house, no job; lands $12.7 million in venture capital; a year later turns down a $1 billion offer from Yahoo; a year after that sells a 1.6 percent share to Microsoft for $240 million (valuing Facebook at $15 billion); and, in July 2010, his site surmounts the half-a-billion member mark, making it the largest social network by a very substantial margin.

It's enough to make your head spin.

When we started training on social media in 2008, we heard a common refrain from business people: Facebook is for kids. I don't think there's any need for us to be there.

Today, an Edison Research/Arbitron study[296] found that nearly a quarter of social network users indicated that Facebook is the social site that most influences their buying decisions. No other site or service was named by more than 1% of the sample, and 72% indicated that no one social site or service influenced their buying decisions the most.

What's so special about Facebook that has made it so popular? To attempt to answer the question, and simultaneously help you become familiar with Facebook features, here are some important milestones in the meteoric rise of the site.

- **2004** — Facebook releases the **Poke** feature with the note: "When we created the poke, we thought it would be cool to have a feature without any specific purpose." Poke allows users to basically nudge one another virtually, kind of like a punch in the shoulder. Facebook sends a notification that tells the user they have been poked and gives them the option to poke you back. That's about it, except that many people consider poking tantamount to flirting. In 2009, a woman was arrested for violating a protection order by poking another woman on Facebook.[297]

- **Fall 2004** — Facebook adds a feature which allows friends to write on a special section of one another's profiles called the **Wall**. It also adds the **Groups** feature, which allows members to create groups and invite members to join.

- **September 2005** — Facebook **opens membership** to high-schoolers — MySpace's primary audience. This may just have seemed a logical extension of the concept, but it proved to be a killer strategic move. With an easier-to-use (and easier on the eyes) interface, Facebook started to siphon off MySpace members who were tired of the garishness and apparent chaos of the site.

- **October 2005** — Facebook adds **photo sharing** of an unlimited number of photos and enables users to tag, or label users in a photo. MySpace only lets users upload 12 photos.

---

[296] Edison Research and Arbitron *The Social Habit II: Internet and Multimedia Study 2011*: **slidesha.re/oZ9JJB**

[297] ABC News' article *Tennessee Woman Arrested for Facebook 'Poke'*: **bit.ly/dcym1A**

- **April 2006** — Facebook debuts **mobile phone access**.

- **May 2006** — Facebook creates **private work networks**. Some forward-thinking corporations were looking for ways to increase collaboration and communication across their vast enterprises. Today there are more than 20,000 networks of employees, from the Central Intelligence Agency and the Internal Revenue Service to Macy's, McDonald's, Time Inc., and the U.S. Marine Corps. Even MySpace has a corporate network of 22 employees on Facebook.

- **August 2006** — Facebook **Notes**, a blogging feature that allows tags and embeddable images is launched. Users were later able to import blogs from Xanga, LiveJournal, Blogger, and other blogging services.

- **September 2006** — Facebook **opens registration to anyone** with a valid email address. This was a bold move and one which was met with mixed reaction from the membership of mostly young people. It wouldn't be the last time Facebook took a controversial unilateral action.

> Facebook has a tenth of the active members as rival MySpace.

- **September 2006** — Facebook creates the **News Feed** feature. This innovation is now a standard feature on other social networking sites such as LinkedIn, and is the central feature of Twitter: a scrolling list of the comments, statuses, actions, and other activity of your friends. Facebook added this feature without warning or input from the membership. This caused a great hue and cry as a violation of privacy, despite the fact that information in the News Feed could previously be accessed by friends.

  Angry members used the Group feature to create a group called Students Against Facebook News Feed (Official Petition to Facebook) that attracted nearly a million members. Of course, this served to cement the importance of Facebook among the protestors, and also widely publicized the News Feed feature itself.

  Zuckerberg posted an apology, saying "we did a bad job of explaining what the new features were and an even worse job of giving you control of them," and his staff worked around the clock for three days to add privacy features to News Feed. In May 2010, the company was granted a US patent on certain aspects of News Feed.

- **November 2006** — The **Share** feature, which allows members to post to their News Feeds from other Websites, launches on more than 20 partner sites.

- **February 2007** — Facebook launches **Gifts**, which allows users to send virtual gifts to their friends. Gifts costed a dollar each to purchase, and a personalized message could be attached to each gift. This feature was removed in August 2010.

- **April 2007** — Facebook debuts **Status**, which enables members to inform their friends of their whereabouts and actions by posting short status messages. Status has become a common feature of social networks ever since.

- **May 2007** — Facebook launches **Marketplace**, which lets users post free classified ads.

- **May 2007** — Facebook launches **Facebook Platform** including apps from 65 developer partners and more than 85 applications from developers such as Microsoft, Amazon, Red Bull, Washington Post, and Digg. Unlike MySpace, which inhibited third party app development, either by shutting them down or acquiring them, Facebook opens its core functions to all outside developers.

Facebook has 20 million users, is growing at a rate of 3 percent per week — adding 100,000 new users a day — and is the sixth-most-trafficked site in the US.
Facebook's photos app is the most popular photo site on the Internet.

- **September 2007** — Facebook **bans** breastfeeding pictures, causing an uproar among moms. The controversy rages for years.

- **October 2007** — **Microsoft takes a $240 million equity stake** in Facebook, valuing the company at $15 billion.

- **November 2007** — Serena Software adopts Facebook as their **intranet**.

- **November 2007** — Facebook launches **Facebook Ads**.

At year end, Facebook has more than 50 million active users.

- **January 2008** — Facebook begins offering multiple languages as it expands internationally. The site enlists members to install the **Translation** application, enabling them to translate words on Facebook from English to their native languages. Using a crowdsourcing technique (see footnote 92 on page 116 about the wisdom of crowds, and also **bit.ly/cpyFhG** for more information), Facebook invites other translators to vote on the quality of a particular translation by giving it a thumbs up or thumbs down.

- **February 2008** — Facebook encroaches more onto MySpace's turf by launched its **new music section** for bands, in partnership with iTunes. Just like MySpace, the new section lets bands offer streamed music, photos and music videos to fans as well as selling tickets and merchandise through a deal with the Music Today service.

- **April 2008** — Facebook **begins partnering with other social sites** to pull external data into profile pages, displaying a user's activity from places such as photo-sharing site Flickr and review site Yelp.

- **April 2008** — Facebook **Chat** released. Members can instant-message each other while on the site.

> Facebook ties MySpace in number of users worldwide at 115 million.

- **May, 2008** — Facebook **Connect** is announced and is generally available at year end. Members can use their Facebook identities on sites across the Web, including profile photos, photos, friends, groups, events, and other information. This comes after the site banned famous blogger Robert Scoble[298] after he imported his Facebook contact list to online address book site Plaxo. Connect eventually grows into the Open Graph initiative.

- **September 2008** — Facebook begins migrating all users to a **new version** of the site.

- **December 2008** — The Supreme Court of the Australian Capital Territory rules that Facebook is a valid way to **serve court notices** to defendants.[299] New Zealand quickly follows suit.

> Facebook is at 70 million US members, having more than tripled in size in a year.

- **June 2009** — Facebook introduces a **Usernames** feature, which enables members to create simpler URLs for their profiles such as **www.facebook.com/MichaelJEllsworth**. Some people pick funny or impenetrable usernames, such as:
- facebook.com/Bachelor
- facebook.com/marryme
- facebook.com/center.of.universe
- facebook.com/nerdy (our personal favorite)[300]

> Facebook officially edges ahead of MySpace at 70.278 million US members.
>
> Claims 250 million total active users.

---

[298] CNet's article *The Scoble scuffle: Facebook, Plaxo at odds over data portability*: **bit.ly/adhv5w**

[299] The Age's article *Kiwi judge follows Australian Facebook precedent*: **bit.ly/9grwix**

[300] Read more interesting usernames at: **bit.ly/bbJHEe**

- **August 2009** — Facebook acquires **FriendFeed**,[301] a site that aggregates members' posts from almost 60 social media services into a single news feed. At the same time, Facebook debuted **real-time search,** not only enabling members to search all of Facebook, but also search their own stream of friends, including photos, status updates and such over the last 30 days.

  Industry pundits view these moves as a direct threat to Twitter, the king of real-time social media.

- **August 2009** — Facebook debuts **HuffPost Social News**, a collaboration with the Huffington Post Website which enables users to create their own personalized social networking-like news page on the Huffington Post itself.

- **Late 2009** — After opening some member information up to search engines in 2007, Facebook changes privacy settings again so Facebook **public profiles can be indexed by search engines**. In July 2010, security consultant Ron Bowes copies the names and profile URLs of 171 million Facebook accounts from publicly-available information and uploads the data as a 2.8GB file, allowing anyone to download it.

- **April 2010** — Facebook replaces the Share on Facebook feature with a **Like** button, and renames its Fan pages, Like pages or just simply **Facebook Pages**. It also introduces a **Recommend** button. The buttons appear initially on sites such as NYTimes.com, IMDb, CNN.com, TIME.com, NHL.com, and ABC.com

- **April 2010** — Facebook introduces the **Activity Feed** plug-in. Website owners can embed a stream on their pages that displays personalized content from Facebook members when they like or share content on the site. If a member is logged into Facebook when they visit the third party site, the plug-in highlights content from their friends. If they're not logged in to Facebook, the activity feed shows recommendations from the third party site, and gives the user the option to log in to Facebook.

- **April 2010** — Facebook launches their **Graph API**.[302] This enables other sites to personalize a Facebook member's experience, as long as the member is logged in to Facebook. See the Pandora example in the *Connection* section on page 187 for more about how this works.

- **June 2010** — Facebook launches **Live Stream Box**, which enables any Website to embed a live, interactive box on their pages for members to connect, share, and post updates in real-time as they witness an event online. This puts Facebook in the center of online events, games, or any Website where masses of people view — and want to comment on — the same Webpage.

The common thread in Facebook's growth from 1 million users in 2004 to almost 750 million in mid-2011 is innovation. The 32 feature introductions and other notable events in this list demonstrate a commitment to improving the Facebook experience for its members. It also demonstrates

---

[301] FriendFeed: **bit.ly/bxxWip**

[302] Facebook on the Graph API: **bit.ly/9LTili**

a kind of cluelessness about how some features will affect their users as well as a general push to make more and more of members' data available to the public (more on this in a bit).

It's clear from the following table, however, that, while market leader MySpace languished, Facebook's innovation fueled staggering growth in numbers of users and revenue.

Table 8 — Facebook User and Revenue Growth

Date	Users (millions)	Revenue (millions)
2004	1	—
2005	5.5	—
2006	12	$52
2007	50	$150
August 26, 2008	100	$280
April 8, 2009	200	—
September 15, 2009	300	$800
February 5, 2010	400	—
July 21, 2010	500	$1,100
Mid-2011	750	$4,050

These are very impressive results, you'll have to agree. Facebook members must really love the site, right?

Wrong. And far from it. Facebook is one of the most-hated companies, ranking in the bottom five percent of private companies, and jostling for position with companies from traditional hated industries such as airlines and cable companies.[303] We can speculate as to why, and there are probably many reasons, but we think two major reasons are Facebook's tendency to make big changes without warning, without asking what their users want, and their steady erosion of their members' privacy, making more and more of members' information available to the public by default.

The difference between Facebook's default privacy settings from 2005, the year after the site debuted, and after their changes at the end of 2009 and into 2010 is remarkable. Whereas once almost everything was private by default, today almost everything is shared with the world by defaults, according to researcher Matt McKeon.[304]

Over the years, the only two personal details that have remained unexposed to the public Internet by default are your contact information and your birthday. Of course, Facebook enables you to change your privacy settings to prevent the sharing of this information, but doing so used to be quite difficult. Facebook has finally gathered all its various privacy controls in one place, but it

---

[303] MSN's article *Facebook hated as much as airlines, cable companies*: **bit.ly/9PChmc**

[304] McKeon's *The Evolution of Privacy on Facebook*: **bit.ly/cwpQNq**

Setting Up Facebook

still can be a bit of a chore to change them all.[305] Be sure you check out these links at the bottom of the page: *Applications and Websites* and *Controlling How You Share*. It's easy to overlook these, but they are very important.

Of course, if you are using Facebook for your enterprise, perhaps you're not too concerned about privacy. But if you have volunteers or other supports using Facebook on your behalf, and community members connecting with you on Facebook, it's good to know the facts. We cover setting your privacy settings in the *Control Your Privacy Settings* section on page 343.

Why Facebook?

As the world's largest social network, no matter what you used to think about Facebook, your enterprise needs to be there. When we did training on Facebook in mid-2009, many of our students still had the mentality that Facebook was a toy for kids, and many expressed the belief that they would never have any use for the social network.

That was then. This is now:[306]

- Facebook's largest advertisers spent 10 times as much on the site between August 2009 and 2010, and some increased spending by as much as 20-fold or more.[307]
- Facebook is sticky. Nielsen findings indicate members spend on average a whopping 6 hours on the site, by far the most time spent on a Website among the top 10 (Yahoo was a distant second at 2:11.)[308]
- Facebook was the number three video streaming site in June 2010 with more than 26 million unique viewers, trailing YouTube and Yahoo[309]
- Facebook's US user base grew from 42 million to 103 million in 2009 — that's 145 percent growth — and by 22 percent (22,474,900 users) in the first half of 2010
- Facebook's total number of users is on track to overtake China's population total within the next five years
- In April 2010, Facebook had more than 141 million unique monthly US visitors according to traffic measurement company comScore[310]
- Far from being just for kids, Facebook shows great demographic balance:
- While more than half of users are in the 18-34 age group, the 35+ demographic now represents more than 38 percent of the entire user base

---

[305] Facebook's privacy settings: **on.fb.me/bEyk8w**

[306] Stats courtesy of iStrategy Labs 1/2010: **bit.ly/dIB2lg** and 6/2010: **bit.ly/dIB2lg**

[307] Business Week: Facebook confirms huge traffic: **bit.ly/9nLHvY**

[308] Nielsen: June 2010: Top Online Sites and Brands in the U.S.: **bit.ly/9AFFTA**

[309] Nielsen: June 2010: More than 10B Videos Streamed in U.S.: **bit.ly/a2xoML**

[310] TechGenie: Facebook confirms huge traffic: **bit.ly/brmroG**

- The strongest growth segment, 55+, grew a whopping 922 percent in 2009 and 35 percent (3,443,460 users) in the first half of 2010
- Teenagers are just 10 percent of the membership

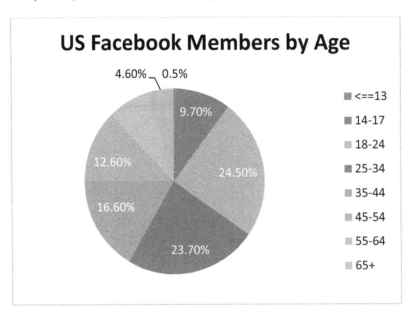

Figure 57 — Facebook Users by Age — June, 2011[311]

Despite topping the 500 million member mark worldwide and being on an exponential growth curve, in mid-2010 there were some signs of slowing US growth for Facebook:

- Facebook growth in the US stagnated in June 2010 — perhaps because of growing fallout from their privacy policies — adding only 320,800 in June after signing up 7.8 million members in May[312]
- Facebook may be running out of available non-members, having reached a 41.1 percent market penetration as of the end of June[313]
- The site actually lost users in the 18-25 and 35-44 age demographics
- Some popular Facebook games, such as the addictive Farmville, may be siphoning off users by establishing their own Websites[314]

Analysts noticed a similar trend in mid-2011, when Facebook gained 11.8 million and 13.9 million users April and May compared with monthly gains of at least 20 million new users over the previous 12 months. The United States lost nearly 6 million users, falling from 155.2 million at the

---

[311] CheckFacebook.com: bit.ly/IBSBBN

[312] Ibid.

[313] MediaBuyerPlanner U S Facebook Crowth Nearly Halts, Saturation or Privacy the Culprit **bit.ly/axDz0R**

[314] Cnet News: Blame privacy woes for stalled U.S. Facebook growth? **bit.ly/aWkI7w**

start of May to 149.4 million at the end of it. This is the first time the country has lost users in the past year, according to InsideFacebook.com.[315]

If we've succeeded in browbeating you into submission and you're ready to get serious about Facebook, the sections that follow will get you started.

Use Facebook Professionally

If you've read the other chapters on getting started with other sites, you'll know lots of the basics, and we're not going to repeat them here. If you're just skipping around, we suggest you read the LinkedIn sections on setting up your profile. Most of the same principles apply to other social networking sites. We'll just hit the differences in this chapter.

It's easy to sign up for Facebook. But you should do some planning first. For example, whose email address should you use to sign up? Facebook does allow you to associate more than one email address with an account, but you might want the first address you use to be a generic or group account, something like *facebook@myorg.com*. Be sure to add at least one more address in case you forget the password, and especially if you use someone's personal address and that person leaves your organization.

Another thing to plan is your name and your profile picture. Among Facebook's terms of service are provisions that state that:

1. You will not provide any false personal information on Facebook, or create an account for anyone other than yourself without permission.

2. You will not create more than one personal profile.

4. You will not use your personal profile for your own commercial gain (such as selling your status update to an advertiser).

7. You will keep your contact information accurate and up-to-date.

8. You will not share your password, (or in the case of developers, your secret key), let anyone else access your account, or do anything else that might jeopardize the security of your account.

---

[315] InsideFacebook.com article, *Facebook Sees Big Traffic Drops in US and Canada as It Nears 700 Million Users Worldwide*: bit.ly/lIRF7h

10. If you select a username for your account we reserve the right to remove or reclaim it if we believe appropriate (such as when a trademark owner complains about a username that does not closely relate to a user's actual name).

Based on these provisions, it's open to interpretation whether you are allowed create an organizational account, but hundreds of organizations do. Just be aware that Facebook changes their terms on an irregular basis, and you should check them from time to time.

Choose your business' logo or other appropriate picture for your organization's profile. If you decide to go with one or more personal accounts, be sure the picture is professional, only of the person, and clearly legible. In fact, you should ensure there are no embarrassing pictures anywhere on your account — this also goes for everyone involved with using Facebook on your behalf.

By the same token, you should only offer information in your profile that you want supporters, prospects, or others involved with your organization to see.

Keep your main Facebook page simple using minimal graphics and widgets. Avoid adding Facebook apps that are not consistent with your business purpose. That means no Farmville!

Post content relevant to your products, your business and its mission. This is no place for gossip or polemic. While your major presence is likely to be your Like page, your friends and fans will probably check out your home page as well, so keep it organized and to the point.

Friending on Facebook

After you've set up your profile, of course you'll need some friends. Friending on Facebook is a little different from other social networks in that you may not be able to see very much detail about the person you're trying to friend. On the other hand, due to the changes in default privacy settings we detailed in an earlier section, this problem may be less of an issue these days.

At any rate, this is a problem whether you are searching for friends to connect to, or evaluating friend requests from others, and it's especially difficult if you or your potential friend have a common name. The following figure shows the small amount of information you can see about members who are protecting their privacy.

Figure 58 — Limited Information Available for Potential Friends on Facebook

Based on this information, would you accept a friend request from Doug?

However, since you're using Facebook for your enterprise, you need to determine your policy for making or accepting friend requests. While it may seem like a good idea to accept all friend requests, remember that these friends have the ability to comment on your status or other activities on Facebook. If they are opposed to your company, are a troll, or otherwise disruptive, you may be forced to unfriend them, so you'll need a policy for that as well. Plus, you'll need to assign someone to monitor your stream and your Like page.

Another reason to choose your friends wisely is the fact that friends can see information about your other friends. Thus you could be the victim of guilt by association, especially if unsavory friends have completely public Facebook profiles, perhaps featuring equally unsavory pictures and comments. Add this to the fact that online customer relationship management software vendor Saleforce.com has a module called Faceconnector[316] that can look you up and see who your friends are, as well as their public information. Perhaps now it's clear why we made a big deal about privacy earlier in this chapter.

Finding Friends on Facebook

Like a lot of social networks, Facebook will allow you to upload your email contact lists and will use them to suggest contacts who are already on Facebook, and allow you to invite those who are not.

If you don't want to do this, Facebook does have a search function that lets you search for people to connect with. Of course, if the people you target have non-public profiles, and common names, this could lead to having to message several "Doug Smiths" to see which one is the one you know. Unlike LinkedIn, there is no penalty for spamming people with friend requests. The recipients can select Ignore if they aren't interested in connecting.

---

[316] Faceforce's Faceconnector demo: **bit.ly/boAZK7**

Your friends can also suggest friends and Facebook will often nudge you with messages in the right column of your main page, suggesting that you help a friend connect with more people.

Grouping Friends

Facebook has a feature that allows you to categorize your friends into groups you can create and name. You can then view a custom News Feed by group and also message all friends in a group.

Typically people may have, for example, a group for family, one for friends, and one for business connections. You can create a group from your Friends page, by selecting the Create a List Button.

To create the group from your Friends page, select the Create a List Button.

You see a form to give the group a name and to select existing friends to add to the group. The group will appear on the left taskbar of your Facebook home page under the Friends heading. Selecting it shows a custom New Feed of the group's activity.

Use Facebook Messaging to Build Relationships

Facebook messaging is a powerful way to build relationships with your Facebook friends. You can message up to 20 friends at a time, but you can also simultaneously message everyone in a Facebook group. This could be a good way for you to distribute your newsletter, for example.

Comment on News Feeds

Your News Feed is made up of activities of your friends. These activities range from simple status updates and picture postings to many other kinds of activities, such as connecting with others, posting on Walls, recommending a link, or requests from within the ubiquitous Facebook games, such as Farmville or Mafia Wars.

If you find a friend's stream is annoying, you can block all or certain kinds of their posts from your News Feed. To remove all your friend's posts, hover over any post and you'll see an X. Click the X, confirm the removal, and that person's feed will be removed. You can also remove messages generated by Facebook Apps by going to the bottom of your News Feed and selecting Edit Options. Here you can restore blocked friends and manage whether apps' feeds are displayed, as in the following figure.

Setting Up Facebook

Figure 59 — Block Messages from Facebook Apps

One way to build a relationship with a friend is to comment on their items in your News Feed. Often you'll find this will spawn a discussion involving friends of the friend, giving you more opportunities to connect to more people.

Change Your Status on Facebook

Like LinkedIn, Twitter, and other social networking sites, Facebook has a status feature. It's at the top of your News Feed and your Profile.

At the top of your News Feed is a box containing the question, "What's on your mind?" When you post in the box, your status appears in all your friends' News Feeds by default.

If you'd like to restrict who can see a post, click on the padlock at the bottom of the box. You'll see options similar to the following figure.

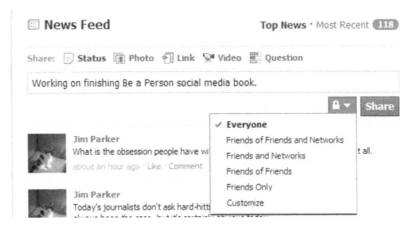

Figure 60 — Selecting Who Can See a Facebook Status Post

If you want even more control over who can and cannot see a status post, select Customize. You see a box similar to the following figure which allows greater control, including the ability to select certain people who can see the post and those to exclude.

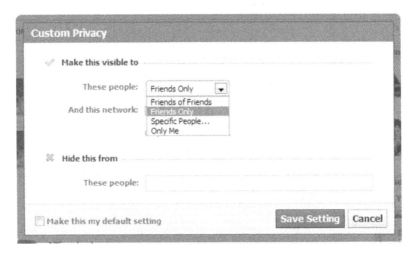

Figure 61 — Custom Settings for Status Updates on Facebook

Changing this setting only works for the current post unless you check the "Make this my default setting" box. If you want to change the setting permanently, you can also do so on your Privacy Settings page.

You can attach a variety of media and features to your status, including pictures, videos, Facebook events, and links.

You can post pithy, meaningful, or funny statuses. Just don't post boring ("Today is the 350th day of the year"), trivial ("Just got up. Looking for coffee"), or obnoxious ("Shots shots shots shots for everybody!!!!!) statuses. Look to post at least one status message a day. If you have trouble coming up with one, there are sites that can help you (you knew there would be).

One such site is FunnyStatus.com. Here are a few of their more interesting canned statuses:

- By the time a man realizes that his father was right, he has a son who thinks he's wrong.
- Leisure is the mother of philosophy.
- Thinking about opening a center for battered fish.
- My GPS says "Estimated Arrival Time." I see "Time to Beat."

If you Like their Facebook page so you can have suggestions when your status well runs dry,[317] or use their Funny Facebook Status Generator.[318]

You can also link your Twitter feed to your Facebook status. Be careful with this if you do a lot of replying on Twitter: People aren't likely to be too interested in "@somebody You're right" status updates. To link Twitter to your status, go to the Facebook Apps page and add the app.[319]

Posting on Walls

A Wall is a Facebook members' public notepad. You can post on your Wall, and friends can post on each others' walls. The posts will show up in both friends' News Feeds. With all the other ways people have to interact, actually posting on Walls seems to be becoming less popular.

Use Facebook Places

In August, 2010, Facebook introduced yet another innovation: a location-aware feature called Facebook Places. Focused primarily on the 150 million active members using Facebook on mobile devices,[320] it has three main features which allow members to:

- Share their current location with their friends
- See friends who are currently near them
- Discover new places around them

It is this last item that has advertisers and business owners salivating. For years the idea of location-based advertising has been tantalizingly close — we've been blogging about it for a dec-

---

[317] The Witty Hilarious and Ridiculously Funny Status Updates Facebook Page: **bit.ly/bqhD3V**

[318] Funny Facebook Status Generator: **bit.ly/cluFZq**

[319] Facebook Apps Page: **bit.ly/aNMIF6** – here are several Twitter-related apps: **bit.ly/aNMIF6**

[320] Facebook Press Room: **bit.ly/biGYNr**

ade.[321] If you're a retail establishment, the attraction of knowing when current or prospective customers are in your neighborhood is strong. You could reach out to them with coupons or other offers to attract them to your store.

Enterprises that hold offline events such as product demonstrations may also benefit from this type of information. Facebook Places offers a way for members who are attending such real-world events to notify their friends of their location and invite them to participate.

At this writing, Facebook Places can be accessed through Facebook's iPhone app or on the Web via **touch.facebook.com**.

Of course, for Facebook members with tons of friends, the addition of another datum to the News Feed may just serve to annoy those who really don't care where you are at the moment. Location-based social media pioneer Foursquare[322] solves this problem by asking its members to specifically subscribe to the location information of friends. It remains to be seen if Facebook takes this step rather than requiring users to opt-out of showing this information on a friend-by-friend basis.

Facebook Places Pages

Facebook also has added a new type of page: the Places page. Enterprises can claim their Places page, associate it with a location, and encourage members to check in from that location, for example when they attend an event.

Every real-world place that is created also creates a standard Facebook Page (often called a Like page; formerly called a Fan page).

When a Place is created it is not technically a page yet. Official representatives of the Place must claim the Page. Facebook says, "Verifying a Place claim requires uploading some kind of official document, such as a local business license or Better Business Bureau accreditation."[323]

More than 1.5 million business pages exist on Facebook, and each one can be merged with the corresponding Places page by claiming it. Facebook has not yet said whether they will be giving away stickers for owners to put on the door like the social media review site Yelp does.[324]

---

[321] StratVantage re: location-based services: **bit.ly/aTn0cw**

[322] Generally acknowledged as the leading location-based social media site, Foursquare has more than 3 million users. Find out more here: **bit.ly/aLqMzc**

[323] Mashable's article *A Field Guide to Using Facebook Places*: **bit.ly/bIG9Lt**

[324] More on Yelp for business: **bit.ly/bdYsZi**

So what can enterprises do with the location information on Facebook members? Currently the information is limited to read access, meaning enterprises can't respond to Facebook members based on their locations although they can ask for permission to see information about the places they are checking in to. But coming soon (and probably here by the time you read this) is the ability to programmatically create places or check people in to places — what's known as a "write API."

Overall, while it may seem that Places will primarily benefit retail businesses that can give coupons and other incentives for people to check in to their establishment — just like Foursquare — the feature really does have potential for enterprises as well — for example as a tool to support couponing and other promotions or as a way to boost participation in corporate responsibility efforts such as blood drives or roadside clean-ups.

But there may be a downside to Facebook Places, and it's kind of typical of Facebook's approach to members' data. It seems that you can tag people using Facebook Places without their consent or prior knowledge. The site does send a notification email when someone checks you in, but if you're out on the town, you're not necessarily following email.

We're sure Facebook considers this nothing more dangerous than tagging someone in a picture of a past gathering, which has been possible for years now. But it is different. You can tag Facebook members who are not actually at the location, and if that location were, for example, a topless bar, problems could definitely ensue. Or imagine you said you were washing your hair Saturday night, but a friend checked you in to the exclusive nightclub you went to instead. Someone could get upset.

Members could also make an event look larger than it actually is by tagging hundreds of absent friends. The possibilities for problems with this feature are endless. Once again, we expected that there will be a hue and cry about the new Facebook feature. And once again, we expected that Facebook will respond by enabling members to change an obscure privacy setting to protect themselves. There was a hue and cry, and Facebook does offer an obscure privacy setting to disable the feature.[325]

---

[325] Controlling who can check you in via Facebook Places: **on.fb.me/aVDSbY**

Top Things to Do on Facebook

Now that you've learned the basics of using Facebook, here are the top things you should do as soon as possible on Facebook and on your site:

- Add a Like Button to Your Website
- Add a Link to Your Business to Your Profile
- Create a Like Page for Your Business
- Invite Friends to Become Fans
- Publish News Worth Sharing
- Create a Group for Your Business

In the sections that follow, we show you why and how to accomplish these tasks.

Add a Like Button to Your Website

Adding a Like button — or the other social plug-ins offered by Facebook, such as Activity Feed and Recommendations — can dramatically boost the traffic to your existing Website.

The Like button gets the most press, and is perhaps the most used of Facebook's social plug-ins. In July, 2010, it was clicked 3 billion times a day, a rate three times greater than when it launched in April of that year. In July, 2011, Carolyn Everson, Vice President of Global Advertising Sales at Facebook, said 50 million Likes are clicked for brands every single day, compared with the one billion Likes that are clicked daily around the Web in general.[326]

The Like button functions a little like Tweetmeme's retweet button,[327] which enables a Twitter user to easily tweet the content of a blog or Website on Twitter. Although Tweetmeme's button has been around for more than a year longer than the Like button, in mid-2010 it was featured on only 200,000 sites and is clicked a mere 500 million times per day.[328]

To use the Like button, a Website embeds some code (interactive text) on its pages. You will probably need to get a techie to do this for you. Visitors who are Facebook members can click the button, which updates the user's News Feed saying they like the site. This often prompts the member's friends to visit the site, and click the Like button themselves. You can see how the use of this simple button can help a site go viral.

---

[326] SimplyZesty.com report on Techcrunch Disrupt conference: **bit.ly/pj4te0**

[327] Tweetmeme's retweet button: **bit.ly/blhpjW**

[328] SocialBeat's article *Facebook serves 3 billion Like buttons a day*: **bit.ly/cbBoki**

The Like button also provides a count of the number of people who currently "Like" something. For the Facebook member, using the Like button provides a list of friends who also Liked the site and includes their profile pictures.

Website owners can add tags to their pages to help Facebook categorize the link. For example, adding a "movie" tag would cause Facebook to add the Website to the member's list of favorite movies. You can see how this would be attractive to site owners.

Sites that implement Facebook's social graph features can indeed experience dramatic increased traffic, but there can be a downside for Facebook members who use the Like button: reduced privacy.

Without getting too technical, we'll try to explain the issue.

Whenever you go to a Website, that Website can deposit a little file on your computer called a cookie. This strangely named file is nowhere near as benign as its namesake delightful confection. While most cookies are used to help you use harmless or helpful Website features — such as remembering your choices from the last time you visited — they also can be used to track your movements and behavior on the Web. Many ad networks use cookies to assemble an anonymous profile of you, your likes and dislikes, and Web behavior.

That's obnoxious, and infringes your privacy, but is not necessarily dangerous. There are more nefarious uses of cookies that are beyond the scope of this book.

Facebook sets a cookie whenever you log in to Facebook, and if you select "Keep me logged in" when you enter Facebook, the system sets a permanent cookie. This offers you the convenience of never having to remember your Facebook ID and password. However, this seemingly-innocent convenience also enables Facebook to track you whenever you use the Like button on a third party site.

Once again, the explanation can get quite technical, so we'll simplify. When you use one of the Facebook social plug-ins when visiting a Website to, say, Like the site, that information shows up in your News Feed. If you happen to be logged in to Facebook at the time you use the Like button, it won't surprise you that Facebook knows who you are, what site you're on, and what you're doing, and that it can deposit your Like into your News Feed. But if you use the "Keep me logged in" feature, Facebook can track you even if you are not currently logged in to Facebook! Even if you don't click the Like button!

This means that, just because you're a Facebook member, the site can collect (and monitor) everything you do on all of the hundreds of thousands of Websites that have Facebook widgets. We're betting you didn't sign up for Facebook to have this done without your knowledge.

That may be creepy enough, but privacy and security advocates are concerned about other aspects of Facebook's social plug-ins: what Facebook does with the tracking information it assembles on you, and how bad guys can use the capabilities of the Like button to steal prestige from popular sites, and worse.

First, let's take a look at what Facebook does with your browsing and Liking behavior. At the very least, Facebook appears to use it to target advertising within Facebook. You may not have ever noticed the advertising on the site. It sits in the right column of your pages, and is personalized for you using the information you put in your profile — presenting come-ons based on age, school affiliations and such.

This information is gold for advertisers, which, naturally, are very important to Facebook. The site is thought to have earned $1.86 billion in global advertising in 2010, and that figure is projected to grow to $2.2 billion in 2011,[329] so targeting is crucial to Facebook. The Like button ropes in thousands of other sites to help feed this information mill that spins gold for Facebook.

OK, you say, not so bad. Facebook makes it so I only see ads that pertain to me. What's the harm?

Well the owners of those Websites that host Facebook social plug-ins can visit Facebook and register to see the number of Likes on their site and view the profile information of who has visited. Remember, in some situations, you don't have to even click the Like button to get tracked by Facebook. Just merely visiting — even by mistake — gets you tracked.

Feeling a bit more creeped out yet?

It gets worse. On the Internet, every innovation eventually provides new ways for the bad guys to do bad things. The Like button has made possible "viral clickjacking" worms that trick users into liking and sharing an unrelated page.

Instead of actually liking a page on Facebook, unsuspecting users are taken to a third-party Website where they are told to click something in order to see a shocking video or picture. They are unaware that by clicking they are actually Liking an unknown, possibly nasty, third-party page, possibly ruining their reputation on Facebook.[330]

Another technique called "Like switching" involves using the Like button from another site with a prestigious Like count that lists familiar friends. When a user goes to click on the Like button, behind the scenes, the button is swapped out for a different one, potentially causing you to Like, for example, a porn site. Would that get your friends talking?

---

[329] Reuters report via Huffington Post: **huff.to/qwU9Vs**

[330] Graham Cluely's blog post *Viral clickjacking 'Like' worm hits Facebook users*: **bit.ly/bnStls**

There are other examples, but we think you get the idea. The Like button and the other Facebook social plug-ins represent a powerful way to get more attention for your site. But there are downsides, and you should remain alert for potential misuses if you want to take advantage of these features for your Website.

How to Add a Like Button

OK, assuming we haven't frightened you off the Like button, here's how to add one to your site.

First off, review Facebook's Terms of Service (TOS) pertaining to the use of their social plug-ins. Here's the relevant portion of the current TOS:

> **Special Provisions Applicable to Share Links**
>
> If you include our Share Link button on your Website, the following additional terms apply to you:
>
> 1. We give you permission to use Facebook's Share Link button so that users can post links or content from your Website on Facebook.
> 2. You give us permission to use and allow others to use such links and content on Facebook.
> 3. You will not place a Share Link button on any page containing content that would violate this Statement if posted on Facebook.

The third point refers to Facebook's restrictions on nudity and other lewd content. We're assuming you're in no danger of running afoul of these policies.

Next, you need to create the programming code you want to add to your pages, known as an i-frame. If this sentence just made you want to skip the whole thing, you'll need to corral a techie to help you. We'll help a bit by explaining what we just said.

An i-frame is like combining two Websites in one browser view. Your main Website appears just as it usually does, but the i-frame is like a window into another Website, showing you what that Website is displaying. In the olden days, you actually saw a dividing line that showed where one site began and the other ended. There are a variety of problems, some of them security-related, in using i-frames, so talk to your techies before proceeding.

Add a Facebook Like Button Using an I-frame

In general, using an i-frame is simple, and lots of sites do it. Here's the code you add to the page to get the button to work:

```
<iframe src="Some Facebook URL" scrolling="no" frameborder="0" allowTransparen-
cy="true" style="border:none; overflow:hidden; width:450px; height:200px">
```

You substitute an URL you get from Facebook for "Some Facebook URL" and change the width and height parameters to specify in pixels how wide and tall you want the button, and you're done. Facebook's developer's page has a configurator[331] to help you generate the code (see the following figure.) Press the Get Code button, copy it into the source of your Webpage and you're done.

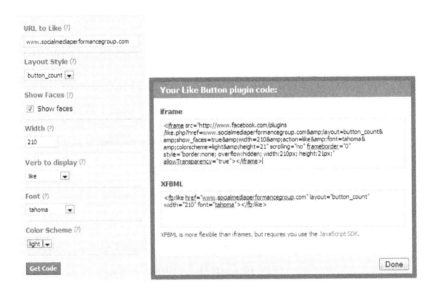

Figure 62 — Facebook Like Button Configurator and Resulting Code

The ease of adding the i-frame version of the Like button is a good reason why lots of sites prefer it. A quick look at using the JavaScript version will demonstrate why.

There are other social plug-ins such as the Like Box, so if you're interested, and have access to a willing techie, you can take a look at the Facebook for Websites manual.[332]

---

[331] Facebook develop's configurator: **bit.ly/bzw78P**

[332] Facebook for Websites manual: **bit.ly/b2uYU3**

Create a Facebook Page for Your Business

The Facebook Page has gone through a bit of evolution over the years. Formerly called a Fan Page, in early 2010, Facebook reimagined it as the Facebook Page or Like Page, and with the release of Facebook Places, added a new dimension: location.

Regardless of the name or features, you should create a Facebook Page for your enterprise. It's easy to do and it's a great way to provide a central location for your community to gather and comment on your organization.

Get started by going to facebook.com/pages.[333]

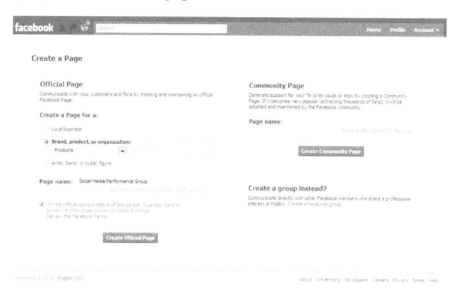

Figure 63 — Creating a Facebook Page for Your Enterprise

Decide whether you want to create an Official Page for a local business, an organization, or a public figure, or a Community Page that might eventually be maintained by your community. You can also create a Facebook group, which allows you to assemble a group of supporters that you can message easily.

Let's say you select organization. Select the category and give the page a name. Make sure the name is unique and memorable, check the box that you're the official representative, and select Create Official Page. You'll see a page template like the following figure.

---

[333] Facebook Pages: **bit.ly/b0ZBaN**

Figure 64 — Facebook Page Creation — Example

Here you can add an image, provide information about your business, and configure other parts of your page. Note the box at the top of the page, which encourages you to create a widget — a bit of interactive code you can incorporate into your main Webpage — to promote your Facebook Page. See our discussion of the Like button, above. Once you have 25 people who Like your page, you can create a user name for the page. This means you can promote it using a simpler URL, for example, **facebook.com/SMPG** rather than **facebook.com/pages/Social-Media-Performance-Group/125722167476231**.

There's a variety of other things you can set up, and we're not going to walk through all of them here, but they include setting up your mobile phone so you can post updates to the page, creating a description of your business and your mission, hooking status updates from your page to your Twitter account, and uploading photos.

Use Facebook's Event Feature

Facebook has a free Event feature that enables you to promote online and offline events to your friends and followers. Not only can you list the event, but you can use Facebook messaging to notify your friends and others who sign up to attend about interesting event features or other information. Since young people think email is for old people, this may be the best way to notify younger supporters about your events.

Use Facebook Notes

Many Facebook members don't know about notes. There's a note that appears on the left column of your main page, and then there is a Notes tab in your Profile view. Writing a note is very much like writing a short blog post, with the exception that you can tag your friends. When you do that, the first part of your note shows up in your friends' News Feeds. In addition, tagged friends are more likely to view your page and profile. Thus, writing a Note is a great way to stay in front of your community. Establish a regular schedule of posting notes to let everybody know what your business is up to.

Periodically a question posed through Notes goes viral, like the 25 Random Things About Me[334] question that garnered more than 5 million lists in a single week not long after it debuted in early 2009.[335] A current search via Google shows 178,000 current 25 Random Things lists on Facebook.[336] Even organizations such as the National Museum of Natural History got into the act.[337]

The craze inspired an offline game that actually sounds lamer than the original idea: "During Game play, you'll try to match fun facts on the game cards with your opponents. Make a match and then add a new, totally random thing about yourself to your list. The first person to complete a list of 25 random things about them wins. It's great fun to compare lists at the end of the game."[338] We'll just bet.

On Facebook your aim is to create a Note that fires the imagination of your community. To help it go viral, be sure to encourage or even require participants to tag their friends.

---

[334] 25 Random Things About Me: **bit.ly/cHmSEt**

[335] According to ABC News and others: **bit.ly/d6j0gg**

[336] Here's the Google search: **bit.ly/bMuKms**

[337] National Museum of Natural History blog: **bit.ly/8YpAEv**

[338] Winning Moves' 25 Random Things About Me game: **amzn.to/9i2Szp**

Control Your Privacy Settings

Changing your privacy defaults can be challenging. Some members report that not only is the process confusing, sometimes changes they make don't stick, and they end up over-sharing.

In the section *Change Your Status on Facebook* on page 330 we showed you how to control the visibility of your status posts. But there are many more privacy settings you can use to change the default settings, which in most cases are to share with everyone, including non-members.

The first step in setting your privacy settings is to go to the Account link at the top right of any Facebook page. In the dropdown, select Privacy Settings. You see something similar to the next figure.

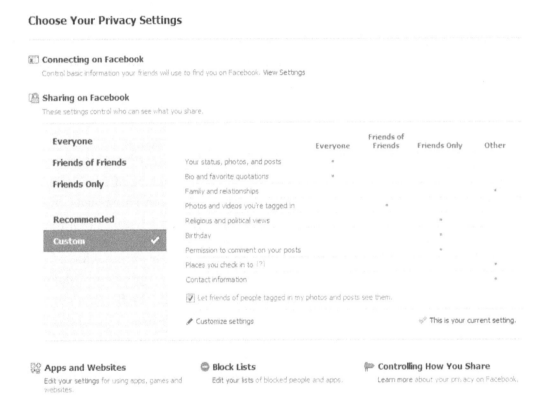

Figure 65 — Facebook Privacy Settings Form

As you can see, there are a number of settings for you to take a look at. Click Customize settings to see further options. The form looks like the following figure.

Figure 66 — Basic Facebook Privacy Settings Form

This page has lots of settings and you should go through each one and determine how you want to set it. For example, you may want to determine who can see things like your religious and political views and your birthday. [339] Note also a very important new setting: "Places I check into." You'll probably want to make sure that's set to show only to friends and you'll want to consider how to set the "Include me in "People Here Now" after I check in" setting. Depending on the "Places I check into" setting, this setting could enable strangers to know you're at a particular place. On this page you can also determine the privacy of photo albums you may have.

Under "Things others share" you'll want to look at the setting for "Friends can check me in to Places." We recommend disabling this setting for the reasons we discuss in the *Use Facebook Places* section on page 332.

Other settings on the Custom page enable you to control what friends of friends can see, and how you share your contact information.

Return to the Privacy Setting main page by clicking the Back to Privacy button. Next you'll want to examine your Applications and Websites settings, toward the bottom of the page. This area controls what personal information applications can see and how they can share it. It's also the place where you can delete apps you don't want anymore.

---

[339] Facebook privacy setting explanations: **on.fb.me/7VrDfW**

Of particular interest is the "Info accessible through your friends" setting. Clicking it produces a form similar to the following figure.

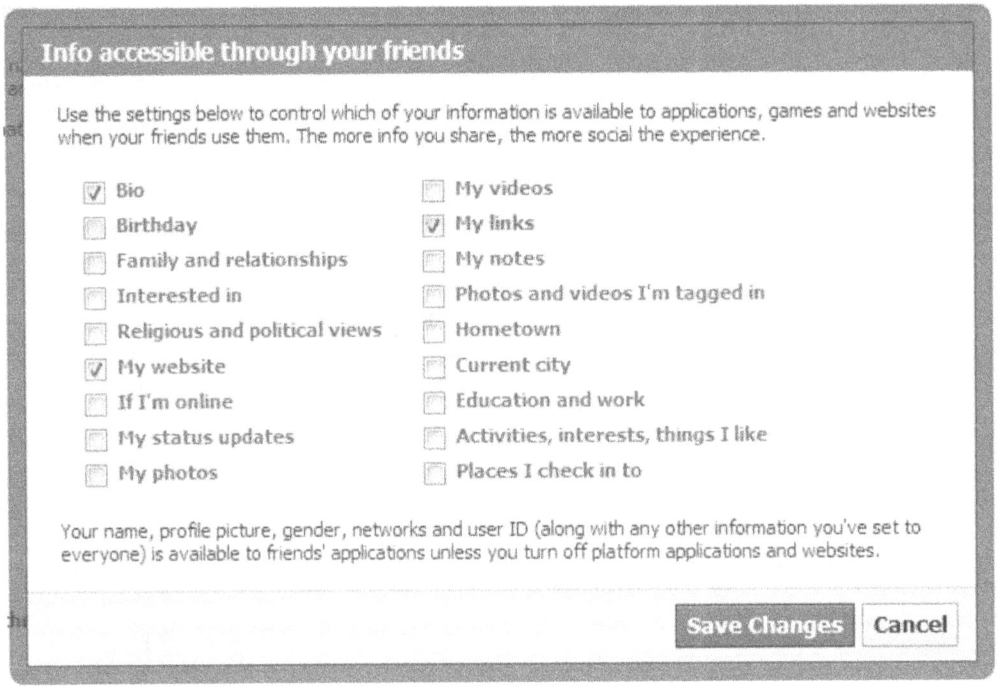

Info accessible through your friends

Use the settings below to control which of your information is available to applications, games and websites when your friends use them. The more info you share, the more social the experience.

- ☑ Bio
- ☐ Birthday
- ☐ Family and relationships
- ☐ Interested in
- ☐ Religious and political views
- ☑ My website
- ☐ If I'm online
- ☐ My status updates
- ☐ My photos

- ☐ My videos
- ☑ My links
- ☐ My notes
- ☐ Photos and videos I'm tagged in
- ☐ Hometown
- ☐ Current city
- ☐ Education and work
- ☐ Activities, interests, things I like
- ☐ Places I check in to

Your name, profile picture, gender, networks and user ID (along with any other information you've set to everyone) is available to friends' applications unless you turn off platform applications and websites.

Save Changes   Cancel

Figure 67 — Info Accessible Through Your Friends Facebook Apps Setting

Did you imagine that by inviting a friend to use a Facebook app that all this information about the friend would be available to the app creator? We recommend restricting this information, even though doing so may affect your ability to use an app.

Return to the Privacy Setting main page by clicking the Back to Privacy button. Next to the Applications and Websites setting is a setting that allows you to block friends and prevent apps from sending you messages should you wish to. There are a few very helpful YouTube videos that can help you better understand Facebook privacy settings, including ones by ConnectSafely[340] and Dummies.com,[341] producers of the "Whatever for Dummies" books.

---

[340] This 10-minute video is a very good overview: **bit.ly/9P88wj** and this video is a little more up-to-date: **bit.ly/mrjsq3**

[341] A good, 4-minute overview of Facebook privacy settings: **bit.ly/cAnqQs**

Join Facebook Groups

Facebook Groups are a great way to meet your community members. You can search for groups to join or create your own. You are limited to joining or creating up to 200 groups, a much higher limit than, say, LinkedIn, which limits you to 50 group memberships. The Groups application page displays updates from your groups as well as groups your friends have joined recently.

You can join or create a group by clicking on the Groups or Create Group links on the left bar of your main Facebook page. You might need to click More in order to see the links. If you've joined any groups, the icons, names, and number of members will be listed there, as in the next figure.

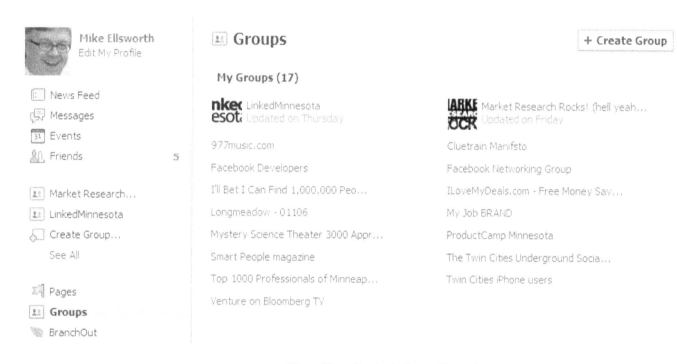

Figure 68 — Facebook Groups Example

You can also see and easily join the Groups your friends belong to by clicking Friends' Groups. Enter pretty much any term you're interested in finding Groups for into the search bar and you'll probably find one or more interesting groups. You can check out the Group and see publicly viewable information before deciding to join.

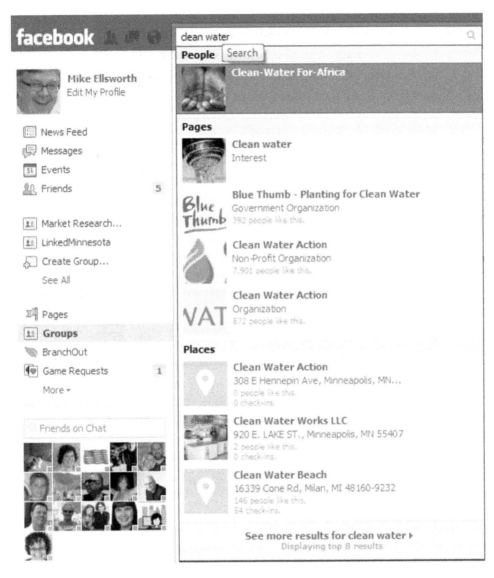

Figure 69 — Search for Facebook Groups

Click the Create A Group button to create your own group. You'll see a form like the following figure.

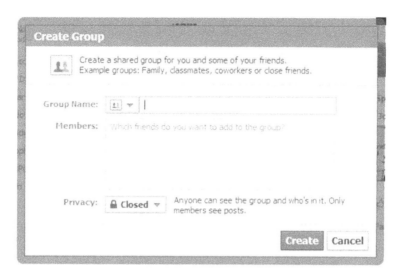

Figure 70 — Create Your Own Facebook Group

Make sure your group's name and description contain keywords your community is likely to use in a search. After you've created your group, invite all your friends to join. You can even create a Like button to post on your Website that will promote the group.

Of course, if you create a group, you need to be the host — or, as we discuss in the *Building Your Community* section on page 393, the experience architect. This means it's up to you to invite your guests, make them feel at home, and get them talking.

Try a Facebook Ad

Facebook offers surprisingly affordable and very targetable advertisings. It's pretty easy to get started, and you can set a daily campaign budget. Just select the Advertising link at the bottom of any page, select Create an Ad, and fill in the form. You'll want to spend some time thinking of the ad title, since this will be one of the main elements that will attract members to click on your ad. You get 135 characters for the body of the ad, less than the limit for a tweet, so make it work for you. Get right to the point; your objective is to get a click.

You also must provide a small image for the ad. You'll want to think about this as well. Come up with something meaningful that makes the member want to click. Don't just go with your enterprise's logo.

Clicking on the ad will send the member to a Website you designate. Avoid the temptation to simply direct people to the main page of your Website. It's far better to create a special page on your site, a microsite, or a special video in your YouTube channel, to receive those who click. This page should acknowledge the visitor, possibly by mentioning where they came from, and it should also get right to the point. You only have seconds to convince the visitor not to leave. Be sure the page has a call to action.

The next section of the Advertising page enables you to target your ad to a specific subset of Facebook members (unless you've got tons of money, you'll definitely want to do this.) You can show the ad by location, age, gender, relationship status, languages spoken, interests, education and work, and even by connections to one of your pages, events, groups, or applications.

For example, you could target an ad to unmarried members from New York who are in college, speak Spanish, and who are interested in clean water. As you can see from the next figure, that's a pretty small bunch of folks.

Figure 71 — Example of a Targeted Facebook Ad Campagin

The final section enables you to name your ad campaign, set a daily budget, and select either a continuously running ad, or one that runs only on certain dates and times.

The last bit on the page is perhaps the most important, and it's easy to miss. Facebook suggests a minimum bid per click, generally under $1. This is the ceiling you will pay when someone clicks on your ad.

Don't just accept this default!

Instead, click "Set a Different Bid (Advanced Mode)" and examine the suggested range that Facebook provides. You can set the per click price to as little as one cent, but we don't recommend this, even if you like to pinch pennies. The reason is that the advertising space on Facebook is quite limited, so your ad is competing with other ads to be shown. Facebook doesn't say how they determine which ads are shown, but it probably involves the amount the advertiser will pay-per-click and the percentage of ads that get clicked on. If your bid is too low, you won't get many impressions — showings of the ad. And if your ad doesn't get shown, nobody can click on it.

On the other hand, the amount per click that Facebook suggests may be higher than is necessary to give you good response. You'll want to experiment with the amount to determine what is best for your ad.

You'll notice that Facebook gives you an estimate of how many clicks per day you're likely to get for your ad. It's a rough guide you can use to set up your daily budget, but don't depend entirely on their number.

Facebook also offers to let you pay for impressions instead of paying for clicks.

Don't ever pay for impressions in any Web advertising unless you really know what you're doing!

An impression means someone saw your ad. One of the reasons you might ever be interested in this is if you're doing a branding-oriented campaign just to get your name out there. And even then it's generally only a good idea if the cost per thousand impressions (CPM) is very small.

To compare the two major options, we recently created an ad. Facebook recommended paying 93 cents per click and estimated we'd get 54 clicks per day. We changed the campaign to pay-per-impression and Facebook recommended paying 40 cents per thousand impressions with an estimated 125,000 impressions per day. Doing the quick math indicates that for the pay-per-click campaign — which delivers 54 members to our Webpage — we'd pay $50.22 a day. For the pay-per-impression campaign we'd pay $50 per day, which doesn't seem too bad. The problem is we have no idea how many clicks we'll get from such a campaign. The campaign might result in the same number, fewer, or many more visitors to our Webpage, but we pay the same even if it only delivers a single visitor to our Webpage.

Because you can't be certain of the return from a pay-per-impression campaign, we recommend staying with the pay-per-click model, at least until you've figured out how Facebook members are responding to your ads. You might also want to go with pay-per-impression after your pay-per-click campaign response has started to decline. This could mean that you've gotten the most-likely people to click and, since they're not going to click twice, it may be more difficult to reach the rest of the audience. At that point, putting your ad in front of more people with a pay-per-impression campaign might make sense.

Whatever kind of ad campaign you select, be sure to read Facebook's advertising help pages before embarking on your first campaign.[342] To maximize your ad spend, you should also consider

---

[342] Facebook help: **bit.ly/9ifotk**

doing split testing, a technique in which you test two or more variations of an ad and measure the results. There's more on split testing in the *Optimizing for Google* section on page 369. Allfacebook.com has a very good post about Facebook advertising that you also should check out.[343]

[343] AllFacebook's article *10 Facebook Advertising Tips For Brilliant Marketers*: **bit.ly/c0cACF**

Setting Up YouTube

"What happens in Vegas stays on YouTube"

Erik Qualman, SocialNomics

"We're still in the process of picking ourselves up off the floor after witnessing firsthand the fact that a 16-year-old YouTuber can deliver us 3 times the traffic in a couple of days that some excellent traditional media coverage has over 5 months."

Michael Fox, founder of Shoes of Prey

YouTube has gotten so big, and is so multifaceted, we had to include two quotes about it to begin this chapter. It's hard to believe that a social computing site that is barely six years old has grown to have such influence in the online and offline worlds.

When Yakov Lapitsky uploaded the first video on YouTube, at 8:27PM on Saturday April 23rd, 2005, he hardly expected he was making history. The 19-second video shows YouTube co-founder Jawed Karim in front of the elephants at the San Diego Zoo. It has had 2,827,204 views as of this writing. And it's really . . . boring. Nothing special. And 2.8 million people have watched it. Big deal, you might say, that's the same as the number of people who watch the USA Network on TV every day (how did you know that?)

Consider, though, that the viewership of oldest video on YouTube represents but the merest fraction of the 15 billion views YouTube garnered in the month of May, 2010. More than 178 million

Americans (**83.5 percent of the Internet population**) watched a video online in April, 2010 and YouTube accounted for 76.7 percent of all unique viewers and 43.2 percent of all videos.[344]

Now surely your business has a much more interesting story to tell than Yakov, who spends most of his 19 seconds of fame talking about elephant trunks. Clearly what you do is more significant than some guy's visit to a zoo. Definitely worthy of a video.

You may think you lack the technical expertise to create a professional-looking video, and you may be right.

But that doesn't matter. Not even a little bit.

The YouTube phenomenon has been built on poorly-produced, shaky camera, fuzzy-but-sincere videos. It almost is better to not be too slick — people tend to equate homemade videos with honesty and authenticity. Forget the lights and special effects and perfectly coiffed actors. Turn your mobile phone camera on some real people talking about your products, and you may be even more effective than slick, Hollywood-quality productions.

One of our clients paid big bucks to have an ad agency make a series of client testimonial videos. These productions had multiple camera views, tracking shots, graphics that zoomed in and out, and the clients were well-spoken and convincing.

They posted them on YouTube and promoted them on their blog. The result: Over six months the 12 videos in aggregate had fewer than 1,200 views. One video has three views, and two of them were from us. The company probably dropped $120,000 on the package, yielding an outlay of $100 per view. You'd do better handing out C-notes on street corners.

On the other hand, take the case of Shoes of Prey, mentioned in the second quote that opened this chapter. This Australian startup company makes custom — also called bespoke — shoes, and a 16-year-old enthusiast (one might call her an evangelist) known online as Juicystar07 and offline as Blair Fowler created a nine-minute video[345] extolling the virtues of being able to design your own shoes. Blair is quite the businesswoman, and she's very much at home in front of a camera. She hosts giveaways and Shoes of Prey paid her to pitch their shoes. Her site is an example of a teen-girl phenomenon called a "haul" site, where girls post their latest beauty or fashion acquisitions for discussion.

The result of Blair's video about Shoes of Prey was more than 450,000 views and more than 90,000

---

[344] ReelSEO's article *13 Billion Videos On YouTube For 135.7 Million Viewers In April*: **bit.ly/0Yrlib**

[345] See Fowler's video: **bit.ly/cXRrlR**

comments on the company's site, making it the fifth-most-viewed video on YouTube worldwide when it debuted.

Small problem, though: The shoes are probably out of the price range of Blair's followers. But they'll grow up someday, and they have older sisters and mothers they can influence.

OK, so they got a big bump in brand awareness among people who probably are not going to become customers in the short term. Shoes of Prey could have left it at that, but they didn't. Take a look at how they took an integrated approach to this promotion:

- They created a strategy to reach their target market — the older friends, older sisters and mothers of Blair's 13- to 17-year-old audience — by encouraging the younger girls' online discussions, and by requiring the girls to comment on Blair's site about their shoe designing experience

- They changed their Website to make it easier for the girls to share the shoes they'd designed on Facebook and Twitter

- They ran searches on Twitter to find every conversation about their brand (see the *Measure Results* section on page 147), and engaged with the people who were talking about them

- They blogged about their experience

- They tweeted about their blog post, with the goal of getting the mainstream media to pick up the story (they did)

- They got retweeted by social media star Robert Scoble,[346] and more than a hundred others, resulting in coverage by lots of media outlets, including the Wall Street Journal blog

In other words, Shoes of Prey followed many of the recommendations you've read about in this book and they achieved a tremendous result: what the company calls "a permanent 300% uplift in sales."[347]

One very important thing about Blair and her community: Although she is paid to review and promote products, she is very upfront with her fans about this. She has established a relationship of trust with them. They know she's picky about what she promotes, and does not accept all offers. They know that when she's enthusiastic about a product, it's because she likes it.

Because she is dealing with her community with integrity, she can get away with making enough money from her venture to necessitate retaining an agent.

---

[346] Robert Scoble's blog: **bit.ly/9NMNyh**

[347] Michael's blog post *How we tripled our sales using YouTube*: **bit.ly/d2qKVz**

Blair's able to do this because of the way she portrays herself in her videos. In the Shoes of Prey video, she suddenly stops her pitch and mentions her bandaged finger. She's lost a nail, and she's pretty bummed about it. But she felt she should explain and share her experience with her fans. This is pure gold. She's **Being a Person**!

The lesson for businesses is not that you can succeed on YouTube if you're a telegenic 16-year-old girl with a perky personality. It is that you can succeed on YouTube if you are authentic, trustworthy, and honest.

Becoming Popular on YouTube

Here's a ranking of the most popular YouTube videos of all time, as of mid-2011:

- Justin Bieber — Baby ft. Ludacris[348] with 561,868,046
- Lady Gaga Bad Romance[349] with 386,769,838 views
- Shakira - Waka Waka(This Time for Africa)[350] with 351,928,810
- Eminem - Love The Way You Lie ft. Rihanna[351] with 344,964,046
- Charlie bit my finger[352] with 335,752,852
- Justin Bieber - One Time[353] with 247,027,414

A quick review of these videos shows they have one thing in common: pop singers. Five of the six are music videos from hot pop singers. OK, that's understandable. Lady Gaga is a great visual artist. Justin Bieber is a tween idols. Number four is a music video by Eminem featuring Rihanna, both hot pop stars. So you can understand, given the marketing hype behind these artists, why they are popular, although the relatively low popularity of Pitbull makes him an outlier.

The #5 video shows a toddler biting his brother's finger. Huh? It's cute, we suppose, but no cuter than the millions of cute kitten, dog, and baby videos on YouTube. Its journey to hundreds of millions of views was chronicled by Slate back in 2009:[354]

> In May 2007, the father of two British tykes uploaded a home video he wanted to share with the kids' godfather in Colorado and a few American colleagues. After three months,

---

[348] Bieber: **bit.ly/d4EsIX**

[349] Lada Gaga: **bit.ly/90FuWJ**

[350] Shakira: **bit.ly/p2fwbZ**

[351] Eminem: **bit.ly/rnPmsp**

[352] Charlie the biter: **bit.ly/duIbfw**

[353] Bieber, again: **bit.ly/q0xtMZ**

[354] Charlie's journey: **bit.ly/96APJb**

Setting Up YouTube

only a few dozen people had seen the video, and he considered taking it off the site. Then, something strange happened: On Aug. 24, 2007, the video was viewed 25 times in California. Three days later, that number was up to 79, with a dozen more coming in from Washington, Texas, and Wisconsin. The number of daily views doubled roughly every week as "Charlie Bit Me" spread around the country and through Europe. On Nov. 5, a couple of guys in Canada filmed a frame-by-frame remake[355] [currently with more than 6 million views of its own]. Two weeks later, CollegeHumor.com linked to the video,[356] and by January it was on *The Ellen DeGeneres Show*.

While this phenomenon is interesting, it's hard to derive any practical principals of viralocity from it. Clearly, however, it shows the power of word of mouth, so try to make your videos so memorable people tell each other about them.

What all these videos really have in common is: They're entertaining.

This is a key element to ensure that your YouTube videos are seen: You must do your best to make your video entertaining. This may be difficult or impossible, depending on the problem you solve (think embarrassing personal hygiene products, for example), but if you want to reach a wide audience, it's a goal to strive for. That said, you may already know a lot about how to reach your target audience, and appealing to their emotions, empathy, or eliciting a gut reaction may work in other venues. If so, be sure you apply these techniques to your YouTube videos as well.

Create Your YouTube Channel

The first thing you should do — really, right now; put the book down at the end of this sentence and do it using the instructions that follow — is reserve an URL for your YouTube channel that matches your Website URL. Go ahead. We'll wait.

Even if you don't want to use YouTube today, you'll want to make sure than nobody else uses your identity.

If you didn't do it in the first paragraph, perhaps you didn't know how. Here's a step-by-step guide to creating your YouTube channel. Before you create an account, be sure you understand YouTube's terms of service.[357]

---

[355] Charlie Bit Me... remix: **bit.ly/bti3O5**

[356] CollegeHumor.com: **bit.ly/9doali**

[357] YouTube's terms of service: **bit.ly/c0KZOT**

- Sign up for YouTube using the URL you want as your username. Go to **bit.ly/bXkY5F** to get started. You'll see a form that looks like this:

Figure 72 — YouTube's Signup Form Example

- Make sure the username matches your Website's domain name or the name of your business. For example, if your name is Widgets, Inc., make your username widgets or widgetsinc. You can create a username up to 20 characters long.

- If you already have a YouTube or a Google account, you can add your new YouTube account to the existing one. If you create a new account, be sure you understand the question about Web History. Consenting to this means Google will track your Web activity while you're logged in to your new account, even on other sites. It will use this information to improve your search experience. But you may not want this type of surveillance.

- When you select Create a New Account and Finish, YouTube will send you a confirmation email that you must act upon before your new account is set up. BTW,[358] the wavy word that you must type into the box is known as a CAPTCHA, which stands for **C**ompletely **A**utomated **P**ublic **T**uring test to tell **C**omputers and **Hu**mans **A**part. It's a way to keep spambots from creating fake YouTube accounts. It's named after a famous early computer pioneer and cryptographic hero of World War II, Alan Turing.

- Once you respond to the email, you're taken to YouTube and logged in.
  You can customize the look of your channel by going to the dropdown by your name, in the upper right of your channel main page, and selecting Channel.

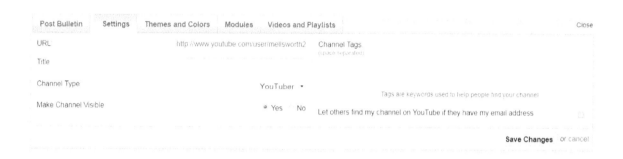

Figure 73 — Change Settings on YouTube Example

- Create tags for your channel so people can find you

Change the theme and colors — We recommend you upload a background image as part of your branding (see the *Triangulate Your Social Media Presence* section on page 204)

- Add various modules such as Comments and Subscribers
- Create Playlists
- On your main channel page, you can:

  - Connect your Facebook account with YouTube
  - Find friends or associates on YouTube

---

[358] By The Way

- On your Account Settings page you can:

    - Use your logo as your channel's profile picture
    - Connect with your accounts on other social media sites

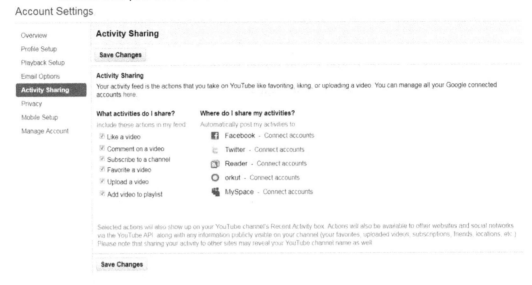

Figure 74 — Connecting YouTube with other Social Media Accounts Example

- Insert a description of your organization in the Describe Yourself field — make sure it's short and to the point — YouTubers are visually oriented, not text-oriented
- Include URLs to your Websites

Now you can create videos — see YouTube's Handbook for Ideas[359] — and start to upload videos. You can post videos of any length up to 15 minutes, as long as the file size is under 2GB. Be sure your videos have a call to action! There's more on that in the section *Getting Video Results* on page 372.

After you've had some views of your videos, go to YouTube Insight[360] in your My Account section to see a demographic breakdown of your audience by age, region, and gender. If you are using an embedded a Google Checkout button, you can also measure success through the number of online sales you have received.

---

[359] YouTube's Handbook for Ideas: **bit.ly/9iduiy**

[360] YouTube Insight: **bit.ly/cYOrmz**

Plan Your Video

Here are some general tips on creating and publicizing your YouTube videos:

- **Create a Video Strategy** — Naturally, we recommend having a strategy before getting too involved in YouTube or other video sites. You should understand what's going on already in your area of interest, who the players are, what they're doing, what kind of community already follows your product category via video, and, most importantly, what you hope to accomplish with video. Create goals out of this strategy, and metrics to measure your progress. Your strategy should encompass not only YouTube, but Vimeo and other video sites, as well as how to get your supporters to embed videos on their sites (more on this in a bit). Finally, your strategy should lay out your Video Search Engine Optimization (VSEO) plan so you improve your findability on Google and other search engines (more on this later).

- **Reach Out** — Post videos that get viewers talking via the comments section on YouTube. It's best to include an invitation to comment at the end of your video — "We'd like to hear your ideas. Please use the comment section below to let us know what you think." Deliver this message with a real person, who points down, indicating the area for comments below. Many users may not be aware of the comments section or how to find it.

  Then join the conversation with your own comments and video responses. YouTube lets anyone post a video response to a particular video, and it can be an effective way to broaden your reach, since each video response will attract its own viewers, who may be interested in your original video.

- **Partner Up** — Find other organizations on YouTube you can partner with and promote each other. Remember, people will spend most of their time on YouTube viewing other videos. Partners can help you build your YouTube community.

- **Keep It Fresh** — Put up new videos regularly. Don't worry too much if you don't have anything earth-shattering to say. Think of the exercise as a way to keep in contact with your community. Report on what your company is doing and planning to do, and give status on ongoing efforts. Remember to keep your videos short—ideally in the two- to three-minute range, and for sure under five minutes.

- **Spread Your Message** — Share links and the embed code for your videos with supporters so they can help get the word out. Embedding means others can copy some simple code that YouTube generates into their Webpages and thus show your video on their sites. You can encourage viewers to embed the videos by having an on-screen person indicate the <Embed> button that appears below your video and asking viewers to use it on their sites.

- **Be Genuine** — High numbers of views come from content that's compelling, rather than what's hip. Make sure your videos and video channel are listed in the YouTube categories that are appropriate.

Create Your YouTube Video

To create a video, you'll need some way to capture images or video. If you have a mobile phone camera, that may be good enough. Otherwise, there are several very inexpensive cameras such as the Flip MinoHD[361] or the Kodak Zi8 Pocket[362] that produce surprisingly good videos.

You'll need a way to get your videos onto a computer (although some cameras will let you post raw video from your camera directly to YouTube). And you'll probably want a way to edit the video and audio, add background music and titles, and integrate video from multiple sources. Many operating systems now come with simple video editing programs such as Microsoft Windows Movie Maker, and Apple's iMovie. There are plenty of free, shareware, and commercial video editors as well, of varying capabilities and complexity.

Using one of these programs, you'll need to save a file in one of the formats YouTube accepts, including:

- WebM files (Vp8 video codec and Vorbis Audio codec)
- .MPEG4, 3GPP and MOV files — (typically supporting h264 and mpeg4 video codecs and AAC audio codec)
- .AVI (Many cameras output this format — typically the video codec is MJPEG and audio is PCM)
- .MPEGPS (Typically supporting MPEG2 video codec and MP2 audio)
- .WMV
- .FLV (Adobe Flash — FLV1 video codec, MP3 audio)

That list may be a bit bewildering for the novice. Just look at your video editor's output or Save As menu and see if it mentions any of the file extensions or types above. More than likely, it will output .AVI and possibly .MPEG4. If it can output .FLV that's probably the best, since YouTube is going to convert your video into that format once you've uploaded it, and it produces one of the smallest file sizes. If you create your video in the .FLV — Flash — format, there are some advanced techniques[363] you can use to get more prominent search placement.

Your video file must be smaller than 2GB or YouTube will reject it. It can have any running time that will fit into that file size. You can get quite a lot of running time into a file that size using compression.[364] However the more the file is compressed, the poorer the resulting video quality is. And speaking of quality, many YouTube experts do not recommend uploading High Defini-

---

[361] MinoHD: **amzn.to/93RodF**

[362] Kodak Zi8 Pocket: **amzn.to/iezAYS**

[363] Tim Nash's *Flash SEO Indexing Revisited Part 1*: **bit.ly/9UrNQu**

[364] Compression refers to reducing a video file size through various means. Some compression techniques are lossless. This means the quality of the video picture is not reduced when the technique is used. Most of those available to amateur videomakers are lossy, meaning the picture degrades in order to make the file size smaller.

tion (HD) video or video with HD's 16x9 aspect ratio. Google these terms to understand what we're talking about.

It may seem daunting, but the basics are actually pretty easy to master with a bit of study.

Be sure that if you use any copyrighted material from other sources that you get permission, and post a notice of that permission at the end of your video. YouTube is committed to removing illegally-posted content from their service.

Script Your Video

While an exhaustive description of this topic is beyond the scope of this book, here are some quick recommendations for the script of your video:

- **Keep it Short** — The average length of a YouTube video is a little more than four minutes, but you should target between two and three minutes. If your issue is complex, break your video into several self-contained pieces and link them together using the tools YouTube provides.

- **Explain Your Solution** — Right up front, tell about your business and the problem you solve, not necessarily the products that solve it. Include enough detail so that the viewer can decide to complete viewing the video. It's best to use a real person on-screen for this portion of your video so you can better engage your audience.

- **Avoid Shocking Video at the Start** — If your solution involves human tragedy or anything icky, don't open with graphic footage. Create a relationship with your viewer and get them involved before hitting them with emotional footage. Such footage can be very effective and dramatic, but should probably be used sparingly, after establishing a connection with the viewer.

- **Build Empathy** — If the problem you solve is emotional, don't be afraid to empathically build a common bond with the viewer. Encourage an emotional response, and then tie those emotions to your call to action.

- **Empower Your Viewers** — If you have a call to action but viewers can't immediately act — by clicking a link to go to your site or by clicking right through to a Buy It Now button — you'll lose the immediacy of the moment. Your video has affected your viewer, and he or she wants to help, now. Give them a way to buy right now, go to your site, follow you on Twitter, join your Facebook page, and subscribe to your blog feed. Show how taking an action will make a difference. Communicate that they can make a difference. Encourage viewers to create a video response to your video and link back to you.

- **Create a Sense of Urgency** — Emphasize why your viewers need to take action now. If you are after donations, indicate a deadline for a sweepstakes or discount or other information to foster urgency.

- **Feed Back** — If you have success with a video, make another video praising those who helped make that success and link it to the first video.

Consider creating a transcript of your video and using YouTube's capability to add it as captioning.[365] This not only improves the accessibility of the video, but it may affect the indexing of it by search engines as well.

Once you upload the video, you'll want to control the thumbnail image that displays in search listings.[366] YouTube offers you three thumbnails, using frames from the beginning, middle, and end (at the ¼, ½, and ¾ marks), and says you can't offer a different one. While this is technically true, Michael Gray[367] figured out that, if you put the image you want to be your thumbnail in the exact middle of your video,[368] you'll be able to select that image from the three that YouTube offers you. You have to be a little bit advanced in your video editor use to do this, however.

In addition to captioning, there are a variety of other things you can do to a video once it's been uploaded. You can annotate it, which means to superimpose little text bubbles on the video. Audio Swap lets you replace your entire audio track with a selected song or other audio track. You can also change the title, description, and tags.

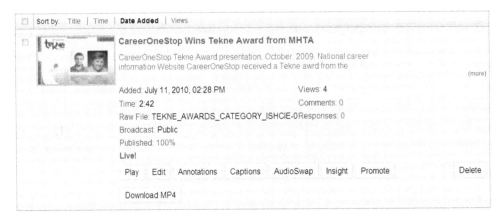

Figure 75 — Post-Upload Modification of YouTube Videos

---

[365] YouTube: Getting Started: Adding / Editing captions: **bit.ly/d3HzpC**

[366] YouTube: Getting Started: Picking a video thumbnail: **bit.ly/9ypBMw**

[367] Michael Gray; Video Optimization: Getting The Money Shot: **bit.ly/c00c0J**

[368] YouTube: How to Change Your YouTube Video Thumbnail to any Picture: **bit.ly/9dztt8**

Publicizing Your YouTube Video

Your first step in publicizing your YouTube channel should be to post comments on related You-Tube videos. You may attract some followers this way. But be careful. It's probably not cool to post snarky comments on competitors' videos. Consider including URLs in comments on related videos and even creating video responses. And don't disable commenting on your channel. See the section on *Dealing with Negatives* on page 209 for reasons why you don't want to limit dissent.

Next, embed your YouTube videos on your Website and on your blogs. This makes them do double duty, and will attract viewers to your channel. There's a bit more on embedding below.

Take a look at your competition and see how they are tagging their videos. Tag your videos the same way. This way, when their video is over, and YouTube displays other videos to view next, your video is likely to come up, as in the following figure.

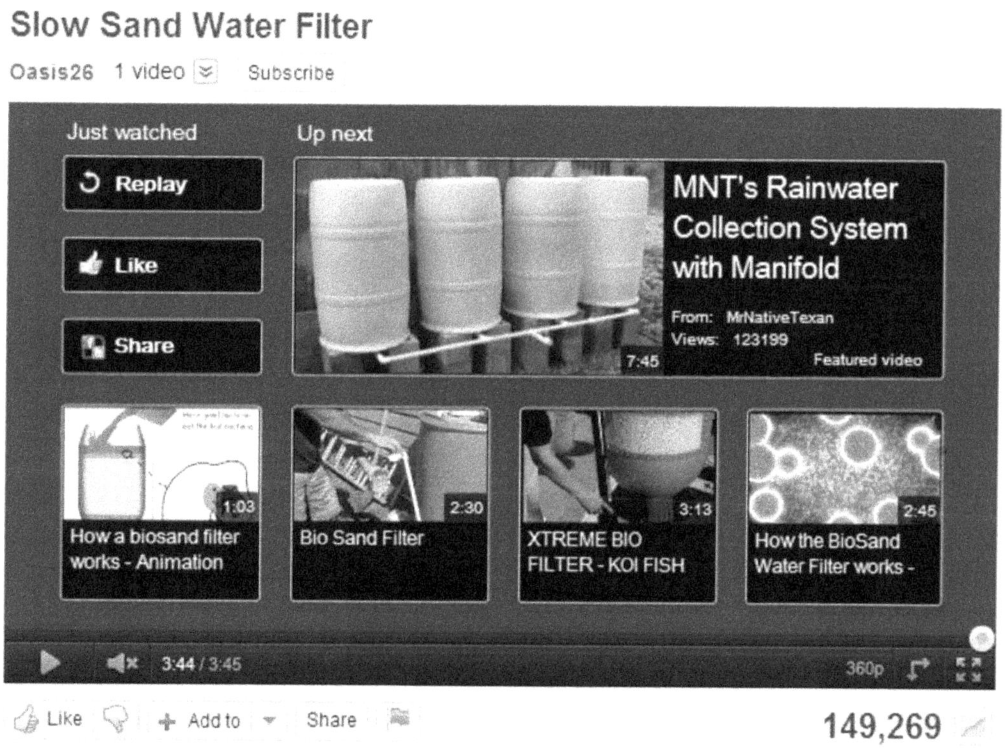

Figure 76 — Suggested Videos Areas on YouTube Page

Subscribe to other channels. Just like following people on Twitter gets you your own followers, subscribing to other YouTube channels will get subscribers for your channel.

YouTube has an active social networking community. Invite your friends, and extend friend invitations to kindred souls. Friend the most popular channels in your field. Thank subscribers for subscribing by posting comments on their channels. Engage members of the various categories of channels, especially the Reporters channel. Participate in the community and you'll attract subscribers.

You should create a special landing page on your Website for each of your videos. This page should be tailored for visitors who have arrived from YouTube, perhaps by addressing them directly — "Welcome YouTube viewer! Here's more information on <the subject of the video>." Be sure to include links to your other relevant videos and to actions the visitors can take on your site. Put buttons for the most important actions right on the landing page.

Creating landing pages is way better than dumping YouTube visitors right onto your main page — never do this — or even to an appropriate generic internal page. Take the time to customize your experience and embrace your YouTube community.

Depending on the video, up to 70 percent of people may view your YouTube videos from other sites, such as sites with embedded players, blogs, search engines, and the like, and thus many people will find your video by doing a search, either on YouTube or on Google or other search engine. Consequently, you need to search-engine-optimize your videos.

Optimize Your YouTube Videos

Like everything else on the Web, your videos are no good if nobody can find them. In addition to maximizing the effect of your social presence on YouTube, as we discussed in the last section, you need to do Search Engine Optimization (SEO) for your YouTube channel. The following recommendations are for YouTube and Google. Optimizing for other search engines will likely be slightly different.

You Tube's search algorithm considers the following attributes of videos when determining ranking, whether they are embedded on your site or on YouTube:

- **Title** — If you've embedded your YouTube video in a page on your site, make sure the title of the page matches the title of the video. You'll do better in search rankings if it does.
- **Description** — Optimize the first 27 characters, which is what displays before truncation in listings. Include a shortened clickable URL (see the *Shrinking Long URLs* section on page 306 for more information). The video's description is shown in the search results on Google.
- **Tags** — Include relevant keywords that describe the video. Make these keywords consistent with those you use in the title and description fields. YouTube has a keyword tool[369] you can use to get suggested keywords. There's even a beta capability to get keywords by demographic group.

---

[369] YouTube keyword tool: **bit.ly/aFQNft**

Setting Up YouTube

- **Number of Views** — You want to focus on getting more views, naturally, so share your videos appropriately using YouTube's social media tools and commenting as well as other social networks. You also want to show up in the list of related videos that appear over a video that's finished playing, and to the right of the video Try to get your videos into this area.

  People tend to watch videos in batches. The average YouTube viewer views more than 100 videos per month.[370] Try to keep your most important videos in the Recent Activity listing[371] on your channel by periodically tweaking the annotation (a text field that pops up over the video) or other text fields of the video. Videos in Recent Activity perform the best on searches.

  The Recent Activity box has a lot of other functionality. Adding new favorites to your channel shows up in the box, as well as new ratings and comments on others' videos. You can broadcast bulletins directly to your channel subscribers, and these show up in your Recent Activity box as well. When you post a bulletin, it will also appear on your subscribers' Recent Activity boxes.

- **Rating** — The rating[372] of your video is similar to the Motion Picture Association of America's movie content ratings. You can rate your video on five categories: Language, Nudity, Sexual Situations, Violence and Drug Use.

- **View counts** — You can only influence this indirectly, obviously.

- **Playlist Additions** — Viewers can add your video to their video playlists. You might consider asking users to add the video to their playlists in your video description or the video itself, since many viewers may not be familiar with this feature.

- **Thumbs Up/Down** — Viewers can rate your video by indicating thumbs up or thumbs down. This type of rating, representing how much viewers like the video, is different from the content ratings mentioned earlier in this list. Consider encouraging thumbs up ratings in your video description or the video.

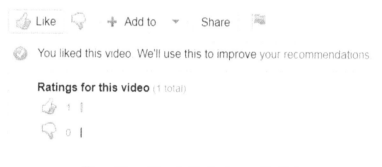

Figure 77 — Thumbs Up Ratings on YouTube

---

[370] comScore press release *comScore Releases May 2010 U.S. Online Video Rankings*: **bit.ly/9Y9D3m**

[371] YouTube Getting Started: Recent Activity privacy settings: **bit.ly/9qdBLs**

[372] YouTube Learn More: YouTube Content Ratings: **bit.ly/c16tqH**

- **Shares/Embeds** — YouTube viewers can share videos they find interesting with their friends. They also can embed your video in their own sites. This social networking capability can be a key to your video's success, so don't be afraid to encourage those who comment positively on the video to share it with their networks. There is a bit of controversy among experts over whether third party embeds are more important than those on your own Website.
- **Favorites** — Viewers can add your video to their list of favorites, which can be seen by visitors to their channels. Encourage this behavior as well.
- **Comments** — It is unclear at this time whether YouTube is evaluating comments for what is known as sentiment — whether the comment is negative or positive. You obviously want positive comments. Your strategy should specify how you will respond to negative comments.
- **Complete Views** — YouTube apparently weights whether the viewer watched your video to completion and factors that into its search algorithm. There's little you can do about this, of course, except create compelling videos.
- **Channel Views** — Another variable you can't really control, channel views is the number of visitors who have viewed your channel page. It is not a summary of all video views, since videos can be viewed via search results and embeds.
- **Authority of Your Channel** — Authority is a complicated concept similar to Google's Page Rank. It basically is an assessment of your channel's influence. A good way to increase your authority score is to leave comments on channels that have a high authority score.
- **Annotations** — Text in the annotations on your video can also influence search results.
- **Flagging** — If your video gets flagged by users for offensiveness, that will negatively affect your search ranking.
- **OneBox Results** — Google often includes a "OneBox" at the bottom of the first page of its results containing a selection of similar sites. If your video appears in OneBoxes, that's likely to increase its search ranking.

Figure 78 — YouTube Video in Google OneBox

- **Number of Subscribers** — Not surprisingly, the more subscribers you have to a video, the higher it will rank.

YouTube gives some guidance regarding search results in its GoogleWebmasterHelp channel.[373]

---

[373] GoogleWebmasterHelp: *What factors influence video results in Universal Search?*: **bit.ly/91Fb15**

As noted in the previous list, one way that YouTube (and, Google, which owns YouTube) finds videos is by looking for keywords in the title, description, and tags fields. So you definitely want to determine the important keywords and ensure that you enter them in those fields.

However, make sure that the keywords are appropriate to the subject of the video, and that you don't jam lots of unrelated keywords into the tags field. The reason: YouTube/Google will penalize videos for using a technique called keyword stuffing — placing lots of irrelevant tags in an item in an attempt to get more traffic. If they determine that you are keyword stuffing, both search engines will penalize your video. So make sure you use consistent keywords in the title, description, and tags fields and that they are appropriate for the actual video they describe.

While you should definitely pay attention to these techniques we've just listed, keep in mind that using the social networking aspects of YouTube will probably be even more powerful in not only getting you more viewers, but more-appropriate viewers. To develop a robust YouTube community for your business, follow our general community-building recommendations elsewhere in this book.

Optimizing for Google

Although in this book we've mostly stayed away from general Website Search Engine Optimization techniques, several factors mean you need to have a Video SEO (VSEO) plan:

- Your YouTube video is competing to be seen — YouTube averages 3 billion views per day of hundreds of millions of videos
- There are 48 Hours of video uploaded to YouTube every minute
- Visitors spend an average of 15 minutes on the site each day and 5 hours per month
- Google may favor videos in search results by as much as 50 times over non-video pages[374]

The Google Website Optimizer[375] is a fantastic tool that can help you determine the effectiveness of your videos and your entire site. You can set up variations of your video pages — or any site pages — and run comparisons of their effectiveness, helping you get to know what your community wants.

This kind of testing enables you to find out what users respond to best, resulting in a Website that is more effective in getting the results you want. Google has a great introductory tutorial[376] that explains common Website testing concepts such as A/B split testing and multivariate testing, as

---

[374] Nate Elliot: The Easiest Way to a First-Page Ranking on Google: **bit.ly/dnFZeQ**

[375] Google Website Optimizer: **bit.ly/bqPlPC**

[376] Google tutorial: **bit.ly/9JhmrR**

well as the use of the Website Optimizer tool. In general, you're going to either need to be somewhat technical, or have a techie help you set up this kind of testing.

The basic process, however, is pretty simple:

- You set up several alternatives to your current Webpage and identify the desired action, such as going to an eCommerce page
- Google assists you in creating the code for these variations, and your technical team implements them
- You record the alternatives in Google Website Optimizer
- Google takes a portion of the search traffic that would otherwise go to the original page and sends it to the alternative pages
- Google tracks each page's success in delivering the users to the target page, a process that is called conversion, because you convert a visitor into someone who takes the desired action
- You can get reports, and copy the test to modify it for more testing

The reports the tool creates include:

- **Estimated Conversion Rate** — Reports how well each variation performs versus your original content displayed as a numerical range or a bar chart

- **Chance to Beat Original** — Displays the probability that a combination will be more successful than the original version

- **Improvement** — Displays the percent improvement over the original, which is a ratio of the conversion rate of a variation to the conversion rate of the original page

- **Conversions/Visitor** — Displays how many visitors took the target action divided by all visitors to that variation. Also known as conversion rate.

- **Page Section Results** — You can test changing just certain sections of a page, and the tool reports the effectiveness

- **Relevance Rating** — Shows how a particular page section affects the success of the variation. For example, if your headline page section showed a relevance rating of 0, that means the headlines did not have any significant effect.

When you sign up for Google Website Optimizer you'll need to create a Google Analytics account. Google offers lots more tools to help you maximize the performance of your site as part of their Analytics offering. And while you're at it, sign up for Google's Webmaster Tools.[377] Among other valuable free tools for webmasters, Google lets you create a video sitemap that helps it in-

---

[377] Google's Webmaster Tools: **bit.ly/dfB5kD**

dex the videos on your site. Further discussion of these and other site optimizing tools is beyond the scope of this book, but there's plenty of free help online.

When you embed a YouTube on your site, be sure to create a separate page for each video, ensuring, as we've mentioned, that the page is the same as the title of the video. Make sure the text is optimized, featuring your best keywords in the copy that introduces the video. Include a text link to your YouTube page, and make sure the text of the link also uses keywords.

Another tip to get indexed is to include keywords in the actual filename of your video. For example, instead of uploading a file called video1234.mp4, rename the file to reflect your keywords, like XYZ-Corp-Sweepstakes.mp4. The result will be an increased search engine rank.

Getting Video Results

You may have various goals for using videos on YouTube. You may want to spread awareness for your products or your enterprise. You may want to counter others who have a different perspective than you on an issue. But one of the most important objectives you may have is to gain prospects, supporters, and evangelists for your organization.

For these and other reasons you'll want to be sure to include a strong call to action in your videos. The results can be amazing.

Here's an example of the power of video to create action. Lynn Rogers, with the Wildlife Research Institute, and the North American Bear Center near Ely, Minnesota, gained an international reputation over 40 years of working in the field with black bears. But Rogers gained international fame by the simple act of broadcasting live on the Web the birth of a black bear named Hope in January, 2010.

The "den cam" video was in black and white and a bit murky, and a mere 25,000 viewers watched it live.[378] Within a couple of days, after becoming the #1 Yahoo.com featured story, the birth video was the #1 most-viewed YouTube video on January 24, 2010 and by late 2010 it garnered more than 800,000 views. The subsequent story of Hope and her mother, Lily, included Hope getting lost for a few days in May, 2010, and again in June.[379] The bear drama spawned almost 300 videos on YouTube, covering the two bears as if they were the latest Hollywood "it" girls.

But all this interest didn't just happen all by itself. The creators of the "den cam," PixController Wildlife Webcam, used social media to help the phenomenon along. According to company CEO Bill Powers, "The day it (the video feed) went up ... it just went berserk at that point. It was the first time anybody had actually seen a bear den. When the bear cub was born, it was kind of neat. That's when we started to use a lot of the social tools like Facebook and those kind of things to get the word out quick, and it just went viral at that point."[380]

The social media efforts included a "Lily the Black Bear" Facebook page[381] with more than 115,000 fans, whose comments on Facebook generated more than 6,000 links.[382]

---

[378] Maker of the "den cam" Pixcontroller reports: **bit.ly/coiR6q**

[379] Lily and Hope reunited: **on.fb.me/9nTQ0I**

[380] Pittsburgh Tribune's article *Export company's webcams follow black bear, cub* **bit.ly/9i2JAa**

[381] Lily's Facebook pages: **on.fb.me/aiCl1Z** and **on.fb.me/cV04zZ**

[382] Lily links: **on.fb.me/as0upZ**

Hundreds of thousands of viewers were fascinated by the experience, and their interest turned into donations totaling $400,000 to the non-profit organizations Rogers heads, Wildlife Research Institute, and the North American Bear Center.[383] In addition, the bear center received a $100,000 grant from Chase Community Giving on Facebook, a program sponsored by JPMorgan Chase in which Facebook users vote on how the charity distributes $5 million. The center received almost 18,000 votes among more than 2.5 million Facebook users who participated.

Demonstrating our recommendation that an organization's main Website must be modified to support social media efforts, Rogers' Website, bear.org, posts blow-by-blow accounts of Lily and Hope, and features a prominent donation button with a funds thermometer.[384] The main page of the Website features various live Webcam feeds, a recent donor honor roll, and the opportunity to buy bear paraphernalia.

What can you learn from the Lily and Hope phenomenon? It's clear that an engaging story supported by video and combined with other social media efforts can deliver for your organization in a big way. Think of the human (or non-human) stories your organization can tell, and how video can help you tell them. It doesn't matter if you have slick production values — look at what was achieved with a low-resolution black and white video. What counts is telling the story, and connecting with your viewers.

For more video tips, Teach to Fish Digital has a free YouTube tutorial.[385]

---

[383] StarTribune's article *The bear whisperer: Scholar plans to expand educational empire*: **bit.ly/cyFqEV**

[384] Bear.org's livecam and journal: **bit.ly/c5ngq4**

[385] Teach to Fish Digital's *YouTube Tutorial*: **slidesha.re/qOp3D3**

Setting Up Blogging

"Blog policy at Microsoft is just two words: Blog Smart."

Lawrence Liu, director of platform strategy for Telligent

Blog is short for Weblog, an old-fashioned term from the turn of the century for a kind of online diary. The original Weblogs were not initially a hit. In 1999 well-known usability guru Jesse James Garrett collected a list[386] of all the known Weblogs — all 23 of them. A year later, his list had grown to almost 300.[387] Peter Merholz, Creative Director at Epinions.com, decided for some reason that the word should be pronounced "wee-blog" which he proposed be shortened to blog, and the rest is history.

As we reported earlier in this book, today there are more than 100 million blogs with more than 120,000 new ones launching every day.[388] Websites such as Technorati[389] exist solely to catalog and classify blogs, delivering a sampling of the best and most-influential blogs. Big money is made by blogs such as Mashable,[390] Perez Hilton,[391] I Can Has Cheezburger,[392] and Techcrunch[393] which staked out claims in niche markets (social media, celebrity gossip, cute (?) cat pictures, tech gadgets) and drawing large viewership.

Along the way, the blog has morphed from a text-only medium to a multimedia extravaganza, featuring audio, video, animations, and games. Technical innovations such as Real Simple Syndi-

---

[386] Jesse James Garrett's list of blogs from 1999: **bit.ly/azc5ox**

[387] Garrett's list of blogs from 2000: **bit.ly/bGAimO**

[388] See the section *Why Social Media?* on page 27

[389] Technorati: **bit.ly/9P2O14** and the Top 100 Blogs: **bit.ly/cIXCWF**

[390] Mashable: **bit.ly/a6Q7e8**

[391] Perez Hilton: **bit.ly/bwaXIR**

[392] I Can Has Cheezburger: **bit.ly/dspJnq**

[393] Techcrunch even has its own URL shortener: **tcrn.ch/cON0ZS**

cation (RSS)[394] enabled blogs to connect to one another, and made keeping up to date on many blogs at once a simple matter of starting a Google Reader account.

Other social networking sites have made it easy to connect blogs to their services:

- You can automatically tweet a synopsis of your new blog post to Twitter and Facebook using Twitter-Feed[395]
- You can add your blog to LinkedIn (use the BlogLink app or Ping.fm[396]) and to Facebook (add to the Notes section)
- You can add your blog to your YouTube channel[397]

As you can see, your blog could be the center of your social media universe, powering a series of satellite sites fed by a single blog post.

So what is this powerful force?

What is a Blog?

At its root, a blog is nothing more than an easy way to publish content on the Web. You could argue that blogs are the original social media application. When blogs arose at the tail end of the 90s, they represented freedom for the average person from the tyranny of the techies. No longer did regular folks need to run the gauntlet of people who had to be involved in putting content on the Web, from the Web designers to the developers to the Webmasters. Anyone could easily start a blog and publish their thoughts on the Internet. It was amazing.

Today, in the midst of hundreds of social networking sites, the blog remains the choice for a personal soapbox. As much as you can rant on Facebook, for example, there's nothing as intimate as your own space to blog. And there is nothing more popular on the Web, with 77 percent of active Internet users reading blogs.[398] However, in mid-2011, there were signs that younger users were trending away from blogs in favor of sites like Facebook and Twitter.[399]

Even today, the modern blog still resembles the diary-oriented Weblogs of old. Simply put, it's a log of your thoughts, ideas, links, photos, videos, or news in a series of posts arranged in chrono-

---

[394] See the section Social Sites Defined on page 19 for a definition of RSS

[395] TwitterFeed is at: **bit.ly/96Lh5X** and Hubpages has the simple instructions at: **bit.ly/c7c8uN**

[396] Ping.fm automatically feeds posts to a variety of sites: **bit.ly/dwbqG3**

[397] YouTube's *Learn More: Adding a blog to my account*: **bit.ly/92ytdo**

[398] The Future Buzz's article *Social Media, Web 2.0 And Internet Stats*: **bit.ly/b4o0bO**

[399] New York Times *Blogs Wane as the Young Drift to Sites Like Twitter*: **nyti.ms/o3bcjy**

logical order. Because of its power and flexibility, the blog can be the cornerstone of your social computing strategy, second in importance only to your main Website.

In fact, we recommend making a blog the centerpiece of your social media strategy. Whether the blog is on your existing site or on one of the blog hosting platforms we detail later, of all the types of social media, the blog offers you an opportunity to state your case with the fewest restrictions. You're not limited by Twitter's 140 characters or by the length of a Facebook or LinkedIn status update. While it's not a good idea to routinely go on at great length, with a blog you have the opportunity to develop a theme or an argument that other venues rarely provide.

So do your work here, in your blog. And link to your blog from everywhere, as we discussed in the *Triangulate Your Social Media Presence* section on page 204. Don't be discouraged by the tens of millions of competitive blogs out there. Make your blog the place you state your case, and most intimately engage with your community. If you offer value — resources, insights, encouragement — and effectively engage your community, your blog can be a hit.

Blogging Glossary

Before we get too far, let's take a look at some blog lingo.

- **Post** — a blog entry; also verb, to create a blog entry
- **Blogging** — the act of posting
- **Blogger** — a person who blogs
- **Blogosphere** — the blogging community
- **RSS Feed** — short for Real Simple Syndication, it's a way for others to sign up (called subscribing; see below) to get updates from your blog without having to visit it
- **Atom** — a feed format that is an alternative to RSS
- **Blog Client** — software installed on your computer that you can use to manage (post, edit) blogs with no need to launch a web browser
- **Blogroll** — a list of other blogs that a blogger recommends by providing links to them
- **Comment Spam** — similar to e-mail spam, unwanted comments posted by robot "spambots"
- **Mommy bloggers** — a particularly cohesive and active group of blogging mothers — see the discussion of the Motrin mommy blogger revolt in the Social Media Hall of Shame
- **Permalink** — a permanent, unchanging link to a single post that can be used when you want to link to a post from elsewhere
- **Podcasting** — originally a contraction of "iPod" and "broadcasting," podcasting means posting audio or video material on a blog and its RSS feed, for digital players (not just iPods).
- **Subscribe** — signing up to be alerted to changes in a blog, or signing up to receive an RSS feed

- **Templates** — the organization structure of a blog page often including content placement, design, graphics, and interactive features; you can find free templates, commercial templates, or have your own designed
- **Theme** — a particular look that can be applied to a blog template, changing the visual elements
- **Trackback or Pingback** — a ping that a blog sends to another blog to notify that their article has been mentioned
- **Tag cloud** — Displaying lists of keywords or tags in a blog as a cloud of words
- **Plug-ins** — bits of interactivity that can add improved functionality and new features to your blog
- **Jump** — the continuation of a story on another page

Components of a Blog

Blogs can be plain or they can be fancy. But most blogs have one or more of the following components:

- **Index page** — The front page, which may contain teasers to other posts
- **Header** — The topmost part of the blog
- **Footer** — The bottom part of the blog
- **Sidebar** — Columns along one or both sides of the blog's main page
- **Categories** — A collection of topic-specific posts
- **Comments** — A section, generally at the bottom, where readers can leave remarks
- **CAPTCHA** — Those squiggly words often seen in a Comments section to prevent automated commenting, it stands for **C**ompletely **A**utomated **P**ublic **T**uring test to tell **C**omputers and **H**umans **A**part
- **Tagging** — Allows readers or bloggers to attach keywords to make it easier to search or collect similar posts
- **BlogThis** — An interactive feature that allows a visiting blogger to blog on their own blog about the entry they are reading
- **Plug-ins** — Interactive features that add improved functionality and new features. Some top plug-ins for the popular blogging platform Wordpress include: Subscribe To Comments, Show Top Commentators, Get Recent Comments, Popularity Contest, and Share This.[400]

Creating Your Blog

It's very easy, and free, to start a blog. It's harder to create a blog that will amass a following, or make a difference. Like all the social media sites we discuss in this book, you should start with a plan that includes your goals, the audience you are trying to reach, the tone of the blog, the name

---

[400] See the list of top Wordpress plug-ins at **bit.ly/ah4Rg9**

and branding of the blog, your marketing plan, and a publishing schedule. Review the section *Elements of an Engagement Plan* on page 115 before starting your blog.

There are all kinds of blog platforms available that will host your blog. The most popular are Wordpress, Typepad, Blogsmith, Blogger and Movable Type. Here's a short list of sites to consider when choosing a hosted blog platform:[401]

- **Blogger.com** — free, by Google
- **Blogspot.com** — free Blogger hosting
- **LiveJournal.com** — free, by SixApart
- **MovableType.com** — paid, by SixApart
- **Typepad.com** — paid, by SixApart
- **Wordpress.com** — free

If you're ready to take on the responsibility of hosting your blog yourself, there are several blogging platforms to choose from, some free, some you need to buy:

- **Wordpress.org** — A free, installable version of Wordpress.com software
- **Movable Type** — Charges for a license for the platform based on number of blogs and whether they are for commercial, personal, educational or not-for-profit use. Also has a free version.
- **LiveJournal** — Open source software that enables you to create a virtual community. LiveJournal goes beyond blogging by allowing you to create self-contained communities and add social networking features.
- **Textpattern** — More than a blogging platform, Textpattern is an open source general-purpose content management system
- **Drupal, Joomla**, and other Web content management systems also have blogging features, although they are primarily designed to run your whole site.

One advantage of self-hosting: You can use your own domain name — blog.yourorg.com. A major disadvantage is that if you don't have a technical staff, the upkeep and maintenance of a blog hosting platform can be baffling and time-consuming.

How to Blog

There are as many ways to blog as there are people on Earth. Each blogger will approach the task of posting an engaging blog in his or her own way. As we indicated above, you should decide how blogging will achieve your online objectives before you start.

---

[401] There's a good overview of blogging platforms and a list of the top 100 blogs and their blogging platforms at: **bit.ly/9ooHQO**

Start by Commenting

Once you've created your plan and figured out your approach, visit lots of relevant blogs and consider posting comments as a way to get the hang of blogging. In doing so, keep in mind the following guidelines for commenting on others' posts:

- **Follow the 4-to-1 rule**: Comment on four posts for every post that you write — Spread the love around
- **Link to other blogs** — Acknowledging a great post on another's blog can help build your reputation and deliver readers for your own blog
- **Comments are a great way to spread the word, but don't spam** — If every comment you make includes a gratuitous link to your blog, or is seen as merely self-serving, you're not going to be successful in luring readers of other blogs to yours
- **Ensure your comments are relevant and on-topic** — This is the other side of the previous rule: Don't comment if you're not adding value. We're often tempted to post something useless like "I agree," or "What he said" but that does nothing but clutter up the comments stream, and readers will immediately gloss over your comment in search of something interesting.
- **Include a link to your blog** — Yes, it's appropriate to include a link to your blog in a comment, but only in context, meaning that your blog amplifies or otherwise is pertinent to the same or a similar topic

Blog Frequently

Once you start blogging, you'll want to establish a rhythm. Try to blog frequently — more than once a week, maybe even daily. The point of you blogging is to get followers. Followers want currency, not stale, month-old posts. Blogging frequently will keep them coming back.

If you can't commit to blog daily, shoot for blogging every few days, or at least weekly. You may need to spread the blogging chores among several authors. If you do, encourage them to maintain a common tone.

Writing Your Blog

One of the most important things to keep in mind when writing a blog is: You have seconds to capture the reader, and it's very easy to lose them after the first paragraph.

Create a Great Title

Your blog needs a great title, and so do your blog posts. Whether it's short and to the point, or long and quirky, your title has to grab the reader. Research shows that people's decision to read

Setting Up Blogging

an article is heavily dependent on the title of the article.[402] If you've read a newspaper or magazine lately (work with us here, GenY), you're familiar with the concept. Chances are good you thumb through the periodical scanning the titles and headlines (and pictures — we'll get to them later) until something looks good. Then you read the first paragraph and decide if you want to read more. If the article isn't delivering what you want, you move on.

On the Web this process is multiplied a thousand-fold. If you're lucky enough for your blog post to make it onto the front page of Google, its title must jump out as the prospective reader rapidly scans the search results. Remember: On the Web, every click is a commitment. You're leaving the familiar comfort of the page you're on to venture into the unknown, in the optimistic hope of finding something useful, entertaining, or informative. And if the article doesn't deliver on the promise of the title, your reader is off to the next adventure.

Here are some title examples drawn from our own blogs. Which blog post title would you be more likely to read?

Boring Blog Title	Better Blog Title
I have lots of new Twitter followers	What's the deal with tons of ghost followers yesterday on Twitter?
Famous Quote About Energy	What Edison Said About Energy
Branding is Changing	The Future of Brands, or Yoda Was Right
The Advantages of Experience	What's Wrong with Young Guys?
Old People Don't Understand Teens	Twitter is for Old Fogies, Teen Says

We hope you prefer the titles in the right hand column.

Create a Great Lead

Blog posts must get right to the point. Study some of the most influential blogs, such as the Huffington Post[403] or Gawker.[404] Watch how they hook the reader in. Here's an example of a recent HuffPost article lead:

> For all his retro failings and inability to open up, Don Draper has always been intrigued, even turned on, by women who are willing to stand up to him and are smart enough to argue with him.

---

[402] Jack B. Haskins' paper *Title-Rating: A Method for Measuring Reading Interests and Predicting Readership*: **bit.ly/cfGcZl**

[403] Huffington Post: **huff.to/9bAbxA**

[404] Gawker: **bit.ly/9czGyt**

Who's that lead targeted to? Yup. Women.

How about this lead from Gawker:

> There's a melodramatic "war" brewing between Facebook and Google, and Facebook's CEO is seizing the opportunity to squeeze more work from his engineers, declaring a "lockdown," keeping the office open on weekends, and putting a neon sign on his door.

Target audience? People like you, who read books about social computing!

Write and rewrite your lead so that it communicates the promise of the post and entices the reader to continue.

Add Pictures

Remember when you were thumbing through the magazine in your imagination in the previous section? You were scanning titles, but you were also looking at the pictures. Since many of your audience members will belong to the post-literate generations, consider including at least one grabber of a picture in each blog post.

Use Pull Quotes

Also known as a lift-out quote or a call-out, a pull quote is a quotation or edited excerpt from a post placed in a larger typeface and embedded in a text box to entice readers and to highlight a key topic. You've probably seen them on the professional news sites and blogs. It's a great way to provide more cues to your readers about what your post is about.

> **This is a pull quote!**
>
> **Notice how it grabs attention.**

Write Scannable Text

Since your prospective readers are going to quickly scan your article to decide on its relevance, be sure to write in a way that enables scanning. This means no long, laborious, clause-laden sentences. Write in a shorter, choppier style that quickly imparts the information. And use lots of white space, especially between paragraphs.

Use bulleted lists. You may have noticed we have a lot of them in this book. Take a moment and scan back 30 or 40 pages. See how the bulleted lists attract your eye, and quickly give you a sense of what's on the page, and what the topic under discussion is?

Notice that we use a lot of white space as well, often setting sentences off apart from the rest of the text.

That's not the way you were taught to write in school, but that's what works in the increasingly attention-deficit world we're living in. So keep your paragraphs short, and don't be afraid to make them only a sentence long. There's a great example of how to lure the reader in on the Problogger site in a post called *How to Craft a Blog Post – 10 Crucial Points to Pause.*[405] Since the author, Darren Rowse, also uses type styles to attract attention, we've reproduced the beginning of the post in the next figure.

Figure 79 — Example of a Great Blog Post Lead

Doesn't this lead make you want to read the rest of the post? Rowse dares you to read on by taking the risk of placing a picture between you and the rest of the post. Brilliant.

By the way, the rest of Rowse's article, and the series it's part of, is killer, and we definitely recommend you read it.

---

[405] Darren Rowse's post *How to Craft a Blog Post – 10 Crucial Points to Pause:* **bit.ly/bGED2G**

Keep it Short

Pundits differ on the precise recommended post length, but pretty much everyone agrees blog posts should be short. We think you should aim for 300-500 words. As a guide, the average 8 ½" x 11" page has roughly 400 words on it.

If your topic is long and involved, split your post into multiple pages, with about 500 words on each. If your topic really demands more extensive coverage, consider making it into a series of posts. We did this recently when a blog site asked us to do a guest post on business use of LinkedIn. They suggested 500-700 words for the whole article. We replied that there was no way to do the topic justice in that amount, and ended up doing a five-part series.

You'll need to figure out the length issue yourself. We suggest you ask your community what they think. Perhaps you always leave them wanting more. Perhaps they get tired of reading you after half a page. Remember that it doesn't matter what you think when it comes to these issues. It's what your audience thinks. And the great thing is: You can ask them.

Good Blog Topics

Once you start blogging, one of your first concerns is going to be, "What do I blog about?"

Chances are you have plenty of possible topics. But what's going to connect with your community? Once again, you'll have to figure this out for yourself, but here's a list of suggestions that may work.

- **Create Top N Lists** — Creating blog posts that offer top 10 (or whatever number) lists is a proven winner. It promises a quick, easily-digestible take on a subject. Google the phrase "Top 10"[406] and see 450 million great examples.
- **Top People/Products** — A variation of top n lists that adds the promise of celebrity
- **Be Contrarian** — Disagreeing with established opinion can be a draw. People often seek this type of alternative to accepted wisdom
- **Be Controversial** — But not too controversial. You're looking to stir up debate, not trouble.
- **Answer FAQs** — FAQs are Frequently Asked Questions. Every field has them. If you promise to answer them, people will be likely to read.
- **Ask Questions** — One pastor we know uses this as an ice breaker: "What's your favorite movie?"

If this short list doesn't do it for you, there are lots of good blog posts that offer ideas for what to write about. Here's a list of great recommendations:

---

[406] Made you look! Here's the Top 10 Google search for your convenience: **bit.ly/cbIMyi**

- *Social Media Content Creation Process*[407] by Geoff Livingston of Now Is Gone
- *Discover Hundreds of Post Ideas for Your Blog with Mind Mapping*[408] by Darren Rowse of Problogger
- *100 Blog Topics I Hope YOU Write*[409] by Chris Brogan of ChrisBrogan.com
- *8 Must-Dos For Aspiring Writers*[410] by Amber Naslund of Brass Tack Thinking

In addition to these bloggers and their sites, check out Dosh Dosh, Buzz Bin, Ittybiz, Copyblogger, Remarkable Communication, Remarkablogger, and Problogger. [411]

Other ways to find blog topics:

- Read something new every day
- Dedicate 20 minutes each day
- Follow Alltop[412] for ideas
- Ask people for ideas, especially your community
- Keep a log of potential ideas
- Bookmark sites you visit
- Use Delicious[413] or Digg[414]
- Read other bloggers
- Find interesting and relevant photos
- Use Flickr[415] — be sure to look for the Creative Commons license so you can reuse them
- Stuck? Try a "Best of" post
- Remember: Fast is better than perfect, and perfect is the enemy of good

Getting Found

There are millions of blogs. How are you going to get found? The first way is, of course, to write compelling, valuable content that matches what your community is searching for on Google and

---

[407] Geoff Livingston's *Social Media Content Creation Process*: **bit.ly/csDMB8**

[408] Darren Rowse's *Discover Hundreds of Post Ideas for Your Blog with Mind Mapping*: **bit.ly/bk5Au1**

[409] Chris Brogan's *100 Blog Topics I Hope YOU Write*: **bit.ly/c7uaM2**, *20 Blog Topics To Get You Unstuck*: **bit.ly/cinHGT**, and *100 Personal Branding Tactics Using Social Media*: **bit.ly/9B04l1**

[410] Amber Naslund's *8 Must-Dos For Aspiring Writers*: **bit.ly/9s82tC**

[411] Dosh Dosh: **bit.ly/bQFgaB**, Buzz Bin: **bit.ly/9FCYE7**, IttyBiz: **bit.ly/bLa2SY**, Copyblogger: **bit.ly/atrUqh**, Remarkable Communication: **bit.ly/9M7ZIE**, Remarkablogger: **bit.ly/cvLuTX**, and ProBlogger: **bit.ly/dghN9l**

[412] Alltop is a blog aggregator: **bit.ly/c0DLPn**

[413] Delicious is a social tagging site: **bit.ly/dzUxVm**

[414] Digg is a social tagging site: **bit.ly/cGXpV9**

[415] Flickr is a photo and social tagging site: **bit.ly/cyVvgU**

other search engines. If you're not doing that, you're not likely to be able to attract many readers no matter what else you do.

The second-best way to get found is to get linked to by more-influential blogs. Build relationships with respected bloggers in your community. (We talked about this in the section *Study Existing Online Communities* on page 100 and in *Synergistic Promotion Activities* on page 138.) Link to them, comment on their blogs, and engage with their audiences.

One common way bloggers collaborate is to guest-author posts on each other's blogs. This has the benefit of offering a blog's audience a change of pace, and can result in increased readers for both blogs.

Recently, however, a powerful new way to promote blogs was introduced: the Facebook Like button. As we discussed in the section *Add a Like Button to Your Website* on page 335, this new replacement for the old Share button can help your Website or your blog go viral. Typepad, a popular blog hosting platform, reported in mid-2010 that the installation of Facebook's new Like Button on the sidebar of a blog boosted bloggers' referral traffic from Facebook by up to 50 percent. For some blogs, adding the Like button to the blog's footer boosted traffic from Facebook up to 200 percent.[416]

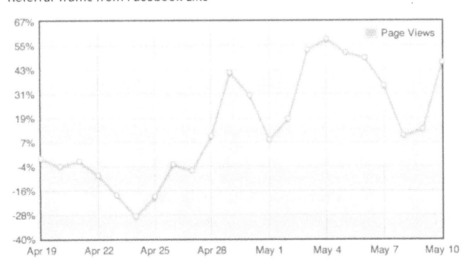

Figure 80 — Referral Traffic from Facebook Like, 2010

Combining the Like button with a campaign on Facebook can boost traffic even further. This way of coordinating your efforts between social sites, described in the *Triangulate Your Social Media Presence* section on page 204, can yield big dividends.

---

[416] Typepad's article *What you should "Like" about Facebook Integration on TypePad*: **bit.ly/936YL9**

Publicize Your Blog

In addition to the general recommendations we made in the section *Get Found* on page 202, you should:

- Add links to your blog on your Website
- Add your blog to your LinkedIn, Twitter, Facebook profiles
- Add your blog address to all your communications
- Embed videos from your YouTube channel in your blog
- Run a contest on your blog
- Ask your supporters to blog about your blog

Publicize Your Blog – Techie

If you or your staff is a bit more technical, try these ideas:

- Add your blog to blog directories such as:

  - Technorati
  - Daypop
  - Blogdex
  - Popdex
  - Blogrolling
  - blo.gs
  - weblogs.com
  - pingomatic
  - Robin Good's list of blog directories[417]

- Enable each post to be its own page
- Set your blog to send pings to search engines via Ping-o-Matic[418]
- Install Email This Post or other plug-in that enables readers to send the post to a friend
- Turn on your site RSS feed and encourage your community to subscribe to it
- Be search-engine-friendly

  - Turn on the search-engine-friendly-URL option on your blog platform[419]
  - See the section *Search Engine Optimization* on page 205

---

[417] Robin Good's blog list: **bit.ly/aynbLz**

[418] Ping-o-Matic: **bit.ly/9LO88F**

[419] Hubpages' *Advantages and disadvantages of each blogging platform*: **bit.ly/8YOKCy**

Advertise Your Blog

There are lots of places to advertise your blog on the Web. One that is quite affordable is a site called StumbleUpon. StumbleUpon belongs to a category of sites called social bookmarking services. Others include delicious and Digg.

StumbleUpon has more than 10 million members who use the site to, well, stumble upon new and interesting sites they might not have otherwise found. Members can rate pages, and when you use the site, StumbleUpon delivers pages or emails that have been explicitly recommended by friends or members with similar interests.

That's great, and it's a great site to subscribe to so you can find interesting topics to blog about. But you can also use StumbleUpon to place your blog or Website in the recommendations that members see.

You can create a StumbleUpon ad campaign for your whole blog or a single post. You can target the audience by selecting dozens of categories, various demographics and/or geography. When users click on the ad, the traffic comes directly to your site. It's a pay-per-click service, which means you pay only for actual views of your site. You can also set spending limits to control your budget, and there's no minimum spend requirements.

What's even better is the cost: 5 cents per visitor.

StumbleUpon reviews all ads and accepts only those that meet their content guidelines.[420]

Write to be Found

As we mentioned, the best way to be found is to write content that appeals to your community, as well as to search engines. First decide on the keywords that your community might use to search for your post. Then, use those keywords throughout the post. Use them in the title, the first few lines, and throughout post.

Another good idea is to use images liberally in your posts. Believe it or not, for some blogs, most visits come from Google Image Search.[421] If you're not familiar with Image Search, it's easy to try it out. Google anything. On the top of the page, to the left, you'll see a list of links, beginning with Web, which is the default Google search type. Click Images. Not only do you see a page full of images that match your search terms, but you can choose from several ways to narrow your

---

[420] Stumbleupon's content guidelines: **bit.ly/aKVSl0**

[421] According to the blog Pictures of Cats org: *Google Image Search builds Traffic*: **bit.ly/dCwj1p**

search, by size, type, and color. When you mouse over an image, Google displays its size and the site it's hosted on. Click on an image, and Google sends you to the site.

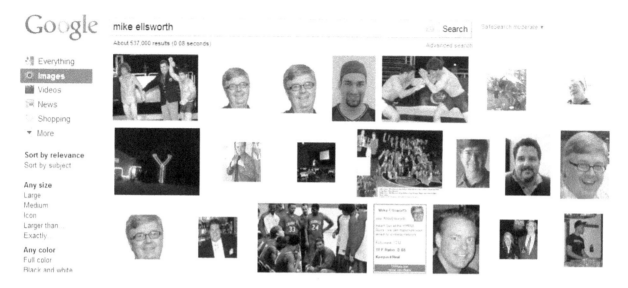

Figure 81 — Use Images in Your Blog — Google Image Search

Google bases its search on the content of the page containing the image. Including, and captioning, images in your blog adds another way you can be found.

Promote Connections

Another way to promote your blog is to pay attention to the people who take the time to comment on it. You should regularly review your comments, and:

- Respond to all commenters
- Acknowledge the comment
- Add your own comment if appropriate

    o   If the comment is negative, encourage further discussion
    o   If the comment is spam, feel free to delete

- Click on commenter's links — when they check their referral statistics, they'll see that you visited their blog
- They may be more likely to return to your blog
- They may start commenting more
- It helps draw them into a relationship

Use MyBlogLog

MyBlogLog[422] is like a social network for bloggers. The service allows you to set up a profile and enter in the particulars of all the social media places you go so you can manage them all in one place. Plus, whenever a member visits a participating blog, the blog owner can know. To make use of this feature, you add a Recent Reader widget to your blog. You'll have to find out how to do that by consulting the help on your blog hoster's site. It's quite easy to do on Typepad[423] and WordPress,[424] and might be a little harder on LiveJournal and others.

When MyBlogLog members visit your site, their photos and links to their profiles show up on the widget, enabling you to learn more about your readership. Using MyBlogLog you can find who is reading your blog, even if they don't leave a comment.

Because the widget captures a link to the member's profile, you can check it out to find out what else they are interested in.

On Beyond

OK, over the last several chapters, we've covered the major social media sites, but there are tons more out there that you may find useful. If you don't believe that, mosey on over to KnowEm[425] and feast your eyes on the more than 400 sites they can help you sign up for automatically.

Not only are there scads of interesting social sites out there, but here are a few utility sites and techniques that you can use to improve your usage of blogs and your other social media efforts.

- **Google Alerts** — A Google Alert is a saved search that you can set to periodically email you results or, if you prefer, you can subscribe to the results via RSS. Set up Google Alerts to track terms related to your product category and your target prospects' names, for example. You can set various preferences such as the type of item (news, blog, video, and so on), the frequency of notifications, and how many results to send.

- **Google Reader** — You can use Google Reader to subscribe to any RSS feed from any site. The reader allows you to organize all this information, search it, and even share it publicly or with your friends. You should definitely subscribe to the top five blogs you need to track for your product category.

---

[422] MyBlogLog: **bit.ly/asxNPI**

[423] Typepad: **bit.ly/aOtEk4**

[424] WordPress: **bit.ly/d4Mgyq**

[425] KnowEm: **bit.ly/cfSBQL**

- **Social Bookmarking Sites** — Use delicious and Digg to bookmark interesting sites you come across. This is useful especially if you use multiple computers, but an added benefit is you can make your bookmarks public, thus increasing the odds of attracting like-minded people.

- **FriendFeed** — FriendFeed,[426] now owned by Facebook, helps you keep track what your friends are posting on several online media. It allows you to create private groups to share information, pictures, and videos with.

- **Plaxo** — We used to think of Plaxo,[427] an online address updating service, as a kind of benign virus. But we actually now just consider it a good way to keep our email address book updated. Plus they added a social media component that lets you pipe in your tweets and Facebook comments.

- **Expert Sites** — Consider joining expert sites such as Squidoo[428] and About.com[429] to build your reputation as you share your expertise. These mostly volunteer sites are a treasure trove of tips and tricks on pretty much any topic. They are great places to showcase yourself as an expert.

- **Location-Based Sites** — Sites like FourSquare[430] and GoWalla[431] aim to exploit the benefits of local social networking and mobile computing.[432] Some may find them creepy or dangerous, but they are a growing segment of the social computing universe.

- **International Social Sites** — We've been talking about the top sites for the US, but there's a whole world out there that isn't American, and lots of them flock to sites like Orkut[433] and Bebo.[434]

  Orkut, owned by Google, is extremely popular in Brazil — making up 52 percent of users — while roughly 20 percent are from India and 18 percent from the US. Okut's age demographics run young. More than 70 percent of users are 18 to 30 years and a whopping 57 percent are in the 18-25 age group.[435] Orkut has roughly 46 million users.[436]

  Bebo is strong in Britain and India. The site was briefly owned by America Online (and now by Criterion

---

[426] FriendFeed: **bit.ly/bxxWip**

[427] Plaxo: **bit.ly/d9SH1m**

[428] Squidoo: **bit.ly/cB2nJ6**

[429] About.com: **bit.ly/cGp3XE**

[430] FourSquare: **bit.ly/aLqMzc**

[431] GoWalla: **bit.ly/c9rZdc**

[432] CRN's article *8 Cool Location-Based Social Networks*: **bit.ly/9AK7Vh**

[433] Orkut: **bit.ly/bR4W1P**

[434] Bebo: **bit.ly/dyvreM**

[435] Emotionally Speaking's article *Some interesting facts on Orkut users and demographics*: **bit.ly/cBHQV8**

[436] The Street's article *Gmail, Orkut Users Hardly Affect Google Stock*: **bit.ly/9ZUFsD**

Capital Partners LLC), and boasts 117 million members worldwide. In addition to overseas reach, Bebo also has a large teenage membership, its largest demographic. Analyst firm Roiworld's 2010 study, *Teens and Social Networks*,[437] indicates teens may be looking for alternatives to Facebook either because they have lost interest (45 percent), their parents have joined (16 percent) or there are too many older people using it (14 percent). So if you want to reach internationally, especially to young people, Orkut and Bebo may be good places to be.

There's lots, lots, lots more out there that we could discuss, but we need to end this book sometime!

With that in mind, we invite you to move on to the last, and perhaps most important, two chapters — all about building your own online community.

---

[437] Roiworld's *Teens and Social Networks*: **scr.bi/9ckbxs**

Building Your Community

> "Community happens when people feel
> they're among like-minded others and when
> they feel their contributions matter."
>
> **Social media expert Chris Brogan**

OK, you've slogged through all the advice in this book, and you've decided you'd like to create a standalone online community for your enterprise. Well, we've got bad news for you: You can't.

Sorry. We hope we haven't led you on by titling this chapter as we have. Community is not something you can create because a community belongs to its members and, as Chris Brogan's quote says, community happens. You can start a community, but the members will create the connections that build and sustain it. You can nurture a community, but the members will decide how long it lives and where it goes.

It's like a party.

You can invite the guests.

You can provide the venue, buy the food and drink, hire the band, and send out the invitations.

But you can't make them have fun. The way that those who show up interact will determine the party's success, not you.

Sure there are things you can do to increase your odds of a successful party: fly everyone to Paris; hire Cirque du Soleil to perform; and give everybody a Dolce&Gabbana bag full of expensive gifts. But you can't ensure that everyone will have fun. And you can't ensure that the party will never end.

It's the same with community. People come of their own volition, share only if they're inclined to, and will leave if the conversation gets boring.

One of our favorite thinkers about community, Amber Naslund, Director of Community for Radian6, lays it all out succinctly:[438]

> You cannot create a community. It creates itself.

> Strong community leaders, in my view, are there as the experience architects.

> It's our job to translate, to interpret, to build bridges and give them chairs to sit in. But ultimately, the community builds and sustains itself, with us nurturing it along the way.

If you're ready to move beyond your need to control your community, the next step is to decide what it is you want to build, um, architect.

What is Community?

We think we probably beat this one to death in the section *Community* on page 190, so go ahead and re-read it if you aren't quite sure what community is.

You'll recall we defined community as:

> A group of people with a shared purpose in a longer-term relationship in which all voices can be heard, and which evolves over time based on where its members want it to go

So that's what you're trying to architect.

So You Say You Want a Community?

First ask yourself, "Why?" We assume if you have decided to take the step of creating your own community space that you've done your homework. You've found your community where it is. You've evaluated the quality of the interactions and of the places, and you've determined there's something missing, something you can provide. You've honestly decided you need to make a contribution — not to mold or lead, or bend others to your will, but to contribute and provide value.

---

[438] Quoted in the comments of Chris Brogan's seminal 2009 blog post, *Audience or Community*: **bit.ly/cs2ogx**

Architecting Community

You are the experience architect for your community. It's up to you to create a welcoming place, filled with cool tools people can use to do the things they do when they're together: tell each other stories, yack, connect, and support each other.

But what kind of community do you hope to design? Physical communities are divided into many categories: urban, suburban, or rural; or neighborhoods, clubs and associations. Some, like the Fellowship for Intentional Community (FIC),[439] enumerate an even larger set of intentional community types that are created because people consciously choose to create them rather than, for example, moving into a neighborhood or apartment building because they can afford the rent.

We are drawn to the concept of intentional communities when thinking about online communities because to us, that's what they are: intentional online gatherings of people with similar goals and values.

A real-world intentional community is a group of people choosing to live in close proximity because they share a common need, belief, or desire, and who have an intent to share resources. The members of an intentional community typically hold a common social, political, religious, or spiritual vision and are often part of an alternative society, for example, a monastery or commune.

The people in online communities share the idea of intentionality with these offline communities. They aren't thrown together by an accident of proximity, such as sharing a birth year (high school) or a locality (apartment building). Although people in such situations may find community with those geographically close to them, they usually did not actively choose to be a part of a particular community. People in online communities intend to be together, take action to join a community that reflects their interests and passions, and stay intentionally.

There is such commonality with offline intentional communities that elements of FIC's mission statement[440] might form a good starting place for your community's mission. Here are these elements transformed and adapted for online communities:

- To embrace the diversity that exists among community members
- To build cooperative spirit within and among community members
- To facilitate exchange of information, skills, and economic support
- To serve as a reference source for those seeking information about our products
- To support education, research, archives, and publishing about our products
- To increase global awareness about our products

---

[439] Fellowship for Intentional Community: **bit.ly/aaicT9**

[440] FIC's mission statement: **bit.ly/dlH7Fi**

Like offline communities, online communities also tend to fall into categories, and one could argue that as many types of communities as there are offline, there that many and more online. And like lots of concepts we've examined in this book, every pundit has his or her list. Here's a short list of categories of communities to consider along with examples for each type:

1. **Social/Leisure** – Communities where people come together socially to talk about games, sports, TV, music. Also included are emotional support communities who exist to help people who are who are living through similar challenges such as loss, disease, addiction, or financial circumstances.

    Examples: Sports team sites (I Am A Trail Blazers Fan[441]), TV show sites (Screen Rant[442]), disease support groups such as the Crohn's Disease Support Group[443]

2. **Place/Circumstance** – Communities brought together by external events and situations such as geographic proximity or a common life experience or position, such as being alumni of a particular school, or members of religious or self-help organizations. Also included in this category are communities defined by age, gender, race, or nationality.

    Examples: DukeConnect,[444] Mayo Clinic,[445] The Twin Cities Online[446]

3. **Interest/Purpose** – Communities of people who share the same interest or passion or a common set of objectives. Charities, political parties and unions can form communities driven by purpose as can people who like shopping, investing, playing games, making music, or taking a class. Members of a fan club, hobby group, or professional organization, amateur woodworkers, and parents are other examples of people who might belong to communities of interest.

    Examples: Social Media Breakfast,[447] Prince.org[448]

4. **Action/Collaboration** – Communities of people trying to bring about change, whether it be political, social, religious, technological, or environmental. Members' bias is toward action in solving real-world problems. Self-improvement communities fall into this category along with job clubs and referral networks. Collaborative communities such as the Linux, AJAX, or Java communities where members actually build software together are good ex-

---

[441] I Am A Trail Blazers Fan: **bit.ly/pG2sGK**

[442] Screen Rant **bit.ly/ruSzsF**

[443] Crohn's Disease Support Group: **bit.ly/aDvyMR**

[444] DukeConnect: **bit.ly/pLHUql**

[445] Mayo Clinic Community: **bit.ly/oTd4JN**

[446] The Twin Cities Online: **bit.ly/r2jX17**

[447] Social Media Breakfast: **bit.ly/r3Gaa0**

[448] Prince.org: **bit.ly/npd3r2**

amples. Another example is innovation and ideation communities, especially within the enterprise, where members solve problems, improve products, and are bound by a common goal. Most customer relations and support communities also fall into this category.

Example: LinuxQuestions.org,[449] Pepsi Refresh Project,[450] GE: Ecomagination Challenge,[451]

5. **Practice** – Communities of people who are in the same profession, undertake the same activities, or who pursue the same vocation or avocation. These communities are distinguished from communities of interest by the degree of dedication they exhibit. For example, amateur airplane pilots may exhibit more dedication than hobbyists who enjoy scrapbooking.

Example: AerHub,[452] Accounting Social Network,[453] Nursing Community Center[454]

In addition to these categories of communities, Rob Howard of enterprise collaboration software company Telligent outlined styles of communities in a post[455] on Mashable:

- **Direct Community:** These are communities owned and managed by a company typically running proprietary community and enterprise collaboration software solutions. Examples include the **National Breast Cancer Foundation's community website**, **Starbucks' blog**, or **Dell's support community**. The organization is responsible for running and managing the community and benefits from rich data and user profiles created within that community. These also would include private B2B and internal employee-targeted communities.

- **Managed Community:** These are communities started and managed by the organization, but run on consumer-facing social networking sites like Twitter, Facebook or LinkedIn. Examples here include the **National Breast Cancer Foundation's Facebook Page**, **Starbucks' Flickr group pool**, or **Dell's presence on Twitter**. The organization is responsible for running and managing the community, but does not necessarily benefit from the rich data and user profiles created within the community. Typically, the facilitator of the community (Twitter, Facebook, etc.) benefits the most from the underlying data.

---

[449] LinuxQuestions.org: **bit.ly/oC0zy1**

[450] Pepsi Refresh Project: **pep.si/od3R4V**

[451] GE: Ecomagination Challenge: **bit.ly/pTbqna**

[452] AerHub: **bit.ly/qMrrop**

[453] Accounting Social Network **bit.ly/o83ctX**

[454] Nursing Community Center: **bit.ly/qPXAH7**

[455] Mashable's How *Businesses can Harness the Power of Online Communities* **on.mash.to/pmqSFN**

- **Participating Community:** These are communities started and managed by individuals or groups of users, typically on consumer-facing social networking sites, but sometimes also with proprietary software. An example here would be a fan site for Microsoft's Xbox or an independent Porsche enthusiast group. Typically the organization whose products or services are the topic of discussion can participate, but has no authority or access to the data created within the community.

It's obvious that all these qualities of communities can be, and often are, combined in a single site. If you decide to create your own community site rather than using a third party site like Facebook, you should consider all of these aspects.

Find Out What Your Community Wants

Before you go too far in architecting a space for your community, you'd better find out what they want. Of course, if you've come this far, you probably have a decent idea based on your listening and engaging. But there's no substitute from actually getting the input from your prospective community members.

As we've mentioned before, you can use Social Media Performance Group's free Social Media Readiness Survey™ [456] online or as reproduced on page 51 and the Social Media Performance Group's Mobile Social Media Use Survey[457] to gather information about your community's preferences. And your leadership should take an assessment such as the Social Media Directors Entrance Exam from Examiner.com,[458] online or using the version we modified and reproduced on page 54. We're assuming you've done all this preliminary work and are ready to really find out if you can provide some value to your community by creating a community site.

While these general surveys can help get you started, consider doing a more in-depth survey to determine what kind of site your community wants. There's a dynamite post by Jim Cashel on the Online Community Report site entitled, *Back to Basics: Want to Know What Community Members Need? Just Ask,*[459] that has some great ideas about conducting member research. We've adapted parts of it below.

The three most important questions you need to answer by asking your community are:

- **What do community members need from you as the host?** What are the member expectations about your level of participation, your effort in developing content, in fostering participation and your commit-

---

[456] Social Media Performance Group's Social Media Readiness Survey: **bit.ly/smpgsurvey**

[457] Social Media Performance Group's Mobile Social Media Use Survey: **bit.ly/c48q61**

[458] Social Media Directors Entrance Exam: **bit.ly/bDlsrx**

[459] Jim Cashel's *Back to Basics: Want to Know What Community Members Need? Just Ask*: **bit.ly/dmoDvA**

ment to hosting the community long-term?

- **What do community members need from each other?** Explore what community members want to get from interactions with other community members

- **What can community members contribute?** How are community members prepared and willing to participate?

In addition to these key questions, ask demographic questions to provide context and a basis for analyzing members' answers. Once you've determined your objectives, create a survey and ask prospective community members to help you design the community experience.

Here's a sample list of questions:

- Name, organization, title, a brief role description
- What information sources do you rely on to find out more about the product category?
- What groups (online or offline) are you a member of related to the product category?
- What products or services do you use related to the product category?
- What is the biggest challenge related to the cause you face in your day to day work?
- How satisfied are you with the level and type of communication you have with [your organization]?
- Do you currently participate in any of the following social media activities: [list relevant sites]?
- What information, insight or content do you want to share with other community members?
- What kinds of information would be helpful for other community members to share with you?
- If we were to offer the following content or features, please rate how useful each would be to you: [list items you are considering providing such as discussion forums, expert Q&A, video previews, blogs, etc.]
- Would you be interested in connecting with other members at local, in-person events?

However you get input from your community, you should definitely take what they say to heart in designing your community space. In fact, it would be a good idea to create an advisory board that you can bounce ideas off of as you make design decisions.

Community Management

The community may run itself, but it's not going to manage itself. You are going to need a community manager, someone who's responsible for the care and feeding of your community. That could be you; it could be one of your staff; or it could be a volunteer, but to succeed, you need to have a community manager. However, no community manager ever does it all by him or herself. A good community manager will enlist the help of trusted community members and organizational management to ensure the smooth running of the discussions and other interactions in the community.

Being a community manager can involve a significant time commitment, so if you can afford it, consider outsourcing this function to an expert. Regardless of what you think about the costs of a community manager, the long-term costs of not actively managing your community far outweigh the required effort. A community in which queries to the management go unanswered, the trolls are running wild, and the friend function has been broken for days is not a community people will hang around. Lack of attention has killed many a community.

Community Manager Tasks

A community manager often wears many hats. When you take a look at the following partial list of tasks that must be done, you can see why.

- Recruit members
- Discover who community members are and what they need
- Help members figure out how they fit — An important manager task is to identify who will fill the various roles in the typical community (see the following list)
- Determine how members want to interact — Do they need real-time chat? To be able to create their own forums? A way to friend one another?
- Design and implement interactive tools
- Help build and maintain the community's infrastructure
- Answer questions or do training on community features
- Help create and evolve the community culture
- Discover the best way to encourage members to connect
- Be the liaison for members to connect with those inside the enterprise
- Convey community feedback to the enterprise and larger community
- Advocate for the community
- Tear down silos inside the enterprise — There's a large component of change management whenever an organization embraces social media. The manager must be a change agent.
- Be an author and an editor for the enterprise's contributions
- Manage community crises — In any community, offline or online, there are going to crises. Online it might be troll attacks or other personality conflicts or it might be members who want to otherwise harm the community. The community manager must also be a crisis manager

That's quite a list! And it may be more than one person can accomplish for your community, especially during startup and the critical 6 to 12 months after the community's debut. You need to think seriously about the resources starting and maintaining your community will require.

Types of Community Members

Telligent,[460] a provider of services to online communities, categorizes community members into seven types. It's as good a classification as we've seen, and we adapt it below, adding the commentary and the final two types, which are often left off such lists.

- **Influencer:** A member who is connected to other well-connected users. Your community manager will want to quickly identify influencers and recruit them to help guide and stabilize the community.

- **Connector:** A highly-connected member who converses with and is linked to many other users. Like the person who knows everyone in town, this type of community member can be extremely important to the growth and sustainability of the community. Your community manager should seek out and engage connectors.

- **Asker:** A member who posts questions. This type of member can be annoying — like the 3-year-old who repeats, "But why?" after every answer. Or they can be stimulating, generating interesting interactions.

- **Answerer:** A member who replies to questions. These members can range from the smug know-it-all to the truly helpful. If you have askers, you obviously need answerers, and optimally, they are civil.

- **Originator:** A member who creates new content, also often called a Creator. This type of member contributes original posts, articles, links, videos or reviews. Obviously originators are important to the life of the community. The community manager will want to ensure originators have what they need to keep producing.

- **Commenter:** A member who replies or links to content created by others. This type of member may rarely contribute any new content. They range from the obsessive who lets no post go uncommented to the judicious and respected critic who inspires further discussion.

- **Moderator:** A member who moderates or curates content created by others. This role ranges from the gatekeeper who must approve all content to a host who sets the tone for the discussion with gentle reminders of appropriate behavior. The community manager can fill this role, but it's better if a community member steps up.

- **Lurker:** A member who very rarely contributes or even comments, but who finds satisfaction in following the discussion. The majority of any community's members will be lurkers, and that's OK. They find value in reading and experiencing the contributions of others. A community manager may be inclined to try to coax contributions out of lurkers, but it's probably best to leave them alone other than checking in from time to time to assess their engagement with the community.

---

[460] Telligent, commits up to 24 paid hours per employee each year to charity: **bit.ly/d9xvco bit.ly/cISEYh**

- **Troll:** A disruptive member who either enjoys stirring the pot or who is actively hostile. Your community will have its trolls. The role of the community manager is to try to temper their effects. See the *Dealing with Trolls* section on page 213 for more information.

Your community management plan should have policies and objectives for dealing with each type of community member, especially potentially disruptive ones. Don't just hope that the community will police itself — yes, that's the goal. It just doesn't happen without planning and support from your organizational leadership and your community manager.

Community Management Benefits

In addition to being an important role in just keeping the community functioning properly, there are a variety of other benefits to be had by having a community manager:

- **Regular feedback from the community means more innovation** — Your community is likely to have lots of good ideas for your business. If nobody's listening — or encouraging — you won't be able to capitalize on their innovative ideas.

- **Continuously evaluate cost/benefit** — You're investing time and money into your community. A community manager can help you evaluate the benefits your enterprise is getting in return. Plus, the manager can help enhance the benefits by ensuring a smoothly-running community.

- **Ensure your business is constantly forming new connections** — A good community manager is not only tending to your community space, he or she is also out on the Web, visiting other communities and prose-lytizing for your business and your community. The manager may contribute guest blogs or invite experts into the community to share their expertise. Generating buzz within and outside of the community is a key community manager responsibility.

- **Always remain relevant** — Without care and feeding, your community can become stale and irrelevant. People will come if they can find you, and if they think you're relevant to their needs and enthusiasms they will stay. The community manager tracks trends relating to your business and your cause and may introduce discussion topics to keep the community informed, and talking.

So the community manager is a critical role for your organization. Yet it's amazing how many enterprises decide they can do without someone to manage their communities. It's not amazing how few of such enterprises produce flourishing communities. Many enterprises try to manage social media and their own communities by committee or by making someone a part-time manager. If your organization can't or won't afford a full-time social media coordinator, perhaps creating your own community is beyond your reach. It's good to be honest with yourself on the cost in commitment and dollars of creating your own community. Doing it poorly can do more harm than good.

Community Building Checklist

"Every webpage is a latent community.
Each page collects the attention of people interested in its contents,
and those people might well be interested in conversing with one another
too.
In almost all cases the community will remain latent, either because
the potential ties are too weak, or because the people looking at the page
are separated by too wide a gulf of time, and so on."

Clay Shirky

The following checklist lays out, step-by-step, how to build your own community site. Be aware of what we said earlier, however, you can't force, impose, or create community. The members of your community will ultimately decide if your community lives or dies. The best you can do is prepare a comfortable place for them to engage. And in many ways, less is more.

It helps if you have a fanatical following. It helps if you don't try to control everything. It also helps if you always keep in mind that this is not a channel for your messages — it's a place where conversations happen; a place where you learn from and about your community. Your job is to close the gulf between people that media and community expert Clay Shirky speaks of in the quote above. Good luck. You'll need it.

The Social Media Performance Group Community Building Checklist™ that follows comprises the following topics, which we discuss in detail in the sections that follow:

- Define Your Goals
- Research Your Community's Needs
- Decide Logistical Approach
- Find What's Already Out There
- Design Your Presence
- Create Your Policies
- Evolve Your Policies

- Create Initial Content
- Launch
- Manage
- Attracting Community Members
- Converting Visitors to Members
- Measure
- What NOT to Do

Many of these topics we've been discussing throughout this book, and some of the checklist consists of bullet points and references to more detail in other sections. Other sections of the checklist introduce new material and have more detail. In general, though, this checklist is light on the explanations. Its purpose is to attempt to list all that you need to consider as you architect your new community.

We'd love to hear what you think about this checklist, and the whole book. You can contribute in our community space at our Website, www.socialmediaperformancegroup.com.

Define Your Goals

- Don't go off half-cocked and just create a community space without goals and a plan
- Review the chapter *Create Social Computing Strategies* on page 65 and *Elements of an Engagement Plan* on page 115
- Determine the potential value you hope to create for enterprise and its clients
- Create your strategy, goals, and measurement techniques (known as Key Performance Indicators, or KPIs)

    - Review the chapter *Measure Results* on page 147

- Know:

    - **What** your community stands for
    - **Who** ideally participates
    - **How** they will create action in the real world

- Identify a Sponsor

    - Key role
    - Must be committed for long term
    - Not necessarily a do-er, but the prime supporter

- Identify a Strategist

    - Plots the development of the community
    - Ensures the community tracks against goals

- Identify a Community Manager

    - Responsible for day-to-day
    - Could be a team

- Estimate the overhead: headcount, budgets and staff time
- Determine who can join the community

    - If under age 18 or 13 are allowed, ensure that you understand the implications
    - In US, must comply with COPPA[461]
    - May need to set a cookie so that if you reject membership and the user returns and tries to change age, they can't register

- Determine who can no longer participate

    - Create a policy for trolls, or objectionable members

Research Your Community's Needs

- Both external community and internal community
- Communication — how will information flow

    - Within enterprise
    - Member-to-member
    - Member to enterprise

- Sharing — how information is shared
- Donating time — how members can help manage and sustain the community
- Gauge community's likelihood of engaging — evaluate alternatives to your community
- Motivation — how to motivate members to join and remain part of community
- Support — what the community expects from the enterprise
- Evaluate the risk, including worst case scenarios — how to disengage if the community doesn't work
- Understand the required culture change — internal and external — for success
- Consider using the Social Media Performance Group's Social Media Readiness Survey

---

[461] The US Children's Online Privacy Protection Act: **bit.ly/cokKI5**

Decide Logistical Approach

- What role should enterprise play?

    - Passive / Background — enabler rather than leader?
    - Engaged / Directing — visible in everyday life of community?

- What type of community culture will be sustainable?

    - Free-for-all — relying mostly on community self-policing
    - Managed — visible role for community manager
    - Controlled — think twice before implementing strict organizational control

- What community activities should the enterprise facilitate?
- What types of content and features should the community have?
- Should the community be a Website extension, built on third party site such as Facebook, or built using customizable social-media-building sites such as Ning?
- Consider extending existing communities
- Understand the costs of creating a new community
- What types of members does the community want to include?
- How to recruit influential / valuable members?
- How do you handle troublesome members?
- What kinds of activities are members prepared to participate in to help your enterprise?
- Should you do fundraising in the community?
- Should you encourage advocacy?
- Should you link online events with offline?

Find What's Already Out There

- Take time to do extensive searches for existing conversations:

    - Mentions of enterprise name
    - Mentions of your product category
    - Issues and topics faced by your target audience
    - Mentions of key employees / board members
    - Advocates or spokespeople for your products
    - Mentions of competitors
    - Use the sites and techniques in the *Find Your Community* section on page 103

- Develop a body of knowledge about:

  - Key news sites
  - Most-active potential community members
  - Influential voices online
  - Thought leaders
  - Active potential partner communities
  - Key blogs
  - In-person meetups and events
  - Where your community isn't, but should be

Design Your Presence

- Don't develop your community as a stand-alone, in a vacuum

  - Create a social presence on Facebook, Twitter, LinkedIn, YouTube
  - Leverage the power of each of your social presences to drive people to your community, and your Website

- Coordinate branding, graphics, messages across your social media presence
- Use your research to determine what features the community needs and will use
- Avoid too much complexity
- Consider creating an advisory board or surveying prospective members to gauge interest in the planned feature set for the community space
- Consider creating user levels
- Reward content creators and question-answerers with recognition

  - Best Practice: Microsoft Most Valuable Professional (MVP) an award for exceptional technical community leaders who voluntarily provide technical expertise within Microsoft support communities — see the section *Run Contests* on page 202 for more information

- Determine how you will encourage connection and participation
- Create guidelines for community behavior

  - Indicate how the community can contribute to the guidelines
  - Ensure guidelines are not overly-restrictive or prescriptive

- Enable community enforcement of behavior

  - Consider implementing a "flag this post" feature
  - Consider implementing voting for posts
  - Consider creating a special area for power users
  - And listen to what they say there

- Select your platform

    - Many create-your-own platforms to choose from:

        - Joomla Community Builder and JomSocial
        - Ning
        - Cisco
        - Capterra
        - KickApps
        - Jive

- Determine your platform requirements — attributes to consider include:

    - Is platform widely supported (or commercially viable)?
    - Forums (of course)
    - RSS Feed support
    - Easy posting
    - Ability to feature posts
    - Security and identity — information security measures and also security features that affect the user experience such as onerous login procedures
    - Privacy
    - Video and other media support (consider embedding from YouTube instead)
    - Mobile support
    - Customization
    - Easy administration
    - Backup
    - Removing posts
    - Approving posts

Create Your Policies

- As part of your social media strategy, consider what policies should govern your enterprise's social computing use
- Establish, in writing, best practices and procedures
- Ensure staff is on message
- Empower staff to be proactive and participative
- Position community as means to engage, not a distraction
- Create Rules of Engagement

    - What to do with negative content
    - What to do with negative members (more later)
    - What to do with staff that blabs

- Study how the US Air Force deals with various types of community members, in the next figure

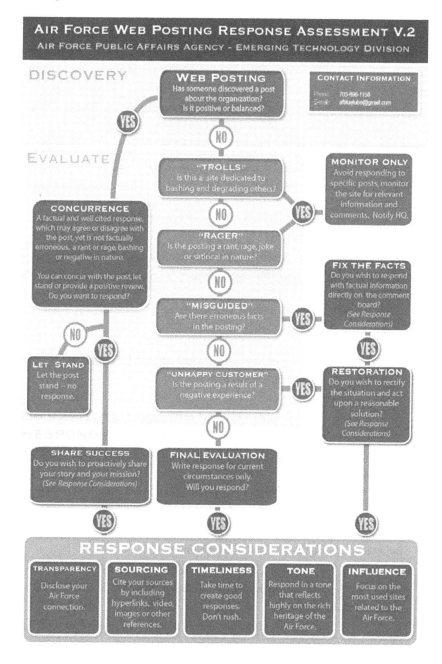

Figure 82 — Air Force Web Posting Assessment Flowchart[462]

---

[462] Air Force Web Posting Assessment Flowchart v.2 (PDF): **bit.ly/dvdtGS**

- Decide whether to hold employees and other community members personally responsible for content they publish
- Decide how staff should Identify themselves in posts
- Decide if staff members who post elsewhere should add a disclaimer to their posts: "The postings on this site are my own and don't necessarily represent [Organization's] positions, strategies or opinions."
- Encourage all members to respect copyright, fair use and financial disclosure laws and set penalties for non-compliance
- Confidentiality: Decide whether to prohibit citing or referencing clients, partners or suppliers without their approval
- Create a linkback policy for material reposted from other sources
- Create a prohibited language policy restricting hate speech, ethnic slurs, personal insults, obscenity
- If you are regulated, ensure all employees understand what can and cannot be said online

  - Understand the legal ramifications of creating a public record or a public meeting by discussing topics online
  - User-Generated Content (UGC) may need to comply with policy, copyright, trademark
  - May need to treat information as part of records subject to retention policies

- Be careful out there: Some laws may restrict your ability to censor employees online:

  - **Political Opinions**
    - Many states, (such as California) prohibit employers from regulating their employees' political activities
    - Unionizing
    - In many states, talking or writing about unionizing is strongly protected; union contracts may permit blogging; states may protect "concerted" speech — protecting two or more people who discuss workplace conditions
  - **Whistleblowing**
    - Many may believe reporting regulatory violations or illegal activities online is protected, but whistleblowers must report problems to the appropriate regulatory or law enforcement bodies first
  - **Reporting on Your Work for the Government**
    - Government workers writing online about their work is protected speech under the First Amendment except for classified or confidential information
  - **Legal Off-Duty Activities**
    - Some states may protect an employee's legal off-duty blogging, especially if the employer has no policy or an unreasonably restrictive policy with regard to off-duty speech activities
  - **Reporting Outside Social Media Site Memberships**
    - Some organizations require employees to report other places where they contribute online
  - **Set Guidelines for At-Work Social Media Use**

- Most enterprises believe at-work use of social media saps productivity, but some studies find just the opposite. See footnote 103 on page 121 for more information.

- Review the following policies for ideas for your social media policy:[463]

  - H&R Block's Response Process — **slidesha.re/q6agAL**
  - IBM Social Computing Guidelines — **ibm.co/bNJl7V**
  - Nordstrom — **bit.ly/oPbXPa**
  - SAP Social Media Participation Guidelines — **scr.bi/pFxUJL**
  - Thomson Reuters — **bit.ly/oLaWbe**
  - Walmart's Twitter External Discussion Guidelines — **bit.ly/nnKcU5**
  - Wells Fargo Blogs and Social Media — **bit.ly/pp5bqs**

Evolve Your Policies

- Once the community is up and running, theory meets community practice, and you may need to evolve your rules
- Establish periodic policy reviews
- Involve your community in reviews

Create Initial Content

- Set the stage by designing various forums around key issues of interest
- Seed each forum with starter questions
- Have a forum for newbies called "Introduce Yourself"
- Have a forum called "What <product> Means to Me"
- Test with a few volunteers, and get the discussions started
- Invite community influencers
- Be careful to not look artificial or staged
- Gradually widen the discussion
- Initial testers invite their friends

---

[463] See SocialMedia.biz for a great list of social media usage policies: **bit.ly/cyou3a**

Launch

- Get enough volunteers to staff the site for initial phase
- Blitz all your online and offline contacts
- Create a media package to distribute if you get press interest
- Target a soft launch to work out bugs and test engagement. A soft launch is where you go live, but don't do publicity, and only invite a small group to participate.
- Launch early in the week, early in the morning

    - Tuesday or Thursday are high traffic days on the Web

- Ensure the initial page tells your story, and includes pictures of your team / clients
- Include a survey or quiz
- Ensure that your site has Facebook "Like" and other social media badges so your members can spread the word
- Give something away
- Reward people for creating a complete profile

    - Perhaps just a white paper or other downloadable content

- Create an offline launch party and invite your board, clients, supporters
- Video the unveiling of the new site and post on YouTube
- Create an online event within the first two weeks
- Plan major new content within the first month

Manage

- Read the community management experts' blogs:

    - Amber Naslund's Brass Tack Thinking[464]
    - Connie Bensen's Community Strategist[465]
    - Tom Humbarger's Social Media Musings[466]
    - Heather Stout's Social Media Building Blocks, in particular her series "Community Implementation Strategic Plan"[467]
    - Mike Pascucci's Online Moderation & Management Musings[468]
    - Ken Burbery's Web Business[469]

- Assign a community manager to:

    - Review all activity
    - Answer questions
    - Stimulate conversation and connection
    - Approve posts (if required)
    - Manage the growth
        - If community grows too fast, members may lose sense of connection
        - If commentary gets too noisy, or too fractious, members may disengage

- Be responsive

    - The community will expect you to respond to issues they bring up
    - Moderators should participate in the community
    - Use moderation lightly
    - Remember, it's the members' community

- Encourage self-policing
- Allow off-topic posting — they're still engaged!
- Model the behavior you'd like to see
- Contact rogue members privately; Confronting publicly may be counterproductive
- Ensure everyone knows the troll policy and other community policies

---

[464] Amber Naslund's Brass Tack Thinking: **bit.ly/al4Ne6**

[465] Connie Bensen's Community Strategist: **http://bit.ly/cdX83j**

[466] Tom Humbarger's Social Media Musings: **bit.ly/bNWsZz**

[467] Heather Stout's Social Media Building Blocks: **bit.ly/dxDWY0** and **bit.ly/aemsl0**

[468] Mike Pascucci's Online Moderation & Management Musings: **bit.ly/9VbRJx**

[469] Ken Burbery's Web Business: **bit.ly/cTb6X9**

Attracting Community Members

- Organic

  - People find you through Google because your site is Search Engine Optimized for relevant search terms

- Referral

  - Get lots of other highly-ranked sites to link to yours
  - Use the Facebook Like button
  - Can use paid links but only as a last resort
  - Pay-Per-Click (PPC)
  - Email
  - You probably already have an email subscription list; use it to promote the community

- Create newsletter articles that draw users to your Website for more info, or the rest of the article

  - Put newsletter subscription widget on all your Webpages

- Personal referrals

  - Run campaigns for current members to invite friends
  - Cultivate evangelists to blog, tweet, Facebook about you
  - Get your board involved

- Promote the community at your live events
- Hold Tweetups[470] — real-world events where everyone tweets
- Give everyone the tools to refer, and connect

  - Ask members to put your badge on their sites
  - Create lists of suggested tweets and topics
  - Encourage members to post pictures to enhance connection
  - Encourage members to put a community link in their signatures

- Run games or contests to encourage lurkers to post

---

[470] Tweetups: **bit.ly/cido0V**

Converting Visitors to Members

- Major requirement: A really good home page
- State the need you meet
- Invite visitors to join your community
- List some of the benefits of membership
- Test various alternatives (see the *Optimizing for Google* section on page 369 for more on this)
- Measure

    - Set quantifiable targets and track progress
    - Use the techniques we've discussed in the *Measure Results* section on page 147
    - Schedule reviews of metrics by your board at least quarterly

Community Building What NOT to Do

- Ignore your community

    - You can do more harm than good
    - People expect response, communication, relationship

- Fail to promote interactions

    - Community may need some help connecting
    - It's your job to see they get talking

- Rule with an iron hand

    - Your goal is to be involved no more and no less than required
    - Let the community guide itself as much as possible

- Betray their trust

    - Obey your own ground rules
    - Enlist community when taking potentially unpopular actions such as banning someone

- Overextend

    - Don't take on more communities, or other social computing activities, than you can handle
    - Your community wants your attention

- Abandon your community manager

    - Ensure leadership's support for the role and the person
    - Understand the cost of managing the community and budget for it

If you've worked you way through this checklist, you're ready to go. You may not want to take all the advice contained in this checklist or this book, but be sure you've considered it so you are making informed choices about social media.

Afterword

> "It's only when technology gets boring –
> that's to say, part of the routine for the majority,
> not just the Geekosphere –
> that it becomes interesting."
>
> **Clay Shirky**

Well, that's it. A quick overview of everything you need to build your social presence online – Fast!

Because social media is so fast-moving, lots of the details in this book will rapidly become obsolete, perhaps by the time you read this. But the overarching concepts, we feel, will survive the constantly changing details. The sites may change; new capabilities may emerge; and certainly some new bright shiny thing will unseat the current 400-pound social media gorillas (we're looking at you, Facebook!)

But people don't change – basically – over the eons. Aristotle's two driving human attributes – pity and fear – remain alive in reality shows and gawker Websites, and the ways we relate to each other are as old as the hills.

We hope we've made some sense of this onrushing phenomenon, and we flatter ourselves to hope the advice in this book will remain relevant no matter how social computing evolves.

We'd like to hear from you, not only about what you think of our advice, but what you learn as you create your own social media practice. You can contribute by commenting on the Social Media Performance Group's Website at:

www.SocialMediaPerformanceGroup.com

In the appendices that follow, we collect lots of pointers to other thinkers and advisors whom we respect, whom we relied upon to create this book, and whom we recommend to you for guidance and inspiration. They are the giants upon whose shoulders we stand.[471]

Be careful out there and remember, Don't Panic!

---

[471] No, this isn't an Oasis reference, but rather Newton: **bit.ly/bItOQl**

Who is the Social Media Performance Group?

The three principals of SMPG have varied and complementary capabilities and experience. We also partner with world class marketing, branding, design, and development resources to offer complete strategy-to-execution services.

Mike Ellsworth

Principal author and founding principal of SMPG, Mike's background includes experience as an IT Program Manager, Chief Technology Officer for a start-up, Vice President of Strategic Planning for an Internet incubator, Senior Project Manager at the Nielsen Company, and as an independent Emerging Technology Strategy Consultant. During his 15-year career at the Nielsen Company in the marketing research business, he helped set Dun & Bradstreet's Internet strategy and developed the vision that resulted in the consumer packaged goods industry's first Web application in early 1995. With his own company, StratVantage Consulting, Mike helped Sterling Commerce create their eCommerce strategy and has helped senior leaders understand and connect rapidly changing new technologies with the organization's existing strategy.

In addition to starting StratVantage, Mike founded CTOMentor, a subscription-based emerging technology advisory service, and The WiMAX Guys, a wireless networking company. Most recently he leveraged more than a decade of social media experience (his first social media proposal was in 2001) by starting Linked InSolutions, a social media training and consulting company.

Ken Morris, JD

In addition to being a founding principal of SMPG, Ken is President and CEO of Aperçu Group Inc., a team of leading scholars and practitioners dedicated to helping organizations improve their financial and operational performance. In addition to social media consulting, Ken consults and coaches on issues of diversity, leadership, conflict management, succession planning, crisis management, team building, negotiation, presentation skills, workplace systems design, marketing, and strategic planning.

Ken's accomplishments include helping improve his customers' financial and operational performance; eCommerce and technology integration; Internet, intranet, networking and information technology; recruitment and retention; business and human resources strategy and execution; marketing and business development; international affairs; executive development, education and training; and community and governmental affairs.

Ken is a former Vice President of Human Resources at Boston Scientific and Guidant, Vice President, Business Development at Professional Development Group, Inc., and previously held positions at Honeywell and State Farm.

Robbie Johnson

A founding SMPG principal, Robbie is an experienced business development manager who has used social media in an innovative way to effectively connect with customers and prospects while driving sales performance. He has worked as Application Sales Representative and Business Development Consultant at Oracle before taking a business development role at Trissential, a Twin Cities IT solutions company. At Trissential, he landed three new customers, including Cargill, and $500,000 in new business solely through the use of social media techniques. In addition, he managed all of Trissential's partner relationships, including with Computer Associates, Oracle, Fujitsu, and others. As a result, Robbie helped Trissential grow from $6 million to $12 million in revenue during tough economic times.

Most recently, Robbie has leveraged his social networking strategy and execution experience to found Strategy Blueprints, a consulting firm that helps companies ensure that their tactical business plans map to their strategic business objectives, especially in the area of social networking and new media.

Acknowledgements

The editing and finishing of this book was an exercise in crowdsourcing. We are grateful for the assistance of the following reviewers, many of whom responded to our LinkedIn Question, who substantially improved this edition as well as the other editions of **Be a Person**:

Laura Bellinger — marketing communications producer and social media coordinator at Care USA. Laura launched CARE's social media and previously worked for CARE as a press officer. **linkd.in/eT2qZH**

Kari Carlisle — writer, archaeologist, museum curator for Fremont Indian State Park and Museum in central Utah where she cares for more than 150,000 artifacts; manages the park's archaeological sites, exhibits, educational programs, and special events; serves on the board of the Utah Museums Association; and chairs the committee for Richfield, Utah's annual Natural Resource Festival.
linkd.in/eLZ52m

Robin Cheung — principal at Cloud 5 Nines.ca. Robin has been a pithy onliner ever since he was first introduced to it in 1987, he holds an MBA from McMaster University (Hamilton); showing his confidence in the future of the Internet, he is currently pursuing his PhD in Applied Management and Decision Sciences (Finance) from Walden University and maintains a business research and education blog at robincheung.ca/.
linkd.in/hMhCFt

Barry Doctor — Product Marketing Manager at Katun Corporation. **linkd.in/hVvkWo**

Deb Ellsworth — creator of the Empathy Symbol, author of the novel, *Earth Portal,* and co-author of *Your Amazing Preschooler.*
empathysymbol.com

Rob Etten — Vice President at The North Highland Company, Rob has experience with Ernst & Young's Management Consulting practice, Price Waterhouse, and Andersen Consulting (now Accenture). His areas of expertise include strategic planning, portfolio management, PMO startup, business process reengineering and merger/acquisition integration. **linkd.in/hE3sV4**

Roger Hamm — an experienced retail / CPG IT professional with expertise in Project Management, Implementation, Product Design and Principal at Viking Business Intelligence Services. **linkd.in/hSKXmj**

Dave Harkins — has helped lead change for nearly 25 years. His background includes extensive experience in marketing strategy, database marketing and direct response, branding, licensing and trademark management, marketing technology, and business development. He's served as VP, Strategic Services at the Jackson Group/Total Response, Managing Partner of Taylor-Harkins Group, Executive VP at Colman Brohan Davis, Chief Marketing Officer and VP, Customer Care at Geneer and VP, Marketing and Product Development at Nykamp Consulting Group. **bit.ly/mi2dxo**

Julie Kendrick — a features writer with a background in Web content development, magazine profiles and marketing communications. She is a contributing writer for minneapolispicks.com, alumni publications including Reach (U of MN alumni magazine) and Teton Thunder (Williston State College) and under contract to provide content and communications for Syngenta, a $12 billion global agricultural company. **linkd.in/ifveBu**

Trevor Lobel — project manager at Oswald Brothers. Trevor is a seasoned project and change manager experienced in software implementations for non-profit organizations and NGOs. **linkd.in/fzdZxc**

Tom Menke — a knowledge management professional known for his ability to leverage technologies, improve business processes, and work with people to improve staff collaboration and client communications to foster the sharing of knowledge and best practices. Tom was formerly Director of Knowledge Management at The Nielsen Company. **linkd.in/fkb0Yu**

Kathy Pettiss — science educator, consultant at Chester County (PA) Intermediate Unit and volunteer StarLab educator at Great Valley School District. **linkd.in/efEkQc**

Paul Phillips — Vice President of Operations at ACORN Research, LLC. Paul serves on the board of the non-profit, HopeWorks (www.whyhopeworks.org) and is a published author. **linkd.in/gSl9vl**

Frances Ponick — principal at Ponick Enterprises. Frances specializes in writing, manuscript evaluation, book doctoring, and training book coaches. Frances has more than 30 years' experience in technical, business, marketing, proposal, and other nonfiction writing, editing, and publishing and has received awards for technical writing, journalism, and formal poetry. Frances worked at a nonprofit for ten years, and has taken graduate coursework on social marketing. **www.franponick.com linkd.in/gfTCaj**

ShaRon Rea — board member at the Harp Foundation and Hope Village Arizona. ShaRon is passionate about building strong community relationships. She is a motivator who believes in possibilities! **linkd.in/hTXhqz**

Mark Rieger — Vice President, Channel Marketing Evangelist for ChannelLine, which helps Technology Companies increase sales through a combination of consulting, research and the industry's only Pay For Performance demand generation program. **linkd.in/gvkjM5**

Alex Rodriguez — marketing director of Baywood Learning Center, a non-profit specializing in the education of gifted children. His many years working at and consulting with non-profits also include working at Trust for Public Land returning and reserving lands and parks for the public and Web consulting for non-profit Cacep. **linkd.in/fXnvHO**

Kathy Rose — a market research, shopper insights, consumer insights professional and principal of Rose Research for Results. **linkd.in/gn61OB**

Anthony Sansone — Senior Technical Editor at EMC Corporation. **linkd.in/iku6vH**

Leanne Storch — Associate Vice President, Pulmonary Fibrosis Foundation. Leanne brings organizational skills and a great empathy to the patients and families who call for support. **linkd.in/eLACSO**

Resources

> "Social media is like teen sex.
> Everybody wants to do it. Nobody knows how.
> When it's finally done there is surprise it's not better."

Avinash Kaushik, Google

We offer this list of resources for quick reference. Like all things on the Web, their location and relevance my change by the time you read this so please remember, Google is your friend. If you want to locate a reference whose link no longer works, try Googling it. And Google anything else you have questions on. The Web abounds with advice, not all of it good, so be careful out there!

The Best of the Best Pundits

These people inspired much of the thinking in this book. They really know their stuff.

Pundit	Link	Pundit	Link
Abbey Klaassen	bit.ly/iDi1ym	Jeremiah Owyang	bit.ly/9aszgM
Adam Christensen	bit.ly/cglyfw	Jesse James Garrett	bit.ly/mp1JQz
Alia McKee	bit.ly/kYpBH1	Jim Cashel	bit.ly/koQWV7
Amber Naslund	bit.ly/aI4Ne6	Joseph Thornley	bit.ly/kNL55p
Amy Sample Ward	bit.ly/jpjLMz	Josh Bernoff	bit.ly/a3ndiq
Andrew Eklund	bit.ly/ldTjCT	Katie Paine	bit.ly/982jqM
Ann Michael	bit.ly/lA2cPq	Katya Andresen	bit.ly/kPLKaq
Avinash Kaushik	bit.ly/m92tZI	Ken Burbary	bit.ly/cTb6X9
Barry Judge	bit.ly/b6H0hY	Kirsten Stanford	bit.ly/l004E5
Beth Kanter	bit.ly/dmp97X	Lawrence Liu	bit.ly/magnW8
Bob Pearson	bit.ly/lavCIq	Lee Odden	bit.ly/cQNLKG
Brian Halligan	bit.ly/iNm4wd	Lisa Barone	bit.ly/ivVfWU
Brian Haven	bit.ly/jgBNhH	Lynn Rogers	bit.ly/jVhxQH
Brian Solis	bit.ly/d8JMJb	Manish Mehta	huff.to/iNnIlg

Pundit	Link	Pundit	Link
Catie Foertsch	bit.ly/iGibLi	Marcel LeBrun	bit.ly/kuME9S
Charlene Li	bit.ly/bV80w5	Mark Rovner	bit.ly/kdu6Ha
Chip and Dan Heath	bit.ly/msAtpQ	Matt McKeon	bit.ly/imc4Kl
Chris Brogan	bit.ly/cXHzNA	Michael Gray	bit.ly/lLRdc1
Chris Lake	bit.ly/iyJE8P	Mike Valentino	bit.ly/kS0r5K
Chris Levkulich		Neal Schaffer	bit.ly/9GtQT4
Clay Shirky	bit.ly/dy9p2j	P.J. Fusco	bit.ly/llxPXK
Constantin Basturea	bit.ly/lWeh7z	Paul Dunay	bit.ly/m5XG9o
Dan Schwable	bit.ly/d3Zuyt	Peter Merholz	bit.ly/iJiHiV
Darren Rowse	bit.ly/dghN9I	Qui Diaz	bit.ly/iIjyaL
David Bohm	bit.ly/b1uCPT	Rachel Happe	bit.ly/blJkdb
David Meerman Scott	bit.ly/lXQGyQ	Richard Seel	bit.ly/kieLSq
David Mothersbaugh	bit.ly/jgSURm	Rick Mahn	bit.ly/aXmSdw
Deb Schultz	bit.ly/ly4iVS	Robert Scoble	scoble.it/9NMNyh
Debajyoti Banerjee	bit.ly/le6OQI	Robin Good	bit.ly/izAtKE
Debra Murphy	bit.ly/lmRO8b	Rohit Bhargava	bit.ly/mlqv0n
Del Hawkins	bit.ly/jMgaHd	Ron Shulkin	bit.ly/jHXgAh
Dharmesh Shah	bit.ly/kSjkwc	Ryan Spoon	bit.ly/kqIXAY
Dr. Ivan Misner	bit.ly/lSSPml	Seth Godin	bit.ly/bdDjWc
Dr. Ralph F. Wilson	bit.ly/ky6awp	Shel Israel	bit.ly/bgr9cM
Ed Keller	amzn.to/kOokqs	Skellie of skelliewag	bit.ly/lWxM3M
Erik Qualman	bit.ly/klLyTu	Tamara Adlin	bit.ly/lKSq2x
Geoff Livingston	bit.ly/lI0bXI	The Cluetrain Team	bit.ly/9jGP3T
Guy Kawasaki	bit.ly/aUJB5m	Tia Fisher	bit.ly/mkbdjR
Howard Rheingold	bit.ly/ktMJRE	Tim Jackson	bit.ly/jF5XsJ
Jake McKee	bit.ly/ioZT9P	Tim Nash	bit.ly/jJhhip
Janet Fouts	bit.ly/mqKfDZ	Vinod Kumar	bit.ly/jDYba0
Jared Schwartz	bit.ly/m3jpSw		
Jason Falls	bit.ly/kuWUYT		
Jennifer Johnston Canfield	bit.ly/jVRMfk		

The Best of the Best Presentations

We've found these presentations invaluable in putting together this book. You may like these or you may want to do your own searches on sites such as SlideShare (**bit.ly/bO2rTk**).

Presentation	Link
Social Media ROI business measurement	slidesha.re/obBZge
Facebook's Best Practice Guide	**slidesha.re/nJMvDC**
B2B Social Media Marketing: Building the B2B Business Case for Social Media	**slidesha.re/pNm67r**
The 25 Basic Styles of Blogging ... And When To Use Each One	**slidesha.re/qpQWob**
8 Digital Trends That Will Change Everything - March 2010	**slidesha.re/n66T1X**
Employees are Social Media Marketers, Too! (they just don't know it...)	slidesha.re/q5xYmL
Hubspot's The Science of Social Media	**slidesha.re/n2UCow**
Effective Blogger Relations: Debunking Myths, Discovering Reality	**slidesha.re/pcf4ow**
Google's The Real Life Social Network v2	**slidesha.re/pywE7L**
FAIL: Social Media Disasters & What We Can Learn From Them	slidesha.re/ofa9yw
Your Company Must Become a Media Company	**slidesha.re/oNCs7u**

Index

Visit the

SOCIAL MEDIA HALL OF SHAME!

SEE RANK SOCK PUPPETRY!!!

THRILL TO EMBARRASSING GOOFS BY OPRAH AND KFC!!!

GASP AT THE WRATH OF THE MOMMIE BLOGGERS!!!

But, seriously, take a tip from Thomas Edison—who said about his attempts to create the light bulb, "I have not failed. I've just found 10,000 ways that won't work"— and check out some of the things **not** to do with social media.

We include many of the 10,000 social media failures in our Social Media Hall of Shame from organizations who should know better, like Wal-Mart, Nestlé, Motrin, and the US Government.

Help avoid your own moments of shame by visiting the Hall at:

http://bit.ly/HallOfShame

You'll be glad you did!

Understanding how to build your enterprise's social presence online — *Fast!*

Get the Enterprise Executive Edition of Be a Person

Written in clear, non-technical language and aimed at enterprise leaders, this version of **Be a Person** is 130 pages of strategy, tactics, and how-to information you can use to understand:

- How social media can benefit your organization by supporting your strategy

- Why and under what circumstances you should build a social media presence – and how to know if your enterprise is ready

- What kinds of tools you should consider to help further your enterprise's online objectives

Use **Be a Person** – Enterprise Executive Edition to answer the questions that executive leaders have about the promise and perils of social media. This book is easily digested in a matter of a few hours, giving enterprise leaders everything they need to understand about one of the most important issues facing enterprises today: What to do about social media.

- The print version of **Be a Person** – Enterprise Executive Edition is available at Amazon or at: **http://bit.ly/BeAPersonE**

Not in the enterprise space? See **http://bit.ly/OrderBeAPerson** for more information about the Small and Medium-Sized Business and Non-Profit versions.